PRAISE FOR *FAKE NEWS NATION*

"This volume makes a useful contribution to the literature on disinformatics. Deceit has always been a constant companion to the tyrant, propagandist, and missioner. What is new to our post-truth era is the digital weaponization of deceit, particularly under the rubric of social media."

—**Hal Berghel**, PhD, author of the "Out of Band" column
in *IEEE Computer*

"This book provides a context for qualifying our current national angst about fake news. It does not promise speculative solutions but situates the reader in a long history of information use and misuse and urges us to think critically and reflectively about a fundamentally human-information phenomenon rather than a contemporarily unique condition."

—**Gary Marchionini**, Cary C. Boshamer Professor,
University of North Carolina at Chapel Hill

"James W. Cortada and William Aspray's brilliantly selected and crafted case studies are must-reads because they bring historical insight to issues of fake news, disinformation, and conspiracy theories of our digital age. "

—**William H. Dutton**, University of Southern California,
author of *Society on the Line*

"For those of us who might believe that we are living in a unique period of history where the emergence of fake news and alternative truths is confounding political and public life, this outstanding volume sheds light on the common use of misinformation across the history of the United States. The authors tell us the story of how lies, fake facts, misinformation, myth-making, and conspiracies have affected American public discourse, political life, business and science policy. They take the reader on a fascinating journey through eight carefully chosen case studies of events from U.S. political, business, and science policy history. These events include the election and assassination of presidents, participation of the United States in wars, the long-lasting popularity of patent medicines, the use of misleading science in defense of the tobacco industry, and the politics of climate change. With these case studies we learn how information has been used and misused. The authors reveal how we experience truth, certainty, and knowledge and where this is undermined by untruth, uncertainty, and ignorance. Through these historical accounts the reader will learn that facts and lies are socially constructed; that information has been weaponized by individuals and organizations to achieve their goals; that facts have been linguistically reconstructed through exaggerations, misrepresentations, conspiracies, and myth-making to create and disseminate fake facts; that support for participation in the Spanish-American War was generated by fake facts published in the media; that the public relations industry has convinced us of alternative versions of truth; that rumors evolve to become facts; and how the current debate over the scientific evidence of climate change has developed, and where this might lead us in the common interest of preserving our planet. I highly recommend this superbly written and researched book. It makes a very important contribution to our understanding of the nature of information, and the role it plays in our daily lives, and a strong argument for the conscientious development of high-level information, technology, and data literacy skills for all people as a necessary foundation for engaged civic life."

—**Harry Bruce**, dean emeritus and professor,
The Information School, University of Washington

Fake News Nation

The Long History of Lies and Misinterpretations in America

James W. Cortada and William Aspray

ROWMAN & LITTLEFIELD
Lanham • Boulder • New York • London

Published by Rowman & Littlefield
An imprint of The Rowman & Littlefield Publishing Group, Inc.
4501 Forbes Boulevard, Suite 200, Lanham, Maryland 20706
www.rowman.com

6 Tinworth Street, London SE11 5AL, United Kingdom

British Library Cataloguing in Publication Information Available

Library of Congress Cataloging-in-Publication Data

ISBN: 978-1-5381-3110-7 (cloth)
ISBN: 978-1-5381-3111-4 (electronic)

♾™ The paper used in this publication meets the minimum requirements of
American National Standard for Information Sciences—Permanence of Paper
for Printed Library Materials, ANSI/NISO Z39.48-1992.

Contents

Preface   vii

1   Introduction   1

2   Political Communication in Presidential Elections and
    the Case of 1828   19

3   Political Communication in the Age of Television and
    the Presidential Election of 1960   39

4   Ultimate in Conspiracies 1: Assassination of
    President Abraham Lincoln   53

5   Ultimate in Conspiracies 2: Assassination of President
    John F. Kennedy   73

6   Fake Facts and Mythmaking in War: Cuba and the
    Spanish-American War   89

7   Rumors and Misleading Advertising in Business   123

8   Information and Misinformation in the Tobacco Industry   159

9   Misinformation, Politics, and Climate Change   175

10 Conclusions   211

Notes   227

Bibliographic Essay   279

Index   287

About the Authors   305

Preface

After the election of Donald Trump as president, people in the United States and across large swaths of Europe, Latin America, and Asia engaged in the most intensive discussion in modern times about falsehoods pronounced by public officials. In the United States, shock and disbelief in the wide use of "fake news," "alternative facts," and other similar concepts such as misinformation, disinformation, rumors, and lies dominated both the media and private conversations. The shock was caused in part by the belief that pronouncements by President Trump and others, challenged by the mainstream "trusted" media, represented a new phenomenon in American life. Political scientists had known for a long time that less egregiously incorrect statements had been part of the rhetoric of political elections, particularly from extremists on the far right or far left. However, an examination of the historical record exposes a very different reality, one in which lies and misrepresentation are much more widespread.

Fake facts and fake news in their various forms have long been present in American life, particularly in its politics, public discourse, and business activities—going back to the time when the country was formed. In different times, lies and misrepresentation have taken many different forms in American public life. And what counts as true has been taken as open to debate. Historians, so far, have done little to study the role of lies and misinformation in American public life, even though they have paid considerable attention to the role of conspiracies, which often involve lies and misinformation.

This book begins to fill the gaps in our understanding of the role of fake facts, in their various guises, in American history. It is one of the first historical studies to place the long history of lies and misrepresentation squarely in the middle of American political, business, and science policy rhetoric. We do this by presenting a series of case studies that describe how lies and fake facts were used over the past two centuries in important episodes from American history. Not only do we focus on the roles that lies and misrepresentations play in these particular episodes, but we also establish patterns and provide comparisons to other episodes so that we can better understand the role of information and misinformation in wars, presidential assassinations, presidential elections, business advertising, and science and health policy debates.

Our goal is to give the educated reader a perspective on fake facts and fake news as they appear today and as they are likely to appear in the future—for one thing we are convinced of from our historical examinations is that that the current behavior of lying and misrepresentation in American public life will not disappear in the years to come. As individuals, and as members of companies and public institutions, we need to understand how to judge the value of information. If, as so many Americans believe, we now live in an Information Society; and if, as so many surveys and studies demonstrate, we use vast quantities of facts to go about our daily lives; then people will simply have to become more adept at acquiring, evaluating, and believing (or discarding) information than they have in the past. Given the vast amount of bad information available over the Internet, for example, developing discriminating information handling skills is an urgent task, beginning with children and extending to all age groups.

Your two authors have each been studying the role of information and its technologies as historians for four decades. We are deeply familiar with how Americans use information. We also know that the role of misinformation is so pervasive that to write an integrated account of its long history is not possible at this time. There is too much research yet to be done.

However, like drilling for oil or prospecting for gold, drilling down through specific case studies is a proven method for identifying broad patterns of behavior that quickly gives one insights to understand current behaviors in American life. That is why we chose the case studies presented in this book. The reader can quickly get the gist of two hundred years of American misinformation, packaged within a useful framework and with insights that can guide current and future behavior. We also intend this book to offer historians writing on a wide range of topics a path to understanding the role that lying and misrepresentation play in their accounts. We will not be as prescriptive as some might want; we wish to leave room for individual behavior. Axios CEO Jim VandeHei, speaking to college students in October 2018, provided suggestions on how politicians, the traditional media, social media companies, and individuals should behave. Speaking to individuals, he argued, "Remember: If your Facebook feed is filled with garbage, it means you were reading garbage in the first place. The algorithm simply gives you more of what you crave."[1] We believe the issue of fake facts in American public life is far more subtle, and that it requires us to explain in more detail its various forms and how Americans use these.

Here is how we do that. The first chapter introduces the reader to the many forms of lying and misrepresentation, the latest thoughts about the social construction of truth, and some cross-cutting themes that we found as we looked at case studies across two hundred years of American history. The final chapter pulls together the commonalities of our case studies and indicates ways in which this material will help you to be a more critical reader of facts in contemporary America.

In between are eight case studies. Two chapters cover presidential elections in which both lying, cheating, and the possibility of misperception had a bearing on the election results: the 1828 election between John Quincy Adams and Andrew Jackson, and the 1960 election between John F. Kennedy and Richard Nixon. Two chapters provide material about conspiracy theories as they related to the assassinations of Abraham Lincoln in 1865 and John Kennedy in 1963. Another chapter provides an account of misrepresentation, especially by the press, in times of war—focusing on the Spanish-American War of 1898 but also providing information about some later wars. Another chapter provides information about misinformation in a business context, examining both consumers' misperceptions about companies and products, and the ways in which businesses misrepresent through advertising—using the patent medicine industry as an extreme case. Two final chapters examine more recent events that involve industries, think tanks, government regulators, and the place of scientific evidence: the claims by the tobacco industry that it is unproven that smoking causes cancer, and the debates over human effects in the environment and the prospects of global warming.

This book would have been difficult to write without the help of colleagues who critiqued our work and made suggestions on how to improve our thinking. These include Michael McDevitt, Burton St. John, Tom Yulsman, and others. We also want to thank the team who worked to produce this book at Rowman & Littlefield. Our editor, Jon Sisk, was an enthusiastic supporter, while we were also served well by Kate Powers, Chelsea Panin, Andy Unger, Lisa Whittington, Garrett Bond, and Sally Rinehart from the Rowman staff.

James W. Cortada
William Aspray

1

Introduction

All control, in essence, is about who controls the truth.

—Joseph Rain[1]

The official philosophies of the totalitarian regimes deny the inherent value of thought. For them thought is not a light but a weapon: its function, they say, is not to discover reality as it is, but to change and transform it with the purpose of leading us towards what is not.

—Alexandre Koyre[2]

It seems that everyone lies. In the mid-1990s, Professor Bella DePaulo, together with some of her faculty colleagues at the University of Virginia, ran an experiment.[3] They asked seventy-seven college students and seventy other adults from the nearby community to keep diaries of the lies they told in a week. These results were anonymously submitted to the researchers for analysis. The researchers then categorized the lies as either self-serving ("told to advantage the liar or protect the liar from embarrassment, blame or other undesired outcomes") or kind ("told to advantage, flatter or protect someone else"). The researchers found that the student telling the most lies averaged 6.6 lies per day, while the adult community member telling the most lies averaged 4.3 lies per day. Forty-six percent of the lies told by students and 57 percent told by community members fell in the self-serving category, while 26 percent of those told by the students and 24 percent told by the community members fell into the kind category. These numbers do not add up to 100 percent because some lies were neither self-serving nor kind but instead functioned to entertain or enable social interaction. Another category, of mean-spirited lies ("to hurt or disparage others"), seldom appeared: 0.8 percent of the lies told by the college students, 2.4 percent of the lies told by community members. The students told approximately two lies per day on average, the community members one.

Returning to this methodology recently, DePaulo used the *Washington Post* tracking of public lies told by President Donald Trump through the first ten and a half months of 2017. In the earlier University of Virginia study, they defined lies by the statement: "A lie occurs any time you intentionally try to mislead someone." But how does this definition apply to political statements and particularly to those of Donald Trump? In analyzing his public statements, DePaulo included falsehoods, misleading statements, and flip-flops as lies—without having any means for determining the intention of the president when making these statements. In his first 298 days in office, DePaulo reported: Trump told approximately six lies per day, much higher than the number told on average by the students or community members in the earlier study. Moreover, between early October and mid-November 2017, the pace had increased to approximately nine lies per day. Trump's lies were harder for DePaulo to code into a single category (self-serving, kind, mean-spirited), presumably because they were serving multiple purposes. In fact, 24 percent fell in multiple categories. Sixty-five percent of Trump's lies were self-serving, higher than the percentage for either the students or community members in the earlier study. Just under 10 percent of Trump's lies fell in the kind category, much lower than either the students or community members in the earlier study. The biggest difference between Trump and the participants in the earlier study, however, was that 50 percent of his lies fell in the mean-spirited category.

Lying has become a popular topic in American public discourse, especially since it is widely believed to have had a significant impact on the 2016 US presidential election and because of the torrent of lies that are being produced regularly out of the White House, led by President Trump himself. These phenomena have led many kinds of academics—communication scholars, economists, folklorists, information scholars, management scholars, philosophers, political scientists, social psychologists, and sociologists, among others—to study fake facts, fake news, and other types of lying.

One of us (Aspray) was in the process of studying urban legends surrounding the 9/11 terrorist attacks at the time that this research field exploded. The other of us (Cortada) was already familiar with the important place of information in American public and private life from writing his book, *All the Facts: A History of Information in the United States Since 1870.*[4] We decided to team up to write a book that intends to illuminate these recent phenomena in American public life. But what value could we add to a scholarly community of hundreds studying these issues, in addition to the thousands of journalists who were following these developments on a daily basis? We noted that most of the journalists and many of the academics thought of fake facts as only a recent phenomenon. But both of us—as historians—know that lying has been a part of public life throughout American history. So, we set out to provide case studies from various eras of American history and involving various aspects of American public life to provide a perspective on what has been happening in recent American history.

LYING AND ITS CONCEPTUAL CORRELATES

Many terms are used regarding lying in American public life: lies, misinformation, disinformation, rumors, falsehoods, fake facts, fake news, urban legends, contemporary legends, false press, and bunk, among others. According to Webster's Online Dictionary, a lie is "a falsehood uttered or acted for the purpose of deception; an intentional violation of truth; an untruth spoken with the intention to deceive."[5] To the degree that a statement is true or false, a lie is associated with having the truth-value of the utterance equal to false. However, sometimes statements have an element of truth without being entirely true. The words *misstatement* or a *misrepresentation* might be used in these cases. Note that this lack of entire truth could be caused by lack of precision in speaking or lack of knowledge of a situation; it might not be consciously intended to deceive someone. *Misinformation* is used to describe information that is false, whether or not it was known to be false when it was spread; whereas *disinformation* is false information that was known to be false when it was spread. The degree to which these utterances diverge from the entire truth, they are said to be *inaccurate*. When someone does lie, they are said to be *mendacious* or to *prevaricate* or *fib* or *falsify* or *tell a fiction*.

The intentionality of a lie may involve telling something that is totally false, but it might instead be told to distort the facts or to provide *subterfuge*, a strategy of using a lie intentionally to gain an end goal. Sometimes people lie with indifference to the truth-value of what they are saying, as in the case of *bullshitting*.[6] Sometimes people exaggerate the details for rhetorical or entertainment purposes, for example, the so-called *tall tale*. Sometimes lies are used to lubricate social interaction, the so-called white lie. Sometimes, lies are used to damage some person's or organization's reputation: *calumny* or *obloquy* or *character assassination* or *vilification*. According to legal terminology, a *defamation* is a libel if written or a *slander* if spoken. The telling of a lie in a court setting constitutes an act of *perjury*.

A *rumor* is a statement or story whose origins are unknown. Its truth-value is unknown, and may be true even though many rumors are false. Rumors have a time sensitivity to them; they are in the present and then tend to die out. A *myth*, which is a belief about something or someone, by contrast to a rumor, tends to be something that becomes established over time and may have temporal staying power. A closely related term is *legend*. The fact-checking site, Snopes, describes the relation between myths and legends:

> Though these two terms are often used interchangeably, they have separate and specific meanings to folklorists. Both myths and legends are stories with casts of characters and plotlines followed to their conclusions, yet their core elements are different. Myths are tales about the acts of godlike or super-natural beings and/or magical animals which serve to explain the creation of the world or how certain elements of our world came to be (e.g., how the rac-coon got its mask) and take place in the far reaches of time (often expressed as "In the days when the world was new"). By contrast, legends are accounts of purported incidents involving ordinary people in more recent times. Al-though both types of stories are told as true, they are not necessarily believed to be literal truth by either the tellers or their audiences.[7]

Urban legends (or as some scholars call them, *contemporary legends*) are a particular type of legend that is often associated with fears associated with living in a complex world. As Snopes describes:

> Urban legends are a specific class of legend, differentiated from "ordinary" legends by their being provided and believed as accounts of actual incidents that befell or were witnessed by someone the teller almost knows (e.g., his sister's hairdresser's mechanic). These tales are told as true, local, and recent occurrences, and often contain names of places or entities located within the teller's neighborhood or surrounding region.[8]

Urban legends are narratives which put our fears and concerns into the form of stories or are tales which we use to confirm the rightness of our worldview. As cautionary tales they warn us against engaging in risky behaviors by pointing out what has supposedly happened to others who did what we might be tempted to try. Other legends confirm our belief that it's a big, bad world out there, one awash with crazed killers, lurking terrorists, unscrupulous companies out to make a buck at any cost, and a government that doesn't give a damn.

While people tend to believe that urban legends are false, they can be true or partially true. Whether true or false, they often serve a real cultural or psychological purpose.

Governments since antiquity have employed propaganda and dissemi-nated falsehoods to serve their aims. The term *disinformation* was apparently coined by Josef Stalin and the practices institutionalized in a KGB unit organized under Stalin in the 1920s.[9] The term came largely into common use in the late 1980s, when reporting on the spread of false information by the Reagan administration to combat Libyan leader Muammar Gaddafi.[10]

A similar term is *lying press* (*Luegenpresse*), which is used pejoratively to characterize the press when it has some political or other goal that is not related to reporting the truth. This term first appeared in Germany, used by Catholics against liberal factions in the German Revolutions of 1848 and 1849, and the term reappeared in common use during the Franco-German War (1870–71), the First World War (1914–1918), the student riots in Berlin (1968), and in far-right political rhetoric in Germany in 2014. The German media used it about Donald Trump in the 2016 presidential election. The terms *fake facts* and *fake news* began to be used in the United States with a similar meaning to lying press.[11]

So, we are left with a certain reality: when we are asked to determine the truthfulness of an assertion or a story, truth is not an absolute. Context matters, the truth is subject to interpretation, and parts of the story might be true without the whole story being true; or the story may be incompletely told. There is a spectrum from absolutely true ("it was 93 degrees at 4 p.m. today") all the way to an outrageous bold falsehood purposefully disseminated for nefarious reasons ("I did not have sexual relations with that woman, Miss Lewinsky")—with many intermediate positions on this spectrum. When a story is partially correct, it may be that the incorrect details are inconsequential, but in other cases—deliberately or by accident—the missing or incorrect information may give a false impression. The range of truthfulness indicates that facts vary, are plastic in that they can be shaped and molded, and that they come in many forms. This book is filled with examples from the eighteenth to the twenty-first centuries, intended to help us gain perspective on truth telling in American public discourse. Only by understanding the variety of representations and misrepresentations, and how they are presented to us, can we begin to constructively understand the nature of facts put before us, whether by a book or magazine or newspaper, or, more often today, by a website.

FACTS AND LIES AS A SOCIALLY CONSTRUCTED REALITY

We begin this section with a longer version of the epigraph that appears near the beginning of this chapter—by the French philosopher of science, Alexandre Koyre:

The official philosophies of the totalitarian regimes unanimously brand as nonsensical the idea that there exists a single objective truth valid for everybody. The criterion of "truth," they say, is not agreement with reality, but agreement with the spirit of a race or nation or class—that is, racial, national or utilitarian. Pushing to their limits the biological, pragmatist, activist theories of truth, the official philosophies of the totalitarian regimes deny the inherent value of thought. For them thought is not a light but a weapon: its function, they say, is not to discover reality as it is, but to change and transform it with the purpose of leading us towards what is not. Such being the case, myth is better than science and rhetoric that works on the passions preferable to proof that appeals to the intellect.[12]

Koyre differentiates between two conceptions of truth. One group of people, for example, including scientists, characterizes truth as "agreement with reality." The other group, in which Koyre includes totalitarian regimes but which we might extend to include most pragmatic politicians today, characterize truth in a utilitarian way, as any thought that contributes to an end goal that is part of a political agenda. As the quotation concludes, for the latter group "rhetoric that works on the passions [is] preferable to proof that appeals to the intellect."

Koyre's statement is very revealing as far as it goes. But it misses the fact that there is a long and honest intellectual debate over how solid facts based in "agreement with reality" actually are. For 150 years, there has been discussion over the philosophical basis of facts. The remainder of this section takes a small detour to consider this honest intellectual debate over the empirical foundations of truth. Of course, this debate matters little to politicians whose only care is for persuading people of their position. The philosophy in this section can be somewhat arcane and difficult to understand, and the reader not interested in these philosophical considerations can skip to the next section without losing much. However, we do come back to these considerations briefly in later chapters, for example, when we talk about the purpose of advertising by businesses.

Throughout the modern history of Western thought, since the time of the Enlightenment in the eighteenth century, facts have generally been regarded as true either because of their logical form or because of empirical evidence, which can be gained through observation or experimentation. However, there is another line of perspectivist thought, which argues that truth is socially constructed. The most influential historical figure who holds this position is the German philosopher Friedrich Nietzsche (1844–1900), but we will also mention a few other major intellectual figures that hold similar views.

Nietzsche rejects positivism; he does not believe in the ultimate ability of human empirical endeavor to establish the basis for facts—for where the positivists believe there are objective facts in the world, Nietzsche believes that there are only human interpretations of what is in the world.

"It is our needs that interpret the world; our drives. . . . Every drive is a kind of list to rule; each one has its perspective that it would like to compel all the other drives to accept as a norm."[13] Nietzsche continues:

> [D]eception, flattering, lying and cheating, talking behind the back, posing, living in borrowed splendor, being masked, the disguise of convention, acting a role before others and before oneself—in short, the constant fluttering around the single flame of vanity is so much the rule and the law that almost nothing is more incomprehensible than how an honest and pure urge for truth could have arisen among men. They are deeply immersed in illusions and dream images; their eye only glides over the surface of things . . . their feeling nowhere leads into truth, but contents itself with the reception of stimuli, playing, as it were, a game of blind man's bluff.[14]

In *Beyond Good and Evil*, Nietzsche uses the phrase "will to truth." He notes that philosophers and scientists have a will to truth, that is, an unexamined belief in the value of "truth, certainty, and knowledge" over "untruth, uncertainty, and ignorance."[15] Nietzsche contrasts this view of philosophers and scientists with ordinary life: he notes that people often live their lives on the basis of untruths, provided that these false beliefs help them to get on with their lives. The belief in a particular fact for Nietzsche is a value judgment about its utility to and conformance with the person's life view. As Nietzsche argues:

> The falseness of a judgment is not necessarily an objection to a judgment. . . . The question is to what extent it is life-advancing, life-preserving, species-preserving, perhaps even species-breeding; and our fundamental tendency is to assert that the falsest judgments . . . are the most indispensable to us, that without granting as true the fictions of logic, without measuring reality against the purely invented world of the unconditional and self-identical, without a continual falsification of the world by means of numbers, mankind could not live—that to renounce false judgments would be to renounce life, would be to deny life. To recognize untruth as a condition of life: that, to be sure, means to resist customary value-sentiments in a dangerous fashion.[16]

Nietzsche thus defines *truth* in a much-quoted passage:

> What then is truth? A movable host of metaphors, metonymies, and anthropomorphisms: in short, a sum of human relations which have been poetically and rhetorically intensified, transferred, and embellished, and which, after long usage, seem to a people to be fixed, canonical, and binding. Truths are illusions which we have forgotten are illusions—they are metaphors that have become worn out and have been drained of sensuous force, coins which have lost their embossing and are now considered as metal and no longer as coins.[17]

Thus, the test of truthfulness—of being a "fact"—is not about how well the assertion mirrors the physical world but instead how well it aligns with these "metaphors." Things are believed to be true because the society shares a common perspective, not because of some underlying physical truth. This defines the perspectivist conception of truth.

The well-known sociologist Emile Durkheim purports a similar line of thought to Nietzsche's. Durkheim, in his *Rules of Sociological Method*, talks about social facts.[18] He contrasts social facts, which consist of "manners of acting, thinking and feeling external to the individual, which are invested with a coercive power of virtue of which they exert control over him," with "organic phenomena [or] physical phenomena, which have no existence save in and through the individual consciousness."[19]

In the last half century, a number of scholars have argued for the power of social norms and social structures to define what is accepted as true—and many of these scholars find an affinity with the beliefs of Nietzsche. Library and information scientists Margaret Egan and Jesse Shera coined the term *social epistemology* in the 1950s. In the 1960s, the influential intellectual historian Michel Foucault and the influential historian and philosopher of science Thomas Kuhn both introduced arguments about the social basis of fact. As one scholar describes Foucault's position:

> Foucault . . . was referring [to] . . . the epistemic status of facts. Facts, as Foucault repeats his power/knowledge analysis in the various fields of profession, are socially constituted and produced by the result of regulation within the system of knowledge. For instance, medical practices and the knowledge applied for them are defined by the power relations within the healthcare system and the hospital, in which there is an agreed consensus of what is deemed to be "knowledge" and "correct practice." This power serves as a converging force that all practitioners can seek agreement from and defines what we do. It can be seen as a meta-structure that frames our practices without explicitly doing so.[20]

Thomas Kuhn's *The Structure of Scientific Revolutions* argued for the importance of community in defining what is accepted truth and what is regarded as anomalous.[21] Bruno Latour and Steve Woolgar, in their book, *Laboratory Life*, go beyond Kuhn with their arguments in favor of the social construction of facts.[22]

In the philosophy community, there has been a similar increase in the study of social epistemology. It is the principal subject of the journal *Social Epistemology*, founded in 1988 by the science and technology studies scholar Steve Fuller; and also of the journal *Episteme* founded in 2004 by the philosophically minded computer scientist Leslie Marsh and the philosophically minded mathematical engineer Christian Onof. As the authors of the *Stanford Encyclopedia of Philosophy* describe the study of social epistemology:

Until recently, epistemology—the study of knowledge and justified belief—was heavily individualistic in focus. The emphasis was on evaluating doxastic attitudes (beliefs and disbeliefs) of individuals in abstraction from their social environment. The result is a distorted picture of the human epistemic situation, which is largely shaped by social relationships and institutions. Social epistemology seeks to redress this imbalance by investigating the epistemic effects of social interactions and social systems.[23]

While these scholars have critical reasons for believing in the social construction of truth, in the recent years known as the "post-truth" era, political advocates—especially, but not only, those of a conservative bent—have adopted an uncritical but politically expedient stance. These political advocates ignore or deny objective facts and appeal instead to emotion and personal belief.[24] Nietzsche would argue that they have a "will to power" rather than a "will to truth."[25]

WHAT IS COVERED IN THIS BOOK

Between the introduction and the concluding chapter, readers will find eight case studies, which present instances of lies and misinformation in American public life from the early nineteenth century until the present day. Our choice of case studies was governed by certain principles. The cases tend to be about multiple events spreading over an extended period of time, involving many people, and of interest to relatively large audiences. Even if a single event—such as a presidential assassination—provoked a situation, the case typically involved additional events such as the contemporary reactions to the assassination, the various theories propounded, and the fact-finding missions engaged in to understand the signal event. These cases are by and large grounded in truthful actual events—that is, the USS *Maine* did indeed sink and President Lincoln indeed was shot. Thus, with only one category of exceptions, we did not select cases where the event did not happen or cannot be verified, such as Martians in Roswell, New Mexico, or Elvis sightings. The one exception involves rumors that took on a life of their own and became the story behind real-life events themselves, such as claims of satanic ownership of Procter & Gamble or snakes residing among piles of bananas imported from Central America to the United States.

Even though our criteria narrowed our choices, there were still too many cases to cover in a single book. It was even more hopeless to try to write a comprehensive narrative chronicling the history of lies in American public life. So, we content ourselves with representative examples. Table 1.1 presents examples of topics we considered but did not have room to present in this book.

Table 1.1. Examples of Case Studies of Lies and Misrepresentation in American Public Life Not Included in This Book

Types	Examples
Rumors	Slave rebellions (1790s–1861)
Rumors	Elvis Presley sightings in supermarkets (1960s–2000s)
Conspiracies	Tonkin Resolution that led to expanded US involvement in Viet Nam (1960s)
Lies	Denial of Roswell, New Mexico, alien landings (1940s)
Lies	Moon landing by humans (1969)
Lies	Russian intervention in US elections (2010s)
Religious	End of the world coming (1840s)
Religious	Visitations of Virgin Mary in Wisconsin (1859)
Military	Leaks of misinformation on Allied invasion site of France (1944)
Scandal	Presidential love affairs denied (1960s, 1990s, 2016–2018)
Political	President Nixon denying Watergate involvement (1970s)
News	Life on the Moon discovered (1835)
News	Death of Mark Twain reported falsely (1897)
News	Toilet paper shortage reported by Johnny Carson (1970s)
News	*War of the World* radio broadcast by H. G. Wells (1938)

So, what do we cover? We have chosen case studies (chapters 2–9) to show that lying and misinformation has been a critical element throughout the history of American public life, and also to demonstrate the wide range of activities that fall under this theme, including national elections, presidential assassinations, wars, trade association coverups, science policy, and rumors harming business organizations.

Chapter 2 examines one of the most raucous presidential elections in American history, that between General Andrew Jackson and John Quincy Adams in 1828. Many of the campaigning practices evident in today's elections first appeared in the 1820s: two national parties, a large direct vote by citizens, and coordinated dissemination of misinformation on a nationwide basis. Various forms of false facts, rumors, conspiracies, and other forms of misleading communications were in evidence. These are described to demonstrate that patterns of political communications evident today were already in evidence two centuries ago.

Chapter 3 explores the presidential election of 1960, which pitted Richard Nixon against John F. Kennedy. While many similarities to the election of 1828 are noted, the 1960 election also introduced two new information elements: tacit information that voters acquired by watching the candidates in televised debates, a development that profoundly influenced campaigning over the next half century; and the impact of highly organized campaign operations that did not last a few months (as in the nineteenth century) but rather years, with the American voter inundated with orders of magnitude more messaging than had occurred even as recently as the Second World War. Lies, misinformation, and rumors dominated much of the discussion of both of these presidential elections.

We turn next to two presidential assassinations as vehicles for exploring the combination of settled and unsettled facts, genuine differences of opinion of events, gross misrepresentations of evidence, and most importantly, the role of conspiracies. The assassinations of Presidents Abraham Lincoln (1865) and John F. Kennedy (1963) are each sometimes described as the "mother of all conspiracies" for good reasons: millions of people engaged in them, thousands of speculators wrote and opined about them, and both remain unsettled today despite the passage of time, massive research, and the continuing discovery of new information.

We begin with Lincoln's assassination in chapter 4, less because it occurred first, more because it established the pattern of interest, research, conspiracies, and rumors that characterized not only Kennedy's death, but also that of other Americans such as Martin Luther King, Robert Kennedy, and Malcolm X. In the Lincoln case, new information—tidbits of data and rumor—kept appearing in articles and books; and each time that happened, new swirls of rumors, implications, speculations, conclusions, and conspiracies attracted the attention of several million people. The Lincoln case also enables us to explore the role of myth-making, first introduced with the example of Andrew Jackson, now extended to the Civil War president, who became a dominant figure in the Parthenon of American saints.

In chapter 5 we explore what clearly was, and is, the largest example of conspiracy theories in American history: the assassination of President Kennedy. The sheer volume of material on the subject generated in the past half century is daunting, as is the number of experts and dilettante historians attempting to uncover various US and foreign assassination plots involving Russians, Cubans, Mexicans, and such iconic American agencies as J. Edgar Hoover's FBI, the White House (with President Johnson as ring leader), Congress, the Department of Defense, the Treasury Department, the State and Justice Departments, and the CIA. And that is before one even explores the roles of rich Texas oilmen, the Dallas Police Department, or the district attorney for New Orleans! As in the Lincoln case, we have the opportunity to explain how the features of information gathered by police and other legal entities could be manipulated, misinterpreted, and communicated for both objective and mischievous purposes.

With chapter 6 we move close to themes that resonate with the 9/11 terrorist attacks, the US military engagement in Afghanistan, and the subsequent engagements in Iraq and Syria. The chapter focuses on the Spanish-American War of 1898, which led to a more activist role for the United States in world events. Historians of this conflict are in wide agreement that newspaper editors played a profound role in pushing the United States into war with Spain to liberate Cuba from its colonial master. Historians of American journalism consider this war the most extreme example of the newspaper media affecting national policy. Thus, we explore what the newspapers did and how they did it—paying attention to the nature of the information, the reporting, and the editorializing they employed. While newspaper editors continued to influence American political events in the twentieth century, never again were they so effective in influencing the nation's views until the *Washington Post* engaged in its Watergate reporting in the early 1970s, leading to the resignation of President Nixon—a first in American history. We conclude this chapter with some contrasts between information in the Spanish-American War and later wars in which the United States participated, in particular the First and Second World Wars and subsequent conflicts to the present.

Because businesses have been active manipulators of information throughout American history, and more so as the percent of the US economy engaged in agriculture began to decline sharply after 1870, we present case studies that begin to define the role of corporations, in particular, in shaping the public's understanding and use of information. We show that there is far more to the story of manipulating information for profit than advertising. In fact, advertising is only a small part when it comes to how enterprises gathered, created, and used information.

To begin analyzing the business facet of American life, in chapter 7 we examine the role of rumors (e.g., a dead mouse in your soda or hamburger) and how corporations dealt with such branding crises, then turn to what might be the most notorious example of nefarious, misleading, malicious advertising in American history, concerning patent medicine merchandizing. Just as we used the Kennedy assassination to demonstrate an extreme case of conspiracies to highlight patterns of behavior, we do the same with patent medicines to accentuate the extremes one could go to in advertising. The reader can be assured that most advertising in the twentieth century was far more benign and truthful than this case would suggest—in part because of government regulations and laws that often were developed in response to the egregious claims made by patent medicine purveyors in the years before the Second World War. It is also a business example similar to the outrageous language that we encountered in the election of 1828, suggesting that throughout American history extreme hyperbole existed with almost complete disregard for truth. Donald Trump was far from the first person to lie so much; whole industries did so as well.

With the emergence of large corporations in the second half of the nineteenth century and their continuing presence as a major feature of the American economy down to the present, there also emerged clusters of companies that economists, government officials, scholars, and businesses call *industries*. By the Second World War, these industries acted as informational ecosystems, complete with trade magazines, associations, and lobbyists; and with shared beliefs, vocabulary, and bodies of information, myths, and similar practices. Members of an industry could act in unison to promote their collective welfare. Their weapon of choice was information—used to influence how government, rivals, and the public viewed them. That practice required new forms of information gathering, manipulation, shaping, and dissemination. Their experiences merged the two strands of case studies we presented in earlier studies—the political and the commercial—representing a relatively new arena of conspiracies, new forms of misinformation, outright lies and falsehoods of many types, all well-oiled with vast budgets devoted to lobbyists, advertising, think tanks, academic researchers, and diverse types of publications and digital communications. To illustrate how these new informational activities functioned, we discuss two cases: how the tobacco industry sought to stave off regulation of cigarette smoking, and the multi-industry initiative to discourage the American government from implementing remediation initiatives regarding climate change (global warming).

The tobacco case study is taken up in chapter 8. The role of the American tobacco industry is one of the best documented examples of how an industry plotted to block Congress and regulators from constraining sales of its product. We know about this history thanks to litigation over the past half century that made available to the public the minutes of meetings, internal correspondence and e-mails, and testimony of its participants. We see how rumors, conspiracies, lies, and criminal activities all interacted over many decades, shaping the public's views of a family of smoking products. This industry's use of information became the model emulated by other industries protecting and promoting their interests, using various shades and forms of information to "have it their way."

Chapter 9 builds on similar themes, by illustrating how multiple industries and constituencies collaborated, conspired, and shaped the informational content of messages available to the American public about human impact on the environment in the so-called global warming debates. Initiated by the petroleum industry, its leaders recruited others to its cause to such an effective degree that today the United States is the only government in the world that does not support global-wide initiatives to control carbon dioxide emissions, which scientists long ago determined to be the primary cause of global warming. The behind-the-scenes manipulation of information is vast and complex, making the rumor-mongering and editorial conspiracies of the 1820s look trivial in comparison. The environmental case study neatly brings us back to the complex nature of the manipulation of information described in the first several case studies in this book.

Chapter 10 provides conclusions drawn from our historical case studies concerning American life today. We pull several main findings from each study and draw parallels and contrasts with the situation today. We explain why this kind of historical perspective provides important context to people living in today's America. We explain how these insights are useful to the media, politicians, educators, and ordinary citizens; and we identify gaps in our knowledge and possible lines of research for us or others.

Cross-Cutting Themes

The final task in this initial chapter is to identify five cross-cutting themes that appear in most of our case studies. These themes were in evidence over the expanse of American history and were consistent with how Americans used various kinds of information, regardless of whether it was truthful, accurate, misinformed, or false. We call them *cross-cutting* because these appeared in almost all cases and often across the entire duration of a case—although they did vary in both intensity and form from case to case. Such seemingly incongruous cases as the 150-year-long debate over President Lincoln's assassination, various forms of advertising, and political and issue-based lobbying all exhibit these themes. We believe these five themes can help scholars, media consultants, and users of information to identify common practices to inform them in their work.

First, all participants in these case studies used information and misinformation as their primary tool for accomplishing specific goals. This practice acknowledges the wide scope in the use of fake (and accurate) information. The most obvious and familiar examples can be found in presidential campaigns. For example, in 1828, some of Andrew Jackson's rivals called his mother a whore. His rivals categorically and incorrectly characterized his attitude towards the expulsion of Indians from territories desired by frontier settlers. In 1960, Republicans portrayed John F. Kennedy as a Catholic who would take orders from the pope; yet he rarely attended church and did not believe in the church hierarchy interfering with public administration. Misinforming, or presenting truth in a jaded manner, appeared in other areas of life when it could support a point of view. For instance, some students of Abraham Lincoln's assassination argued that a small group of senior Confederate officials plotted the deed, tracing the steps of a small group operating in New York and Canada, suggesting they were the main participants; when, in fact, it was actor John Wilkes

Booth who committed the murder in collaboration with an entirely different set of participants.

The use of fake and accurate information, whether accepted as is or manipulated, has been part of a much broader trend in American society. Beginning in the 1600s and extending to the present, residents in North America increasingly relied on facts—information—with which to go about their daily work, to formulate points of view on a wide range of topics, and to persuade others to agree with their point of view. That was made possible by a high rate of literacy, the availability of considerable printed (and later electronic) materials, and a strong-enough economy to support the acquisition, use, and dissemination of information. So, while useful facts circulated, such as how to plow a field or tune up an automobile, lies and fake facts circulated too. No aspect of American life was absent the use of good and bad, true and false information. As many historians believe, the amount of information one relied on to carry out their everyday life activities increased over time.[26] Hence, it is not surprising that Americans took advantage of both information and misinformation in increasing amounts as time passed. This cross-current helps explain why, by the second half of the twentieth century, the tobacco industry distributed many more facts (including numerous fake facts) than had newspapers in the 1890s about Spanish colonial rule in Cuba.

Second, information of all types and degrees of accuracy were presented in the literary and rhetorical style of its day. This practice reflected a genre of information handling commonly deployed. In the 1700s, for example, politicians used language that we would consider outrageous today. In 1828, Jackson's wife was called an adulteress, his mother a whore. In 1960, the thought of this kind of personal attack on the Kennedy family was inconceivable. Calling President Lincoln a "monkey"—a popular word used by his political opponents—was, again, inconceivable in twentieth-century politics. Not until the political campaign of Donald Trump was the use of derogatory nicknames back in style—and even then, only used by him, not by professional politicians. The media that were used also evolved over time, affecting the style of presentation of misinformation and lies. In the 1800s, for example, newspaper articles and pamphlets were widely used for political, religious, and economic discourse; and by the end of the century, books were added to the list. The greater brevity (sound bites, shorter treatments) of expression encouraged by radio and television led to a new genre of statement-without-qualification explanations of adjectives. A 1930s' radio news broadcast might declare that President Roosevelt wanted to "pack" the Supreme Court, when in fact the president was trying to get the justices to stop declaring his New Deal legislation unconstitutional, not necessarily to alter the size of the court, except as a last resort. Declarations of points of view by millions posting on the Internet in an active voice without explanation (or evidence) became normal, so much so that websites appeared to correct statements that on their face value were false and had not been vetted.

The issue of vetting the truth appears in all the case studies. The form of vetting depended on the genre. In the 1600s and 1700s, information was routinely presented without the benefit of scientific knowledge, often by amateurs who did not know better. But beginning in the 1830s and continuing over the next 150 years, the professionalization of experts writing newspaper articles, serving as doctors, and teaching children increased slowly but steadily, picking up momentum in the mid-twentieth century. Professionalization was advanced through formal education such as a college degree, membership in an academic organization such as the American Medical Association, and licensing such as an electrician authorized by the state to practice a trade. The public came to rely on properly trained experts to inform them. Experts increasingly relied on truth, rather than misrepresentation, in their normal work practices. But, in the late 1990s and into the twenty-first century, anyone could access the Internet and post whatever they wanted to say, regardless of their status as an expert. The number of commentators using the Internet so outnumbered the experts that people had to start looking for "trusted sites." We learned that the American public faced two problems: that they did not always know how to discriminate between true and fake news, and that they could often not discern the true identity of a source. For example, was a perspective or fact coming from a friend on Facebook or was it a Russian attempting to foment discord in an election? Was the friend an expert on the topic at hand?

Third, people and organizations weaponized information to accomplish their objectives. This practice reflected the value of using misinformation for practical purposes. Americans have long viewed information as a tool, something to be used to solve a problem, improve an activity, make it more efficient, or persuade someone of their point of view. Information had to have purpose, and not be some abstract intellectual activity done for amusement. A good example of weaponizing information is advertising. Case studies in this book explore the rise of professional advertising in the nineteenth century, the controversial use of that form of information handling by patent medicine vendors and the tobacco industry, and the more modest use by groups lobbying on both sides of the climate change debates. Politics, of course, is rife with the deployment of information to achieve some political goal.

Compare the 1960 presidential election to that of 2016. In both cases, each party wished to create an image of its presidential candidate that it felt would result in the candidate's election and to do the same to the opponent so as to make that individual unattractive to voters. Kennedy's

Democrats spoke of him as healthy (when he was not) and of his opponent as dishonest and unethical—Tricky Dick (when more recent historical analyses has shown that he was more ethical than suspected at the time). In 2016, Trump created effective negative images for all of his opponents—such as "Little Marco" Rubio and "Pocahontas" Elizabeth Warren—while Democratic candidate Hillary Clinton characterized Trump's supporters as "Deplorables." Each candidate's characterizations worked inasmuch as they caused some voters to embrace them and to reject their opponents. One could argue that in the case of the 2016 election campaign, the divisiveness that emerged proved more intense than had been seen in American politics since the 1820s. Heating up the base occurred in all three elections—1828, 1860, and 2016—continuing beyond the national political campaign and after the election to disseminate false information and insults aimed at specific audiences that could be largely counted upon to accept them at face value. Although bloggers on Facebook carried this out in 2016, partisan newspapers in the nineteenth century were just as effective at this task.

Fourth, as ever-larger organizations formed, they too (and not just individuals) used misinformation. This practice demonstrated the role of scale in the ever-widening use of information. Prior to the fourth quarter of the nineteenth century, government and private organizations were small, and large companies and large public sector departments did not begin to emerge in any quantity until the early 1900s. Only then did large corporations become widespread. General Motors, AT&T, Ford, Sears Roebuck, Wells Fargo, and IBM were important corporate examples; the military was the first large department within the US government. Superimposed on these, primarily in the private sector, were national industry associations, unions, and lobbyist and nonprofit issue-oriented organizations—not the least of which included religious denominations and political parties. Almost from their beginning, larger groups became aggressive users of information and misinformation, and even of bold-faced lies (e.g., tobacco industry) to promote their causes. These activities resulted in far more information diffused than any individual or even small collection of newspapers could distribute. By the second half of the twentieth century, these large organizations could afford to hire people skilled in advertising, lobbying, writing, and the law, who they employed to manipulate information in promoting their points of view. They could be amoral, as in the case of the tobacco industry; outrageously unethical, as in the case of the patent medicine industry before government regulators began to rein in their exaggerations and lies; or they could simply spin arguments and data to promote their causes (e.g., medical advocacy groups promoting support for their particular disease research agendas, or climate change advocates arguing for control over factory emissions).

All of these organizations professionalized the collection and presentation of information, ranging from absolute truths based on science and other academic research to outright lies, to a far greater extent than possible before. They dominated messaging from a top-down and out form beyond what occurred prior to the 1900s. In short, weaponized information scaled up through an expanded media that included various forms of direct mail, print, radio, television, and the Internet. The case studies of the tobacco industry and climate change advocates demonstrate how this cross-current worked in American society for more than a century.

Fifth, the impact of individuals declined, although never disappeared, while the importance of institutions grew in importance. This cross-cutting practice reflected the kinds of shifting sources of power and influence in evidence since the early 1800s. There was a partial switchback to the voice of individuals that occurred largely after the adoption of the Internet and social media, which gave individuals a new voice that millions adopted. These individuals often had neither the desire, the responsibility, nor the capability to scrutinize the materials they produced or forwarded for its factual basis. Thus in a striking way, the Internet era is like the practice that existed before the 1870s, when individual newspaper editors would reprint articles that appeared in other newspapers they favored and even earlier to the practice of individuals publishing pamphlets sold in bookshops and general stores opining on a topic without any vetting by the printer regarding the accuracy of the content or qualifications of the author. Thus, we arrive in the early decades of the twenty-first century at a situation in which bottom-up communication competes with institutional bottom-down messaging. The two are often intertwined, sometimes without a reader understanding the original source. In the process we see the situation in which one can believe that the Internet gave back a voice to individuals, but not to the extent that Internet dreamers imagined, because the institutional voices remained loud and determinative.

With the availability of social media, the inadequacy of training of students and adults on how to discriminate between fake and accurate information, and the inherent cognitive behavior that makes people tend to believe that which is already familiar to them, it is readily possible for both true and false information to be widely spread and believed.

2

Political Communication in Presidential Elections and the Case of 1828

American politics has often been an arena for angry minds.

—Richard Hofstadter, 1964[1]

Richard Hofstadter was a historian of American politics with a discerning eye for the details of discourse and intentions. He observed that, across American history, politicians had a way of dealing with information and ideas that tended to be pejorative because their thoughts "had a greater affinity for bad causes than good." He argued that the *paranoid*, the word he used to describe "a style of mind," could be used for good or bad causes. "Style has more to do with the way in which ideas are believed and advocated than with the truth or falsity of their content."[2] Conspiracy and threats to peace and prosperity often were themes found in the rhetoric of political campaigns, and politicos always identified enemies. They and their allies held low expectations that problems would be solved, but at least their "cherished convictions" could be protected.[3] Nowhere in American political history did one see such behavior on display more intensely than in national elections. Over fifty presidential elections have been held during the past twenty-two decades, and every one of them exhibited intense, exaggerated rhetoric and loose play with the truth. Facts were weapons, which were malleable and often not truthful. This observation applied regardless of whether a president was elected by state electors, as was the case prior to the 1820s, or through national elections (although the ultimate decision was made by the Electoral College). The behavior was practically universal.

An election is about persuading voters to select a candidate to be an official, and for over two centuries that has meant it is incumbent on candidates to (a) convince the public that they shared common views on the issues of the day, (b) that they agreed on the goals to be achieved by that official, and (c) that rivals were not qualified by views, experience, or objectives to be elected. It is this third issue (c) that often dominated in speeches, campaign literature, and news coverage over the centuries. It is why Hofstadter could speak about paranoia in American politics. It is also why examining US presidential elections offers a view into the use of fake facts, misinformation, conspiracy theories, and myth building in American life. Presidential elections are large, time-consuming events that grip the nation every four years, often dominating the news and much conversation except in those rare cases where there was a national crisis such as a major war underway, for example, the Civil War, the two world wars, or Vietnam. No other recurring event in American life came as close to riveting the public's attention, and since the First World War also the attention of many people in Europe, Asia, and Latin America. It is why this chapter focuses on the role of information in American presidential elections.

Politicians certainly did not make these elections boring. In this and the next chapter, we see wives accused of sexual improprieties, husband and wife charged with bigamy, and one candidate claimed as being a servant to the pope. We also see cases of corrupted voting processes, and other candidates (not discussed here) of paying cash for votes, getting voters drunk (a practice of long standing dating to the early 1700s in Colonial North America), and insulting individuals, questioning their ethics, and accusing them of other crimes and misdemeanors.

We intend to paint some of the color of these campaigns in this and the next chapter. This chapter first talks generally about political communication in presidential elections, and the last third of the chapter provides an extended discussion of the election of 1828. This and the next chapter focus on two case studies to make several points. First, the behaviors Hofstadter identified are not merely recent phenomena; they have been in evidence for more than two centuries and remain in place today. Some readers of this book may have come to the topic because of the behavior of the presidential candidates in 2016 and the many accusations that President Donald Trump lied about most issues.[4] However one feels about Donald Trump's truthfulness, his behavior is not new; it is simply more extreme than voters had been used to seeing in the previous ninety years of presidential campaigns. The most recent ninety years has been a period of relative calm and sobriety in presidential political discourse compared to the late nineteenth century or the period before the American Civil War.[5] To illustrate this long history, we look at two campaigns. The 1828 campaign, discussed in this chapter, is considered one of the most outrageous in American history—involving blatant falsehoods, shamelessly presented to the public as fact. Yet, the 1828 campaign will seem eerily familiar to those who observed the 2016 campaign.[6] While the intensity of the use of false facts and accusations ebbed and flowed over the next century, the behavior never went away entirely. It did evolve, however, to conform with the style of political discourse of the day. To provide comparison to both 1828 and 2016, in the next chapter we consider the 1960 election. It too set a tone, a style for how election campaigns would be conducted over the next half century.

The elections of 1828 and 1960 allow us to explore issues political scientists have studied with respect to information, going beyond Hofstadter's notion of paranoia. Specifically, we add to our earlier discussions about exaggerations, misrepresentations, conspiracies, and myth making with an exploration of the use of language, which one political scientist dubbed "the linguistic reconstruction of facts," and contribute further evidence that people can hold views about issues not based on hard evidence.[7] In other words, facts did not always need to be considered before taking an action such as voting. These two case studies also allow us to explore how fake facts diffuse in American society.

WHAT POLITICAL SCIENTISTS TEACH US ABOUT FAKE FACTS

As political scientist Murray Edelman observed, facts that bother or reassure and stimulate conflicts often conform to an individual's beliefs "about what should be happening."[8] People take ambiguous facts, or those that are difficult to accept, and repackage them in ways they understand, enabling them to either accept them or dismiss them as untrue. For a presidential candidate, using ambiguous language made it possible for his (or rarely, her) followers to interpret what they were hearing in any way they wanted—that is, in ways matching their preconceived opinions and beliefs. Such behavior by candidates and voters has proved to be highly effective. That is why, for centuries, a presidential candidate could demonize adversaries, call them traitors, racists, unpatriotic, or enemies of the state.

Edelman spent decades studying how Americans responded to information served up by politicians and government agencies, arguing that governments shaped opinions of large numbers of people and set expectations. They did this through behaviors that, after two centuries, one could categorize as ritual. These rituals might include the use of ambiguous language, draping over a point of view the American flag or patriotic language, as President Ronald Reagan did in the 1980s when he talked about the "City on the Hill," or as President Abraham Lincoln

did earlier, when he spoke of what the Founding Fathers did "Four score
and seven years ago"—not to mention the routine setting of presidents
speaking with a row of American flags behind their podium. It is in such
language that political myths nestle as points of view, as preconceived notions held by the public. President John F. Kennedy's presidency became
"Camelot," a magical time that, in reality, was as harsh and politically
dangerous as many others in American history; or seeing President Lincoln as the "martyred" president, when in reality a year before his death
political observers seriously doubted he would be reelected by his Union
and noting that he was already hated by the Confederacy.[9] Sometimes
these myths are developed during a national campaign, as in the case of
a vigorous John Kennedy in 1960, when in fact he was ill. At other times,
they are perpetuated, as in the case of Andrew Jackson in the 1820s as a
crude, ill-mannered, rough-and-tumble frontier hero who fought Indians
and the British.[10]

The political scientist Edelman concluded, "political beliefs and perceptions are very largely not based on empirical observations or, indeed,
upon 'information' at all."[11] As Edelman argues, what is not known from
empirical information is often "the most resistant to revision based on
observations of the world," thus reducing or totally eliminating the possible influence of actual—truthful—information.[12] Experienced politicians
acquired this insight and used it during national elections. It often was
best deployed in stirring public controversy: In addition to examples concerning Andrew Jackson and John Kennedy in this and the next chapter,
was Franklin D. Roosevelt a Socialist or, equally troubling, eager to enter
the Second World War when Americans wanted to stay out? Were any of
many dozens of candidates for president pro-labor or anti–Big Business
racist or too liberal? The list of issues is endless, but every campaign had
its own special examples. There is nothing like a good dose of uncertainty
to create doubt and suspicion based on preconceived notions and old-
fashioned prejudice. Sound bites and lack of intellectually rigorous discourse served the purpose of enabling ambiguous statements to fit nicely
into preconceived worldviews of potential voters: Southern candidates
were anti-black, those from New England did not understand the South
or the needs of Midwestern farmers, rich politicians would not be able to
help the poor on welfare and could instead be counted on to reduce funding for those in need—certainly if they were Republicans. Democrats, of
course, would raise everyone's taxes, spend too much money, and drive
the nation into greater debt.

People in general do not change their worldview other than in minor
ways. When people changed their worldviews, it occurred slowly, as
we see in later chapters with respect to smoking causing cancer and air
pollution causing climate change. A voter's instinct was to continue de-

fending his or her political beliefs.[13] So, metaphors and myths provided meaning to otherwise complex issues and facts that stimulated anxiety. Often a politician did not have to define an issue or point of view; he or she could simply assume it. The public was more interested in reinforcing impressions in their mind than in accumulating and analyzing data about an issue.[14] Thomas Jefferson assumed most Americans wanted to optimize farm life; Donald Trump assumed that his political base believed Mexican immigrants were bad people; Richard Nixon assumed that most Americans saw Communists as enemies of the United States; and all post–Second World War candidates assumed that voters wanted to defend freedom. So, the public accepted simple explanations for complex issues: push the Indians west to rid the nation of their threat (Jackson), keep Europe out of Latin America (James Monroe and his Monroe Doctrine), a "New Deal" for every American to solve the Great Depression (Franklin Roosevelt), the "New Frontier" is a way of energizing a new generation and economy (Kennedy), or "Make America Great Again" (Trump) when it was already the world's most prosperous economy with its lowest unemployment rate in a half century.

In each presidential election, one could identify common themes in support of mythic expressions. Often these involved identifying outsiders as enemies, for example, immigrants by Trump and by almost every presidential candidate from the 1840s through the 1920s on the conservative side. Abolitionists were a threat to Southern pre–Civil War voters. Urban citizens and rural Americans were pitted against each other, rich vs. poor, white vs. black, educated vs. less educated. The "other" was always dangerous, un-American, and to be guarded against by the candidate who offered to save the nation—or at least his or her adherents—from the "undesirables." Presidents and candidates routinely call upon the public to work together, to implement the leader's plan, to protect the nation from its enemies and problems. Kennedy spoke of "Ask not what your country can do for you. Ask what you can do for your country" in his inaugural address. To strengthen the "call to arms," politicians reinforce perceptions by blaming problems and other unwanted developments on some group accused of deliberately taking action not in the interests of the nation. In the Progressive Era of the early 1900s, Big Business was regarded as harming workers; in the 1950s, Senator Joseph ("Joe") McCarthy saw Russian spies and Communists lurking in every government agency and in Hollywood; and, in the 1960s, Nixon identified enemies in the antiwar student movement. Whether these claims were true or not was beside the point.[15]

Communication scholar Dan F. Hahn has identified features of ambiguous language, which is the discourse commonly used by politicians, and not only during elections. See textbox 2.1.

> **Textbox 2.1.   Features of Ambiguous Language—as Typically Used by Politicians***
> - Language choices which we might disagree with
> - Simplifications that are oversimplifications
> - Generalizations regarding policies, which can be variously interpreted
> - Technical or pragmatic language used to deliver the truth
>
> ---
> * Hahn, *Political Communication*, 89–91.

Each of these features leads to a degree of ambiguity in the utterance. So, truth can be distorted or misrepresented by candidates on purpose (usually) or by accident (rarely during the message-conscious twentieth century). Misrepresentations of facts are brought about most often by the use of euphemisms, simplifications, generalizations, and the art of attempting to say nothing. On this last point, Hahn has an equally useful list of techniques in evidence in most national elections (see textbox 2.2).

> **Textbox 2.2. Communication Techniques Used by Politicians in National Elections***
> - Memorable phrases, such "military-industrial complex," "New Frontier," "Great Society"
> - Earnestness, such as Nixon's, "let me make one thing perfectly clear"
> - Grand vision, such as Senator Barry Goldwater in his 1964 presidential campaign, speaking about "flowering of the Atlantic Civilization"
> - Political jargon, such as "hard work," "God," or "lawless crime"
>
> ---
> *   Hahn, *Political Communication*, 102–106.

While various forms of information packaging have routinely been in evidence in American elections, the voting public incongruously has held fundamental faith in the value of information. While it seems that respect for facts is momentarily suspended during a national election—later even by the elected president seeking support for implementing a particular policy—in all eras, the public nevertheless expected facts and truth to be applied by public officials in the course of doing their daily work.[16]

The situation of a presidential candidate exaggerating or disseminating misinformation on the one hand, while on the other running government agencies that assiduously collect and use accurate facts, must seem confusing. But as political scientist Bruce Bimber reminds us, government in a democracy "is an apparatus for assembling and managing the political information associated with expressions of public will and with public policy."[17] Ruling elites use information, "to influence public opinion, set agendas, mobilize citizens into collective action, make decisions, and implement policies."[18] Therein lies the intersection between truth, misinformation, falsehoods, and outright lies, all driven by the need to get elected, organize public opinion, and carry out the work of government. Nowhere in the life of a democracy do all those elements come into play in the most public manner more so than in a national presidential election.

This behavior evolved over time. Prior to 1800, individuals making decisions about who should be president were largely politicos in the national capital and the political elites in the few states that made up the nation. In the first thirty years of the nineteenth century, national political parties emerged, characterized by simple national organizations and newspapers aligned with them to promote partisan points of view. These parties came quickly to dominate the creation of public opinion and to shape discourse and implementation of policies in government. The next major change in that process occurred between 1880 and the First World War: large political party infrastructures, interest groups focused on one or a few issues, and the use of large amounts of information thrust into society through print media. These were characteristics of the Spanish-American War.

By the early 1950s, politicians could command the attention of everyone in the nation. The extent of this shift can hardly be exaggerated. Radio, then television, and since before the Second World War general news magazines, made that possible. Interest groups (now usually called "lobbyists"), research and propaganda arms of national political parties, and influential opinion makers all used newly developed methods for acquiring and communicating information in ways effective in influencing the public, as evidenced in the cases of smoking and climate change discussed later in the book. These techniques were by this time in full use by all candidates for the presidency and other national and most state elected positions. In the post-1950 period, television played a profound role, as we see in the next chapter with the 1960 presidential campaign. To a large degree, dissemination of false and true facts remained centralized at the national level.

Political scientists also began to think of political communications that occurred in recent decades, together with their influences and features, as evolving—documenting their "more diverse, fragmented, and complex" forms. For example, targeting specific audiences became more precise over time (Catholic voters in Wisconsin in 1960, anti-Vietnam messaging aimed at college students in the 1970s). Historians think in terms of "eras," which are similar to the notion of "phasing." Both are essentially describing similar patterns of communications. A politician might deliver lengthier explanations of their views tailored to different ethnic groups in the 1940s through articles and pamphlets; yet in the 1960s through television, therefore, using different words and style of presentation, often to more massive audiences that television reached. However, these practices were already evident in earlier times, such as in the 1820s. But their frameworks proved useful in organizing discussions about the role of information (accurate, inaccurate and so forth), such as phasing offered by Jay G. Blumler and Dennis Kavanagh.[19] The growing insistence in parsing definitions of different types of information is also useful, indeed essential. The definition of "fake news" and its role as potentially harmful news-like content is an example.[20] We see in both chapters a conformance to the definition of disinformation increasingly favored by political scientists looking at recent times, that this form of information seeks a result using the most effective message needed.[21]

Beginning in the 1990s, however, a new tool was added to this information dissemination ecosystem: the Internet. The immediate effect of so many tens of millions of voters using it was the multiplication of lies, facts, and misinformation—as well of grassroot organizations and individual voices. That decentralization of information creation and dissemination added massively to the mix of facts and rumors, as well as cries of conspiracies, which now are so much in play in twenty-first-century national elections.[22] The use of disinformation has been with us since the nineteenth century for military purposes, but it has also been used in political discourse since the earliest days of American political affairs.[23] Misinformation has been studied more than disinformation within the political arena, and that difference in maturity informs our discussion.[24]

From the beginning of the United States, politicians wanted to control what people knew and, to use the phrase Alexander Hamilton deployed in 1787 to explain the concept, "the center of information." He used the word "information" some three dozen times in *The Federalist* papers.[25] Like a media expert of the twenty-first century, Hamilton linked the word to another word, "communication," using it a dozen times.[26] He thought of the use of information in positive terms, envisioning the national government as the prime creator and communicator of facts. So, it would be natural that the president would do the same in the political arena. Before his elevation to the presidency, James Madison worried about "secret wishes of an unjust and interested majority" or minority that would lead to the improper use of information.[27] Both voters and politicians in the eighteenth and much of the nineteenth centuries had limited access to accurate and inaccurate information, compared to Americans since then, so people often relied instead on impressions and unsubstantiated facts. Use of the telegraph beginning in the 1840s, the telephone in the 1870s, the radio in the 1920s, television in the 1950s, personal computer networks in the 1980s, and the Internet in the 1990s changed that circumstance, as did the parallel growth in the aggregate educational levels of American citizens and the massive availability of printed material.[28]

The press was a critical delivery mechanism for fake news from the early 1800s—as we see in the Jacksonian case—through to the end of the twentieth century, with television being a strong second source, beginning in the mid-1950s. In the years prior to Andrew Jackson running for president, the press was largely the property of political factions and was extremely biased in its coverage of issues of interest to political factions and parties. While that bias continued into the twentieth century, beginning in the 1820s more independent newspapers began to appear and they increasingly covered more than political issues. By the end of the 1800s, newspapers were aspiring to provide objective news coverage. Beginning in the 1820s, newspapers stationed reporters in Washington, DC, to collect information for their readers. That activity included the dissemination of information and messages from political parties and politicians.[29] One could argue that the ability of a politician or political group to disseminate its point of view had been institutionalized, made into a body of practices still used today.

The press is how Americans learned about every president, including the most obscure, such as Millard Fillmore, who served from 1850 to 1853. Fillmore let it be known that he thought German and Irish immigrants were dangerous and unwelcome, and that they would drive down wages and be criminals. For thirty years, he spread rumors that Freemasons were murdering people. He blamed Catholics for his failed bid to become governor of New York in 1844. There was no truth in any of his accusations, but the press did not hesitate to share them with their readers; and it seemed to work for him. He continued to run on this kind of negative messaging, serving as the failed presidential candidate for the American Party (better known as the Know Nothings), and fomenting hostility toward immigrants and Catholics in 1852. His messages and habits of administration sound eerily familiar today, as historians have documented.[30]

What types of information did presidential candidates need? Once they had determined the arguments to use to persuade voters to elect them, they sought out facts in support of their positions. Declaring a candidate immoral or a wife beater was best supported with "facts" that they had bad marriages or a violent temper, which then could be presented as factual truths through their favored communication channels. From the beginning of party politics, most candidates (or at least their parties) conducted "opposition research," to learn as much as they could about the bad things their opponents did or said, which could then become fodder for negative campaigning and advertisements. Mayor Richard J. Daley of Chicago was a crooked Democrat, so he obviously rigged the election in favor of Kennedy. Andrew Jackson was sexually promiscuous so, of course he was a bigamist. Lincoln was not one of the most handsome men to run for president and a frontiersman with limits to his education and the polish of his manners, so he was a "monkey."

Opposition research was extremely useful in challenging a candidate through negative advertising. In 1800, the Federalists accused Thomas Jefferson of having slave mistresses and of fathering a child. In the late twentieth century that fact was verified, but in 1800 it was merely a rumor.[31] Grover Cleveland supposedly fathered a child out of wedlock with a person named Maria Halpin, according to supporters of James G. Blaine in 1884. Their chant was "Ma, Ma, where's my Pap? Gone to the White House, ha, ha, ha." Cleveland supporters accused Blaine of using his congressional position for financial gain, and had their own chant: "Blaine, Blaine, Jay Gould Blaine! The Congressional Liar from the state of Maine." On election night, Cleveland's winning team came up with yet another chant: "Hurrah for Maria, Hurrah for the Kid. I voted for Cleveland, and I'm damned glad I did."[32] It mattered not whether Cleveland had fathered the child; opposition research and messaging carried the day because it convinced many people that he had, and by the standards of the day, this was unacceptable behavior by a president.

Political scientists attribute several advantages to opposition research. First, newspaper reporters often could not do adequate amounts of research on an issue, but political parties increasingly could and did, and then fed their results to the press. In the process, they controlled the press with their own point of view. The public has commonly been influenced by negative commentary and advertising. Tricky Dick (Nixon) was seen as likely to be a crook, and in the 1970s, after the Watergate break-in, historians agreed with that assessment. These misinformation campaigns distracted attention from a candidate's weak spots (so-called negatives) by shifting attention to the weaknesses or failures of their rivals. Criticizing an opponent in a false and negative way was almost always an effective use of opposition research. Bog Squier, a political media consultant, put it well: "I love to do negatives. It is one of those opportunities in a campaign where you can take the truth and use it like a knife to slice right through the opponent."[33] Add in bad or biased reporting and one could multiply the impact of negativism, creating a situation that one expert described: "seems to many [in the public] to be simply voyeurism."[34]

One could even take an attribute of a candidate's personal life—as done with Jefferson in 1800 and Jackson in 1828—and imply a falsehood. Two political scientists recalled the case of a Senate campaign in Montana in 2002, in which one candidate, who had been a hairdresser in the 1970s, was seen in a photograph of that decade applying beauty cream to another man's face. The implication was that he was not manly enough for the voters of Montana. Of course, that he had been a hairdresser twenty years earlier was irrelevant to whether he could function effectively as a

US senator.[35] The ex-hairdresser was not elected. Barack Obama was accused of being born in Africa (fake news), while a whispering campaign about Kennedy's health circulated (although it failed to catch on), while he promoted his vitality and, by implication, his virility.

Candidates needed to package information in ways that facilitated their transmission to voters. Historians often characterize the election of 1896 as "epic" because in that year Republican William McKinley gave over three hundred speeches, possibly heard by over a million people who came to the front porch at his home in Canton, Ohio. At the same time, the fiery and energetic William Jennings Bryan spoke all over the nation during a difficult economic time, arguing that the Democrat's money policy of linking gold to currency was harmful to workers. Bryan's frequently quoted message resonated and was disseminated across the nation and routinely still appears in American history textbooks: "You shall not press upon the brow of labor this crown of thorns, you shall not crucify mankind upon a cross of gold."[36] That was heady messaging that mixed in facts, fake facts, and opinions tailored to a specific voting sector. To win, McKinley individually tailored his messages to Germans, African Americans, merchants, blue-collar workers, and women (who he counted on to influence their husbands since women did not yet have the right to vote). Each constituency received pamphlets and heard professional speakers crisscrossing the nation. Perhaps unique for the time, McKinley hired a professional political consultant (Marcus A. Hanna) to craft the messages and implement a nationwide distribution of his points of view.[37] Every election since that one has engaged professional campaign experts who focus on packaging points of view tailored to increasing support from subsectors of the voting public.

These professionals did a considerable amount to generate both accurate and inaccurate information over the next century. It became standard practice to package criticisms of an opponent's morals, religious affiliation, political views, past performance, sway of forces hostile to the nation, and their misuse and misrepresentation of the truth. In the process, the professionals were able to protect their candidate in the public's eyes from being seen as the one making these personal attacks; the candidate could be portrayed as being above the fray. Richard Nixon, for example, was portrayed in 1960 as "Tricky Dick," largely because he looked sketchy. The press questioned some of his activities of the early 1950s, while Kennedy supported these characterizations but did not personally utter them.[38]

The two case studies presented in this and the next chapter illustrate how these facets of fake news, misinformation, rumors, plots, and myths have worked. They demonstrate that fake news in presidential campaigns has a long history. As recently as the 2016 election, concern over the role of fake news led academic researchers to conduct an initial study of their effects. Fourteen percent of Americans reported that social media was the "most important" source of information for them, but not quite the dominant source of facts about that national election. Known "fake news" circulating on the Internet in the three months prior to the election were disseminated unequally: pro-Trump viewers shared information thirty million times on Facebook; Clinton supporters eight million times. The authors of the study reported that "the average American adult saw on the order of one or perhaps several fake news stories in the months around the election, with just over half of those who recalled them believing them." These investigators reaffirmed what generations of political scientists already knew, that "people are much more likely to believe stories that favor their preferred candidate, especially if they have ideologically segregated social media networks."[39] In other words, fake news stories were influential and reassuring to voters. Their predilections and prejudices were reaffirmed.

THE PRESIDENTIAL ELECTION OF 1828

Upon first consideration, the election of 1828 may seem too far in the past to offer insights about how Americans use information in a political context. But historians would argue differently. A leading biographer of Andrew Jackson, H. W. Brands, neatly summed up its significance: "His [Jackson's] election, though not unexpected by the time it happened, turned the American political world on its head. Not since Jefferson's victory in 1800 had there been a hostile takeover of the presidency, and no one expected Jackson to offer an olive branch like that put forward by Jefferson."[40] It was that "hostile takeover" that makes the election relevant to our study of the varied uses of misinformation, lies, conspiracies, and mythology. This election also has a modern quality to it in that it began taking shape by the 1824 election, with many of the libels offered up at that time being repurposed for the 1828 election. These libels included accusations about Rachel Jackson's character and the legitimacy of her marriage to "Old Hickory" Jackson.

During the first quarter-century of the American republic, East Coast elites from New England and Virginia took turns being president. By the mid-1820s, however, the frontier had expanded so greatly that a national political divide existed between East and West, not to be reshaped into the more familiar North and South divide until the late 1840s. Historian John Lewis Gaddis observed that the East-West divide changed national politics as "the deference that allowed American dynasties" of the East Coast to rule gave "way to a boisterous irreverence. Elite's did not wear well on an expanding frontier, in cut-throat competitive newspapers, or among freshly franchised voters."[41] Jackson was nominated for president in 1824 to run against John Quincy Adams, whose father had been the second US president. Jackson won the popular vote with a plurality, but just as with Hillary Clinton in 2016, that victory in the popular vote did not translate into a majority in the Electoral College.

In 1824, the presidential election had to be resolved constitutionally by the US House of Representatives. Adams's allies collaborated with the third runner-up, Henry Clay, to line up sufficient votes to elect Adams as president. Adams named Clay his Secretary of State, positioning the latter by tradition and practice to someday become president. Jacksonians immediately suspected a back-room deal had been made; the historical record is not clear on the matter. Nevertheless, the suspicion was believed and affected how people reacted in the 1828 election. These voters recalled the "corrupt bargain," and one byproduct of that belief was the bare knuckles political fight in 1828. Any pretense of holding back rhetoric through the use of polite language, for example, was dropped; so too, any attempt to stick to the facts, as creation of "fake facts" became normal. Historian Sean Wilentz characterized what happened in 1828 as "a complete failure of political intelligence and imagination."[42] Any semblance of political politeness was gone. Nicknames, lighthearted attacks and humor, cartoons, campaign emblems, and nursery rhymes all punctuated speeches of the day.[43]

Note the environmental circumstances at play. One group of politicos and their supporters thought the election of 1824 had been stolen. Both sides used falsehoods and negative campaigning, which had existed in milder forms since the election of 1800, but now intensified. The political balance of power was shifting from dominance by New England and Virginia to a larger geographic split of East and West, introducing new participants and ways of campaigning. Combine these circumstances and one had a recipe for intense, crude, misleading campaigning. The election of 1828 did not disappoint—it became one of the most infamous in American history and a perfect laboratory for exploring how fake facts, together with libelous and slanderous accusations played out in national politics. While such behavior had been in evidence since 1800, it had all been aimed at a small electorate. In 1828, the electorate was larger and more diverse, which one historian described as more engaged with "more meetings, more broadsides, more pamphlets, and more books" than ever before, with propaganda becoming "the means for not only advocating a cause but mobilizing for it as well."[44]

While a number of issues were inaccurately raised, the most contentious one, the one that drew the greatest amount of attention—then and later by historians—involved stories surrounding General Andrew Jackson's marriage to Rebecca. For historians of fake facts and misrepresentations, it is an example of how actual facts, confusing but not ill-intentioned actions, and cynical manipulation of truth could be used to defame a person. Then as now, sex sells; and the slander of the 1820s involved charges considered outrageous given the social and moral standards of the day by voters in New England and in the South, less so in the West. They involved the most famous man in the United States at that time, the hero of the Battle of New Orleans of 1815, the candidate who had almost won the presidency in 1824, the Indian fighter who made the frontier "safer" for settlers, the general who helped bring Florida and neighboring regions into the American fold by seizing territory from the British and Spanish, a soldier who had fought against the British during the Revolutionary War. Opposing him was an old nemesis, John Quincy Adams. Allies on both sides conducted their opposition research. Deciding what to do about this giant American hero, "Old Hickory" Jackson, opponents reached for every idea to denigrate his moral qualifications for holding the highest office in the land.

Born in 1767, Rachel Donelson grew up into an attractive young lady, and married just after her seventeenth birthday to Lewis Robards in Kentucky. Several years into the marriage, he became jealous of another man who was attracted to her and kicked her out of his house. She arrived in Nashville at roughly the same time as Andrew Jackson. Rachel and Lewis reconciled, but soon after he became jealous of the handsome Andrew Jackson. Jackson and Lewis confronted each other, and Lewis again left his wife. By now, in 1789, Jackson seemed to have fallen in love with Rachel. Robards became involved with other women himself, and Rachel with Jackson. Jackson had heard that the Virginia legislature had passed an act allowing Lewis to sue for divorce from his wife because "the defendant hath deserted the plaintiff, and that she hath lived in adultery with another man since such desertion."[45] Jackson and his friends denied he was living with Rachel. One of his leading biographers, however, concluded the charge of adultery was true.[46] For a while they lived in Natchez but returned to Nashville in 1791, presenting themselves as husband and wife. No record ever surfaced that they married before returning to Nashville. So, they probably eloped, he at the age of twenty-two, she twenty-four years old. However, neither realized that the divorce actually was not granted until 1793, meaning any marriage that might have occurred in 1790 or 1791 was illegal. In January 1794, the two married before a justice of the peace in Nashville. By all reports of friends and family they remained a happily married couple until her death in December 1828. In 1808 they adopted a boy they named Andrew Jackson Jr. Those are the facts as best known to modern historians about the Rachel and Andrew Jackson marriage.

Years passed. Then came the campaign of 1828, considered by historians as "one of the most vicious in the nation's history." Jackson set the tone, because he thought he had been robbed of the presidency in 1824. He accused Adams and his confederates of corruption, cheating, and bribery when the Congress, required by the Constitution to pick the next president from the top three contenders, selected Adams. The fact that the Congress thought him less qualified for the position than Adams was irrelevant to him. Jackson's allies bellowed out "Corrupt bargain!" for four years, especially against Henry Clay, the third candidate. Clay never shook off the charge, leaving the political battlefield to Adams and Jackson in the next campaign. Robert V. Remini, a highly regarded biographer of Andrew Jackson, explained the context of what happened next with Rachel, pointing out that the campaign "splattered more filth in more different directions and upon more innocent people than any other in American history."[47] Adams's side fought back, doing a thorough job of opposition research on Jackson and in the process uncovering details of Jackson's marriage. Recall that there was a paper trail—the Virginia law passed specifically to authorize Robards to file for divorce, later the actual divorce documents. Jackson's enemies accused him of adultery because she was not divorced when the Jacksons claimed they were married. He was called a "wife-stealer," son of a prostitute, a Negro, usurper—and, as if none of that was enough, was accused of gambling, cockfighting, dueling, brawling, drinking too much, of being ignorant, illiterate (he misspelled words, as does Donald Trump)—and thus he was regarded as morally and professionally unfit for office. The Jacksonians accused Adams's wife of having been born out of wedlock, and that Adams had lived with his wife before they married.

Historian Norma Basch has studied the moral debates of that election and in the process examined the many pamphlets and newspaper articles that appeared on the matter at the time.[48] She was interested in learning about the moral values of the day, which ranged from the expectation of formal marriage to adoption of common-law practices on the frontier. The relevant point for our exploration of the marriage is that the election "was no less innovative in its organized manipulation of a sexual scandal."[49] Adams's side based its charges on eighteenth-century marital virtues. For them, "adultery represented political chaos."[50] How could the nation elect a seducer? For them, approval of such an individual challenged the civic order of society. Basch took seriously that both sides were sincere in their moral views. Brands has argued more recently that the Robards affair was more about trying to win a close election than to proffer a moral stance.[51] But the attacks went on for some time, with the earliest accusations starting in the spring of 1827 and continuing throughout the election cycle. The accusations were couched in the language of morality, which would not resonate well with a twenty-first-century reader.

For example, an anonymously signed 1828 pamphlet, *View of General Jackson's Domestic Relations, in Reference to His Fitness for the Presidency,* characterized Jackson's relations with Rachel as an "unmanly and dis-honorable act." The pamphlet called upon "the community" to "assign to seduction and adultery their appropriate estimation."[52] Other critics were similarly blunt. Another line of argument held that the Robards affairs should be hinted at but still accused Jackson of spending "the prime of his life in gambling, in cock fighting, in horse racing," and who "tore from a husband the wife of his bosom."[53] Here one sees Jackson portrayed as an abductor rather than a seducer, and Basch's reading implied that this ac-count was about "wife stealing" among men, "in which one man violated the sexual rights of another"; thus, "one of Jackson's most heinous crimes" occurred because he could not obey one of society's basic contracts.[54]

While newspaper editors decried discussions of the privacy of domes-tic affairs, they simultaneously recounted the whole story of the Jackson marriage.[55] Jackson's critics argued that how a man handled his marriage was a test of how he would handle public affairs. The *Daily National Jour-nal*, for example, argued that Jackson, "provoked if not invited an investi-gation of his character," as all aspects of his life when he stood for election to the presidency. Another pro-Adams writer argued that this marriage was "an affair in which the National character, the National Interest, and the National morals, were all deeply involved," hence, "subject of public investigation and exposure."[56] Adams's marriage was counter-posed as pristine by his supporters. Jackson's allies were less vociferous in their accusations of sexual or other wrongdoing by Adams. The closest claim accused Adams of soliciting a woman for Czar Alexander I when Adams was the American ambassador to Russia and of using federal funds to buy a pool table. The problem here was the lack of legal documentation so conveniently available with respect to the Robards divorce.[57]

So, the mudslinging continued. Rachael was accused of being a "mod-ern Jezebel," while others asked the singularly critical question, "ought a convicted adulteress and her paramour husband to be placed in the highest offices of this free and Christian Land?"[58] Jackson's enemies po-sitioned Rachel as a central character in the political theater of the day. Adams's allies wanted her morals to be a consideration of a candidate's qualification to be president. She was now a negative model of the Ameri-can political wife. How could she lead American women if she was a "convicted adulteress"? By being the defendant in the divorce, she was guilty of exercising her "unbridled passions." One pamphleteer put it this way: "When the rein is so given to indulgence, that it runs the whole race, and ends in divorce and marriage, the most favorable estimate we can make of the parties, is that they are mere creatures of passion, and the victims of its ungoverned predominance."[59] That Jackson had been married successfully to this woman for nearly four decades was deemed irrelevant and never brought up. She was simply a "fallen" woman:

Who is there in all this land that has a wife, a sister or daughter that could be pleased to see Mrs. Jackson (Mrs. Roberts [Robards] that was) presiding in the drawing-room at Washington. THERE IS POLLUTION IN THE TOUCH, THERE IS PERDITION IN THE EXAMPLE OF A PROFLIGATE WOMAN— HER WAYS LEAD DOWN TO THE CHAMBER OF DEATH AND HER STEPS TAKE HOLD ON HELL.[60]

For potential Southern voters, Jackson's enemies also turned on his mother. Charles Hammond, editor of the *Cincinnati Gazette*, let his readers know that "General Jackson's mother was a COMMON PROSTITUTE . . . brought to this country by the British soldiers! She afterwards married a MULATTO MAN, with whom she had several children, of which member General JACKSON is one!!!" A Kentucky newspaper added that Rachel was like "a dirty black wench."[61] To a potential Southern voter concerned that Jackson might support the emancipation of black slaves, these were inflammatory statements.

The Adams side let such language spread across the nation, as one historian explained, "because it encapsulated everything they feared about Jackson, and their fears about Jackson went to the heart of their campaign. Those fears were the fulcrum about which they defined and asserted their moral authority as an emerging political coalition."[62] Indeed, the Adams supporters needed to damage an American icon with anything they had if they were to win the election for an unpopular sitting president. That the Jacksons had an irregular start to their married life could hardly be avoided in the campaigning.

As if the Robards affair was not enough, there were other controversies that lent themselves to charges, including false and misleading information to satisfy almost any political appetite. Jackson was accused of being a slave owner (a charge that played well with Adams's New England supporters) and of dueling a great deal (true, but many people did). Both of these issues were less controversial than the issue of Jackson's marriage. Still, selling slaves was frowned upon, so his enemies began accusing him of "negro speculation," and even his dueling practices were challenged as violating the gentlemanly rules involved. His harsh treatment of his troops as a military commander was another accusation. For example, his authorization of the execution of a soldier, John Wood, was portrayed as harsh action against a young and innocent boy.

The most sensational charge not involving Rachel became known famously as the "coffin handbill." The broadside published silhouettes of six coffins, representing six troopers Jackson authorized for execution during the War of 1812. They were members of a group of some two hundred militiamen who had been charged with desertion, mutiny, and other violations related to desertion of their duties at Fort Jackson in late

1814. The soldiers argued that their term of military service was over and they were going to go home; their officers claimed they had three more months to serve. Jackson sided with his officers. All the militiamen were court-marshaled, and most were fined and dishonorably discharged three months later. Six leaders of the mutiny, however, were sentenced to death. The request to carry out the sentence came to Jackson in New Orleans, and he examined it just after the Battle of New Orleans, while not knowing that the United States and England had already settled the war. General Jackson believed he was still in a state of war and could not brook any break in discipline in the ranks, so he approved the execution.

Figure 2.1.   The most infamous illustration from the 1828 presidential campaign, blaming Andrew Jackson for the execution of American soldiers. Published by John Binns in Philadelphia. Courtesy Library of Congress.

Nobody took notice until 1828, when the anti-Jacksonians told the story of these men, characterizing Jackson as a heartless monster who crushed people like a despot. The coffin handbill, distributed by Philadelphia editor John Binns explained: "The act was as cruel as uncalled for," that he "had no pity for his fellow man."[63] In the same document, Binns included an account of killing Indians at the Battle of Horseshoe Bend in 1814 and of other confrontations with people. "He has ever been a man of blood and carnage." A supposed eyewitness warned in the broadside, "prepare yourselves for a recital that must make the blood of the most obdurate curdle; that must make every man's hair stand on end; a recital at which the stoutest heart must sicken; and the very contemplation of which must make human nature shudder at her own depravity!!!" About Jackson's crimes, Binns continued:

> Would you believe it, "gentle reader," this monster, this more than cannibal, Gen. Andrew Jackson, eat the whole Six Militiamen at one meal!!! Yes, my shuddering countrymen, he swallowed them whole, coffins and all, without the slightest attempt at mastication!!!!!! . . . can you, my deluded countrymen, even think of making this horrible anthropophagian monster President of the United States?

The reader is told that Jackson would roast and eat any cabinet member who displeased him.[64] Less remembered by historians were other charges of cannibalism. John Taliaferro, a Congressman from Virginia, accused Jackson of killing one thousand Indians; then took a nap among their corpses, afterward eating a dozen or so for breakfast. Would he do the same to governors and congressmen who opposed him after he became president? This is the same Congressman who apparently wrote the supplemental text for the Coffin broadside.[65]

So far, we have not discussed the role of information in making Jackson a hero. In fact, he was a national hero, mythologized over the years by his achievements.[66] That process began nearly twenty years earlier, but it was seized upon during the 1828 election—his roles as a successful Indian fighter, defeater of the British at the Battle of New Orleans, greatest public figure/leader since George Washington, and so forth. Negative charges as well as the hero-worship contributed to obfuscated discussions about the substantive issues facing the nation. One Jackson scholar, Edward Pessen, concluded about the election that all this rhetoric and misleading charges and countercharges had an effect: "demagogy, barbecues, concentration on personalities, slander, and insult had the serious role of fostering a political system dominated by major parties that follow expediency rather than principle."[67] The process worked; Jackson became president. However, as Pessen observed, "the politics of expediency provided a cover for charlatans, contributed to miseducating the public about specific issues,

Figure 2.2.   This image of General Andrew Jackson, published in 1815, mythologizes him as a result of his winning the Battle of New Orleans, beginning a process that he and others deployed to launch his national political career. Courtesy Library of Congress.

and propagated dangerously simplistic notions about complex problems. It has fostered the dubious notion that thorny problems are easily solved."[68] That was the informational contribution this election made to future American presidential campaigns.[69] It was all facilitated, too, by the existence of a nationwide collection of newspapers, which Jackson's leading biographer argued was one of the most important contributions of the politicians of the early nineteenth century.[70] Echoes of the behaviors of 1828 were evident in the election of 1960.

3

Political Communication in the Age of Television and the Presidential Election of 1960

Style has more to do with the way in which ideas are believed and advocated than with the truth or falsity of their content.

—Richard Hofstadter [1]

Nothing is simple to understand about John F. Kennedy because so much of what is known by the public, and even by many historians, remains shrouded in myth, misinformation, false facts, conspiracy theories, and thus in controversy. It has been easier to understand and document the lives of his contemporaries—Richard M. Nixon, Hubert Humphrey, and Lyndon B. Johnson—all of whom vied for their party's nomination to be president in 1960. Kennedy's run for the presidency generated its own controversies and myths—to such an extent that over a half century afterward, much is still not settled, such as who really won the majority of the popular vote, Kennedy or Nixon? Most readers would only know, at best, that in 1960 Kennedy ran for president and won; a few might recall that in his inaugural speech he made his famous declaration, "Ask not what your country can do for you." Some readers are convinced that Chicago mayor Richard Daley "swung" the election to Kennedy by stuffing ballot boxes and by allowing dead people to vote.

Every presidential election is consequential in its own way, and the 1960 election is no exception. Understanding its significance is as important as knowing what happened. As to the role of information, this election both continued long-standing traditions in data handling, while at the same time introducing new forms that have been used ever since. These long-standing practices included editorial opinion-making by newspapers and radio programs, opposition research resulting in dissemination of misinformation or outright falsehoods, exaggeration of potential conflicts of interests on the part of opponents, "sound bite" slogans and phrases, hints of conspiracies against a campaign or subsets of the electorate, superficial discussion of issues, purposefully misleading use of data and statistics, and the wide use of campaign literature, posters, rallies, and speech-making at community events such as county farm fairs and political rallies. Complicating the story of the 1960 election is the fact that it and so many other aspects of Kennedy's life were subsumed into the larger mythology of the "martyred" president cut down in the prime of life in Dallas. Kennedy remains a young, handsome president in our minds when, had he lived a full life that one would expect given the longevity of many of his relatives, he might have been a grandfather as these words were written in 2019.[2]

The leading expert on the 1960 election, Edmund F. Kallina Jr., has argued that the election was significant for several reasons. Three of the four candidates vying for office that year became presidents: Kennedy, Johnson, and Nixon; Hubert Humphrey was vice president and losing presidential candidate. No other election had so many runner-ups who eventually occupied the White House. Nineteen sixty was one of the most tense years of the Cold War, with a dangerous crisis between the Soviets and Americans in Berlin, growing problems in Vietnam, and deteriorating relations with the Soviets over Cuba. The future of America was at stake in the minds of American voters. The election was the closest in American history, yet voter turnout was the highest in fifty years. Critical to our study: it was the first election to include televised debates, the first Catholic president, and the most organized campaign in American history (up until then).[3] This last observation is crucial because every national campaign since then has emulated many of Kennedy's practices, including how information and false facts are deployed, including the early start on campaigning (four years before the election). As Kallina concluded, this campaign "matched two outstanding candidates against each other. The men were remarkable and so were their campaigns."[4]

However, it was also a typical campaign in many ways. Several Democrats competed for the presidential nomination, but Kennedy won that round largely due to the growing popularity of primaries. The Republicans selected Vice President Nixon as their standard-bearer. The campaigns continued all summer and fall, before the election in November. The typical history of this campaign marches the reader through, week by week, as the candidates differentiated themselves from one another and misrepresented the positions of their rivals. Issues gave both sides the opportunity to misrepresent the other, or themselves.[5] As journalist Theodor H. White elegantly put it:

Each of the great tribal communities of American life is split between Republicans and Democrats in different proportions; but these different proportions are among the most enduring realities in our political system. They change slowly; the past holds imagination, prejudice and dreams fixed. And what each candidate must do in the campaign is to chip away at this grip of the past within each subgroup by holding out some vision of a new future.[6]

White took his comment to its correct logical conclusion: "It is generally held that 80 percent of American voters vote by inheritance and have made up their minds by the time the conventions are over."[7] So, the battle was for the final 20 percent, and in 1960 that effort became the most expensive campaign up until that time, with the costs driven up sharply by the expense of television advertising and by both sides fielding large national campaign organizations.

Yet, almost the entire population—not just the undecided voters—paid attention to the ebb and flow of issues. In particular, three issues rose above all others to teach us about the role of fake facts, rumors, and conspiracies in national politics: Kennedy's health, his Catholicism, and the accusation that the Democrats stole the election.

The issue with the least effect on the election was Kennedy's health because it did not surface sufficiently to influence events, but it was of concern to both presidential contenders. Kennedy suffered from Addison's disease, which reminded him of his mortality even though he was only in his early forties, since it could be lethal. He also had painful back problems. To dispel this issue, Kennedy purposefully exuded an image of vigorous health and energy. Rumors of his poor health had circulated in the 1950s. But Kennedy lied to Gore Vidal when challenged on the matter, answering, "I don't have Addison's disease."[8] The Johnson team learned the truth before the convention, while Johnson was still competing with JFK for the nomination. Kennedy took cortisone shots to keep the disease under control. In fact, Kennedy had used the health card against Johnson, spreading rumors that Johnson's health was weak based on a heart attack the Texan had had in 1955, and circulating rumors about the possibility of a more recent heart attack. Bobby Kennedy, Jack's brother and his campaign manager, denied the health rumors and publicly stated that "John F. Kennedy does not now have nor has he ever had an ailment described classically as Addison's disease. . . . Any statement to the contrary is malicious and false." Instead, Bobby dissembled that, in the postwar period, his brother had a "mild adrenal insufficiency," but that it was "not in any way a dangerous condition," and was probably the result "of his wartime experience of shock and continued malaria."[9]

Individuals broke into JFK's doctors' offices in New York, but they failed to find his records as they had been hidden in another folder. The doctors issued a letter during the primaries stating that Kennedy had a "superb physical condition" and that, given the stress he experienced in campaigning, it was clear, "that [he is] able to hold any office to which [he] aspire[s]."[10] Senior Kennedy campaign operatives, however, worried that Nixon's people had stolen copies of the files.

Both Kennedy's and Nixon's campaigns were concerned that their candidate's medical records would become public (since Nixon had visited a psychoanalyst in the 1950s).[11] Each feared that if they revealed their opponent's health records, the other side would too. Indeed, these worries persisted until the last few days of the campaign, when both sides saw from the polls that the election was too close to call. On November 3, Nixon decided to strike first with the news, using as a surrogate John Roosevelt, the youngest son of former Democratic President Franklin D. Roosevelt. The younger Roosevelt challenged both men to publish their records, knowing that in Nixon's case he meant problems the candidate had with his knee, not his head. That day, a reporter asked about Kennedy's Addison disease. Roosevelt spoke of "rumors . . . that Senator Kennedy. . . has or has had Addison's disease."[12] Nixon offered to make public his own record over the weekend before the elections, the implication being that Kennedy should too. Nothing came of it on Monday, and the next day the nation went to the polls.

Historian Edmund F. Kallina Jr. reported that throughout the campaign and the subsequent presidency, Kennedy kept up a brave front. Regarding the half year of campaigning in 1960, Kallina observed:

> with the pain and courage came concealment, deception, and a search for relief. As Joe Kennedy's [father of JFK] and JFK's ambitions advanced, public knowledge about his physical condition became a major threat. Any revelation, admission, or leak of the true state of Kennedy's health, especially of the Addison's, might have doomed his presidential ambitions.[13]

These fears explained why it was essential to deny and keep from the public knowledge of the truth. The evasiveness began in the 1950s and extended long after Kennedy's assassination. His political operatives had concluded there was no way to explain clearly to the public the nature of his illness. So, they denied anything was wrong and when pressed, obfuscated. JFK even told his staunch supporter, Arthur Schlesinger Jr., in 1959, that he did not have the disease "and have never had it," moreover, even denying taking cortisone.[14] Upon the conclusion of the election, the disease went into remission only to reappear years later.

A greater threat to JFK's candidacy, however, was his Catholicism. This threat was evident throughout much of the campaign and influenced how some voters responded on Election Day. Kennedy was of Irish descent and raised Catholic, but he was not particularly devout—in contrast to his mother. So, it seemed unfair, or at least ironic, to him and his family that he was being criticized by political foes and some voters for being Catholic. In the 1950s, he began publicly to distinguish his Catholicism from his duties as a public official. For example, in 1957 he argued: "What church I go to on Sunday or what dogma of the Catholic Church I believe in is a personal matter. It does not involve public matter. It does not involve public questions of policy or as the Constitution defines responsibilities of the President, Senator, or member of the armed forces."[15] Two years later, in an interview published in *Look* magazine, he argued that "for the office-holder nothing takes precedence over his oath to uphold the Constitution and all its parts—including the First Amendment and strict separation of church and state."[16] He held to that position until his death.

American Catholics were generally pleased that a person of their faith was running for president. The Catholic press seemed offended that he would have to explain his position vis-à-vis the church when Protestant candidates did not have to do so.[17] Most Catholics were simply pleased, including Catholic bishops and cardinals in the United States. However, commentary from Rome proved confusing and harmful to Kennedy's cause. In May 1960, the Vatican newspaper *L'Observatore* criticized politicians who separated "the Catholic from the ecclesiastical hierarchy," and "proclaiming the believer's full autonomy in the civil sphere." The editorial continued, "The Catholic may never disregard the teaching and directions of the church but must inspire his private and public conduct in every sphere of his activity by the . . . teachings of the hierarchy."[18] Kennedy's rivals now had ammunition to fire at him, which they did, and he now had to constantly fight back.[19]

In some of the primaries, notably West Virginia, he faced hardcore Protestant prejudice against his "papist" background, but also criticism from liberal Democrats who considered Catholicism a reactionary force in society. In the 1950s during JFK's early political career, much of this feeling was kept out of the newspapers, but not during his presidential campaign. He found critics in both the *Nation* (liberal leaning) and the *Christian Herald* (Baptist leaning). Even Eleanor Roosevelt, widow of Democratic President Franklin D. Roosevelt, made subtle comments critical of JFK's Catholic connection.[20] A Gallup poll taken in 1960 reported that 20 percent of Americans would not vote a Catholic into the presidency.[21] Eleanor Roosevelt reportedly was shocked that 80 percent would be willing.[22] Once Kennedy was nominated, however, Roosevelt backed him.

The Protestant Midwest and South were both difficult regions for Kennedy. In August 1960, Protestant leaders met secretly in Switzerland to work out how to block his election. That same month, the Minnesota Baptist state convention declared a Catholic president would pose a "serious threat to America," and that "we cannot turn our government over to a Catholic President who would be influenced by the Pope and by the power of the Catholic Hierarchy."[23] A North Carolina Baptist preacher labeled Kennedy's candidacy a "hellish, world-wide plot to enslave men and women."[24] One of the best known religious leaders in the United States, the highly respected Norman Vincent Peale, on September 7 led 150 clergymen representing 37 Protestant denominations in questioning the wisdom of electing a Catholic president. Their tone was sober and cautious, but nevertheless they posed the crucial issue of concern to many voters: "Is it reasonable to assume a Roman Catholic President would be able to withstand altogether the determined efforts of the hierarchy of his church to gain further funds and favors for its [Catholic] schools and institutions, and otherwise breach the wall of separation of church and state?"[25] In 1928, the first Catholic presidential candidate, Al Smith, had faced the same question. One student of the 1960 campaign described the anti-Catholic mindset as still alive and "still festered in both shouted Southern sermons and discreet Northern whispers."[26] Peale, however, was criticized and eventually he disengaged himself from the clerical position, admitting, "I was just stupid."[27] But the damage had been done. The central concern was out in public for all to discuss. To his credit, Richard Nixon refused to take advantage of the issue, although others in his Republican Party did not hesitate to do so, particularly during the state primaries that spring.

The South was particularly challenging for Kennedy. Newspaper editors and politicians observed that the Republicans would probably carry Texas and Arkansas (at a time, unlike today, when the South was Democrat-leaning) because of Kennedy's religion. The same prognostication circulated about West Virginia at the time of its primary. In a widely covered speech, Kennedy fought back on September 12 at the Greater Houston Ministerial Association:

> I believe in an America where the separation of church and state is absolute—where no Catholic prelate would tell the President (should he be a Catholic) how to act and no Protestant minister would tell his parishioners for whom to vote—where no church or church school is granted any public funds or political preference—and where no man is denied public office merely because his religion differs.[28]

This pattern continued throughout the fall, with people questioning his allegiance, Kennedy defending his independence from the Church.[29]

The issue had not popped up in this campaign until March 1960, after which it increasingly became the subject of debate; at the time, November's election was far away. The controversy began when anti-Catholic pamphlets were mailed to Wisconsin voters, including many Catholics.

At the end of the month, a pro-Humphrey advertisement appeared in some 250 local newspapers stating that Humphrey was not going to get a fair deal in the upcoming primary because local Catholics would vote for Kennedy. The suggestion was obvious: get out the Protestant vote for Humphrey.[30] The Minnesota candidate repudiated it, but now both pro- and anti-Catholic voices accused the other side of plots and of fostering dissent and suspicion. The press enjoyed covering this controversy.[31] Kennedy won the Wisconsin primary on April 5 and the one in West Virginia on May 10.[32] On election night, television correspondent Walter Cronkite stated that it appeared "religion is playing a rather large role in this election," arguing that Catholic Republicans were crossing over and Protestant Republicans were going the opposite way.[33] The press now began to speak of Humphrey as Kennedy's "Protestant opponent."

The issue was exaggerated, however. A postmortem analysis of voting in Wisconsin demonstrated that people "did not vote their rosaries or their hymnals."[34] Each side instead gained votes based on more traditional political considerations.[35] Five weeks later, in the West Virginia primary, similar issues resurfaced and proved in historian Kallina's assessment, "more controversial."[36] Political experts thought Kennedy entered West Virginia behind in the polls because of the religious issue. The state had a much smaller percentage of Catholics than Wisconsin did. In West Virginia, Catholics represented 5 percent of the votes, Protestants 35 percent—and the latter were characterized as "militant" by the press. This turned out to be a false representation. Everyone else (59 percent) had no declared affiliation with any religious denomination. Unlike in Wisconsin, where Kennedy ducked the issue, in West Virginia he aggressively repeated his mantra about separation of church and state. The press, politicos, and experts all exaggerated the role of religion in West Virginia. Kennedy won because he convinced enough voters that he could advance their political and economic interests more than Humphrey could. In the end, the religious dialogue was inconsequential. With primary season almost over, Kennedy focused on the national convention and his nomination, but rounds of religious mudslinging continued against him. The religion issue tailed off until the last couple of weeks of the campaign, when polls showed the election was very close. But by then, other more typical campaign issues were predominant.

An issue concerning corrupt voting practices surfaced slightly during the campaign, but then took on importance in the period after the election but before the Electoral College voted in December—and is still heard occasionally today. This issue overshadowed concerns about health and religion and did more than those other issues to raise suspicions about corruption in American presidential elections during the second half of the twentieth century. This new issue involved various types of corrupt voting practices, ranging from vote buying to ballot box stuffing to voting by dead Chicagoans. The odor of ballot box corruption had often lingered over national elections since the 1820s but rarely became a stink. The 1960 election reminds us of the alleged Russian interference in the 2016 presidential election. The 1960 election concern did not involve use of the Internet, of course, as it did in 2016. Instead, the media of corruption in 1960 were the purchase of votes in various ways and the falsification of or prevention of voter turnout, often characterized as "ballot stuffing." The pattern was for one political party or candidate to levy accusations before anyone had time to methodically investigate the facts. In 1960, the Republicans quickly accused the Democrats of voter irregularities immediately following the election. As a result, conspiracy talk and dissemination of misinformation and lies gained attention. These kinds of behaviors had appeared in earlier national elections, ever since 1800. Usually, the truth was of limited importance during the heat of the moment of accusation. Often, the results and possible corrections by local and state election officials were something of a letdown.

In 1960, this story began as the Democrats competed for their party's nomination prior to their national convention. In April in the West Virginia primary, Humphrey and his allies suspected foul play. As the leading historian of the election described it:

> There were charges of vote buying. There was a messy campaign smear. Later, it developed that elements of organized crime had actively supported the Kennedy candidacy. From almost the beginning of the contest, rumors circulated that Kennedy bagmen roamed through the state, handing out money to politicians willing to sell themselves and their organizations to Kennedy.[37]

The Kennedy organization supposedly was sending donations to small Protestant churches, particularly to African American congregations. Humphrey believed this was fact and in April declared, "I don't think elections should be bought" and said to colleagues, "I can't afford to run through this state with a little black bag and check book."[38] Nixon was never so adamant, even after the election was over and electioneering problems had surfaced in Chicago.

But the main event that triggered the controversy of voter fraud was the closeness of the national election in November. After Nixon lost, by less than 150,000 votes in total, Republicans immediately began complaining about voter fraud. Once these accusations began appearing, they continued for months, then lingered for years. Even though the election had been extremely close, both Eisenhower and Nixon concluded that the Republicans had not executed their campaign as well as the Democrats had. The Republican ticket suspected irregularities had occurred, but they chose not to lodge a formal complaint of fraud. Between election night and December 19, when the Electoral College voted for the next president, a mounting chorus of complaints erupted among the Republicans as a grassroots effort.[39] The complaints quickly coalesced around events in Chicago, although Republicans also suspected problems elsewhere in Illinois and in other states. Kennedy won Illinois by a margin of only 8,858 votes, but had a 456,312 lead in Chicago, a city with a reputation for corrupt politics, including decades of election tampering. Local Republican vote watchers complained on Election Day that ten thousand voters had been removed from the voting rolls. Republicans observing voting across Cook County, which included Chicago, charged that Democrats had stolen one hundred thousand votes. While none of these observers could provide proof, they nevertheless complained loudly to the press. Complaints also flowed into the national headquarters of the Republican National Committee (RNC) from other states, but the RNC decided not to pursue them because they believed that the national election results could not be overturned. Even so, the RNC sent staff out to investigate charges that surfaced in Illinois, Texas, Missouri, New Mexico, Nevada, South Carolina, New Jersey, and Pennsylvania. None of their investigations found significant evidence of wrongdoing.

Meanwhile, in Chicago in late November, the *Chicago Tribune* and the *Chicago Daily News* both published stories accusing Mayor Daley's political machine of having acted improperly. For example, on November 24, the *Chicago Tribune* stated, "It is a good guess that in an honest election Mr. Nixon would have carried Illinois by 100,000 votes."[40] The *New York Herald Tribune* carried four articles by pro-Nixon reporter Earl Mazo in early December that offered evidence of voter fraud in Chicago, which in the mind of this reporter was sufficient to have cost Nixon the election.[41] The Democrats remained quiet about the charges, waiting for the Electoral College to officially elect Kennedy. The national press hardly paid attention to the issue. In Chicago, however, it was front-page news. Mayor Daley did not avoid criticism, not surprising given that he had a less than spotless record in such matters, running one of the tightest political operations in the country. He was later reported to have told Kennedy on election night, "with a little luck and the help of a few close friends, you're going to carry Illinois."[42] In time, local investigations found errors, some intentional and others just sloppy voting practices, for example, not being able to use voting machines properly. Some voter registration officials were found guilty of inappropriate behavior. But all of these findings happened after Kennedy had been sworn in as president.

The Republicans had the problem of explaining why they lost the election and, in facing that challenge, created their own mythology. This appeared at the same time that the Democrats were circulating their own account of why the nation picked young Kennedy. The Republican story was partly about Nixon not running as effective a campaign as he needed to, but also about the Democrats' voter fraud. This claim of fraud survived for decades. A leading student of this election observed that "vote fraud became the most popular GOP interpretation of why the election was lost. Quickly, it became the great Republican myth of 1960, which lives on fifty years later in a different century."[43] Historians have considered the story as plausible because of repeated election irregularities. The South, in particular Texas, the home state of Kennedy's running mate, Lyndon Johnson, was the subject of some of these rumors. Voter fraud in large northeastern and Midwestern cities was also common, with Daley's operation in Chicago considered "a model of efficiency when it came to getting out the vote and making sure that it came out correctly."[44] Mazo's articles ensured the myth received national attention, and, as the historian Kalinda observed, the reporter's point-of-view "infiltrated into countless books and articles about 1960, where it became the conventional wisdom, at least in Republican and independent circles."[45]

Democrats promoted a different story that also lingered for decades: about voter prejudice against a Catholic candidate. The evidence shows modest truth to both the Democrat and Republican accounts, but of insufficient consequence to have decided the election. While some voters rejected Kennedy because he was Catholic, and some officials committed voter fraud, it was the life of these accounts that is of importance to us here. As Kalinda explains: "The Republican focus on voter fraud permitted the party faithful to view themselves as the party of good government and the upholder of clean, honest elections."[46] It did not help Nixon that he and the national press did not get along well. Theodore H. White in his best-selling book about the election admitted that the press was prejudiced in its reporting and so could be counted upon to dismiss more easily the charges of voter fraud.[47] It was a charge that added to the Republican mythology about the outcome of the election.

What effect did television have on this election? To be sure, all during the campaign both candidates accused each other of not supporting one issue or another, such as Kennedy criticizing Nixon for being hostile to Social Security, when it was not true; while Nixon claimed that Kennedy was "running America down and giving us an inferiority complex," or that the cost of living would go up if the Democrats came into office.[48] But television had a greater effect on voters than any individual speech by either candidate, or than the charges one made about the other. For the first time, the way in which voters responded to the images they saw on their television screens shaped their perceptions of the two candidates. What the candidates *said* on television did not sway them as much as the portrayals of their facial expressions, intonations of their voices, body language, and overall appearances. It was a new source of information and it did more to distinguish them than what they said; for the truth was, they differed less on national issues than their campaigns would have one believe. Television made such a difference that of all the events recalled about the election of 1960, none has stood out more so than the television debates, and most particularly, the first one.

The two leading candidates agreed to participate in four televised debates—a first in American presidential campaigns—with the first, and most watched, one occurring on September 26. Regarding the issues and questions asked, they skillfully held forth, representing their points of view with answers that were remarkably similar. Those who listened to the debate on the radio reported later that the debate was a "draw," some even thought Nixon "won" it.[49] But the television viewers had an entirely different reaction. Kennedy looked straight into the camera, had a nice tan, was good looking, and seemed relaxed to viewers. He was, to use a term coined later, "telegenic." In contrast, Nixon looked gray, tired, as if he had not shaved, nervous, even sweaty, and he slouched. He did not look directly at the camera as consistently as Kennedy did and his voice seemed nervous. In other words, he came off as not telegenic. There were other problems, too: Kennedy wore a dark suit, Nixon a gray one that blended into the background; Kennedy was more handsome, Nixon sported jowls; Kennedy looked younger and more energetic, while Mayor Daley remarked that Nixon looked like he had been "embalmed."[50] Nixon improved his performance in the next three debates, but the audiences for those final three television debates were much (millions of viewers) smaller. Nixon's moment to make a positive impression had passed.[51] Jackie Kennedy thought her husband was "brilliant" in his first debate; Nixon's mother asked son Richard if he was sick.

After the election, pollsters established that over half of all voters had been influenced by the television debates to some degree. The debates displayed an enormous amount of tacit knowledge that propaganda or written materials could not: one's sense of humor, speaking skills, ability to react quickly to comments and questions, and ability to display intelligence.[52] How was it possible that this debate proved so influential? In 1960, 88 percent of American households had a television set and an estimated seventy-four million people watched the debate.[53] Many voters decided on Kennedy that night. This debate also had the effect of scaring off future presidential candidates for sixteen years from agreeing to debate one another on television. Finally, incumbent Republican president Gerald Ford agreed to debate Democratic candidate Jimmy Carter on television. Since then, all candidates have participated in nationally televised debates.

Information, misinformation, criticisms about Kennedy's Catholic background, charges of Nixon's truthfulness and honesty, and the two

Figure 3.1. Taken during the second Kennedy-Nixon televised debate, held on October 7, 1960. These debates left the impression on the American public that Kennedy was younger and more vigorous than Nixon. Courtesy Library of Congress.

candidates' positions on issues were filtered through the impressions voters acquired that evening. Returning to the point made earlier in this and other chapters that individuals tend to adhere to their preconceived impressions, television reinforced this behavior. If a voter was already suspicious about Nixon before the debate, his TV performance confirmed their hunch. If a voter was inclined to dismiss the potential influence of the pope on Kennedy, after the debate it was clear he was an American first, a Catholic second. Over the next five decades, political campaigns had to craft their messages in ways that leveraged the vast amount of tacit information voters absorbed from television. As one historian put it, the effect of TV was immediate, calling it "the invigoration of the Kennedy campaign," which the Democrats needed at that moment; while immediately, "on the Republican side, it was mostly doom and gloom."[54] The speed of the reaction to the debate caught everyone by surprise. It did not take weeks to gauge the effect, but instead only hours. For the next month, Kennedy rode a wave of growing acceptance and popularity, with the more traditional back-and-forth campaigning not returning to normal until the final month of the campaign, by which time the race tightened up to a nearly dead heat by Election Day.

What our narrative demonstrates is that much of the political behavior in this election centered around communication, largely managed by two political parties. As political scientists Jay G. Blumler and Dennis Kavanagh characterized this period in American political history, it was a "golden age" for political parties: "In this period, the political system was regarded as the prime source of initiatives and debates for social reform" and voters had long-lasting party affiliations, accompanied, as others have noted, "by a high level of confidence in political institutions."[55] Political scientists have observed that voters did not sift through options and issues, but instead voted and thought along party lines. This raises the question of how interested the voters were in the events described earlier, or whether this was a creation of the political parties and the media. However, the large number of viewers who watched the first television debate demonstrates that a great many Americans were interested, even if only momentarily.

Debates about the role of misinformation and falsehoods flowed in defined ways. Blumler and Kavanagh observed that in this period of the 1960s, "political communication was a top-down affair," compliments of the two major political parties and their spokesmen and candidates.[56] While one can see the inchoate role of information and misinformation in the 1828 election, the decades of professionalization of communication skills was much more readily evident in 1960. In that election, one can see the purposeful, carefully crafted messaging and agendas at play.

4

Ultimate in Conspiracies 1

Assassination of President Abraham Lincoln

People are still debating the Lincoln assassination. It's understandable.

—Chief Justice Earl Warren[1]

In American history, misinformation, outright lies, and falsehoods often go hand in hand with conspiracy theories. These theories are often fed by speculation and rumors and marginally rooted in empirical data. These theories may live on, even in the face of incontrovertible facts that do not support them. There is often doubt of what transpired and why, and plausible explanations can live on despite mounting evidence to the contrary. Nowhere does the interaction of all these elements appear so frequently, for so long, or in such detail as with the assassination of an American president. Conspiracy explanations can be fueled by mystery, by unexplained aspects of the event such as the lack of answers to obvious questions, or by issues never resolved. The assassinations of American Presidents Abraham Lincoln in 1865 and John F. Kennedy ninety-eight years later share a common note of mystery: was there a plot to kill the president involving multiple people? If so, who were they, and how and why did they do it?

In both instances the individuals who did the deed are known: John Wilkes Booth in the case of Lincoln, Lee Harvey Oswald in the case of Kennedy. But enhancing the mystery of each of these assassinations is that both men were killed before law enforcement could interrogate the killers properly to determine whether others were involved. In both instances, officials had to piece together what might have been a conspiracy, and in both cases the possibility of conspiracy was never resolved to everyone's satisfaction. In Lincoln's case, dozens of people were arrested, eight were tried, and four were hanged; and today some amateur and professional historians question whether all of the hanged parties should have been executed. In Kennedy's case, no grand plot was ever satisfactorily uncovered that warranted arrests and prosecution to the extent the various conspiracies suggested were involved. So, the central point of discussion in both assassinations remains open.

There are common features to the two assassinations. The subject of the assassination instantly captured the attention of anyone hearing about it. The time scale of dissemination was different (for Lincoln, within two hours if you were in Washington or as much as two weeks if you were in a more remote part of the United States; for Kennedy, within minutes everywhere), but the reaction whenever one heard the news was similar. If you ask anyone today, more than fifty years after the Kennedy assassination, they can tell you where they were on that Friday afternoon at about 1:15 Eastern time. The news broke through radio and television broadcasts as well as announcements in classrooms, conference rooms, offices, and on the street. With both assassinations, there was widespread and intense interest in both the event and the subsequent evaluations as they unfolded. People followed every nuance, bit of information, fact, rumor, and lie. "Everyone" had a theory about what happened and who was involved. Many of the adults who lived at the time of these assassinations maintained an interest in the subject for the rest of their lives. Media on these topics—whether it was books, newspaper articles, or television programming—were widely viewed. It was only after the passage of the first generation of people who had been present at the time of the assassination that the intensity of interest waned. Even today, more than fifty years after the Kennedy assassination and more than 150 years after the Lincoln assassination, interest remains.[2]

The volume of commentary and speculation, and the level of detail to which these discussions were taken, is massive and obsessive. Almost seven hundred books have been published on the Kennedy assassination (an average of one every month since the assassination), and even more about the Lincoln assassination. Many are substantial tomes, running four hundred to five hundred printed pages. Especially with Lincoln, but also with Kennedy, the speculative nature of some accounts and the ardency of the conspiracy theorists have driven professional historians away from the topic in fear for the safety of their professional reputation.[3]

The assassinations have been documented to such a level of detail that they are among the most described events in American history. The two most documented minute-by-minute events of the nineteenth century in American history were clearly about Lincoln's assassination (largely not written by historians) and about the Battle of Gettysburg on July 1–3, 1863 (largely written by military historians and memoirists). Kennedy's death has been documented at almost the same level of detail as Lincoln's. This documentation provides details down to the minute of the activities and whereabouts of everyone associated with the assassination: the shooters, their alleged confederates, and various public officials suspected of involvement—including vice presidents, key cabinet officials, the military, and civilian law enforcement. Foreign involvement is one common thread of conspiracy theory discussion: the role of the Confederacy in masterminding Lincoln's assassination; and the Soviet Union, Cuba, Mexico, and American organized crime in the case of Kennedy.

In this chapter, we begin by summarizing what occurred in the Lincoln assassination, reflecting existing consensus among historians about the settled facts of the matter. We summarize and analyze the conspiracy theories, which drove so much of the debate about what happened, illustrating the ways in which facts and falsehoods were presented and woven into conspiracy story lines.[4] We conclude with a discussion of the patterns of behavior of conspiracy theorists and their audiences, and how these patterns fit into the larger story of information use in the United States.

THE LINCOLN ASSASSINATION

On April 14, 1865, while Lincoln was attending a play with his wife at Ford's Theatre in Washington, DC, a well-known actor, John Wilkes Booth, entered the president's seating area and shot him once in the head. Booth jumped from the balcony of Lincoln's theater box, and in doing so broke his leg but nevertheless escaped on a saddled horse he had ready by the alley next to the theater. Lincoln was carried across the street to a private home, where the following morning he died from his gunshot wound. The larger plan had been for collaborators to kill various cabinet officials. Only Secretary of State William H. Seward was attacked. Lewis Powell wounded Seward in the face but was not able to kill him because others in the Secretary's house intervened. Another collaborator, George Atzerodt, was assigned the task of killing Vice President Andrew Johnson but instead got drunk and never attempted the assassination.

Key to the story were Booth's escape and the rapid realization that he had collaborators of some sort. Booth's escape has become the stuff of legend, but the basic facts are that he and a colleague, David Herold, crossed into Maryland, stopped at the home of Dr. Samuel A. Mudd to get his leg set, hid in a wooded area near the border of Virginia until April 21, and then made his way south with Herold. Nearly two weeks after the shooting, on April 26, Booth was cornered in a tobacco barn in Bowling Green, Virginia. Union troops set fire to the building, then shot him. He

died the next morning from his wound on the front porch of the farmhouse where he had been trapped. His capture was the result of a massive manhunt involving thousands of troops and civilians, directed by
Secretary of War Edwin M. Stanton. Stanton learned the names of some
conspirators, and he had soldiers seeking them. Although many dozens
of suspects were arrested in April and May, ultimately a military court
tried eight conspirators, three were sentenced to life in prison on June 30,
and four others were hanged on July 7. One additional person, John Surratt, escaped from Canada to Europe and was arrested by an American
official in Egypt in November 1866. One of the hanged conspirators was
his mother, Mary Surratt, who ran a boardinghouse that Booth occasionally used. The hanging of a woman was an extraordinarily rare event in
nineteenth-century America, and the first by the US government.

The reaction of the nation and the government made the assassination
a complicated historical event. The Civil War, which had begun in April
1861 and resulted in nearly seven hundred thousand deaths and the
destruction of massive parts of the South, was winding down—indeed
finished for all practical purposes at the time Booth shot Lincoln. The end
of the war should have dominated media coverage, but it was largely
crowded out for months by news of the assassination and the hunt for
and prosecution of conspirators. Meanwhile, with pomp and ceremony
befitting the death of a president, Lincoln was buried in his hometown
of Springfield, Illinois, in May. Northerners mourned his death because
they had lost their leader, Southerners mourned because many believed
he would have controlled Northern impulses to punish them severely.
Lincoln's funeral parade in Washington, DC, held on April 19, brought
out hundreds of thousands of viewers. Millions more stood along the
railroad route that brought him back home to Illinois for burial. It was an
extraordinary turnout for a nation (the Union had a population of twenty-
two million people). Within two weeks of the assassination, all of North
America, as well as much of Latin America, Europe, and parts of Africa
and Asia had heard the news.

CIRCUMSTANCES THAT STIMULATED CONTROVERSY OVER THE LINCOLN ASSASSINATION

One could hardly have asked for a more complex, rich source of factors
leading many to create and spread rumors, false facts, and speculation.
These factors included the existence of multiple participants, the rapidity
with which trials and executions occurred, widespread and conflicting
theories about what happened, the length of communication time in the
mid-1860s, the death of the key perpetrator and other conspirators before

they could be properly questioned by law enforcement, and widespread public interest.

The situation was further complicated by the instantly changed image of this president. During the Civil War, Lincoln was highly unpopular. Northerners were not always convinced that the Union should be preserved or the slaves freed, especially as the number of military deaths climbed into the hundreds of thousands, with many more wounded or incarcerated in prisoner of war camps. Southerners blamed Lincoln for bringing on the Civil War (not true), destroying their world, and causing so many deaths and hardship.[5] He was personally attacked on all sides for his frontier ways, sloppy dress, and simple language. He was called a "monkey," and was regarded as all-round unsophisticated by Eastern standards.

But his death changed everything. Northerners now viewed him as having saved the Union. He was called "The Martyr of Liberty."[6] His Secretary of War, Edwin Stanton, present at Lincoln's bedside at the moment of death (7:22 a.m. on April 15), immediately uttered, "Now he belongs to the Ages," instantly starting the mythologizing of the president. To this day, Lincoln remains one of the most revered presidents in American history, ranked number one or two with George Washington—and he

ABRAHAM LINCOLN,

THE MARTYR DIES, BUT FREEDOM LIVES.

Figure 4.1.   Image of assassinated President Abraham Lincoln presented as a martyr, published circa 1865. Such images circulated for decades. Courtesy Library of Congress.

achieved this status instantly.[7] Easter Sunday occurred the day after the shooting, and so his shooting was the subject of sermons across the North, which had heard the news quickly thanks to an extensive network of trains and telegraph lines. Southern leaders expressed sadness, including the head of the South's military forces, Robert E. Lee.[8]

The *New York World* had not always been kind to Lincoln, but on April 15 it reported, "today every loyal heart must suffer the terrible shock, and swell with overburdening grief at the calamity which has been permitted to befall us." The newspaper used the word "plot" to describe the source of the murder and wrote "that the same political fury and hate which lit the flames of the great rebellion inspired these hellish deeds."[9] Two days later, the *World* argued that:

> the loss of such a man, in such a crisis; of a man who possessed so large and growing share of the public confidence, and whose administration had recently borrowed new luster from the crowning achievements of our armies; of a ruler whom victory was inspiring with the wise and paternal magnanimity which sought to make the conciliation as cordial as the strife had been deadly; the loss of such a President, at such a conjuncture, is an afflicting dispensation which bows a disappointed and stricken nation in sorrow more deep, sincere, and universal than ever before supplicated the compassion of pitying Heaven.[10]

Horace Greeley, editor of the *New York Tribune* and the nation's most prominent newspaper editor, mythologized the chief executive: "President Lincoln fell a sacrifice to his country's salvation as absolutely, palpably, as though he had been struck down while leading an assault on the ramparts of Petersburg," blaming Booth as "an avenger" of the South.[11]

Individuals confided to their diaries, a popular practice at the time, the grief they felt. New York lawyer George Templeton Strong had anticipated Lincoln might get in trouble, but also that he would go down in history as a great man: "I foresaw most clearly that he would be ranked high as the Great Emancipator twenty years hence, but I did not suppose his death would instantly reveal . . . the nobleness and the glory of his part in this great contest."[12] Politicians and poets gave speeches and eulogies across the North. George Bancroft, a historian living in New York in the 1860s, declared on April 25 that:

> the grave that receives the remains of Lincoln receives the costly sacrifice to the Union; the monument which will rise over his body will bear witness to the Union; his enduring memory will assist during countless ages to bind the states together, and to incite to the love of our one undivided, indivisible country.[13]

Even Walt Whitman, one of the nation's greatest poets, reinforced the president's new image in May 1865 in his poem "Hush'd be the Camps To-Day": "O Captain! My Captain! Our fearful trip is done," and continuing, "But O heart! Heart! Heart!/O the bleeding drops of red,/Where on the deck my Captain lies,/ Fallen cold and dead."[14]

Given the extensive coverage of the Lincoln assassination, how best do we deal with the role of fake facts in this instance? We can see a multitude of types of misinformation that dominated the nation's understanding of the events in the spring and summer of 1865. The leading authority on the conspiracies surrounding the assassination, William Hanchett, remarked "that every American thinks they know what happened."[15] Civil War historian Bruce Catton observed that "the mere words 'Ford's Theatre' and 'Our American Cousin' immediately evokes the entire story for every American."[16] But Hanchett, although he agreed with Catton's comment, concluded that:

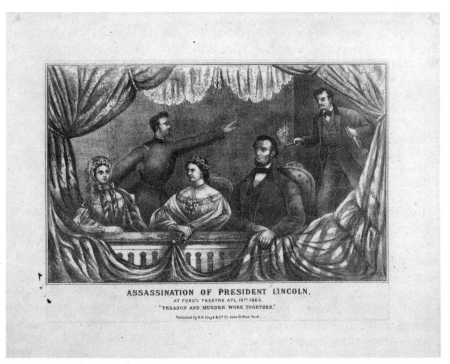

Figure 4.2.   This is an early image published before 1870. Courtesy Library of Congress.

the public has little understanding of the passions of the Civil War that led to it and that so deeply affected the way with which it was dealt. We have not only been ill-informed, we have been misinformed about the assassination; there may be more popular misconceptions about the Lincoln murder than about any other event in American history.[17]

Hanchett expressed this conclusion in his 1983 study of the assassination, after having witnessed two decades of extensive debate about President Kennedy's assassination. The debates that have continued to the present have sustained his assessment. In 2014, another authority on the Lincoln assassination, Edward Steers Jr., made a similar point:

The traditional story of Abraham Lincoln's assassination is littered with myths, from the innocence of Mary Surratt and Samuel Mudd to the escape of Booth to Oklahoma (or Guwahati, India), where he died by suicide several years later. That a subject so widely written about is so filled with falsehoods is interesting in itself. Perhaps it speaks to the greatness of Lincoln. That a man so great could be struck down at the pinnacle of his success is difficult to accept.[18]

Why was there so much interest in this event? Hanchett waited until the end of his book, where he considered what various commentators theorized or promoted as facts, to answer the question:

Among the reasons why the sensationalists, the charlatans, and the crackpots have been able to make such a big thing out of Abraham Lincoln's assassination is that the assassin never had his day in court, not even military court: he denied it to himself by refusing to be captured alive. Had he lived to answer questions and explain his motivations, much of the mystery of his murder conspiracy would have been dispelled, no matter whom he implicated or failed to implicate.[19]

In a more mundane way, however, we can explain the interest as well by several factors: the curiosity of the public, for it was a human interest story with genuine mystery to it; a desire for reconciliation or recovery from the shock of the war and from this event; mischievous behavior by some authors to advance their personal or political agendas; the need to secure the nation's safety by rounding up conspirators who could possibly kill other cabinet officials; and a desire to punish the guilty to both avenge and support the rule of law. Each of these elements supported Hanchett's central point that this was all about a mystery never resolved. The Kennedy assassination was similar in these respects.

The Lincoln case has a multitude of elements that enrich the narrative: conspiracy theories and rumors; suspicious behaviors; creation of mythology, lies, and misrepresentations; curiosities and human interest stories;

even prophecies most notably from the president himself, who predicted he might be the subject of an assassination (he had been briefed on potential plots during each year of his presidency); heroes and exemplary behavior; religious overtones; involvement of famous people; widespread public interest; wars; propaganda; and disasters. It seemed that the story had something for everyone, both in 1865 and throughout the next century.

The passage of time enabled many individuals to conduct highly detailed research, thinking (or speculation), and writing on the topic. Most of the settled facts of the assassination that stood the test of time were known within a couple of years of the shooting. While minor details were added over the next 150 years, the known fundamentals of what actually happened did not change much.

Over time, the reputations of key players evolved. Booth was instantly the evil force at work, but by the 1970s he was also sometimes cast as a misguided, well-meaning, likable person; even while others confirmed his ruthless nature.[20] Secretary of War Stanton's reputation as a possible mastermind behind the conspiracy thrived for some seventy-five years before historians began casting him not as a conspirator but instead as a competent cabinet official loyal to both Lincoln and the president's immediate family, and as a highly effective crisis manager in the way he handled the pursuit of the fugitives and suspects in the case.[21] The same can be said of Judge Advocate General Joseph Holt, the War Department official responsible for the day-to-day investigations and judicial processes of the assassination.[22]

Lincoln's martyrdom remained unchanged in the mind of the American public, despite efforts by some historians to present him as a man with clay feet more than as an almost God-like figure.[23] The first statue in honor of Lincoln appeared in Washington in 1868, only three years after the assassination. The Lincoln Memorial, dedicated in 1922 and now on the National Register of Historic Places, reinforced his stature; it remains on tourists' "must see" list when visiting the nation's capital.[24]

The number of commentators engaged in the subject of Lincoln's demise, as well as the amount of misinformation, increased during the 1930s. It became difficult to ferret out truth from fiction. In that decade, new information and widely sold books renewed interest, reinforced by the celebration of "final encampments" of veterans, such as that at Gettysburg, which were filmed and shown as news reports in theaters across the United States. Academics fled in retreat, with only a few daring to step gingerly back into the fray.[25] Books with "new" information about the assassination continued to appear, some even becoming "best sellers," such as Bill O'Reilly's 2011 book, *Killing Lincoln: The Shocking Assassination That Changed America Forever*.[26]

Fake Facts and the Lincoln Conspiracies

Conspiracy theories became the most enduring driver of fake facts surrounding the Lincoln assassination. There was talk of two separate conspiracies: one to kidnap Lincoln and whisk him away to the Confederacy. When that did not materialize, there was conspiracy talk of the assassination. Some of the actors in these stories were the same in both conspiracy theories. One version had Vice President Andrew Johnson involved in some way, alleging that he had an acquaintance with John Wilkes Booth.[27] The most commonly held conspiracy theory had John Wilkes Booth organizing a group of eight people to carry out the assassination.[28] The earliest of these theories argued that Confederate public officials arranged the assassination. Although this theory was quickly superseded by others, it had a revival in the late 1970s.[29] Various accounts involved Southern merchants selling cotton in the North or in Europe, international bankers, and the Vatican Church (either directly involving the pope or through the actions of North America priests). A theory, given serious credence for a while, held that Lincoln's Secretary of War, Edwin Stanton, developed and executed both the assassination and a coverup. The Stanton conspiracy was consistent with many mid-twentieth-century writings about the assassination, but in recent decades historians have discounted this theory and raised Stanton's historical image to one of an outstanding cabinet official.[30] Other conspiracy theorists believed that disaffected Northern politicians, including various Congressmen, might have been responsible.[31]

The first newspaper accounts of the assassination appeared on April 15–16 and simply reported the basic facts. The *Herald*—the largest newspaper in the country at the time, with a circulation of one hundred thousand—quickly published the news that Lincoln had died a mere one hour and twenty-three minutes after being shot on the morning of April 15.[32] By the end of the next day, however, various papers began to publish multiple editions, presenting more details and using lurid language. For example, the New York *Herald* published seven editions in one day. On April 16, the *Herald* declared that "the heart of this nation was stirred yesterday as it has never been stirred before. The news of the assassination of Abraham Lincoln carried with it a sensation of horror and agony which no other event in our history has ever excited."[33] On April 15, the *Cleveland Morning Leader* had run the headline on page one in an unusually large font size, completing the headline with seven exclamation marks. Several newspapers reported that Secretary of State William H. Seward was "also assassinated," which later proved false as he was only wounded. By noon on April 16, residents in San Francisco knew that the president had been killed and that John Wilkes Booth had done it, thanks to the transcontinental telegraph that had been opened in 1861.

On April 18, the Selma, Alabama, newspaper printed in bold letters: "GLORIOUS NEWS. Lincoln and Seward Assassinated. LEE DEFEATS GRANT. Andy Johnson Inaugurated president." The article assured readers of their impeccable sources, that the news "is said to be true beyond a doubt," and that Lee "had affected a junction and whipped Grant soundly. Passengers, wounded soldiers and officers confirm this."[34] The errors are egregious: Seward was not killed and Robert E. Lee did not defeat General Grant; nevertheless, the newspaper had no qualms assuring its readers that it had the facts right. We can probably attribute this misinformation to bad reporting, normal confusion close after an event, and wishful thinking.

Harold Holzer, the leading Civil War newspaper historian, has carefully documented how partisan the press had been throughout the war, pointing in particular to three competing newspapers in the highly contested New York City market. The *Herald*, the *Tribune*, and the *New York Times* competed in this most contested media market in the country. These three newspapers represented distinct political positions.[35] Nevertheless, on the first two days following the assassination, the three newspapers showed remarkable similarity, across multiple editions, in the way in which they headlined their stories. At first, all three emphasized the "National Calamity" and "Our Loss." It was only after a few days that differences in their coverage began, as each of the newspapers began to examine the events through its own well-honed political lens.

Both the political stance of the newspaper and the censors played a role in reporting the assassination. Consider the case of the pro-Confederacy *Richmond Whig*, published in Richmond, Virginia. On April 17, it became perhaps the first newspaper in the South to report Lincoln's death. However, by this time, the Union Army had already occupied Richmond—the capital of the Confederacy—for two weeks; thus, the city was completely under Yankee control. Lincoln had even visited Richmond after its fall on April 4. The local Union occupation force had allowed the newspaper to publish, but only under the supervision of US military censors. Its reporting illustrated the changed editorial policy of the newspaper:

> Assassination of President Lincoln!
> The heaviest blow which has ever fallen upon the people of the south has descended! Abraham Lincoln, the President of the United States, has been assassinated. The decease of the Chief Magistrate of a nation at any period is an event which profoundly affects the public mind, but the time, manner and circumstances of President Lincoln's death render it the most momentous, most appalling, most deplorable calamity which has ever befallen the people of the United States.[36]

The conspirators' trial received near constant and detailed coverage from the press. The Washington, DC, *Evening Star*, for example, provided lengthy reporting down to the level of reproducing quoted exchanges in the courtroom, including legal procedural matters among the lawyers that were not routinely covered by the press then or now. The testimony made available by newspapers to the public and to subsequent writers about the assassination was so detailed that it fed conspiracy theories for over a century—as students of the event questioned the actions and motives of all involved. For an example of the level of details published by the press, consider a report of the investigation of the boardinghouse where the conspirators and Booth had stayed:

> This was on the night of the 15th of April. I then went out into the bar room, and while I was there a friend came up to me; I say a friend, because it was a man whom I see about the streets every day. He said there was rather a suspicious-looking man there who had taken a room the day previous, and that I had better go and look at the book. I went and found the name as near as I could make it out: G. A. Atzerodt. It was written very badly; In fact, nobody could make it out until I went to the book. The proprietor of the house could not make it out. I then went upstairs to the room. I saw one of the clerks or men attached to the house, and asked him to go up to the room with me, saying that I should like to go and see it. I went upstairs to the room. The door was locked. The man said that he thought the party who had taken the room had carried the key away with him, I did not altogether like the appearance of things, so I went down to one of the proprietors, and asked him if he had any objection to going up to the room, and if he could get a key to fit the doer. He said he had not one that would. I went upstairs again to the room, tried all the keys, and could not get one to fit. I asked him if I had his permission to burst the door. He said he had no objection, and I burst open the door into the room. There was a black coat hanging up on the wall on the left hand side as you go in the door. Right opposite was the beds' end. I went towards the [illegible], and underneath the pillow I found a Pistol loaded and capped.[37]

On cross examination, one of the residents at Mrs. Surratt's boarding-house testified:

> I boarded at Mrs. Surratt's house up to the time of the assassination. Booth called frequently at Mrs. Surratt's. He generally called for Mr. John H. Surratt and in the absence of John H. Surratt, he would call for Mrs. Surratt. Their interviews were always a part. I have been in the company of Booth in the parlor, but Booth has taken Surratt out of the room and taken him upstairs, and engaged in private conversation in rooms upstairs. Booth would sometimes when there engage in a general sort of conversation, and would then say, "John, can you go upstairs and spare me a word!" They would go upstairs and engage in private conversation, which would sometimes last two or three hours. The same has occurred with Mrs. Surratt. I have seen

the prisoner, Atzerodt, at Mrs. Surratt's. He came to Mrs. Surratt's house, as near as I can remember, about three weeks after I formed the acquaintance of Booth. He inquired for John H. Surratt or Mrs. Surratt, as he said. I have never seen him in the house with Booth. He must have been at the house ten or fifteen times. The young ladies of the house could not comprehend the name that he gave. They understood that he came from Port Tobacco, the lower portion of Maryland, and, instead of calling him by his proper name they gave him the nickname of "Port Tobacco." I met him at the corner of 7th street and Pennsylvania Avenue about the time that Booth played the part of Pescara, in "The Apostate."[38]

Other witnesses added to and contradicted this testimony at the 1865 trial, and again at John Surratt's trial in 1867. Reproducing this testimony illustrates the level of detail in which commentators of the assassination would engage over the next 150 years, almost recounting their versions of the minute-by-minute flow of events, not just of the trial. Conjecture and misinterpretations befuddled historians for decades afterward.

The day before the military court was to seclude itself to render a verdict on the charged conspirators, an Ohio paper informed its readers that:

the impression seems to be that all will be convicted, but that Payne, Harrold and, Aizaroth only, will receive the death sentence. When verdict and sentence, in each case, are agreed upon, the sentence will be sent to the Advocate, General Holt, who reads [illegible] then lays it before the Secretary of War, by whom it, is referred to the President for his approval.[39]

These minutiae became fodder for speculation in future years. In this instance, those who believed that either Secretary Stanton or Andrew Johnson masterminded the assassination thought they could use their governmental authority to have the military court approve the death sentence quickly and move forward to rapid execution before the conspirators could talk more widely.

In understanding the news coverage of the Lincoln assassination, one must have a tolerance for misinformation that inevitably results from the immediacy of a situation with its rush of events—the urge to report "breaking news." However, the situation is different after a few days of coverage, and it is here where one sees more clearly the broader patterns of fake facts identified in this book. The first problem to address is the role of perception reinforced by commentary, supported by either true or fake facts. Recall that Lincoln was highly unpopular in both the North and South, accused of being backward and boorish, mean, cruel, and autocratic, violating laws, and causing thousands of unnecessary deaths. The press and campaign material hammered on these points so intensely that there was widespread belief that Lincoln would not be reelected president in the 1864 election. In the end, his greatest electoral supporters were Union soldiers, together with just enough civilian voters to provide him with a majority. Many writers held it against Lincoln that he was socially unpolished, which contributed to his image as an incompetent president. For example, one commentator described Lincoln as "a barbarian, Scythian, yahoo, or gorilla." A Southerner who met Lincoln alluded to him as the "vulgar monkey who now rules Washington." A New York editor called him "an uneducated boor. He is brutal in all habits and in all his ways. He is filthy. He is obscene. He is vicious."[40] Add in his "cowardice" and being "a drunk," and one can see how true and fake facts mixed together to create an image that stayed with him until he was assassinated. Then, overnight, he became a martyr and his public image was transformed.

Some descriptions of Lincoln also can be characterized more as exaggerations than as falsehoods. The editor of the La Crosse, Wisconsin *Democrat*, Marcus Mills Pomeroy, illustrated this feature of information handling blended with his own political point of view during Lincoln's first presidential election in 1860: "May Almighty God forbid that we are to have two terms of the rottenest, most stinking, ruinworking small pox ever conceived by friends or mortals."[41] These kinds of statements were more than just inaccurate or hurtful; they were dangerous. They encouraged the spread of rumors of assassination even before the president was sworn into office, for example, forcing him on his way to Washington, DC, to pass through pro-Southern Baltimore in the dead of night without fanfare. Throughout the war, rumors of assassination attempts and actual plots circulated, made more credible by Lincoln's negative reputation. As one historian reported, "After the war, newspapers and magazines carried innumerable articles about conspiracies against Lincoln by men and women who claimed to have been involved in them or to have known someone who was."[42]

After the assassination, these rumors found fertile ground and flourished for the next century and a half. As would also happen with President Kennedy's assassination, people were quick to believe theories of complex conspiracies. Even senior public officials bought into the rumors, often with little or partial evidence. Secretary of the Navy Gideon Wells's reaction to Lincoln's death was "Damn the rebels, this is their work."[43] Former Attorney General Edward Bates opined that Wilkes could not have operated alone, "for this assassination is not the work of *one man*."[44] A federal judge in a less than judicious tone exclaimed, "damned be the assassin," and "doubly damned be the instigators to the crime. May the infernal gods sweep them all to hell in a hurricane of fire!"[45] The New York *Herald* rode that wave, arguing that pro-Southern or anti-Lincoln political comments about the president in the Northern papers were the sources of the plots. Yet, within days, government investigators concluded that some plotting had occurred in Canada (true) and that the Confederate government in Richmond had approved these activities (uncertain). Collectively, the Northern press and the government in Washington subscribed to the hypothesis of a "grand conspiracy." Only over time would the grand-ness shrink as evidence surfaced that only a handful of individuals were involved, largely centered around Wilkes's inner circle of acquaintances. The Secretary of War, once suspected of having been part of the grand conspiracy and perhaps even its leader, was one of the first to diminish the validity of the theory as his department conscientiously conducted the investigation of the assassination and trials. The only senior official to remain committed to the grand theory was Joseph Holt, the War Department official responsible for holding the trials.[46] For the next half century, hundreds of commentators sifted through trial evidence, wrote memoirs, and speculated about the conspiracy, generating much of the vast literature that has appeared on the assassination.

It took nearly seventy-five years before the vast majority of the facts of the event not only had been established but also largely accepted by experts and the public. The only open question, never resolved, concerned the character of the assassin himself. Who was he? What was he like? What was he thinking? Was he a terrible human being or a likable but gullible actor? As one historian put it in the mid-1980s, Booth remained "a riddle."[47]

Although there was growing consensus about the assassination, it did not mean that new conspiracy theories did not rise. In 1937, a chemist named Otto Eisenchiml published his own account of the assassination, the result of his amateur historical sleuthing. His account hyped the conspiracy theory to a level not seen since the mid-1860s. His account was riddled with misinformation, but nevertheless it profoundly influenced the public's perception of the assassination for decades. He wove existing facts together to raise concerns and suspicions in the minds of his readers, often asking questions without answering them.[48]

Eisenchiml accused War Department Secretary Stanton of wanting to silence his prisoners to protect the Secretary of War, who had allegedly masterminded the assassination plot. This account ignored the realities this cabinet official faced in the days and weeks after the shooting. Historian William Hanchett has studied Eisenchiml's work closely and concluded that "when scrutinized point by point . . . [his] grand theory thus falls apart."[49] Stanton remained a defamed figure for several decades until more careful historical scholarship published in the 1990s describe his role more accurately. Hanchett summed up the problem with how Eisenchiml used information: "he has shaped the facts to fit his theory, rather than his theory to fit the facts. His assertion that Stanton aspired and plotted to become the nation's postwar leader is pure fiction."[50]

One technique that Eisenchiml used was to ask multiple questions, not always answering them in any definitive manner, but peppering his text with speculation, leaving the reader to suspect foul play. Why wasn't Lincoln better protected at the theater? Wasn't Stanton responsible for providing that security? Why was the guard who was at the theater never punished? Why could telegraph messages not be transmitted out of Washington for the two hours immediately following the shooting? Why was Booth shot, when the orders were to bring him in alive? Why were the conspirators' heads covered with sacks that would have prevented them from talking with anyone? Why were conspirators jailed on an island off the coast of Florida instead of in a regular federal penitentiary? Answers were less than definitive. For example, considering Lincoln's protection at the theater, Eisenchiml blamed the guard for making it possible for Booth to shoot the president by stepping away from his post for a few minutes, and noted that the guard was not disciplined by Stanton. Not being punished for dereliction of duty became "one of the unexplained mysteries of those eventful days." Readers were left wondering what could have been going on.[51] Eisenchiml found other ways to bring suspicion upon Stanton's motives and behavior, such as the momentary loss of telegraphic communications, which, it was later learned, was caused by a short circuit in the main batteries of the telegraph system. Eisenchiml did not consider in his book any alternative theories to his own.

Nonetheless, Eisenchiml had written a compelling narrative. *Why Was Lincoln Murdered?* sold well and was serialized in *Reader's Digest*. His themes were repeated by others and retold in television dramas. Television programs repeated many of the discussions that had earlier appeared in books, introducing the assassination to millions of people who were perhaps unfamiliar with the details. For example, PBS aired *The Assassination of Abraham Lincoln* in its program, *American Experience*, in 2009. Commercial networks had their version also, such as *Lincoln Assassination: Mystery at the Museum Specials*, an episode first aired in 2018 on the show *Mysteries at the Museum*. Even the prize-winning Lincoln scholar Harold Holzer appeared on a program in 2014 called *Person of the Year* in an episode titled *Harold Holzer on Abraham Lincoln*. Dozens of television programs about Abraham Lincoln appeared on American television in the run-up to the 150th anniversary of the Civil War—and these re-communicated the various rumors and theories of the assassination.[52] Whether on television or in books, Hanchett's conclusion was that Eisenchiml misrepresented and falsified the evidence, and many scholars today went to "the logical next step" of assuming that Eisenchiml participated in the "manufacture of false evidence."[53] Hanchett's analysis, in particular, convinced professional historians over the next thirty years, even if the public was slower to agree. As Hanchett noted: "But whether farcical or foul, or simply superficial and uninformed, most interpretations teach us more about their authors and about human nature than they do about why what happened at Ford's Theater."[54]

For historians of information, there are also other lessons to be learned. Many of the enduring true facts were quickly brought to the surface, even though they often were not accepted because of prior attitudes toward the event. If someone disliked Lincoln, he was disposed to think the worst of the situation and to look widely for conspiracies. More balanced accounts emerged, but they fell largely on the deaf ears of the generation that lived through the experience because they had a lens through which they viewed new facts and the arguments put before them.[55] It would take the passing of that generation before a more open-minded view was possible.

In the case of Lincoln, one enduring feature that transcended generations was the mythologizing of the president, and it began almost immediately upon his death. The experience is worth revisiting. On May 1, 1865, just two weeks after the assassination, a group in Washington, DC, began the campaign, picking up on the momentary praises of the press of all political stripes for the dead president:

> It is earnestly hoped that every newspaper throughout the country will call attention to the object of this Association, and give it such editorial encouragement as shall secure a general recognition. It is the desire of the Association to raise a monument that shall properly commemorate the sublime life and character of the lamented deceased, one that shall be creditable alike to the city and nation.[56]

On May 30, 1922, the Lincoln Memorial was dedicated in Washington, DC. It has been depicted on the back of the five-dollar bill since 1929 and was on the back of the American Lincoln penny from 1959 until 2008. Nearly eight million tourists annually visit the memorial.[57]

HOW THIS ASSASSINATION CONSPIRACY FITS INTO THE LARGER ISSUE OF AMERICAN CONSPIRACIES

Lincoln's assassination, much like Kennedy's almost a century later, reflects the nexus of misinformation, falsehoods, and conspiracies that scholars have increasingly come to understand are features of conspiracies. Lincoln's assassination, more than Kennedy's, however, has been less studied by experts as an example of the form taken by conspiracies, and yet this earlier event presents clear evidence that it followed patterns evident in other cases studied in this book and that, as historians have begun to establish,[58] public interest in conspiracies predates events of the late twentieth and early twenty-first centuries. Mistrust extended to beliefs in conspiracies. Students of political behavior tend to dismiss conspiracies as the work of crackpots, but at their own peril because the core of conspiracies is the use of misinformation, lies, or true facts situated differently than actual events would call for.[59]

Two political scientists reflected the salient features of conspiracies introduced in our first chapter and evident in the story of Lincoln's assassination: that conspiracies are, "animated less by misinformation, paranoia, or political mistrust, and more by . . . compelling narrative structures," as we saw with the publication of Eisenchiml's account.[60] While most scholars disparage conspiratorial thinking and behavior, these two political scientists point out that belief in conspiracies is a form of public opinion.[61] One could see that in the Lincoln assassination in all the editorial commentary in the media, and in Kennedy's times in the polling of the American public. Scholars observe that conspiratorial narratives, which are necessary to establish public opinion, share three features, which existed in both presidential assassinations. First, the event is intentionally hidden from sight and always involves evil forces at work. Second, the conspiracy narrative interprets events as a battle between good and evil (e.g., Booth was avenging the South, or he killed a political saint). Third, the narrative challenges mainstream versions of the story (Booth and Oswald were lone assassins), positioned this way to hide the work of powerful forces. The role of narrative in the way it presents bits and pieces of information fits neatly with how humans reason and organize their memories.[62] In both assassinations, but with Lincoln's an early example, conspiracists were able to link events and causes in a sufficiently compelling way to make it possible for ordinary citizens to accept them as plausible or true.

As noted in chapter 1, the final piece needed was that the assassination had to align with and reinforce preexisting knowledge of events. A preexisting condition had to exist—in this case four years of violent civil war that had engaged the attention of all adults in the nation and shaped their opinions on a vast scale.[63] Increasingly, historians and political scientists have been able to document that believing in conspiracies did not require someone to be ideologically, say, on the political right or left. Belief in conspiracies was democratic; everyone from any walk of life or belief could and did participate because "a conspiracy narrative may provide a more accessible and convincing account of political events," as we see in the next chapter that again others did regarding Kennedy's assassination.[64]

In both assassinations, we find a recurring theme that appears as well in all the case studies in this book: the role of power, of conspiracies used to marginalize or exclude people. In the North, Lincoln's assassination further marginalized Southerners out of the mainstream of how the

United States was evolving; with Kennedy, there was a further marginalization of Castro Cubans, the Soviets, Texas politicians, the FBI, and the CIA, among others. Political scientists, in particular, have long noted this feature of the use of information in conspiratorial narratives.[65] The role of power in society is a complex notion that we do not take up in this book, but merely call it out as playing a role in the manipulation of information, the narration of assassinations, plots by the patent medicine and tobacco industries, even by some protagonists in the climate change debate, all demonstrated in subsequent chapters. In Lincoln's era, fear and threats played major roles as Confederate officials were seen as attempting to kill off the senior leadership of the Union, with untold dangerous consequences made possible by such an act. In Kennedy's case, was it the FBI trying to silence critics, or the Soviet Union striking with surgical precession at American leadership during the Cold War? Add rumor to the mixture and one has the makings of a plausible conspiracy fraught with the unknown, or to use President Trump's expression of it, "People are talking about it." Opponents then can be marginalized and their power and influence diminished or discredited. One student of the process, art scholar Eleanor Heartney, observed that Americans enjoyed their conspiracies, "they are a grand old American tradition—the mother of them all being the speculation surrounding President John F. Kennedy's assassination" because "paranoia sells." Her observation was correct—"old American tradition"—but as demonstrated in this chapter, vibrant and extensive in Lincoln's case too.[66] The result was the emergence of fear, uncertainty, even anxiety, in the American culture, induced by the misuse of information.[67]

In the next chapter, we take up the role of misinformation and fake facts in President Kennedy's assassination. While historians have linked the two assassinations in the superficial way of categorizing them as the deaths of two presidents, we contend that the links are much stronger, the bonding agent being the role of information in how these two events were investigated, later studied by scholars in multiple disciplines, and how the public shaped their perspectives on what actually occurred. It is to that story that we now turn for it helps us understand patterns of conspiracy and the use of misinformation that transcend the four presidential assassinations that have occurred in American history.

5

Ultimate in Conspiracies 2

Assassination of President John F. Kennedy

There has to be more to it.

—Edward Kennedy[1]

President Kennedy was assassinated in the early afternoon of Friday, November 22, 1963, in Dallas, Texas. Millions of pages of investigatory material spun off from this event, including over four million pages of previously sealed materials released between 1994 and 1998 by the US Assassination Records Review Board.[2] Approximately one thousand books have been published on the assassination.[3] Despite these massive collections of materials and seven US government investigations, not to mention those conducted by the local police department in Dallas and the Mexican government, the actual events of that day, its participants, and reasons for the assassination remain unsettled facts. As this chapter was being completed in 2019—fifty-six years after the assassination—the combination of so much information and so many unanswered questions make any authoritative description of what happened difficult, if not still impossible to write. Responsible students of the event have documented and cited sources in excess of what historians normally see. The Wikipedia entry on the assassination includes over 160 endnotes and is the length of a book chapter.[4] A separate Wikipedia entry, titled "John F. Kennedy Assassination Conspiracy Theories," is twice the length of the assassination overview entry and contains nearly 450 citations.[5]

Because we are closer in time to the Kennedy assassination than the Lincoln assassination, the intensity of public interest in it remains high. The Kennedy assassination was the first time that television and radio coverage ran nonstop, without interruptions for commercials. This pattern lasted throughout the weekend of the shooting and into the next week. More Americans collectively and simultaneously experienced unfolding events than ever before. Hundreds of thousands of people passed in review of Kennedy's coffin in the rotunda of the US Capitol that Sunday, just forty-eight hours after the shooting. Most Americans alive in November 1963 remember where they were when they heard the news, including children in elementary schools, similar to the experience of most Americans at the time of the 9/11 terrorist attacks in 2001.[6] Tens of millions of people processed the same information as it came over the radio and television in the United States, as did many millions more in other parts of the world. There was no delay in reporting news—no sorting, filtering, and distilling. As soon as a story was reported on the Associated Press wire, the media would report it to the public. Books on the assassination routinely became best sellers—not only immediately after the shooting but even a half century later.[7] Public opinion pollsters periodically conducted surveys, consistently resulting in two findings: (a) intense public interest in knowing facts about all aspects of the assassination, and (b) belief that Kennedy was assassinated by a conspiracy, even though for over two decades official accounts presented by the US government held that only one shooter killed the president. The polls typically showed that two-thirds of respondents suspected a conspiracy involving multiple shooters, although there was never agreement as to whom the conspirators were.[8] This lack of consensus was at least in part the result of the ways in which settled facts, withheld information, contradictory evidence, spinning of information, rumors, and outright lies were circulated in the United States and other parts of the world.

Theories of who killed the president and why spawned what one US District Attorney calculated were the involvement of 42 groups, 82 possible assassins, and 214 people criminally charged in the event.[9] Conspiracy theories ranged from the single shooter theory to theories involving small pro- and anti-Castro groups, "nut cases," Fidel Castro's Cuba, Russia, Mexicans, Texas Republicans, rich people or oilmen in Texas, the CIA, FBI, Vice President Lyndon Johnson, and the Mafia in the United States. Each of these cases has been argued multiple times. While there are similarities to the Lincoln assassination, the complexity and volume of facts, rumors, and conspiracy theories about the Kennedy assassination are far greater. Allegations included the whole spectrum of witness tampering (foul play, suspicious deaths), suppression of evidence (ignored facts, confiscated film and photographs, autopsy notes, withheld CIA and FBI documents), evidence tampering (photographs, Zapruder film, autopsy reports, Kennedy's head and brain tissue), and fabrication (bullets and cartridges, Oswald's weapons, number of shots fired, eyewitness testimony, film and acoustical evidence), among others.

Theories about the Lincoln assassination tend to chronicle the story in a time frame measured in hours. Compare these theories to a widely read history of the Kennedy assassination written in 1967 by the respected jour-

Figure 5.1. Formal photograph of President John F. Kennedy, published in 1964 in the Warren Commission Report. It is the image most widely seen of the president over the next half century. Courtesy US Government Printing Office.

nalist William Manchester. It begins on the inside of the hardcover edition
even before the title page, with a minute-by-minute chronology of events,
for example, at 1:33 p.m. "LHO leaves TSBD, passing NBC's MacNeil,
1:34 p.m. First UPI Flash, 1:37 p.m. Caroline leaves White House," and
so forth.[10] Government investigations of the assassination also engaged
in that level of detail, most notably the federal investigations conducted
in 1963–1964 (known as the Warren Commission) and the US House of
Representatives investigation (1976–1979), both of which described many
events of the assassination in increments of seconds.[11]

Television kept the story in the news through participant interviews,
conversations with experts and theorists, amateur films and sound recordings of the assassination, and photographs. Newspapers and magazines carried thousands of stories about both the Lincoln and Kennedy
assassinations, although the Kennedy assassination generated a larger
number of stories. Unlike in Lincoln's time, however, the bulk of the
debate about Kennedy's death was conducted in books, not newspapers,
with summaries published in newspapers. Books were a logical medium
to use, given the large amount of information someone with a point of
view needed to present to make the case. There were also substantial roy-
alties to be made. After the period of news led to the period of theorizing,
television also became involved. For example, in 1988 the highly regarded
CBS correspondent Walter Cronkite hosted an hour-long program on the
Public Broadcasting System science show NOVA, titled "Who Shot President Kennedy?"[12]

What facts about the Kennedy assassination do we know with some
certainty? President Kennedy was shot twice while riding in an open car
in a motorcade in Dallas at 11:30 a.m. Central time on Friday, November
22, 1963. His wife, Jacqueline, sat next to him and also in the car were
Texas Governor John Connally and his wife, Nellie. The governor was
wounded in the attack by one of the bullets that penetrated Kennedy.
Some of the shots reported to have been fired came from the sixth floor of
the local book depository building in Dealey Square, where the shooting
took place. Within two hours, Lee Harvey Oswald had been arrested as
the prime suspect in the crime. Between the time of the assassination and
his arrest, Oswald shot police officer J. D. Tippit, although some students
of these events have argued variously that perhaps someone else shot the
officer.[13] Oswald was charged the same day for the murder of that officer.
On Sunday morning, at 11:21 a.m., while Oswald was being transferred
from the police station located one block away from the assassination site
to a more secure facility, a local cabaret operator named Jack Ruby shot
Oswald. Oswald subsequently died from this wound. For the suspicious,
here we have fodder for alternative theories: the president's assassin was

killed—silenced—while a potential second shooter (the police officer) was also silenced, both before they could talk.

Immediately upon being shot, the president and governor were transported to a local hospital, where at 2 p.m. the president was pronounced dead. Connally recovered from his wounds. The nation heard of the shooting at about 1:15 p.m. and soon after 2 p.m. learned about Kennedy's death. Kennedy's body, together with his wife and Vice President Lyndon B. Johnson, were quickly transported to the president's airplane and flown back to Washington, DC. As part of the transition of power called for in the US Constitution, Vice President Johnson was sworn in as president of the United States by a local justice of the peace on the airplane at 3:38 p.m. On Sunday and Monday morning, President Kennedy lay in state at the US Capitol. Later that Monday, a state funeral was held and then he was laid to rest in nearby Arlington Cemetery.

Figure 5.2. This photograph was taken just a second before Jack Ruby shot Lee Harvey Oswald (the man to the right of the white-suited police officer), November 24, 1963. Ruby is shown holding out his gun. The picture appeared in most national newspapers and on all three television networks. Courtesy Library of Congress.

Immediately, there were questions about what happened and speculation concerning conspiracies; and these have continued to the present day in much the same form. The first book on the assassination appeared in May 1964, *Who Killed Kennedy?*, setting the tone for future speculation. Investigations of the events by the Dallas police, the US Secret Service, the FBI, and the CIA occurred without delay. However, the major investigatory event was carried out by the president's Commission on the Assassination of President Kennedy, better known as the Warren Commission (named for its chair, Earl Warren, Chief Justice of the United States), established by Lyndon Johnson on November 29, approximately one week after the shooting.

The Warren Commission submitted its final report on September 24, 1964, months after other individuals had begun publishing articles in magazines and books on the topic. Thus, the Warren Report appeared after the public had already been exposed to considerable information about the events. The activities as described in what became the "official" account of events and conclusions fueled criticisms and speculation about the assassination for decades. Its fundamental conclusions were that Oswald operated alone in the assassination and that he killed Kennedy. The Warren Commission recognized, however, that speculation and rumors abounded. It even cataloged the ones that existed at the time of its report. These included questions about the assassin, sources of the shots, Oswald's movement, Tippit's murder, Oswald's activities after his arrest and also earlier his time in the Soviet Union and his later trip to Mexico City, Oswald's relations with US government agencies, various conspiratorial relationships, and miscellaneous rumors and speculations.

Ongoing concerns about the findings of the Warren Commission led the US House of Representatives to launch a second investigation with the US House Select Committee on Assassinations (HSCA), which reached overall similar conclusions but also three additional major findings: that the FBI had conducted a "flawed" investigation; that the Warren Commission failed to explore sufficiently the possibility of an international conspiracy against the president; and that there was a "high probability" a second shooter participated in the killing, hence raising the possibility of a conspiracy. Subsequent blue-ribbon panels during the 1980s and 1990s investigated various activities of the CIA; and these touched on the assassination. Congress passed the President John F. Kennedy Assassination Records Collection Act in 1992 to make public the records of the event and all related investigations. Through October 2017, the US National Archives and Records Administration and other repositories released records of the assassination. At the present, public officials at the archives have stated that only a few thousand documents have not been released and they remain under seal for reasons of national security considerations, some eligible for disclosure in 2027.[14]

Public attitude drove much of the concern of the American government that resulted in multiple investigations and statements in support of the Warren Commission's report. Unlike in Lincoln's day, late twentieth-century America had many organizations that polled public attitudes, including ones about their beliefs in whether or not there was a conspiracy to kill the president. Other polling organizations measured the degree of the public's agreement regarding the findings of the Warren Commission. It seemed that everyone had an opinion; millions of people had either read the government report or summaries of it. Every major poll taken in the past half century reported that over half the public believed in a conspiracy and that Oswald had not acted alone, thereby disagreeing with the Warren Commission's findings.[15] A Gallup poll in 2003 reported that 75 percent of its respondents did not believe Oswald operated alone, while an ABC poll the same year reached the same conclusion, with 70 percent suspicious of the lone shooter theory.[16] The following year, a Fox survey reported that two-thirds of respondents believed in a conspiracy and 74 percent believed the government had been or was continuing to cover up what really happened.[17] The lowest percentage of respondents believing there had been a conspiracy surfaced in a Gallup poll in 2013, but even this poll reported that 61 percent still believed in a conspiracy.[18]

In all of these polls, however, Americans disagreed on who was involved in the conspiracy. Neither government reports nor well-researched and well-written biographies of key participants disabused this belief. For example, the multivolume biography of President Johnson written by Robert Caro, which had been well received by the public and was a best seller and prize winner, could not dissuade people when volume four appeared in 2012 stating, "nothing that I have found in my research" suggested Johnson's involvement.[19] In 2003, a Gallup poll reported that nearly 20 percent of its respondents believed Johnson had been involved, largely because it was widely known that he disliked the Kennedys (borne out by Johnson's biographers, including the Caro study) and his fear of being dismissed from the Democratic ticket for the upcoming 1964 presidential election.[20]

The most definitive account of the Warren Commission, written by Philip Shenon, which was awarded the prestigious Francis Parkman Prize by the Society of American Historians, stated the challenge for historians of information concerning this particular assassination:

> I became a victim of the dual curse faced by anyone who tries to get closer to the truth about the assassination—of too little information and too much. I made the astonishing, nearly simultaneous discovery of how much vital

evidence about President Kennedy's murder has disappeared and also of how much has been preserved. There is now so much material in the public record about the assassination, including literally millions of pages of once-secret government files, that no reporter or scholar can claim to have seen it all. Whole collections of evidence have still not been adequately reviewed by researchers, almost exactly fifty years after the events they describe.[21]

That circumstance goes far in explaining why conspiracy theories about this assassination continue to bloom and why others have characterized it as "the mother of all conspiracies."[22]

CIRCUMSTANCES THAT STIMULATED CONTROVERSY OVER THE ASSASSINATION

Several circumstances led to the fabrication or manipulation of information related to the shooting. Within hours of the assassination, reporters in Texas were receiving phone calls with spurious tips, with one Texas journalist complaining that he was "inundated with them."[23] The same reporter pointed out that there were always "loonies" but there were also those who sought to make money out of the situation by selling an absurd story: "Nobody pays for the truth. They pay for a conspiracy."[24] Early accounts in this category involved defending Oswald for being "framed" or about conspiracies involving the Dallas police, Cubans, and others.[25]

But the principal cause of the heightened level of speculation was the Warren Report. In his meticulously researched study of the report's history, Shenon concluded that it "was flawed from the start." He explained:

The commission made grievous errors. It failed to pursue important evidence and witnesses because of limitations imposed on the investigation by the man who ran it, Chief Justice [Earl] Warren. Often, Warren seemed more interested in protecting the legacy of his beloved friend President Kennedy, and of the Kennedy family, than in getting to the full facts about the president's murder.[26]

Shenon explained that the young lawyers who did most of the research advocated for full disclosure, but the FBI and CIA, which were tasked with much of the interviewing and background research, seemed more interested in making sure they were not blamed for possible collusion or dereliction of duty than they were in supporting the commission. In the 1990s the family of a deceased CIA operative who had followed up leads to the Kennedy assassination in Mexico during the early 1960s made public his unpublished memoir documenting the considerable amount of information about Oswald's attempts to obtain a visa in Mexico City to go to Cuba two months prior to the assassination, his relations with anti-US conspirators in Mexico and elsewhere, and how much of the agent's findings the CIA destroyed to keep them from the Warren Commission.[27] Congressional investigators in the 1970s confirmed that the CIA and Robert Kennedy, then the US Attorney General deputized by his brother the president to assassinate Fidel Castro, had collaborated on the failed initiative, recruiting Mafia leaders into the project. So, when Oswald began bumping into some of the conspirators, his activities as well as rumors and reports about them fed the discussion concerning cover-ups and conspiracies.[28]

The FBI also withheld information from the Warren Commission; in particular, the fact that it had been watching Oswald since 1959.[29] Clarence Kelly, J. Edgar Hoover's successor as head of the FBI, quickly uncovered this behavior of the Hoover-led FBI and did not hide it from the public. He wrote later about the FBI's cover-up: "Why did the FBI people do this? The reason, at least in the beginning was easy enough to understand: hide the news from Hoover."[30] Then he got to the heart of the matter: "To the world at large, they must have reasoned, it might look as if the FBI had the assassin within its grasp—and then let him get away. To J. Edgar Hoover in Washington, it most certainly would have looked that way." Disclosures of that magnitude "would have ignited an inferno of retribution in Hoover."[31] In fact, careers in the FBI, CIA, and the US Department of State were broken over the assassination during the several years following Kelly's disclosure.[32] Kelly summed up his conclusion about what would have happened if FBI agents had been more forthcoming in sharing information from their Dallas field office with Hoover before the assassination: "without doubt JFK would not have died," and "history would have taken a different turn."[33]

The CIA was never candid about its behavior. Shenon rendered this conclusion based on his investigation: "what is clear to me is that over the last fifty years . . . senior officials of the United States government, most especially at the CIA, have lied about the assassination and the events that led to it."[34] Shenon was similarly harsh in his judgment of the FBI:

> Hoover and his deputies went out of their way—from the first hours after the assassination—to avoid pursuing evidence that might have led to the discovery that Oswald had coconspirators. It was far easier for Hoover to blame the assassination on a disturbed young misfit who had no recorded history of violence than to acknowledge that the FBI might have been able to foil it.[35]

Warren prevented his staff from interviewing some individuals who might have had insights and facts about a possible conspiracy, a few of whom later went public with their stories. He also prohibited his investigators from examining autopsy photographs and X-rays. That latter decision, supposedly imposed at the request of the Kennedy family, "all but guaranteed the medical evidence would remain hopelessly muddled today."[36] Even members of the Kennedy family told friends that they, too, believed in a conspiracy, especially one involving the Mafia.[37]

In the early 2010s, David Slawson, one of the young lawyers working for the Warren Commission and now in his eighties after a long and distinguished career, concluded that Kennedy had been the victim of a "massive cover-up" by many government officials who had not acted upon the information they had in hand prior to the assassination that would have prevented his death. Slawson now believed that some people—though not senior US officials—knew that Oswald wanted to kill the president and encouraged him to do so. Slawson's bottom line: "I know that Oswald was almost certainly not a lone wolf," and that Robert Kennedy and the CIA conspired to keep facts from the Warren Commission to hide their efforts to kill Castro as a means to prevent the destruction of Kennedy's political career.[38]

This is not the place to debate the details of what happened, rather to recognize that the machinations of various officials, when combined with the continuous unveiling of new facts (and misinformation), documents, and different points of view fed the half-century discussion about the assassination, particularly regarding possible conspiracies. However, an example of how information was used opens a window into how fake facts, misinformation, and creative interpretations affected what we know about the assassination. There were so many examples that could have been chosen. In addition to shared data and concerns—such as about the bullets or rifle used—each participant became the locus of additional information, such as Oswald's widow and his mother; Cuban operatives in Mexico City; members of the CIA, FBI, and Dallas police department; and high-profile individuals including Robert Kennedy and Lyndon B. Johnson.

One would think that with so many witnesses to the assassination, including recordings of the sounds of the gunshots, even film of the event (especially the Zapruder film), and the bullets themselves, there would be no controversy about how many shots occurred or how many hit the president. The film was particularly influential. Abraham Zapruder, a bystander with a silent, color motion picture camera, provided the most complete film of the assassination, including the shots almost in front of him. But, even that film did not quell the controversy. The Warren Commission concluded that "the preponderance of the evidence indicated that three shots were fired."[39] That language alone ("preponderance of the evidence") stirred suspicion for the next fifteen years. The congressional study of the assassination published in 1979 sustained the debate by concluding four shots had been fired: three by Oswald in the Book Depository building and a fourth from the grassy knoll just beyond it. That implies a second shooter and hence a conspiracy. From the day of the assassination to the present, debate has continued about which shots hit the president and how. Both government studies concluded that one bullet entered the back of Kennedy's neck, passed through his throat, then struck Governor Connally three times before settling in his left thigh. This theory came to be called the single bullet theory.[40] Another bullet hit the president in the head and was deemed the fatal shot. But others argued that there were more shots and that they came from other locations.[41] Even the governor's wife said there were other shots. Reportedly, fifty-one eyewitnesses said the president was killed by shots from a nearby grassy knoll, not the building housing Oswald.[42] Over the years, people reported having seen shooters on the grassy knoll.[43]

The FBI dismissed a reported bullet hole in the president's limousine, arguing it had occurred prior to the assassination. Does a president ride in a car with a cracked windshield? The Zapruder film was studied by numerous conspiracy theorists to determine the paths of the various bullets. Students of the shooting proposed that the president might have been hit in the head twice simultaneously. In this way, the debate continued for decades. The government retrieved bullets, supposedly one in nearly perfect shape that had killed the president, another from the gurney carrying the governor at the hospital, and fragments at the scene of the shooting. But the third bullet was never found. The contradictory, incomplete autopsy reports also added confusion to the story of the bullets. The FBI's account of how the president was hit by the bullets contradicted that of the doctors in Dallas and those who subsequently conducted the autopsy of the president in Bethesda, Maryland.[44] Ballistics tests conducted by the government supported the single bullet theory and that three shots were fired.

Much of that evidence was swept aside by conspiracists. Jim Marrs, who conducted the study that became a basis of Oliver Stone's 1991 movie, *JFK*, which argued the case for a US government assassination of the president and cover-up, declared that "a world-class assassin was recruited," although not named; and that Oswald was simply the "patsy" who could be blamed for the shooting.[45] Joseph McBride, a long-term student of the assassination, argued that a police officer on the grassy knoll shot Kennedy even though the recovered bullets came from a rifle, not the service pistol carried by the officer.[46]

Disputes over the autopsy reports became entangled with discussions about the number of bullets—and all these issues were debated in the press and in books. For example, one reporter in 1965 challenged the single bullet theory that claimed to hit both the president and the governor:

That bullet that presumably entered the President's back on a downward course turned inexplicably and exited in an upward direction. To complicate matters more, the same bullet, according to the Warren Commission, then changed direction again and raced through Connally's body on a downward course.[47]

After pages of narrative about conflicting accounts of the wounds and gunshots, Sylvan Fox ended the discussion in the same way as had hundreds of others suspicious of the forensic evidence: "That means it is altogether possible that more than three shots were fired and that at least one came from a place other than the book depository. Where might it have come from?"[48] Although the Warren Commission reported that three shots were fired, this same writer simply reported that the commission's evidence "about the number of shots" fired was "inconclusive" and that "doubts" lingered "about the direction of the shots, the flimsy basis on which the Commission decided that Governor Connally and President Kennedy were hit by the same bullet—all compel the belief that we have gotten something less than the full story of Kennedy's assassination."[49] On the more fanatical fringe, Oswald's mother, Marguerite Oswald, defended her son and was accused of trying to make money off her newfound celebrity status. She queried, "maybe Lee Harvey Oswald was the assassin . . . but does that make him a louse?" She added, "it is possible that my son was chosen to shoot him in a mercy killing for the security of the country. And if this is true, it was a fine thing to do and my son is a hero."[50]

More than with Lincoln's assassination, there was conflicting data, including the testimony of over five hundred witnesses before the Warren Commission, and facts were twisted or used in support of one argument or another in the Kennedy assassination. Mrs. Oswald's theory of the "mercy killing" has been dismissed by responsible students of the assassination, but her idea made the rounds in the 1960s, while other theories concerning possible multiple assassins continued to appear in the second decade of the twenty-first century.[51]

Alfred Goldberg was a military historian recruited onto the Warren Commission staff. He was responsible for being the on-staff expert about the conspiracy theories. He cataloged ten types and wrote the rebuttals to these that appeared in the final report from the Warren Commission. Recalling his experience in preparing the commission's analysis of these conspiracies, he read hundreds of articles and commentaries that appeared soon after the shooting and continued to follow this literature for years afterward. His observations summarize what has happened to facts about the assassination: "There was so much literature. There was an underground network operating already—all kinds of allegations, speculations, rumors." Shenon, who interviewed Goldberg decades after the assassination, observed that Goldberg "was so offended by the way so many supposedly legitimate scholars and journalists did not trouble themselves to research the basic facts of the assassination before rushing garbled conspiracy tales into print." Goldberg argued that "it was a good money-making thing for a lot of people," characterizing the theorists as "in the main, either ignorant, crazy or dishonest" in taking advantage of the American public, which had difficulty accepting the idea that an American president could be killed by one person. It would have been more plausible that a plot was afoot involving powerful people.[52]

MYTHOLOGY, FACTS, AND PRESIDENT KENNEDY

Beginning the weekend of Kennedy's assassination, his family began creating the mythology of the great, martyred president, including the organization of a state funeral modeled after but exceeding the ritual held for President Lincoln. The funeral played a crucial role in launching Kennedy's mythology.[53] There was the lying-in-state at the White House and the Capitol, a parade down Pennsylvania Avenue, and numerous eulogies. Mike Mansfield, the Majority Leader of the US Senate, captured the tone and mood of the moment: "There was a man marked with the scars of his love of country, a body active with the surge of life far, far from spent and, in a moment, it was no more." Mansfield went on to say that a piece of everyone died that Friday:

> Yet, in death he gave of himself to us. He gave us a good heart from which the laughter came. He gave us a profound wit, from which a great leadership emerged. He gave us of a kindness and a strength fused into a human courage to seek peace without fear. He gave us of his love that we, too, in turn, might give.[54]

The head of the Warren Commission, Chief Justice Earl Warren, a close friend of the Kennedy family, declared that "the whole world is poorer because of his loss. But we can all be better Americans because John Fitzgerald Kennedy has passed our way."[55] Speaker of the House of Representatives John W. McCormack, summed up the new image within forty-eight hours of Kennedy's death: "President Kennedy possessed all the qualities of greatness."[56] McCormack's contribution in creating the myth of the martyred President Kennedy mirrored gestures made in April 1865, "Now that our great leader has been taken from us in a cruel death, we are bound to feel shattered and helpless in the face of our loss . . . he has now taken his place among the great figures of world history."[57]

Like Lincoln before him, prior to his assassination Kennedy did not receive the admiration that the eulogies suggest. He could not persuade Congress to pass any of his significant legislative initiatives, conservative Texans bitterly opposed him as too liberal, the Mafia resented his administration's crackdown on their activities, he had faltered badly with the Bay of Pigs invasion, and he had hostile relations with both Fidel Castro and the Soviet Union. But, as in Lincoln's case, all that was swept away by a bullet.

Larry J. Sabato, a distinguished political scientist at the University of Virginia, and also the author of a Kennedy assassination book, wrote upon the fiftieth anniversary of Kennedy's death that much of what the public knew of the president was still incorrect, even if in consonance with his legend—in particular Sabato questioned that: the Kennedy-Nixon TV debates ensured his winning the election in 1960, the president was a liberal, he was determined to land people on the moon, President Johnson slavishly followed and implemented Kennedy's civil rights agenda, and all the facts had been presented on the assassination. Sabato argued that each of these five beliefs about Kennedy was not entirely true. Regarding the assassination "fact," Sabato wrote that "even a half-century later, we don't have the complete story. This is because many government documents remain classified and hidden."[58] In November 2013, a British reporter reported the obvious:

> out of JFK's death, the legend of Camelot was born, and just like Lincoln, Kennedy entered history as a US president gunned down in his prime, part of whose greatness could never be taken away from him. Over the last five decades, it is true, there have been those who have tried their best to revise downwards the Kennedy legend, but as this week will demonstrate, it has unquestionably endured in the American popular imagination.[59]

Why? Sabato argued that Kennedy's rhetoric was powerful, especially recordings of his speeches that were comparable to those of Winston Churchill during the Second World War; his positive "can do" attitude, such as suggesting that humans could land on the Moon, resonated with the populace; and the photographs of a young and vibrant First Family, all becoming part of a fairy-land Camelot, helped to create this myth.[60] The legends continued to accumulate so long as his mythical presence remained. Even the fact-checking site snopes.com was engaged, for example, in refuting a widely held belief that the president killed off the practice of American men wearing hats because he did not wear one at his own inauguration. As snopes showed, citing photographic evidence, Kennedy had worn a top hat to the inauguration.[61] The myths and facts about Kennedy reflect a point made by Sabato, that "Americans in any century can be too inclined to accept consultant-crafted images of flesh-and-blood people.

Just as important, the courtiers of the powerful, including many in journalism, can conspire to deceive us, or acquiesce in the deception, as they did with JFK."[62] Jackie Kennedy's "Camelot" was pure fiction.

Before moving to the next chapter and its discussion of the role of fake facts and manipulation of information in war, there is still the lingering issue from the Kennedy assassination of the role of information becoming immediately available through television, later the Internet. Unlike with the Lincoln assassination, events unfolded in real time in Kennedy's death: the actual assassination, the shooting of Oswald as viewers were watching on television, the funeral, and later the broadcasts of the Warren Commission hearings. These events had an immediacy that involved the public almost as participants. That sense of participation as events unfolded has remained a feature of American life to the present in major national activities. One consequence dating to Kennedy's assassination was the intensification of the public's opinions about events, most notably its views regarding conspiracies. That intensification required public officials to engage sooner and more frequently with a public more engaged and passionate about events than in earlier times.[63]

Controversy over the effects of television on government responses has continued since the assassination, with much of the debate on the part of political scientists and media experts, for example, siding with the negative consequences, in displaying the effects of President Ronald Reagan's influence on television, and even today on the influence of President Donald Trump. Students of the effects of television have suggested that public mistrust of government already existed by the early 1960s; and of course the public's constant resistance to officials' statements about the single shooter theory remains. Clearly established and understood by public officials is that television, and later the Internet, shaped public opinion, and therefore they had to present their points of view on television (later on the Internet) and quickly, in almost real time, as did Mrs. Kennedy in mythologizing her "martyred" husband. She started this process the day he died when she insisted that the American public see her wearing the blood-stained dress when boarding Air Force One returning to Washington, DC.[64] Studies of the interactions of public opinion, media coverage, and the role of public officials in such an arena of immediate discourse has focused more on the role of the media and advocacy groups, and less on the role of officials shaping opinions in periods of intense crisis or interest. In the Kennedy case, we saw government agencies avoiding public pronouncements other than to calm citizens, with only President Johnson wishing to influence views by moving quickly to form the Warren Commission and pressing it to do its work quickly.[65] The effect of television in the Kennedy assassination as a vehicle for transmitting fake and actual facts remains a subject warranting further study.

Long before television or radio or the Internet, there were newspapers that shaped public opinion and government responses. No case in American history more dramatically demonstrates that interplay among the public, officials, and proponents of multiple views than the Spanish-American War of 1898. It so influenced subsequent uses of information and misinformation by all sides that we need next to explore that American experience. It is to that case study we turn next.

6

Fake Facts and Mythmaking in War

Cuba and the Spanish-American War

The horrible tales of suffering sustained by the reconcentrados and the destruction of the "Maine" seemed likely to arouse public opinion to such a pitch that nothing but immediate war would satisfy it.

—J. B. Crabtree, 1898[1]

Fake news has a long history dating back to the founding of the United States. Some of these stories have long histories. This chapter examines how Americans viewed Spain's colonies in the Caribbean during the nineteenth century and how these perceptions led to armed conflict with Spain in 1898. By the time the United States engaged in war with Spain, Americans had been discussing Cuba, Puerto Rico, and Spain's treatment of these colonies for decades. Nothing makes this reality more obvious than a book published in 1897, before the war began, titled *Facts and Fakes About Cuba*.[2] Written by a reporter working for the *New York Herald*, like reporters today, he had an agenda— in his case, to critique the pro-Cuban independence movement. This newspaper became an important voice in the national debate about the Cuban situation, so its coverage is crucial for understanding the role of information in this war. For more than half a century, most Americans had favored Spain losing its colonies, many recognizing the benefits of acquiring Cuba and other Caribbean islands as colonies or new states. The history of US-Spanish relations concerning these Caribbean colonies was riddled for decades with false and misleading reports—what we would call fake news today.

The question of what Spain should do with its Caribbean colonies, and how the United States should respond to this European colonial power, resurfaced several times during the nineteenth century. The discussion began in the 1820s. Fake news regarding Cuba flared up first in the 1840s and 1850s, again during a significant revolt in Cuba against Spanish rule between 1868 and 1878, and finally between 1895 and 1898 when another revolt broke out involving the United States in a war against Spain (known today as the Spanish-American War). Events and consequences led to intense media coverage in each period, including a postwar debate that lingered until 1914. Concern about Spanish colonialism in the Caribbean came to an abrupt end with the start of the First World War, when the nation's attention turned to larger concerns.[3]

Over time, the number of issues subject to rumors, false or inaccurate facts, or misrepresentations grew in volume and variety. For example, during the second major Cuban revolution (1895–1898), Spain's cruelty to its colonials, use of concentration camps, treatment of arrested American citizens, brutality of the fighting on both sides, speculation about how the USS *Maine* blew up in Havana harbor, and the role of future president Theodore Roosevelt as a mid-level US Army officer commanding the Rough Riders in the bloody battle of San Juan Hill in eastern Cuba became fodder for fake news. Although the war lasted only four months, for the United States it generated numerous books, hundreds of academic and other serious articles, and thousands of press reports.[4]

We present here the major lines of discussion surrounding the "Cuban question"—those that account for the majority of the fake news that was generated. Collectively, these expose characteristics of American fake news that one will recognize as still being in evidence today in the current national discourse about the role of the United States in world affairs. It has often been a dramatic event that has riveted the public's attention and generated national interest, such as the destruction of the World Trade Towers in New York in 2001, the Japanese attack on Pearl Harbor in 1941, the complete destruction of General Custer's command in 1876, and the sinking of the USS *Maine* in 1898. However, each of these events was preceded by a trail of fake news and misinformation that conditioned the public framing of the event. We begin this chapter by discussing US-Cuban-Spanish relations prior to the Cuban revolt of 1895, then consider Spain's controversial suppression of Cuban rebels and its public, which was followed by the destruction of the USS *Maine* that so animated discussions about Cuba. The war created new images, fake facts, and mythologies regarding the roles of Theodore Roosevelt, his Rough Riders, and the Battle of San Juan Hill.

In the nineteenth century, residents in North America received nearly all of their information about the Caribbean from newspapers; very few books were published until the eve of the war, and most of them appeared only after its conclusion. Coverage of Spain's Cuban colony—and to a far lesser extent the colony in Puerto Rico and even less the one in the Philippines—was almost constant for decades. This coverage focused on four topics: (1) US economic interests in the colony shaped by the ownership of sugar plantations and the exports of sugar and tobacco to the mainland; (2) the "cruel" treatment by Spanish officials of Americans who they arrested, tried, and sometimes executed for supporting the activities of Cuban revolutionaries and their North American allies (often individuals, never the US government), known as *filibusterers*; (3) debates over whether Cuba should become a US colony, whether the United States should pay Spain to give up the island, whether Cuba should be given greater political and administrative autonomy from Spain, and whether Cuba should be given outright independence; and (4) whether the United States should extend its policy of "Manifest Destiny," to control a major trading route of military importance.[5]

Press attention animated discussion in the US Congress, the White House, and the Departments of War and State, as well as in Spanish government and media circles. Editorials and news stories argued the various cases for independence, autonomy, and US acquisition. This media attention stirred interest in the topic, led to local meetings across the United States, and stimulated individuals to sign up to be filibusterers to fight the Spanish in Cuba. In the 1890s, several newspapers, located principally in New York City, stirred up sentiment among their readers through direct actions such as using their reporters in Cuba to "rescue" imprisoned female prisoners who they reported were abused and inappropriately maltreated by "evil" Spanish officials.

Generations of historians have debated whether the "yellow press" of the time was a principal cause of the war between Spain and the United States.[6] For more than two decades, most historians argued that the press had substantial influence on the course of events.[7] But increasingly over the past half-century, historians have identified other causes and motives that complicate the story of how Spain and the United States ended up at war over a colony recognized by both countries as economically impoverished. Some of the historians have noted, for example, race and class issues—how some white Americans saw the Cuban situation (as well as those in Haiti and Santo Domingo) as being about illiterate, unruly black rebels fighting against middle- and upper-class white Cuban businessmen and plantation owners. On the Spanish side, it was about the end of Colonialism, the difficulty of giving up one of its last remaining colonies despite the poor management of the island.[8] Regardless of what stance one took, two realities existed: the coverage provided on Cuba in the American press was so extensive that no newspaper reader in the United States could avoid the subject, and American officials responsible for making the decision to wage war (president, Congress) were pressured by their constituencies to take action. Historians have only recently documented how measured the response of the US government was in the light of frenzied public sentiment: that government officials attempted to understand the facts surrounding the incidents that occurred, worked in a calm and measured way with the Spanish government to resolve issues, and left a detailed paper trail demonstrating their desire to understand each circumstance so as to avoid war at almost all cost.[9] That quiet collection of information and documentation of rational public administration occurred within the corridors of government, even as some members of the media were relentlessly screaming for action by the late 1890s: whipping up public animus toward Spain, even though after each major incident they often called for calm to allow the facts to unfold.[10]

US-CUBAN-SPANISH ISSUES PRIOR TO 1895

American national discussions about Cuba became frequent in the 1820s and routine by the end of the 1840s. Information about Cuba available in the United States was commonly inaccurate during the nineteenth century for multiple reasons: intentional misinformation, sloppy reporting, and inability to verify reports of events and circumstances. Editorial opinions were mixed with selective use of data but presented as a factual representation to advance a newspaper's editorial agenda. Stories reported by large newspapers on the East Coast, especially in New York and Washington, DC, were typically picked up and repeated, sometimes with modifications, by other newspapers around the country.[11] Rumors were routinely passed off as verified facts, while outright lies and propaganda spread as well. In each decade, advocacy groups spread inaccurate information about Cuba and Spain. These included revolutionary groups in New York, Washington, DC, New Orleans, and south Florida that were bent on fomenting verbal and military attacks on Spain. The goal of these stories was normally to recruit volunteer fighters and raise money to arm them. Political parties sought to use the Cuban issue to further their own agendas. During the first half of the nineteenth century, newspapers typically promoted a political point of view, much as Fox News does today for the political right and the *New York Times* does for the political left.

Nineteenth-century stories about Spain and its Caribbean colonies have a striking similarity to the stories about the 9/11 terrorist attacks: rumors followed by legends; accounts of suspicious or awful behavior; extensive publication of editorials, articles, and speeches; dramatic accounts of human interest stories; celebrations of milestone dates; and in particular, conspiracy theories, especially ones describing the destruction of American ships and buildings.[12] The sinking of the USS *Maine* was an iconic example, but not the first.

How does this case compare to that of the 9/11 terrorist attacks? We did not find accounts of foreknowledge, pareidol, numerological accounts, or religious interventions and miracles—even in the Spanish press.[13] However, stories of heroes abounded, notably about Teddy Roosevelt, the Rough Riders of San Juan Hill, and the sailors who destroyed in spectacular military engagements the Spanish navies assigned to Manila and Santiago de Cuba. Prophecies about Spanish colonies in the Caribbean appeared throughout the nineteenth century, but many of them simply seemed to speak to the tacit knowledge of the day in which either Cuba would be separated from Spain (most likely through US intervention) or Spain would find a way to accommodate the political desires of its colonial citizens.

There was widespread use of visual imagery in the accounts about the Spanish colonies—in particular about the sinking of the USS *Maine*. This is not unlike other famous episodes in American history such as the massacre of Colonel Custer's cavalry at the Battle of Little Big Horn and the attack on Pearl Harbor or the World Trade Center. However, there are two important differences. It was only near the end of the nineteenth century that portable cameras were available, so the visual accounts of these events were typically drawings rather than photographs, film, or television coverage as there was with the 9/11 attacks. The second difference was that there were few eyewitness accounts of these nineteenth-century events, and those that did occur had the extra complication that the process of delivering images to publishers was a slow one in the nineteenth century. While sketches of events supposedly prepared by eyewitness artists graced the pages of American and Spanish newspapers and magazines, many of these were prepared in Florida or New York rather than at the site of the event. For example, *Harper's Weekly*, a widely read and well-regarded mid-nineteenth-century newspaper, published scenes of one captured American vessel, the *Virginius*, with the headline, "The Spanish Butchery." But its artist was not on that ship at sea.[14]

Why did US-Spanish-Cuban relations keep cropping up in American diplomatic, economic, and domestic affairs, and in the press throughout the nineteenth century? Over the first half of the century, unrest on the island led various groups to seek to free Cuba from Spanish control. These insurgents used the United States, primarily Louisiana and Florida, as their base of operations (Cuba is only ninety miles from the American continent) as a source of military recruits for these invasions and as a place to raise funds. These groups encouraged the American government to become involved in the invasion or the purchase of Cuba. Ships with contraband traversed the waters between Cuba and the United States from time to time, transporting filibusterers and military materiel to the island. Meanwhile, the normal trading with the United States meant there were regularly ships in the area that Spanish colonial officials monitored for being rebel ships. The century was regularly punctuated by Spanish seizures of ships, looking for military supplies or filibusterers (who often were US citizens), but often these ships were not involved in rebel activities and were simply plying normal trade and sailing under the American flag. When the Spanish colonial officials captured a ship, they dealt harshly with their captives.

In light of these seizures, the American government advocated for the rights and safety of its citizens and compensation for seizures of ships involved in legitimate trade. When Americans were executed by the Spanish, the United States typically entered into diplomatic negotiations, seeking official apologies as well as compensation for the affected families. These events were covered extensively in the American press, and American political parties often used these episodes to criticize Spanish rule and Spain's disrespect for American property and its citizens—primarily as a means to gain advantage in the American political arena. There was widespread interest in having the United States buy Cuba from Spain, but Madrid was not interested in such a deal. Cuba was also a pawn in American North-South politics. Because the island had slaves, Southern politicians sought to acquire Cuba to increase their political bloc in Congress, while the North resisted those efforts. This issue fueled discussion in the American media about America's strategic interests, domestic politics, and expansionist feelings, especially after the US success in the Mexican-American War of 1846–1848, which added extensive new territory to the United States.[15]

From the 1820s through the 1890s, filibustering and seizure of ships commonly led to the spread of rumors, false facts, and extensive editorializing. One of the earliest and most dramatic examples was the expedition of Narciso López, who prepared to liberate Cuba through military expeditions launched from the United States in the 1840s. In 1850, he landed in Cuba with six hundred volunteers but had to retreat. He returned the following year with a smaller force and this time was captured.[16] Most of the prisoners, including a number of American citizens, were executed, López as well. This incident outraged the American press. The American filibusterers were portrayed as brave young men, one quoted in the press as saying, "The only thing I was afraid of was that I would not get there in time to see any of the fun." The *New York Tribune* reported these young men as having "flocked to the standard" for the "noble cause."[17] Numerous stories appearing in the American press between 1849 and 1851 detailed the men involved and the cruelty of the Spanish authorities, criticized the American government for discouraging these expeditions, and rallied support for them. The press commonly treated López as a hero who was facilitating "Texinization" of Cuba,[18] or as someone consuming "the flower of American chivalry."[19] The lack of facts did not discourage the press, as one newspaper story candidly admitted: "A startling rumor reached here last night." Newspapers routinely embellished and republished reports appearing in other publications; the sources of these stories were often sailors and other visitors from Cuba, and the stories were mostly spurious.[20] The leading historian of the López expedition, Tom Chaffin, reported that the American press relied "heavily on stories from the *New Orleans Delta*, the *New York Sun*, and other papers with ties to the filibusterers. Those papers, of course, had strong political motivations to skew stories to favor or even protect the filibusters."[21] López's last expedition was reported by the *Herald* as Cuba's "Lexington," and the paper reported that Spanish "troops are deserting in squads to the insurgents," when in fact that did not happen.[22]

Reactions to the defeat and execution of López led to predictable press coverage and outrage. He was referred to as a "fallen hero," "martyr," and as Cuba's "Washington."[23] In the end, however, there was no mass uprising in Cuba as the press anticipated, and thus López's campaign failed. As one observer noted, the extensive, often exaggerated and inaccurate reporting "led the way in fanning the flames of his ambitions and popularity."[24] The *Southern Press* (Washington, DC) criticized Southern newspapers for this incitement: "There is the result of your diragrations, of your iniquitous falsehoods, of your placards with large black letters, and your detestable extras."[25] But this enabled American publishers to sell many newspapers to a growing readership.

Ship incidents continued to be covered by the press. The most notorious cases in the mid-1800s involved two American vessels, the *Black Warrior* (1854) and the *Virginius* (1873). The *Black Warrior* was seized by Spanish officials for minor infractions of port regulations in Havana harbor. That action expanded quickly into an international incident when Southern politicians used it to try to buy Cuba from Madrid. Spanish officials were offended, while American officials and politicians used the incident to posture on slavery and Cuba. The incident nearly led to war with Spain.[26] Congress published an extensive report on the terrible things the Spaniards supposedly did in confiscating the ship and its cargo.[27]

The "*Virginius* Affair," as it was dubbed by the press, resulted in diplomatic tiffs between the two nations from 1873 to 1875. This affair occurred during the first major Cuban revolt against Spain (known as the Ten Years War). The *Virginius* was outfitted to carry filibusterers and military supplies to Cuba. The Spanish captured the ship, including American and British citizens who were onboard. Spanish officials wanted to execute everyone on the ship and started to do so, executing fifty-three people before the British government insisted that these executions stop. The incident has been recorded in history as a victory for diplomacy because the American and British governments negotiated a settlement of payments to the affected families. But these discussions dragged on for nearly two years, during which time the press and politicians continued to urge war with Spain to finally resolve these continuing misdeeds of a harsh Spanish regime. The affair was also a catalyst for modernizing the American Navy.[28] The *New York Herald* kept published sensational reports about Spanish cruelty, injustice, and unfairness; presaging its behavior toward Cuba in the 1890s. The language was inflammatory in many newspapers, as these four examples attest:

> Loving the island of Cuba as a rare and wonderful portion of our star, knowing the vicissitudes of its history, feeling indignation against the horrible massacres of American citizens and Cuban students by the nation whose flag is a river of blood between banks of gold.[29]

> If Spain chooses to consider our defense against savage butchery as a cause of war to her, we must meet her also in war.[30]

> [On the shooting of American sailors] "It is a crime for which no explanation or apology can atone," and "the Peninsulars [Spanish authorities] are doing the work their victims could never have accomplished. Their mistakes are ringing the death knell of Spanish power in America."[31]

> [Spanish officials had added] another page to the dark history of bloody vengeance and cruel disregards of the rules of civilized war, and of common humanity, which the military and other officials in Cuba have but too frequently made part of the history [of their rule in Cuba].[32]

The *New York Times* and the *New York Tribune* acted with more prudence, in contrast to the reporting of the *New York Herald*. Most newspapers took sides on whether to negotiate a settlement or dispense justice to Spain and bring a final resolution to the Cuban Question.[33]

Reporting involved rumors and misinformation about who and how many prisoners there were, how many were executed, and the lack of a trial for these people (a summary court-martial was held). The haste with which the Spaniards began executing crew members fired up many newspapers. To add color to its coverage, the *New York Herald* fabricated stories when it was unable to obtain on-the-ground reporting. The paper called for war with Spain after news of the "massacre" of the crew began circulating in North America.[34] That aroused the public in meetings where Americans heard such messages as, "We are on the brink of war."[35] Reports of various Americans willing to raise volunteer regiments to go fight Spain in Cuba were reported by the media for two years. With the exception of the *New York Herald*, which was not seen as respectable by other newspapers but which had a wide national readership in the way that modern tabloids do, the press as a whole did not enjoy the massive experience that it would in the 1890s at the time of the sinking of the USS *Maine*. Nevertheless, the precedent of repeated spreading of exaggerated or misleading information was established. No future incident regarding Cuban matters would garnish as much prudence from the press as did this incident.[36]

SPAIN'S SUPPRESSION OF CUBAN REBELS AND CITIZENS

On February 28, 1895, Americans began reading in their newspapers that yet another revolt had broken out in Cuba. This time the rebels applied lessons learned in their prior revolution of 1868–1878; and three years into the new fray, the United States declared war on Spain. While the rebels were clear in their objective to win outright independence for Cuba, North Americans vacillated and considered a range of options, such as negotiating for Spain to grant its colony autonomy, purchasing Cuba, or conquering it. The war ended with Spain losing Cuba, Puerto Rico, the Philippines, and miscellaneous islands in the Pacific to the United States through a humiliating outright military defeat that overnight made the United States an international military and colonial power.

A defining feature of this revolt was the thoroughness with which the Cuban rebels organized, recruited soldiers, raised money, and established an effective, national propaganda and lobbying effort in the United States.[37] The media became a major outlet for fake news, propaganda, and editorializing; and, for the first time, the press had considerable influence over citizens to organize pro-Cuban rallies and shape public opinion, even if the press was unable to completely dictate American policy toward Cuba and Spain.[38] The American press was extensively wired up with telegraphic communications and belonged to the Associated Press news service, so information both real and fabricated circulated rapidly around the nation. By this time—compared to twenty years earlier—the number of newspapers and newspaper readers had vastly increased. Newspaper managers in New York understood that the Cuban situation could be exploited to sell more newspapers in their highly competitive media market, and some of the New York newspapers published as many as a half-dozen editions every day, with circulations approaching a million copies.[39]

The situation in Cuba energized reporting and encouraged the spread of information, misinformation, exaggeration, rumors, and opinions. The fighting bloodied both sides. A scorched-earth approach adopted by both sides led to the destruction of sugar plantations, entire communities, and sources of animal and crop foods; and this resulted in famine conditions in the countryside. The Spanish practice of concentrating urban and rural populations in camps or within controlled urban spaces increased the incidence of disease. A harsh military regime with strong support from the Madrid government had no reservations about using force of whatever degree necessary to crush the rebellion. The American government was reluctant to get involved in the war until very late, leaving a political and military vacuum. The Cubans and the Spanish hardened quickly into intractable positions, extending the conflict and its brutality—all of which became fodder for the American press and propagandists on all sides.

When the revolt began in February 1895, the Spanish ambassador in Washington, DC, declared it a "fiction" and argued that the insurgence had collapsed; and for a couple of months the American press and public believed him. In that first year of rebellion, however, tens of thousands of insurgents engaged in two dozen battles against the almost two hundred thousand Spanish troops on the island. The high-water mark for the revolutionaries' military success had just been achieved; and while the American press and pro-Cuban propagandists would report many new victories in 1896 and 1897, in reality there were few of them. At that high-water mark, Madrid sent a new captain general to Havana, Lieutenant General Valeriano Weyler y Nicolau. He was a tough, no-nonsense soldier with prior experience in the Ten Year's War[40] and wasted no time getting to Havana and ratcheting up the conflict. In the process, he acquired the nickname "Butcher" from the Hearst newspapers; while the *Chicago Times-Herald* tagged him as "the most brutal and heartless soldier to be found in a supposedly civilized country."[41] Weyler remained a lightning rod attracting negative press coverage and exaggerated accounts of his actions and those of his army in the United States and (later in) Spain.[42]

Weyler quickly launched his scorched-earth campaign across the countryside to prevent Cubans not engaged in revolt from being able to supply food and shelter to the rebels. Lacking sufficient resources to concentrate hundreds of thousands of civilians in controlled areas, misery spread across the land, stimulating more resentment against his rule than any other action that he took. Known as the reconcentración, he gave civilians—pacificos—eight days to move to army-fortified sites with their cattle and goods. Then their homes and fields were destroyed. His concentration campaign did as much to bring the United States into the war as any other factor, by conditioning the American public to expect harsh rule and inhumane treatment from the Spanish regime. So, when the USS *Maine* blew up in 1898, Americans were ready to take on the Spanish. Meanwhile, rebels were destroying sources of food and crops that sustained the Spanish, thus also contributing to the spread of disease, malnourishment, and hunger. Images of the results were published in American newspapers for the next three years and for a decade afterward in the numerous general histories of the war published in the United States.

For years, press reports exaggerated the number of deaths resulting from Weyler y Nicolau's concentration policy. Reports also exaggerated military victories of the rebels. Success for both sides slowed in 1896 and 1897. The number of deaths remained a controversial subject of propaganda and hyperbole. Not until 2013 was any historian able to arrive at reasonably accurate statistics. Whereas reports from the time stated that the number of deaths ranged from 60,000 to 500,000, the most accurate estimate by historian Andreas Stucki now places the total number of deaths closer to 170,000, which was 10 percent of the island's population.[43] It was a high number since deaths in extensive civil wars conducted in the nineteenth century typically involved population losses of 4 to 5 percent.

In the 1890s, the largest newspapers in the United States sent reporters to Cuba—dozens in fact, representing an innovation over prior practices.[44] Editorial and reader appetites for reports from the front drove up circulation of newspapers, particularly on the East Coast of the United States. Cubans living in New York seeking support for the rebellion had formed the Cuban Junta in September 1895 and successfully encouraged establishment of other pro-Cuban clubs, rallies, and fundraising efforts across the United States. The Junta adopted the conceit that it was a "legation" of the Republic of Cuba, and it advocated for total independence. The Junta fitted out more than sixty supply ships with soldiers and munitions, although they had only moderate success at avoiding the American and Spanish naval patrols. The Junta published over one hundred pamphlets and distributed what one historian called "a deluge" of propaganda materials to the American public.[45] Around the country the American press proved sympathetic to the Junta's filibustering activities, while federal politicians remained largely permissive.[46] As living conditions became harsher on the island, both the Junta and the press played on the humanitarian sympathies of the reading public and held "Sympathy Meetings" all over the country. The messages were unambiguous: "The Cuban cause is just" and "in time Cuba shall be free."[47]

When the Spanish authorities increased censorship and effectively slowed the telegraphic flow of stories out of Cuba, newspapers sought content from the Junta, which gladly provided generous quantities of it—often daily—which it claimed was pouring in from Cuba every day. One historian concluded that the Junta had "formulated a very systematic propaganda program" emphasizing themes of Cuban successes and Spanish failures, and calling on American humanitarian and military support.[48] Cubans falsely reported achieving significant military victories over outnumbered Spanish foes; and their accounts celebrated the brilliance of the rebel leaders Máximo Gómez, Antonio Maceo, and Calixto García—all who became familiar to the reading public. The Junta reports predicted Cuban victory over Spanish incompetence and portrayed Spain "as the sick man of Europe" on the verge of collapse.[49]

By 1897, stories of Spanish atrocities could be found in most large urban newspapers and magazines in the United States. Newspapers as diverse as the *Omaha Daily Bee, Chicago Record, Detroit Journal*, and *Chicago Times-Herald*, in addition to the New York papers, routinely carried these stories. The Junta created a useful scandal in February 1898, when it made public a purloined letter written by the Spanish ambassador to the United States, Enrique Dupuy de Lôme, critical of US president William McKinley. The pro-Junta *New York Journal* published the letter, and from there it spread widely across the American media, which reprinted phrases that were regarded as "humiliating to the President."[50] The central issue of the day remained brutality: "the most brutal and heartless soldier to be found in a supposedly civilized country."[51] Weyler's arrival in Cuba was bigger news because he was going to "cause the island to flow with gore."[52] The slaughter of women and children was a particularly favored theme of press coverage. Reporters for the New York newspapers *World, Sun, Journal*, and *Herald*, together with others from the Washington *Post* and the New Orleans *Times-Democrat* were posted in Cuba, sending back reports of atrocities. James Creelman of the *World* provided a typical report of the atrocities in Cuba:

> American citizens are imprisoned or slain without cause. . . . The horrors of a barbarous struggle for the extermination of the native population are witnessed in all parts of the country. Blood on the roadsides, blood in the fields, blood on the doorsteps, blood, blood, blood! The old, the young, the weak, the crippled—all are butchered without mercy. There is scarcely a hamlet that has not witnessed the dreadful work.[53]

Another widely circulated report described "skulls of all were split to pieces down to the eyes. Some of those were gouged out. All the bodies had been stabbed by sword bayonets and hacked by sabers until I could not count the cuts." Mutilation stories were also common: "The tongue of one had been cut out, split open at the base and placed on the mangled forehead in a ghastly likeness of a horn."[54]

A June 1896 report published in *World* informed readers how a Spanish officer induced cooperation from a female prisoner:

> "I'll make you," said the Spaniard, and he proceeded to tear off her clothing. He then questioned her anew and receiving no answer from the woman who was crying hysterically he unsheathed his sword and fell to cutting and

slashing his victim, until her blood covered the floor and she fainted in a corner. Her shrieks and entreaties only served to provoke the brutal laughter of the soldiery, while the woman tried to shield her child with her own body, but the merciless bullets did their work.

Because the baby did not die outright, "one of the soldiers, moved by a sort of barbarous pity, crushed the little one's skull with the butt of his rifle."[55] Another correspondent supposedly interviewed other Spanish soldiers about these sorts of events, reporting they "spoke of massacres as if they were everyday occurrences with them."[56] "Even children are slain by the Spanish; bodies sometimes shamefully mutilated."[57] These were strong narratives for Victorian Era readers. The *World* also spoke of atrocities committed on American citizens during 1896 and 1897, with the Spanish motive for violence attributed to the "unpardonable crime of being Americans." Regardless of whether Cuban or American, women were "shockingly abused and three girls were severely clubbed while striving to defend their honor."[58]

The American press declared that over three hundred thousand people had already been killed or died of maltreatment by the summer of 1897. There was no basis for knowing the truth, however, inasmuch as record keeping was poor, creating problems even for historians attempting to catalog the numbers later.[59] These accounts were illustrated with sketches showing dead bodies and atrocities, often published across multiple columns on the front pages of American newspapers. Cartoons were used to illustrate articles and editorials in the period 1895–1898. Printing technology had improved to the point that it was easy to publish these photographs and sketches along with the reporters' stories. Historian Marcus Wilkerson has noted the relentless coverage: "One illustration, showing carrion crows picking the body of a dead Cuban while starving children stood nearby, bore the caption, 'Last of a Family of Seven Waiting for Death.'" Wilkerson quoted the article that accompanied this illustration:

A third of the population has died. Hundreds more are dying daily in Havana and its environs alone; dying with accompaniments of misery and suffering almost inconceivable, wholly undesirable. They fall dead in the streets; they die before your eyes as you stand in the wretched pens where they are huddled together; they die with an agony of body which is equaled only by the hopeless anguish and forlornness of their minds . . . unpitied and uncared for.[60]

Ultimately, this kind of coverage supported editorials that asked,

How long are the Spaniards to drench Cuba with the blood and tears of her people? How long shall old men and women and children be murdered by the score, the innocent victims of Spanish rage against the patriot armies they cannot conquer? How long shall Cuban women be the victims of Spanish outrages and lie sobbing and bruised in loathsome prisons?[61]

Congress could not ignore the constant stories of the atrocities in Cuba. Congressmen spoke out on the floor of the Congress, asking in "impassioned language" about the "shooting of boys, the ravishing of women, and the sale of young girls," and the "herding of famishing American citizens in the small towns and villages."[62] As the rebellion dragged on and stories continued to appear about the problems of Americans in Cuba, one might imagine that the US population in Cuba was massive, when in fact it numbered only about three thousand, with many concentrated in Havana, Santiago de Cuba, and on sugar plantations on the western end of the island; whereas the majority of the fighting occurred at the other end of the colony. The Congress ordered detailed reports on the situation in Cuba, publishing intra-government memoranda as well as letters and materials from the press and the Junta.[63]

Exaggerated and colorful reporting by the American press became everyday faire once Weyler arrived in Cuba and lasted until his dismissal and return to Spain in November 1897, for failing to squelch the revolution or to win the public relations wars in Spain and the United States.[64] For eighteen months, atrocity stories were often the lead story of the day. Wilkerson made the point:

[The] partisan press, particularly the New York newspapers, was resorting to one of the surest methods of striking a responsive chord among their readers—the attack of Spaniards on defenseless prisoners, their wanton disregard for the rights of non-combatants, and their abuse of the rights of American citizens.

These themes all appealed to the reading public.[65] But they also substituted for facts. One historian pointed out that Spanish censorship stymied attempts at more accurate reporting.[66] Even supposedly hard facts were often not reported accurately. For example, in late 1895, the *New York Herald* represented that Havana was about to fall to the rebels, and, on January 6, newspapers began reporting that Havana had fallen. The press learned quickly that the reporting was a hoax, which irritated editors, but nevertheless they allowed the story to continue to circulate.[67]

DESTRUCTION OF THE USS *MAINE*

In 1897 and continuing in 1898, tensions between the United States and Spain increased. There were multiple causes: a recent seizure of an American flagged ship, the growing sympathy of Americans for the Cuban cause for independence, the relentless media reporting of Spanish behavior, and other political concerns. The American consulate in Havana reported to Washington its serious concern about the safety of US citizens in Cuba and requested the presence of a naval vessel in Havana should US citizens need to be evacuated on short notice. The USS *Maine*, a new battle ship commissioned in 1895 using a now-aging nautical design, was reluctantly dispatched to Havana. The Spanish were not pleased, and American officials in Washington hoped the ship would not need to anchor in Havana for long. On the evening of February 15, 1898, the ship suddenly exploded in the harbor, sinking, killing 260 men (three-quarters of its crew) and injuring 78 others; only 16 remained uninjured. It was an enormous and dramatic tragedy guaranteed to rivet the attention of the American reading public. Within two hours, telegraphic reports of the explosion arrived at the US naval base in Key West, Florida, and in Washington, DC.[68] Rumors had circulated for some time in Key West that the US Consulate in Havana would be blown up and that other Americans around the island would be killed, so the report of the explosion was readily believed and was quickly confirmed. Naval officials in Havana and Washington, as well as the White House, urged people not to jump to any conclusions about the cause of the explosion. Much of the media took the same position in its editorial comments over the next several days.[69]

The explosion became the subject of naval inquiries and extensive speculation in the media; and the cause remained a mystery for over a century. The reaction of the American public to the *Maine* affair, however, was not dissimilar to the reaction to the Japanese attack on Pearl Harbor in 1941 or the 9/11 attacks in 2001.

The US Navy convened a board of inquiry to determine the cause of the explosion in 1898; a second board met in 1911, and a third published a report in 1976.[70] The Spanish Navy also conducted an inquiry the year of the explosion. Often overlooked in both contemporary reporting and in American history textbooks for a century was the fact that every naval inquiry agreed that explosions in the forward part of the ship where munitions were stored likely caused the massive destruction, although there was some disagreement over how those explosions occurred. The question was whether the ship was destroyed by an internal explosion, not an external one, as would be claimed by those who sought to blame Cubans or Spaniards for the destruction. In 1998, yet another investigation was conducted—this time by the *National Geographic* magazine—reaching similar and not fully definitive conclusions.[71]

The evidence that mounted over the years, based on the experiences of European navies with similar types of exploding ships, led to consensus among experts that the cause in all probability was coal dust near the boiler, which was located near the ammunition. However, no study has definitively proved the cause.[72] One historian reminded us "that arguments driven by the *Maine* have persisted for so long, and with such prominence, underscores (sic) some of the more enduring characteristics of the historical literature."[73] Here, the ship is the object of intense and voluminous rumors and false facts in much the same way as there were surrounding the crash of planes into the twin towers of the World Trade Center.

One popular alternative explanation of the sinking of the *Maine* was that the explosion was the result of a torpedo or a mine. This position was held not only by many members of the American public, but also by some American civilian and military officials, and even by a few Spaniards in Havana. The details of the explosion were sensationally reported in the American media. The Cuban Junta and others quickly took advantage of the incident to promote US military intervention in Cuba. The public in the United States soon came to the belief that the ship had been blown up on purpose. Some believed the Cubans did it to force the United States to enter the war, while others believed that Spain was behind the attack. Calls for revenge appeared within days on the editorial pages of newspapers across the United States, and local "sympathy meetings" held across the country were well attended. A new battle cry entered the American lexicon, "Remember the *Maine*."

Because this event occurred so long ago, it is easy to conflate the milieu of information in the period from 1895 to 1914, when the greatest interest existed in the subject of the *Maine*, and the discussions that have continued to the present among historians, journalists, and naval enthusiasts.[74] Those writing about the incident after the First World War relied heavily on the literature produced beforehand, specifically naval reports, US government records, contemporary press coverage, celebratory books of the Spanish-American War, and historical scholarship. Blended into all these accounts were both confirmed and unconfirmed facts, together with intensive speculation and debate about how the ship exploded. We leave aside this ongoing dialogue to focus instead on the creation and diffusion of information—fake and actual facts—that occurred in 1898, with emphasis on what happened closest to the event.

While a saddened nation came to terms with this shocking event, the press scrambled for every piece of information it could find. Immediately and for days afterward, the *New York Journal* printed more than eight pages of coverage each day, including news articles, photographs, and editorials, relying on a staff quickly assembled in Havana to provide a continuous flow of material for months. Its practice mimicked what all the major television networks did after the 9/11 terrorist attacks. Newspaper publisher William Randolph Hearst offered a reward for the conviction of the guilty party.[75] Hearst's paper, the *Journal*, operated in other more sensational ways. On February 17, its headline read "THE WARSHIP MAINE WAS SPLIT IN TWO BY AN ENEMY'S SECRET INFERNAL MACHINE," reporting that the ship's captain, Charles Sigsbee "practically declares that his ship was blown up by a mine or torpedo."[76] In fact, Captain Sigsbee did not make such a statement, but a million readers read the message in multiple editions of the paper. The next day the *Journal* published the headline "THE WHOLE COUNTRY THRILLS WITH WAR FEVER," and then the most famous headline of all, "REMEMBER THE MAINE!" which in its original form continued with another screaming headline, "TO HELL WITH SPAIN!"[77] Joseph Pulitzer, Hearst's arch rival in the New York media market, showed only slightly more restraint in his paper, the *World*: "THE MAINE EXPLOSION WAS CAUSED BY A BOMB—SUSPICION OF A TORPEDO." Less than a week after the explosion, Pulitzer's newspaper reported that the "World's discoveries prove the mine theory," followed the next day with the headline, "Government accepts mine theory of the World." The article went on to argue that Spain was clearly engaged in "treachery, willingness, or laxness" because it had failed to protect the ship in the harbor that it controlled. To atone, the writer argued, Spain must grant Cuba its independence.[78] The other major New York newspaper, the *Sun*, called its rivals "shriekers of sensations" and of publishing "freak journalism." Given the facts of the case as it was known then and after the various naval boards of inquiry, the *Sun* had a good point. New York's anti-interventionist newspaper, the *Evening Post*, sided with the *Sun*: "A thousand different explanations have been offered by editors and reporters who were not there, and a thousand different pictorial illustrations of the scene have been given by persons who did not see it."[79]

Thus began a nationwide discussion about the cause of the *Maine*'s explosion. Nobody discussed the possibility of multiple causes; it seemed reporters and readers wanted simple answers, such as mines, torpedoes, or Spaniards. Historians examining what was published agree that many newspapers played up the story, as it was the largest news event since the assassination of President James A. Garfield in 1881. Newspapers in New

York, Boston, Chicago, and San Francisco covered their entire front pages with this story day after day.[80]

The New York papers published what they called "suppressed" cables from Captain Sigsbee to the Navy Department, asserting that the explosion was no accident, that Navy divers found the munitions chambers had not exploded, and that there were "new proofs of treachery." None of these claims were accurate. One historian studying the reporting out of New York concluded:

> The influence of the Journal in publishing "faked" news articles is clearly shown in the fact that the Associated Press carried news dispatches similar to the Hearst accounts concerning evidence uncovered by the divers. These reports were broadcast throughout the country and it seems reasonable to assume that thousands of Americans had made up their minds that the explosion was the result of Spanish treachery before an official investigation of the disaster was started.[81]

Editors reinforced their messages by commissioning artists to draw sketches demonstrating the theory of an external explosion. Other images depicted the Spanish using their own divers to hide evidence of a mine explosion. In fact, these divers were in the water helping to recover the dead that the Spanish buried a few days later in a Havana cemetery with full military honors. The *Journal* published multiple issues daily and rented trains and ships to bring back information from Cuba.

The *Journal* began propagating the rumor that war with Spain was imminent, creating a war scare. The paper reported on February 18, just three days after the explosion, that the "whole country thrills with the war fever," Americans are ready to take up arms, and the "union is ablaze with patriotism"; one week later, on February 25 the paper reported that Congress was ready to act if the president did not.[82] The *World* reported that, regardless of the cause of the explosion, Spain was legally responsible. It also reported on war preparations all over the country (February 24), and of "the warlike spirit of the multitude" (February 25). Pulitzer's newspaper declared that the nation could quickly raise an army of five hundred thousand and that the House of Representatives had committed to allocating $200 million for home defense. It also explained how New York City could defend itself against the Spanish. Illustrations in the paper editorialized for a "Free Cuba."

While some newspapers around the country urged caution until the information of what was going on in Cuba was more complete, at the same time they went against their own advice and reprinted stories that did not have solid foundation in facts.[83] For example, the *New York Herald* suggested patience in its February 17 newspaper but soon made the business decision to carry articles on war preparations in order to compete for a readership now energized to consume whatever content appeared about the *Maine*. The *San Francisco Chronicle* was more creative. It sided with the *Herald* in urging caution but at the same time published articles suggesting the explosion was caused by "treachery" (February 17), based on material from the *Herald*'s wire service about war preparations. The *Chicago Tribune* urged quick action by Congress to prepare for war because the Spanish were "exulting over the Maine disaster" (February 21).[84]

One historian concluded that, with the nation inflamed over the Cuban question, the mystery surrounding the disaster and the rumors that arose as to the probable cause of the catastrophe presented opportunities for the sensational newspapers. They had been urging intervention of the United States in Cuba, to send out columns of dispatches, many of which were based upon nothing more tangible than mere speculation.[85]

Historians concur that the media had at least some influence in getting the United States to head to war with Spain.[86] For example, historian Joseph Wisan concluded, "reporters, aware of the policies of their papers, produced the type of news most acceptable to their editors. Hearst's famous reply to the artist Remington's complaint that there was no war in Cuba—'You furnish the pictures; I'll furnish the war,'— illustrates the degree of objectivity that prevailed."[87] Stories about the *Maine* were every bit as much at the forefront of news reporting as were the stories about Spanish savagery and concentration camps. The difference was that the latter appeared in the media over a three-year period, whereas stories about the *Maine* were prominent only for a few months until war was declared. After the war, stories of outrageous Spanish behavior waned, while speculation about what "really" caused the destruction of the *Maine* lingered as the reporters began to write book-length accounts of the war. Later historians have varied in their beliefs about the importance of the media—and in particular the role of fake facts—in creating the Spanish-American War. One middle-of-the-road assessment argues: "we do not find the yellow press started the war . . . but we do find that sensational and conservative newspapers together created an enabling environment for going to war."[88]

Early historians pored over the browning pages of old newspapers of the period and were amazed at how brazen false facts were disseminated with little regard for the truth. Speaking about the coverage over the entire Spanish-American War and the events leading up to it, one historian gave this typical assessment:

> Artists far removed from the Cuban scene illustrated reports vividly but inaccurately; cartoonists magnified atrocities; feature writers, Sunday supplement writers, even contributors to women's pages added their prejudiced efforts. With so much information and misinformation from which to choose, editorial writers knew no bounds.[89]

Figure 6.1. While there were many images depicting the explosion of the USS *Maine* on February 15, 1898, this particular rendition, made in 1898 by Kurz & Allison, was the most widely distributed, hanging in bars all over the United States. Note the images of American sailors being flung into the sky while the ship is destroyed. Courtesy Library of Congress.

The extent of media coverage was impressive. Between March 1895 and April 1898, when the United States went to war, there were fewer than twenty days in which there was no reporting in the national press about Cuba. As time approached the beginning of the war, reporting became more detailed, taking up increasing numbers of column inches, even entire pages in the paper. By the time the war began, it had become impossible for a reader to avoid the issue, creating an image of Spain as "arrogant, insulting, vindictive, cruel, that Weyler and his cohorts were brutes in human form."[90] These images were in stark contrast to the reality of the Spanish attempting to work with the American government to diffuse the situation, while simultaneously trying to retain their island colony. As one historian concluded, the "average reader" had been indoctrinated to approve of war against Spain.[91] Even historians who portrayed some American newspapers as less rabid on the Cuban question than New York's media acknowledged that the sinking of this battleship prepared the public for war with Spain.[92]

Unlike the facts that purported to describe specific events, such as battles, rapes, and the brutal treatment of Cubans, stories about the sinking of the *Maine* focused more on speculating about the cause of the incident, given that many facts about the time and place of the sinking, and the number harmed and killed were quickly established and generally not disputed.

How unusual was the professional behavior of these newspaper reporters? Validating stories and the facts they contained had started ever so gingerly in the 1850s, but did not become the normative professional practice until after the First World War. Such blatant widespread disregard for the truth that seems so shocking to a reader in the twenty-first century was routine and widely accepted in the 1890s—not only in the case of reports about Cuba but about news reporting in general.[93] The people who were the subjects of this kind of reporting often complicitly abetted the practice—none more obvious than Teddy Roosevelt and his Rough Riders in Cuba.

The behavior of newspaper editors and reporters changed after this war. Starting in the post–Civil War period, there had been growing a slow movement of reform to professionalize journalism, meaning reporting factually, but the Spanish-Cuban situation temporarily sidelined some of that reform. In the years immediately following the Spanish-American War, however, newspapers and journalists increasingly subscribed to standards of truthfulness that were in contrast to their prior behavior.[94] This transformation changed the relationship between the press and the national government as the nation faced other wars and existential threats to its security.

TEDDY ROOSEVELT, THE ROUGH RIDERS, AND THE BATTLE OF SAN JUAN HILL

Mythology had a long history in the United States, beginning with the reverence with which the nation worshipped George Washington and later Abraham Lincoln. Even today, comedians still believe it is irreverent to joke about Lincoln's assassination. The Spanish-American War created two new heroes of mythic proportions, although not of the same stature as Washington and Lincoln. The first was Commodore (quickly promoted to admiral) George Dewey, whose naval force annihilated the Spanish navy in the Battle of Manila Bay on May 1, 1898, with the consequences that the Spanish colony of the Philippines fell into the arms of the United States and America became established as a Pacific Ocean power.[95]

The second new hero was Theodore (Teddy) Roosevelt, who began his military career in the spring of 1898 with his commission as a lieutenant colonel in the US Army cavalry. His exploits in Cuba, coupled with his strong family connections led to his rapid rise in American politics: governor of New York in January 1899, within a few months after the war ended; US vice president in 1901; and upon President William McKinley's assassination later that year, the youngest president in American history (thirty-nine years old).

While his combat service in Cuba was real and respectable, it was the storytelling surrounding his time in Cuba that helped catapult his political career. He was a force of nature—with high energy, charisma, strong oratorical skills, and a genius for political posturing and bold decision-making that aligned with a rising nation on the world's stage. The mythology surrounding his role in Cuba was also enabled by the kind of reporting done by the media and the language they used, which strayed from the truth to an extent not witnessed again during the twentieth century.

In the spring of 1898, Roosevelt was the assistant secretary of the Navy and already advocating intervention in Cuba, having already prepared the Navy for confrontation against Spain in the Pacific. Once war was declared in April 1898, he resigned his post at the Navy Department and joined a volunteer cavalry regiment being assembled by Colonel Leonard Wood. The men under Lt. Colonel Roosevelt soon became known as the "Rough Riders," thanks to the quick thinking of their commander. They consisted of cowboys, ranchers, miners, and hunters—many of them coming out of the southwestern United States, plus some East Coast college athletes. Their nickname came from the term used by the nation's most popular western show of the 1890s, led by Buffalo Bill Cody. Roosevelt's men thus instantly acquired a reputation for being tough, excellent horsemen and for embracing the independent, reliable ethos of the American cowboy. Roosevelt was an easterner and had been a sickly child, but he had spent some time in the West as a young man, admired the values and lifestyle of the cowboys, and identified with them in the popular way Americans thought of cowboys.

It turned out that Roosevelt's command was one of the few that actually saw combat in Cuba. The Rough Riders engaged in the Battle of Las Guasimas on June 24, 1898, attacking Spanish soldiers in a thickly wooded area. In the confusion of the fighting, it was mistakenly reported that Colonel Woods had been killed. Upon hearing the news, Lt. Colonel Roosevelt immediately assumed command of the troops, as appropriate under the circumstance, and spurred his troops forward. This action resulted in the Americans taking full control of the targeted Spanish outpost. They suffered eight deaths and thirty-one wounded, but Roosevelt had displayed bravery and leadership, and his decisive action had led to success. He now held the respect of his soldiers, his superiors, and most importantly the reporters who had accompanied the Americans in the quest to seize Santiago de Cuba.[96]

The Battle of San Juan Hill followed on July 1. Facing yet another hill with a Spanish fort at its crest, Roosevelt was ordered to work his way up but was pinned down by Spanish infantry and artillery. He took it on his own initiative to rally his men for a spurt up the hill, which they did on foot, while he rode up and down the line on horseback encouraging them onward, exposing himself to Spanish fire. Within an hour of heavy firing, his men reached their objective. Both sides suffered heavy losses of life and injury. Roosevelt credited the success to the use of a Gatling gun.[97] In the days that followed, the Rough Riders played a key role in completing the encirclement of Santiago de Cuba, Cuba's second largest city, which triggered a second naval defeat for the Spaniards as devastating as the naval battle Dewey had won in Manila Bay.

The Rough Riders rotated back to the United States in August—to Montauk, New York. By the time they arrived stateside, the New York press had already reported Roosevelt's victories. Since he was from New York, the local press was filled with stories about "local boy makes good." He and his cowboy Rough Riders were celebrated as heroes. His men admired him and recognized his contributions with the gift of a bronze statue, "Bronco Buster," depicting a cowboy riding a bucking horse. The US First Volunteer Cavalry—the Rough Riders—disbanded on September 15, 1898, but kept meeting in reunions in Las Vegas, holding their last one in 1967. Roosevelt immediately went on to campaign for the governorship and did not hesitate to wear his Rough Rider uniform occasionally that fall. He often brought veterans of his command in uniform to his campaign events. He published a memoir of his Cuban experiences the following year.[98] Myth-making was now well underway. The brutality of war, naked American soldiers whose uniforms rotted in Cuba, widespread fever among his troops, lack of strong senior army leadership above him, and absence of decent food were all forgotten, not to be remembered until historians reported on these elements of the story a century later.[99]

A professor of American literature, Christine Bold, who has studied cowboys as well as the West and its mythologies, has convincingly argued that the Rough Riders derived from western frontier culture and created the American hero that the American public might see depicted in a John Wayne movie. Bold argues that the experience of the Spanish-American War allowed the United States to extend its notion of the advancing frontier beyond what it had been in North America, which had essentially been closed as the West filled with ranchers, farmers, and urban residents. Cuba, Puerto Rico, and the Philippines became the new American frontier. Advocates of expansionist imperialist aspirations, along with entertainers and writers, "aligned the new imperialist purpose with the established imagery of the heroic frontier."[100] Roosevelt projected his self-image as a rough and tough cowboy into that imperialist perspective when socializing with his East Coast college graduate friends. Bold's study of popular entertainment of the early 1900s led her to conclude, "the most popular forms of entertainment presented events in Cuba and the Philippines as spectacles conducted according to the rules of gamesmanship," making it possible to portray events such as Custer's Last Stand or the Battle of San Juan Hill as the resolution of social and psychological tensions of both military and political issues.[101] Buffalo Bill's Wild West Show presented in a circus-like format a dramatization of these events to vast audiences who could "witness and applaud this symbolic assertion of America's power in the world."[102] This is an act of mythology creation, and pouring it right into the cauldron of its creation was Teddy Roosevelt.

Roosevelt was not the first to build legend around the meme of cowboys and Indians. As early as the Chicago World's Fair in 1893, skits involving cowboys and Indians attracted many visitors. At the fair, William Cody introduced the viewing public to Buffalo Bill's Wild West and Congress of Rough Riders of the World. Rough riders were characterized as tough, independent-minded cowboys, heroes of the lost Wild West, sporting an image that originated before the Civil War when they were seen as bronco busters.[103] Roosevelt had built a log cabin at the fair, while the artist Frederic Remington displayed fifteen illustrations.[104] Cody helped to create the myth of the cowboy in the 1890s, and when the Cuban war came along at the end of the decade, he identified the Rough Riders as a battlefield extension of the western cowboy. In 1899, Cody hired sixteen of Roosevelt's Rough Riders to participate in his show's reenactment of the Battle of San Juan Hill. He cast the people who had played Indians in earlier skits as Spanish soldiers and, of course, the Rough Riders needed their hero commander—"Teddy" Roosevelt. In Cody's world, the messy reality of war was plastered over by having the Rough Riders on horseback, participating in a highly synchronized battle. The Americans had won that fight, the Cuban War had been short and popular, and the consequences spectacular. Cody had a winning theme on his hands.

Roosevelt's fingerprints were all over this mythology-building exercise. After naming his troops after Cody's troop, Roosevelt transported the myth and the veterans themselves from his command into his political life, not even waiting for 1898 to end. By wearing his uniform and placing veterans on stage with him while running for governor of New York he positioned himself at the heart of the public's image of the western cowboy as the personification of the American hero in its most current form. In speeches, books, articles, and press coverage for years to come,

COL. THEODORE ROOSEVELT U.S.V.

Figure 6.2. The most celebrated US Army figure to come out of the Spanish-American War was Colonel Theodore Roosevelt because of his role in the Battle of San Juan Hill. Note the mythologizing of Roosevelt that began within weeks of his return to the United States from Cuba. This print was published by the same printers that produced figure 6.1 of the USS *Maine*. Courtesy Library of Congress.

Roosevelt made sure that the Rough Riders always appeared as eternally youthful. Fiction writers and others who wrote books for boys created a genre of this kind of mythology.[105] Richard Harding Davis, a frequent contemporary commentator and reporter about the war, recognized what Roosevelt had done: "Now we can refer instead to the courage of the young men of the university and of the Knickerbocker Club when they forced the pass of Guasimas and charged up the hill of San Juan . . . and the men are Americans."[106]

By writing of warfare in Cuba much like a boat race, polo match, or fun at the beach, newspaper reporters reinforced the games-like attitude and bravado that Roosevelt and his Rough Riders presented.[107] For example, the *New York Herald* described their behavior using the following language: "Sharp-shooters and cowboys were firing at Spanish guerrillas in the trees as impressively as though they were contesting for badges in the rifle range."[108] Davis also used the sports analogy, describing events at San Juan with the soldier's "eyes on the ball, and moving in obedience to the captain's signals." Book titles continued this equation of heroic and sports metaphors, such as Thomas W. Hall's 1899 publication, *The Fun and Fighting of the Rough Riders*.[109] Roosevelt was not above adding to the mythology of hero-sportsmen: "I've had a bully of a time and a bully fight! I feel as big and as strong as a bull moose!"[110] He applied the analogy of a strong bull moose throughout the rest of his career.

Roosevelt's image as a tough western fighter was enhanced by reporters who were as keen on selling his image as they were in hawking their stories about Spanish atrocities, American victories, and the "evil" done to the USS *Maine*. On May 4, 1898, even before Roosevelt had fought at San Juan Hill, the *Daily Oklahoma State Capital* had characterized him as "a cowboy early in his life" who was "willing to take desperate chances. He does not know the meaning of fear."[111] His Rough Riders enhanced their army uniforms by wearing cowboy bandanas, and upon their return to the United States they held small rodeos for the public and other army units. On the occasion of receiving the gift of the bronze statue of a cowboy on a bucking horse, Roosevelt told his Rough Riders: "The foundation of the regiment was the 'Bronco Buster,' and we have him here in bronze." He was already linking cowboys and average-Joe army soldiers who had fought on foot rather than horseback to the mythology of the rugged western American.[112]

Spain was portrayed as old, rotten, and decadent, while the American soldier, "The Boys of '98," and Roosevelt were portrayed as young and strong. Jerome B. Crabtree's account, published in 1898, captured the mythology in its title: *The Passing of Spain and the Ascendancy of America*.[113] Roosevelt is described as young, personifying the contribution being made by a new generation, similar to the portrayal of John F. Kennedy six decades later. Crabtree was effusive in his language: "The young giant of the West stands on a continent and clasps the crest of an ocean in either hand. Our nation, glorious in youth and strength, looks into the future with eager eyes and rejoices as a strong man to run a race."[114] Roosevelt was "vigorous," "manly," "dashing," and a "young leader." Woodrow Wilson, who became US president four years after Roosevelt left office, wrote more disdainfully but in the same meme, calling Roosevelt "a great big boy."[115] The fact that, as president, Roosevelt displayed an extraordinary level of vigor, energy, and bold domestic and international policies compared to the presidents of the prior quarter century solidified for decades the mythology of his persona, the Rough Riders, and the American experience in Cuba. In 1901, he acquired another label—"cowboy president"—and the media presented him in text and cartoons as an international Rough Rider prepared to take on the enemies of the nation.

Although all this imagery and language embellished the reality of what had occurred in Cuba, Roosevelt was able to successfully play on it, matching his image to the mood of the times using concepts and terms already shaped by the public relations success of Wild Bill Cody. As Christine Bold summarizes:

> In the midst of frightening social disorder and incredibly rapid change, Cody, Roosevelt, and Remington reformulated the frontier West according to certain organizational patterns, then set within this scene the part-military, part-Western figure of the Rough Rider. With this creation, they acted out a healing of domestic tensions, by presenting the Rough Rider as the harmonious meeting point of various regions, races and classes in modern America. Then they demonstrated America's power abroad by pitting these national Rough Riders against an array of savage enemies, often in the context of a rule-bound game.[116]

Roosevelt rode that mythology, accompanied by a regiment of entertainers, reporters, and veterans.

THE MYTHOLOGY OF THE IMPERIALIST HEROES

With the end of the war and the American occupation of Cuba, Puerto Rico (acquired as an almost last-minute decision by the Americans), the Philippines, and a few islands in the Pacific, the American public saw their country as a global imperial power. Events over the next two decades confirmed this belief, no fake news was required for that conclusion. Newspapers had a more difficult time after the war in driving up their sales or promoting their editorial stance with stories of America's colonial empire. Occupations and nation-building are not as exciting as men charging up hills or decisive naval battles with whole fleets sinking to the bottom of the ocean. But myth-building continued, as we saw with Teddy Roosevelt. A small book publishing industry emerged overnight as reporters, politicians, and veterans rushed into print with memoirs, analyses, and histories of the war. Book salesmen knocked on farmhouse and city apartment doors peddling subscriptions to these products, some of which were issued in editions of more than five hundred pages in less than a year after the end of the war. So much for judicious research and scholarly analysis! The public had an appetite for the sensationalism right up until the First World War.

These beautifully illustrated tomes continued to spread the images and the false facts that had first appeared in the newspapers. J. Hampton Moore's 678-page book, published in 1899, has a long title beginning *Reminiscences and Thrilling Stories of the War by Returned Heroes Containing Vivid Accounts of Personal Experiences by Officers and Men, and Continuing as Daring Deeds of Our Brave Regulars and Volunteers at the Battles of La Quasina, El Caney and San Juan . . . Exciting Experiences in Porto Rico and at the Capture of Manila*. The book was dedicated "To the Gallant Soldiers and Sailors of Our Army and Navy Whose Heroic Sacrifices and Superb Achievements Gained for the Stars and Stripes Such Magnificent Victories in Our War with Spain This Volume Which Narrates in Glowing Terms the Thrilling Stories of Their Splendid Triumphs Is Respectfully Dedicated," with the dedication continuing for another six lines.[117] Dozens of books of this genre were published in the first decade following the war.

Another genre consisted of biographies of generals, common sailors, and, of course, Lieutenant Colonel Roosevelt. Consider the book of Joseph L. Stickney, an aide to the naval commander in the Pacific, Admiral Dewey, titled, *Life and Glorious Deeds of Admiral Dewey Including a Thrilling Account of Our Conflicts with the Spaniards and Filipinos in the Orient*. Like most books published soon after the conflict, this book was replete with photographs of heroes draped in bunting.[118]

Even the Cubans joined the act of memorializing the Americans. A Cuban "diplomat" in Washington, DC, Gonzalo de Quesada, collaborated in 1898 with "the well-known author," Henry Davenport Northrop, to write a long, illustrated (with phototype engravings) account titled *America's Battle for Cuba's Freedom Containing a Complete Record of Spanish Tyranny and Oppression Scenes of Violence and Bloodshed; Daring Deeds of Cuban Heroes and Patriots, Thrilling Incidents of the Conflict . . . Secret Expeditions; Inside Facts of the War*.[119] This book represented the Junta's agenda. At the time, there were no Cuban diplomats inasmuch as there was no Cuban Republic recognized by the United States, only Cuban advocates for total independence self-organized into a "Legation" in Washington, DC. When the fighting ended, the United States occupied Cuba, and a formal national government was established in Havana only in 1902. The purpose of the book was given away on its lengthy dedication page, after acknowledging "the Army of Cuban patriots" and their deeds: "this volume is dedicated with the hope and belief that their great struggle for independence will be crowned with success." This account diverges considerably from the narrative written by later historians.

The mythology and misinformation continued in a different form over time. The Rough Riders became the subject of pulp fiction, just as had the 7th Cavalry and their mythical hero leader, George Armstrong Custer, almost immediately after their deaths. Christine Bold points to boys as the emerging market for Spanish-American War mythology. Between 1904 and 1907, a pulp magazine called *Rough Rider Weekly* spun tales of the protagonist, Ted Strong, who came from the East, lived on a ranch in the West, had a mustache like Roosevelt, and wore clothes reminiscent of the uniform worn by the real Rough Riders. Strong fought outlaws and Indians and engaged in military-styled combat described much like the mythical accounts of charging up the hill in San Juan. When the magazine deviated from this theme to fight city criminals, it folded; but so long as it retold the Roosevelt and Rough Rider story, it prospered.[120]

THIS WAR'S INFLUENCE ON SUBSEQUENT AMERICAN WARS

Given that the Spanish-American War is the only war we study in detail in this book, we will take a few pages to talk about the role of information and misinformation in subsequent American wars. All American wars informed the next generation of senior military officers and public officials about how best to conduct the next war. The Spanish-American War proved no exception. Although historians focus largely on the effects of a war on future military strategy and weaponry, wars leave an information legacy, too. In every subsequent war fought by the United States, senior military and civilian leaders had personal experience in managing the prior war, and this influenced their actions. Thus, during the First World War, national political leaders acted based on their experience in the Spanish-American War, Second World War leaders responded from their personal experiences gained in the First World War, and so forth down to and including the American wars in the Middle East and Afghanistan. The gap in time from one war to another was generally within the professional lives of the next generation of leaders. Regimental commanders in the First World War had fought in Cuba; Normandy's Supreme Commander, Dwight D. Eisenhower, had served in France during the First World War; President Lyndon B. Johnson, who presided over the bulk of the Vietnam War, had some experience with the Second World War, and President Richard Nixon had served in the US Navy. Nineteen years separated the Spanish-American War from the start of the First World War for the Americans, twenty-two years between the First and Second World Wars for the United States; the Korean War began barely five years after the Second World War, and Vietnam occurred less than two decades after the Second World War. The US president during the first Iraqi war was a Second World War navy pilot, Herbert W. Bush, who also was a senior public official during the Vietnam War; while his commander on the ground, General Norman Schwarzkopf Jr., was a veteran of the Vietnam War, as was General Colin Powell, then Chairman of the Joint Chiefs of Staff.

Senior military and political leaders learned lessons that inform both the history of information in general and, more specifically, the dissemination of disinformation, misinformation, the role of censorship, and the control of facts. Americans and their historians normally think that the War of 1898 was the result of fake facts and yellow journalism, and this chapter supports that conclusion. The American government learned, too, that it was reluctantly forced into that war by an out-of-control press, which whipped up war fever. When the First World War came around, senior officials proved far more cautious about rushing into combat and carefully nurtured the opinions they wanted Americans to have, beginning in 1914 when the Europeans went to war, not waiting to shape perceptions until the United States entered it in 1917.[121]

But when the United States did enter the war, public officials immediately placed strong hands on the management of information about the war, to avoid the out-of-control situation that occurred barely two decades earlier. First, they weaponized information to control how the American public supported the war, better known as spreading propaganda about the benefits of neutrality, later about the evilness of the German cause. Second, they purposefully disseminated false information to confuse the enemy, and expended novel efforts to engage the public in supportive activities. President Woodrow Wilson had concluded, long before the American public did, that the nation would probably need to enter this war; and to prepare the public, he established the Committee on Public Information (CPI).[122] It energetically encouraged newspapers to self-censor themselves to avoid providing useful information to the Axis powers. To facilitate censorship, federal authorities established the Censorship Board and the Chief Cable Censor's Office to deny the Germans and their allies information deemed useful, while at the same time allowing some to seep through that would mislead them. Officials explicitly told the American public what information not to share, such as about troop movements and weather. These various agencies published posters, pamphlets, newspaper articles, and booklets to keep the American public engaged in supporting the war while blocking information from the enemy.[123] The primary vehicles they used were newspapers and pamphlets; while radio would be used extensively during the Second World War. Some of these publications included *The War Message and the Facts Behind It*, with 2.5 million copies printed; *The Government of Germany*, over 1.6 million copies; *A War of Self-Defense*, 722,000 copies; and *German Militarism and Its German Critics*, over 300,000 copies.[124] Meanwhile, censors read mail, and the military and civilian agencies spread misleading information intended for German consumption.

At the end of the First World War, these various agencies stopped their work, but—and this is a critical point to make—most federal agencies prepared final reports documenting lessons learned, and provided advice in anticipation that these activities would be needed in a future war. When the United States entered the Second World War, the federal government was able to resurrect similar agencies and activities based on these reports.[125] Because the American public and print media had the recent experience of learning what to say and what to suppress, the nation largely self-censored itself, requiring less micromanagement by officials. The First World War had taught the military a great deal about how to deploy misinformation, and nowhere did this prove more effective than in the planning that went into the Allied invasion of Normandy, France, which successfully brought the war to the Germans on European soil, in June 1944. The Germans were led to believe that the Allies would invade France at a different location from the five beaches where the actual assault began. Similar uses of misinformation in the Italian campaign in the Mediterranean had already proven effective. Americans still wanted to know about military campaigns and for that purpose, the widely circulated weekly *Newsweek* magazine hired a retired American general, Stephen O. Fuqua, to write a weekly column explaining current military campaigns and activities in terms understood by its readers and that at the same time did not compromise military plans and intelligence. Fuqua had served in Cuba in 1898, Philippines in the early 1900s, and in France during the First World War, and there he had learned a great deal about the role of information in war.[126]

When at war during the second half of the century, the United States increasingly used techniques evident in other parts of American society to hide information, misinform, or mislead.[127] The best-known example that increasingly is becoming evident as historical research unfolds is the case of the Tonkin Gulf Resolution. Briefly told, allegedly two US naval destroyers off the Vietnamese coast were attacked by North Vietnam. President Johnson immediately requested and received from Congress passage of the Gulf of Tonkin Resolution to authorize him to retaliate on August 7, 1964. The resolution authorized the president to take military actions he believed appropriate to retaliate for the attack and to maintain the security of Southeast Asia, providing him the legal basis for escalating US involvement in the area. The Johnson administration wanted to engage further militarily without a formal declaration of war, and this resolution provided sufficient legal permission to proceed. The problem, however, was that the actual assault on the ships was publicly characterized inaccurately, suggesting that President Johnson used a minor event to obtain permission to engage in his wider purpose of attacking North Vietnam. Subsequent releases of naval reporting in 2005 suggested there might not have been an incident at all. In 1965, the president commented privately, "For all I know, our Navy was shooting at whales out there." In time, political enemies and historians questioned whether the incident even occurred, accusing Johnson of fabricating or exaggerating a trivial event to obtain his larger objective.[128] In 1971, the public and its representatives in Congress had had enough with the suspected incident, called the "Credibility Gap," and also weary of the war, they rescinded the resolution.[129] For many Americans, it had been a shoddy, deceitful affair, a modern tale of mistrust in their government, driven by lies from the White House that tainted information put out by the federal government regarding subsequent war-related events. As one historian reported, Johnson had lied and deceived the American public. His deceptions increased as the conflict escalated, contributing to one of the worst debacles in American history. In 1971, two years after Congress repealed the Gulf of Tonkin Resolution, it passed the War Powers Resolution setting limits on a president's ability to send troops into combat without congressional approval, a power it refused to use in the Vietnam War and has refused to use in subsequent conflicts."[130]

Just when the government thought it was controlling messaging, television got in the way. During the Vietnam War, TV reporters were allowed considerable access and so they reported US failures and deaths of American troops, presenting images that no amount of government propaganda or counter-data could overcome. So, the military decided in the next series of wars, involving Iraq and Afghanistan, to control and even block reporters from presenting the truth of what was happening on the ground. TV intruded on occasion, however, as on the evening of March 20, 2003, when the United States attacked Iraq, covered by CNN reporters. US, European, and Iraq officials monitored developments by watching CNN's live coverage of the event! Fortunately for the Americans, it went well, but quickly the military restrained access, as a lesson from Vietnam and the earlier invasion of Iraq in 1990–1991, in order to control the messaging. In other words, the Spanish-American War taught the military and the US government to control what people learned about war and to shape the messaging about progress. For years, Johnson and

Nixon officials told the Americans that the war was going fine, only to lose what most Americans considered their first failed war. Fake facts, misinformation, and control of access to information had become an essential element of American warfare. Beside the Spanish-American War thrusting the United States on the international stage, it launched a profound change in how civilian officials and the military conducted warfare—teaching them to weaponize information.

While the Spanish-American War teaches us about the role of the press in facilitating the nation's entry into military conflict, other forms of information manipulation also affected profoundly the attitude of millions of citizens. We turn in the next several chapters to a set of case studies that demonstrate other roles of various kinds of fake facts and news, misinformation, rumors, and conspiracies in other aspects of American history.

7

Rumors and Misleading Advertising in Business

Everybody says it, and what everybody says must be true.

—James Fenimore Cooper[1]

To be effective, information must be calculated to stir an audience, to provoke an enduring psychological bond between the public and the corporat[ion].

—Stuart Ewen, 1996[2]

Businesses have been both the subject and source of rumors, misinformation, fake facts, and conspiracy theories in North America since the 1600s. In chapters 8 and 9, we will see additional examples of corporations and their industries propagating rumors, doubts, and conspiracies—in those cases to minimize the public's perception about the dangers of tobacco and the fallacies of taking seriously the warnings about climate change. This chapter focuses on two long-running forms of misinformation in the world of business: (1) the role of rumors and (2) false or misleading advertising.

Like presidential assassination plots or manipulations to generate public support for a war, kernels of truth often exist in the information put forth by businesses, which makes it possible to spin new perspectives that are exaggerated or otherwise misleading. Some ingredients sold as homeopathic or wellness medicines may help to improve the appearance of skin, but they do not cure cancer; perhaps a dead mouse did make it into a can of beans or a bottle of Coca-Cola sometimes, but that does not mean the manufacturer systematically or even commonly sells adulterated products. Spiders do not commonly hide in blouses imported from Asia. Seldom does a ship's cargo of bananas from Costa Rica include poisonous snakes. Yet, each of these stories floated in and out of the American press for decades. They kept folklorists busy, made the life of public relations professionals in corporations more difficult, and even attracted the attention of social psychologists and economists.[3] People did not segregate rumors and misinformation from advertising; they assumed both shared the common feature of some mistruth. It is no wonder that American consumers view advertising with skepticism.[4] Their association of it with various forms of misinformation has not been unfounded.

In the cases of smoking and climate change discussed later in this book, companies usually initiated rumors; and when those companies advertised, they did so to promote points of view regarding tobacco and climate change and to sway the public's opinion about regulatory issues. In this chapter, however, the rumors we consider are typically launched against firms, and the firm must then respond to defend its operations and public image.[5] Advertising by businesses has been used overwhelmingly to promote the benefits of a product, announce the existence of goods and services, and explain their functionality. In the examples discussed next, advertising is typically aimed, for example, at persuading a customer to smoke one brand of cigarettes rather than another; or to convince the public that one brand of aspirin is better than another, even when scientists and manufacturers explain that aspirin is aspirin, regardless of brand. Most large businesses encounter rumors about their firm, their competitors, or their industry—and these rumors are usually negative. Every business has to inform potential customers that the company exists and describe what it sells, hence the need for advertising. In this chapter, we differentiate between rumors and advertising but acknowledge that both deal with information—ranging from verifiable facts to outright falsehoods.

We first explore the range of attributes of information contained within rumors and advertising, and then demonstrate the breadth of false rumors, drawing largely on examples familiar to readers from the past several decades. To reinforce the argument made throughout this book that false information has existed in the American public domain for more than two centuries, we explore the long history of patent medicines, which takes us from New England of the 1600s to today's supermarket. This is an extreme case of falsehoods and chicanery, purposefully chosen to highlight the variety of false facts and the bad behavior adopted by vendors—together with the responses of customers. Patent medicines have been pervasive throughout American history, and these "medicines" have reached every corner of American society.

Because so many academic disciplines currently study rumors and advertising, a word about language is in order. For decades, most scholars of rumors were folklorists. They rarely used such words as "business," "retail," "manufacturing," or "management." They preferred to rely on the now antiquarian term, *mercantile*, which in the nineteenth and early twentieth centuries was used to describe only stores—retail operations—whereas folklorists have applied the term to all types of commercial activities except farming.[6] To focus on retail operations leaves out banks, manufacturers, transportation companies, fast food restaurants, large department stores, and software producers, among others, which constitute over 80 percent of today's economy. So, we instead use the term most currently deployed, *business*, to encompass all "for profit" enterprises. In this practice, we are widely supported by the language of business writers, corporate managers and employees, economists, historians, public relations experts, newspapers (which are businesses, too), and social scientists. But we rely extensively on the pioneering work on mercantile rumors conducted by folklorists and cultural anthropologists to identify various forms of information and how organizations and people responded to them.

THE ROLE OF MISINFORMATION, RUMORS, AND FALSE ADVERTISING IN BUSINESS

Rumors and advertising are two facets of a larger consideration about the role of truth (in particular, established facts), conducted not only in this book, but, more broadly, in the literature about the so-called Age of Information. It is appropriate to ask, what is truth in a business environment? Is it a timeless verity? Is it something verified by research, or proven by statistical or mathematical argument? These are well-established means for establishing truth in science and engineering, but what is their place in business practice?

The American philosopher, William James, argued in 1907 that truth is no absolute verity; rather, it evolves.[7] He may have identified a feature of how businesses thought about how to use truth at a time when public relations (PR) experts were attempting to ground factual statements in hard certainty. He argued that events make a factual statement true. Historian of public relations, Stuart Ewen, built on that idea by arguing that truth emerges from a continuous "audit in the public mind."[8] He explains: "When that audit fails to substantiate the validity of a truth or of a previously accepted body of truth, an entire system of belief, a worldview, stands in jeopardy."[9] This is in line with the more philosophical discussion of the social construction of facts that we discussed in chapter 1. If we believe McDonald's makes a bad hamburger, it will always be so—even if its burgers are proven to be healthy and tasty. If IBM is believed to be *the* premier vendor of large computers, that is the truth even though today less than half of IBM's revenues come from selling machines. James's words accurately describe the behavior of customers and advertisers then and now, not unlike their beliefs about their expectations of the outcome of a presidential election or the causes of a presidential assassination.

This is not the place to focus, as we did in chapter 1, on the difference between the belief of most scientists and many philosophers that truth is based in either mathematics or the state of the physical world, in contrast with the perspectivist view that truth is not absolute but instead socially constructed.[10] More salient to this discussion is the fact that "fake news [facts] is not simply news that is false; it is *deliberately* false," emphasizing the intention to mislead.[11] Tension and ambiguity about facts, truths, and beliefs in the business context have been particularly interesting since the 1870s for at least four reasons. On the one hand, the public was increasingly attracted to factual proof of events by scientific evidence that became irresistible as a way of thinking about facts.[12] On the other hand, from the 1870s until after the Second World War, newspapers and magazines were powerful institutions in American life, shaping American public beliefs about realities in the world, even though these media were rife with rumors (often reported as facts) and with advertising (promoting what the advertiser wanted the public to believe rather than what might actually be true). The American corporation was created in the middle of the nineteenth century, and, from 1870 on, these corporations became one of the largest users of public relations—in particular, of newspaper and magazine advertising. Partly in response to this growing market, advertising itself became larger and more professionalized; and these professionals quickly came to see the public as malleable, "controllable" in what they believed. The public's changing attitude toward the role of Spain in Cuba in the 1890s, for example, exemplifies this power of the media in swaying American public opinion.

The public relations industry believed that, when properly positioned, a statement could be sold to the public as truth; and that proper positioning was about collecting facts that presented one's point of view more convincingly than an opponent's. As one public relations professional in 1916 expressed it, "What is a fact? The effort to state an absolute fact is simply an attempt to . . . give you my interpretation of the facts."[13] By the 1920s, social psychologists were weighing in with their own views. For example, Harry Overstreet thought having proven facts did not always result in actions that logically stemmed from the truth. He called for an argument "to arouse the more important but slumbering wants into action."[14] He urged use of colorful language and exaggeration to create the desired image a firm sought. As advertising historian Roland Marchand has argued, the central message that corporations wished to communicate through their texts, pronouncements, publications, and advertising was a positive corporate image of solidity, ethics, and quality.[15]

Rumors differ somewhat from advertising. We discuss rumors among the many kinds of lies and misrepresentations in chapter 1, but let us look in more depth at the nature of rumors here. A rumor can be an idea (or supposed fact) that one proposes be believed. A rumor is normally spread by word-of-mouth, person-to-person, although since the 1990s the Internet has become a widely used mechanism for disseminating rumors. A key feature of a rumor is that what is pronounced is unsubstantiated, lacking any authenticity or verification.[16] Unlike gossip, which is largely about people and often intended for entertainment, rumors may have a dark side to them, also a sense of urgency and foreboding.[17] Gossip might be, "I hear that the new CEO likes to play a lot of golf," while a rumor might have it that "the new CEO is planning on replacing lots of senior executives."[18]

Rumors share common features. They reflect anxiety (e.g., worry that the replacement of executives could harm one's job security). But they can also reduce anxiety ("I heard they are not going to lay off people at our plant"). Situational ambiguity of any sort—a lack of information about a particular issue of interest to the local population—encourages sharing of rumors among colleagues and friends.[19] Rumors are also uncertain. They help people to understand and explain some ill-defined situation, or what one sociologist a half century ago called "improved news."[20] If a company does not communicate well to its employees about a situation important to them, rumors fill the communication gap. Some rumor scholars call this function "a form of collective problem solving."[21] Rumors generally concern topics important to people. For example, learning that mouse meat was used to make hamburgers by one's favorite fast food restaurant would be of far more than casual interest, whereas the use of mouse meat in a restaurant in an obscure location around the world would only invite discussion if the details made it a curiosity. Ambiguity alone is insufficient to cause the spread of a rumor, but a personal importance to the topic motivates rumor dissemination. Finally, rumors have to be believable ("Yes, I can imagine KFC accidentally including chicken poop in their products"). Credibility is key; it makes rumors believable ("I can see my union going on strike"). These four features—situational anxiety, ambiguity, personal relevance, and believability—influence the creation and dissemination of rumors.[22]

The content of a rumor often makes exaggerated claims ("IBM plans to shut down the entire plant and lay everyone off by the end of the year"). Rumors also tend to recur. For example, it seems every few years fast food chains have to deny rumors of rodents in their sandwiches, as does Coca-Cola have to defend against claims of dangerous chemicals in its drinks. The same anxiety and ambiguity that caused the original rumor is often the cause of a recurrence of the rumor.

Distortion is a common feature of rumors. As people retell the rumor, it gets modified much as occurs when children play the telephone game of whispering to each other what they heard from the previous person. The children's story of the tailor who killed seven flies in his shop ending up being the emperor discussing how he had to kill seven dragons is the familiar example. Distortions can have a negative impact on businesses by influencing stock values.[23] If Facebook tightened its practices to reduce the spread of false facts, as it did in 2018, analysts could argue that this damaged the company's way of doing business because it potentially limited the influx of advertisements and traffic to this platform—as happened in late July 2018, causing the value of its stock to drop 18 percent. Twitter lost approximately 15 percent of its stock value for similar reasons. In both instances, these firms were cleaning fake facts off their computers but analysts speculating about the matter did not have hard facts on how much, how many, and when—data they needed to inform investors whether to buy or sell stocks in these firms.

No rumor is of value unless it is communicated to an interested audience. Of course, rumors predate the Internet. However, when the Internet became a common medium for public discourse, we entered a Golden Age of Rumors because the technology enabled people to circulate rumors quickly and easily to ever-larger audiences.[24]

Folklorists have characterized rumors for over a half century in a slightly different way. They observe that rumors are shaped by the identity and structure of the audiences to which they are directed, such as social class, company of employment, race, ethnicity, age, gender, or profession.[25] Rumors are intended to shape one's worldview, to reinforce preexisting perspectives or prejudices. Social influences make it possible to keep introducing these rumors, many of which were of older formulation, such as the mouse in the food. The credibility of a rumor might depend on the audience's worldviews (or perceived worldviews), for example, that customers believe advertisers exaggerate; that salesmen believe customers always want them to lower prices; that police officers believe most young ethnic minority males engage in criminal activities; and that political liberals believe all CEOs make too much money. Rumors pander to these beliefs or perceived beliefs. Folklorists also emphasize that the narrative has to be "performed" in an "appropriate setting."[26] Spreading a rumor that a company is going to close its factory in, say, Rochester, Minnesota, plays best if it is spread within that plant by local employees, such as through a blog read by those employees or other residents of that city. New Yorkers probably would not even know that this rumor was making the rounds; and if they did, they might not be interested; and, thus, they would likely be neither influenced by it nor willing to spread it themselves. (But if a group of New Yorkers were deciding where to have lunch, that would be the time for someone to tell the story of rats being found in a fast food restaurant, embellishing it with the fact that they were Norwegian rats and that the food came from somewhere in Minnesota!)

The discussion of the past several pages raises the question of urban legends in the business arena, what folklorists and sociologists call "mercantile legends."[27] Unlike advertising, which is massive and extremely diverse, there are essentially only four types of business-themed urban legends. Sociologist Gary Alan Fine has summarized these as being about the Evil Corporation, the Deceptive Corporation, the Careless Corporation, and the Beneficent Corporation.[28] An example of the Evil Corporation urban legend is that Satanists control the company, for example, a charge that has been leveled periodically against Procter & Gamble (P&G), or that IBM helped the Nazis carry out the Holocaust.[29] An example of the Deceptive Corporation urban legend might involve the claim that McDonald's intentionally puts worms in its hamburger meat as filler.[30] Product contamination is a common theme in examples of the Careless Corporation urban legend, particularly directed at food manufacturers but also at makers of patent medicines, as we discuss later in this chapter. Urban legends falling under the Beneficent Corporation category often hold that a company will provide a monetary or in-kind donation to a group if the company sells a certain amount of its goods to that group, such as a cigarette company supposedly prepared to donate kidney machines. This kind of legend even has its own name, Redemption Rumors.[31]

These four classes of urban legends became particularly widespread—even popular—since the First World War, thanks to the existence of so many large enterprises, "the modern Leviathan" agents in society. As one folklorist explained, "the scale of these entities is so large as to provoke trepidation among some consumers. Their size removes a sense of control from the consumer."[32] This is the same point made by both historians of advertising and public relations professionals for why advertising needs to make corporations friendlier, more approachable, more sympathetic, and less anonymous and distant if the advertising is to be effective.[33] Thus, it is not surprising that the highest proportion of these mercantile legends involve companies that directly interact with consumers, such as restaurant chains and national retailers, including online providers such as Amazon and Google; while mercantile legends are less common about insurance companies and business-to-business (B2B) manufacturers, where direct business-to-consumer contact is less common. These memes were common in the nineteenth century, too, with "the theme of the greedy businessman versus the trustworthy housewife," constantly reformulated over the past two centuries.[34]

RATS AND RUMORS

While the media enjoys publicizing rumors and fake accounts about companies doing terrible things as human-interest stories, companies take these stories seriously because they represent a threat to the company's sales and reputation. They affect a firm's credibility. One particular genre of mercantile legends that has been popular for a long time involves imported goods from other countries that threaten to displace jobs in the United States. Mexico in particular, but also South Asia and China, have been regular targets. One story that has circulated since the 1960s involves a shopper in a department store bitten by a snake or a poisonous insect, often a big spider hidden in a piece of imported clothing. This rumor even has its own name, The Department Store Snake, and is well documented to have occurred many times (the rumor, not the biting!); but there is no verification that the biting ever actually happened.[35] In one instance, a lady went to the hospital, was diagnosed with a snake bite, and in explaining her comings and goings that day, reported trying on a blouse at a Sears store in Massachusetts. The clothing she tried on was inspected and, of course, a snake was found hiding in the lining of the piece of clothing imported from Taiwan.[36]

Recall that, during the 1960s, the United States was experiencing the Vietnam War, Japanese imports were displacing American vendors with inexpensive consumer products such as toys and household items, and foreign clothing and textile firms were having a negative effect on clothing manufacturers in North Carolina. Women's clothing was imported from South Asia, Taiwan, the Philippines, India, and Israel (and a little later, from China). So, Asia was the larger threat to Americans, and it had a reputation for having many poisonous snakes. But it could have just as easily have been a threat from Latin America, for example, bananas from Costa Rica or in pots and clothing from Mexico. Many of these countries had a reputation of being exotic places and simultaneously for making inexpensive but shoddy goods; Japan was on this list of countries in the 1950s and 1960s.

A byproduct of these perceptions for American consumers was a rumor reflecting an underlying economic fear. Snake stories were situated in stores such as Sears, Kmart, and more recently Walmart, which all import from these mysterious countries about which consumers knew little. Americans criticized these stores and sued them, not their Asian suppliers. The retail outlets and the country of origin are typically named in the stories. Heard enough times in their various forms, these rumors evolved into fact, a statement of the realities one faced in purchasing imported goods.[37] Although these shoddy goods stories declined in popularity in the 1980s, by the end of the twentieth century they were back in circulation.[38]

Gary Alan Fine reminds us that such rumors were also evident in the importation of raw materials. For decades, stories circulated that Chiquita Bananas shipped from Central America frequently hosted snakes and spiders. We have found evidence of these rumors appearing as early as the 1950s, but the rumors may go back as far as the 1920s, when the banana import trade began. The banana continues to be the subject of rumors. In 2016, there were press reports of bananas being injected with HIV-infected blood. CNN reported that these bananas had been found at a Walmart in Oklahoma, while other reports established that this was the work of Satanists.[39]

Yucca trees from Africa, the rumor goes, were loaded with spiders exported throughout the world, but especially to the United States, England, France, Sweden, and Finland.[40] Competing rumors had biting spiders attacking innocent customers, which arrived in trees or cacti from Central America. Fine quotes the spouse of a "victim" in Michigan: "We [she and her husband] purchased a cactus from Frank's Nursery and Crafts [in Kalamazoo]. When we took it home, I noticed that it seemed to move on its own." After calling the store, an employee called back "and said get out of the house at once. People from Frank's arrived and said that the motion was caused by a tarantula having babies inside the plant."[41] That the plant was raised in Florida—hence from the United States and therefore "safe"—did not matter; the story circulated around Michigan. As in other variations, the "victim" is not harmed, lives to tell the tale, and waxes eloquently about employees in "white suits" arriving to fix the problem.

Some rumors involved specific countries: in the 1970s, it was cheap Japanese cars that were thought to be dangerous to drive; in the 1980s, it was Korean cars with the same problem; and a continuous American favorite has been Mexico—that "third-world country" so few Americans know much about, but which seems to take jobs away from Detroit and elsewhere, thanks to NAFTA and other reasons. As one story goes: innocent American tourists return home to North Dakota (or someplace else far, far away from Mexico) from a Mexican vacation with a new pet. What they thought was a cute pet—a Chihuahua dog—and had smuggled into the United States, their veterinarian informed them was instead a "Mexican water rat."[42] This was another 1980s case of an undocumented alien illegally entering the United States—a "rat," that is, a scavenger, which might also be rabid. In 2016, then-candidate Donald Trump called Mexicans "vermin," not just "rapists" and "criminals."[43] Fine suggests that the story of the Mexican pet was a cautionary tale to US citizens not to become emotionally attached to Mexicans.[44]

Another rumor blames Mexicans of filling up bottles of Corona Beer with their urine, which explains why the liquid has such a distinctive yellow hue. People would tell each other that they heard the story on the respected television news programs *60 Minutes, 20/20,* or *Nightline*; so, it must be true. This story apparently dates back to the mid-1980s, to a beer distributor in Reno, Nevada, possibly started by a salesman who had to compete against the rising popularity of this Mexican beer. The rumor soon spread to Boise, Phoenix, Seattle, Minneapolis, Milwaukee, and Chicago.[45] The color alone made the story *plausible*—a requirement of all good rumors—and plausibility was enhanced by the geographic source of the product: Mexico, which was perceived to be highly *untrustworthy*. The rumor fit with a long-standing suspicion and fear of Mexicans that dated to before the Mexican-American War of 1846–1848, which continues to the present. Folklorists discovered a subtext of American concern about contamination and competition in each of these rumors.

Other rumors struck at American corporations. What people believe about a corporation influences what they accept as true about it. This is an important observation because most companies face image problems at one time or another—and large corporations continuously so, because they affect so many people. A continuous challenge for public relations professionals is to correct faulty images and dampen fake facts and news about their firms. In the act of doing so, the public relations professionals developed a large body of beliefs and practices.[46] A couple of examples illustrate the information challenges faced by corporations.

In 1991, a rumor circulated that the Ku Klux Klan (KKK) was bottling Tropical Fantasy Soda Pop, resulting in sterility in black men.[47] In fact, this drink did not cause sterility. Nonetheless, sales quickly declined by 70 percent. The bottlers' trucks were attacked, and retail outlets refused to carry it. Another example involved Pop Rocks, a candy falsely charged with causing the consumer's stomach to explode if consumed together with a soda beverage. Pop Rocks sales dropped precipitously. Bubble Yum bubble gum was rumored to contain poisonous spider eggs. In all three instances the bad "news" traveled quickly among prior users, even though all of these claims were false.[48] Firms experience more than declining sales; they also lose customer trust.[49] Probably most readers have heard stories of terrible ingredients supposedly found in almost every fast food restaurant chain they can think of, and how consumption of these products would result in illness or worse.

Within an organization, rumors circulate constantly. Common ones include the CEO or some other popular executive or manager leaving the firm (with dire consequences for those remaining), enemies of one's division are to take over key positions in the firm, layoffs are imminent, a branch office or factory is about to close, the business is changing from direct to mail-order sales, the company experienced a massive unexpected loss in revenue and profit this quarter, entire product lines are to disappear after an impending merger, the company is moving to another location, or older employees are being pushed out the door. All these issues involve common themes: turnovers, pecking orders, job security, or customer concerns. No corporation is immune from these rumors. The fact that every one of these kinds of events does occur at some time and place reinforces the plausibility of these rumors.

IBM publicly experienced each of these types of internal rumors, first in the early 1920s, again in the late 1950s, and more recently in the 1980s; and these rumors were still circulating as this book was being published.[50] IBM is not different in this respect from many other corporations. The rumors are believable. They make sense and are consistent with prior experience. IBM employees who saw layoffs in the early 1990s were more apt to believe additional layoffs would occur in the 2000s, because the tradition of lifetime employment at the company had already been broken. What is remarkable is how fast these rumors spread, often in hours or days without benefit of the news media to help. Given that these rumors appeared reasonable, it is prudent for the employee to take them seriously and pass them on to colleagues.

Other rumors seem less reasonable and prudent on their surface. Satan remains a popular protagonist in many rumors. The power of profits plays a definitive role too. One scholar of business rumors explained: "It is slightly more credible to believe that large corporations might be owned by or contribute monies to extreme political organizations or controversial social movements," for nefarious reasons. "To accept that a large fast-food chain is owned by the KKK requires a leap of faith, but religious and political organizations do make investments in corporations, and most corporations contribute to charities."[51]

P&G seems unable to escape the persistent rumors that the company is a property of the Church of Satan.[52] McDonald's reportedly has been using worms in its food since the 1970s, while Kentucky Fried Chicken (KFC) was not to be outdone, offering up fried rats on its menu in the 1970s.[53] There were also rumors based on ethnicity, race, or religion: Jews were said to control the banks, perhaps the most continuously circulating rumor in the Western World.[54] Masons and Catholics were said to own businesses they ran to help their religious organizations. Satanists supposedly run Arm & Hammer; while Celestial Seasonings is reportedly controlled by the Unification Church, Coca-Cola by Mormons, and Exxon-Mobil by the Satanists who also operate McDonald's. According to these rumors, the Mormons were apparently quite busy, because they also reportedly ran Marriott Hotels, Ralph's Super Market, and Safeway. All these organizations, of course, had employees who were members of these churches or cults, but the companies operated independently of these churches. These rumors are similar to the accusations that John F. Kennedy worked for the pope (see chapter 3). Alleged ties between religious groups and specific businesses were repeated many times in both the United States and Europe.

In the period following the Second World War, P&G wins the prize for most frequently being associated with one religious group or another. In the mid-1980s, one hundred thousand customers complained to the firm about its involvement in Satanism.[55] During the 1980s alone, the company experienced three separate waves of criticism. Crest toothpaste was constantly attacked more than any other P&G product. Its logo seemed Satanic to some people; and since the CEO was never a public figure, that "unknown" executive was accused of being a Satanist by people appearing on various television news programs.[56]

Political rumors have been attached to major enterprises as well. It is interesting to see how, at various times, the Adolph Coors Company was once connected to Nazis, the Central American Contras, the KKK, the Moral Majority, and the National Rifle Association. KFC, as a Southern US enterprise, was not surprisingly attached to the KKK; but also to the American Nazi Party. Pepsi-Cola was claimed to be managed by the Palestine Liberation Organization (PLO), and Stroh's Beer by the gun control lobby; while Uncle Ben's Rice was rumored to be subservient to both the KKK and PLO.

In some instances, a small element of truth sparks a rumor. Consider the case of Coors, a family-owned beer manufacturing business. Joe Coors, who served as president of the firm in the 1970s, was a member of the arch-conservative John Birch Society during the 1960s and 1970s, as well as being affiliated correctly with the Heritage Foundation and the Stop ERA movement. President Ronald Reagan was a family friend. So, it was easy to associate the firm with far-right political and religious fringe groups.[57] Sometimes an accidental discovery of an unintended ingredient in a bottle can initiate rumors. Coca-Cola has been accused of bottling a mouse on occasion, as has 7-Up.[58] Every rumored claim described in the past several pages was untrue; but every one of them had at least an iota of plausibility, and, because of that, some people believed these rumors.

We offer one final example because it literally appeared the week one of the authors began writing this chapter in July 2018. Posted to a *Facebook* account of retired IBM employees, the rumor spoke to the long-standing tradition at IBM of wearing white shirts, blue suits, and regimental silk ties, even after the computer industry began to dress more casually in the 1990s. The post was an article from a magazine, *The Week*, which had come to the attention of a retired employee: "Scientists in Germany have discovered that wearing a tightly secured necktie can reduce the flow of blood to the brain by some 7.5 percent, potentially diminishing the wearer's brain function." A respondent to this posting wrote that when he became a manager at IBM, in 1988, he had seen such an article. He brought it to the attention of his manager, who seriously told him that if he wanted to remain a manager he would have to wear ties to work.

This is an interesting, if almost humorous instance because for decades employees lightheartedly questioned the need to dress so formally, particularly those who repaired computers and, while doing so, regularly destroyed suits and ties. There was always a mild undercurrent of resistance to the dress code. Yet, even that was part of the mythology of the firm, with stories about the dress code dating back to the early 1900s that were not "official" but accepted practice. In this instance, restrictive use of neckties and pants too tightly strapped around one's neck or waist can reduce blood flow in the body, but here the hint is that wearing ties could create a medical problem that could constrain one's ability to do the job. In reality, it was more wishful thinking, because shirts of course came in various neck sizes and employees knew how to tie a Windsor knot without choking. One of your authors (Cortada) worked at IBM and remembers seeing similar stories circulating in the mid-1970s in a culture where photocopied cartoons and rumors were constantly in evidence.[59]

All these examples represent episodic, if repeated, examples of rumors circulating—many of them serious threats to the reputation of a firm, others lighthearted. Closely related to these rumors were jokes, which similarly were based in something plausible. The question, "How do Ford Motor Company employees change a flat tire? They replace all four of them," speaks more to the corporate value of completed work done properly than to the truth that the only way to change a flat tire on a car is to replace all of them. "How many IBMers does it take to change a light bulb? Three: one to change it, and two to supervise the task." This joke speaks to the high intelligence of IBM employees but also to the overmanagement of the firm, which many employees criticized. Plausibility is essential; then the public relations professionals step in to address the negative image, rightfully seeing the threat to the company's reputation. In Ford's case, the correct way to fix a flat tire, of course, was to replace the one that was flat; to replace all four was wasteful. The IBM joke spoke to the nagging concern that existed for decades that the company was too bureaucratic, with too many levels of management.

TRUTH IN ADVERTISING: PATENT MEDICINES

Patent medicines are mixtures of ingredients prepared to cure some perceived illness but not normally designed as the result of scientific research that proves their curative effectiveness. Also known as *nostrums* (Latin for "our remedy"), they acquired the "patent" portion of the name in the seventeenth century, when some elixir or combination of ingredients secured the approval of English kings with letters of patent, which gave the king's endorsement that a vendor could use for the purpose of promoting the product. Not until 1925 could one patent chemical combinations in the United States, and rarely were any patent medicines patented because they typically could not prove their efficacy.

Almost all these patent medicines were concoctions with little or no medicinal benefit, and almost all were routinely sold deceitfully to the public. They promised—but did not deliver—remedies promising cures or relief from serious diseases or chronic health conditions. As their lack of efficacy became more widely known, they were sometimes called *quack medicines*. Kenneth L. Milstead, at the Food and Drug Administration (FDA) in the 1950s and 1960s, provided an elegant definition used by the US government, based on what these vendors did:

> When an untrue or misleading health claim is deliberately, fraudulently or pretentiously made for a food, drug, device or cosmetic, this is quackery. . . . It matters not whether the quackery is practiced by the witch doctor or the licensed medical practitioner, the Indian medicine man or the pharmacist, the proprietary drug manufacturer or the prescription drug manufacturer; the health facturer or the prescription drug manufacturer; the health food manufacturer or the clerk in the health food store; the health lecturer, the self-styled nutritionist, the doorstep diagnostician, the fly-by-night operator or some of our most respected food, drug, device and cosmetic manufacturers —it is still quackery.[60]

Reaching closer to our concern about information, Milstead added: "It matters not which mask it wears—ignorance, superstition, fear, gullibility, folklore, myth, half-truth, or falsehood—it is still quackery."[61] As one report explained, the "prevailing wisdom" held that "patent medicines promised to cure everything from cancer and epilepsy, to kidney disease and tuberculosis, but left the patient no better off than before treatment, and often had deleterious long-term health consequences."[62]

Historians have long studied the use of these concoctions, and we draw upon this scholarship to understand the role of fake information in this setting.[63] There is hardly a more long-standing example of fake facts in business than patent medicines. People knew that these curatives were useless, so why did they spend so much money on them, and why did

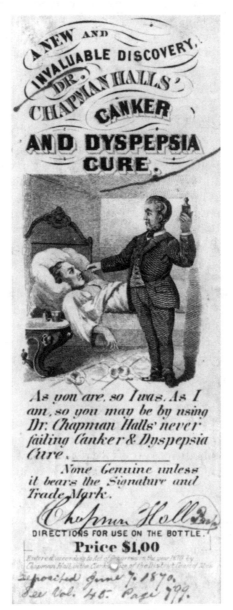

Figure 7.1. Dr. Chapman Hall's canker and dyspepsia cure, circa 1870. Courtesy Library of Congress.

this behavior persist over the course of several centuries? As scientifically developed "ethical drugs" reached the market through the work of pharmaceutical firms and medical doctors, and as patients in the United States became increasingly educated and had more ready access to truthful information, how were such nostrums able to persist for the past century? Why is it that one can walk into a modern supermarket and find entire aisles of these products? If the reader is taking "enriched" vitamin pills, or "enhanced" forms of fish oil tablets, or "herbs," he or she is consuming patent medicines. The debate over patent medicines is complicated by the fact that some of these products might actually be helpful, such as cod liver oil, but not its enhancements; similarly for vitamin pills with their enhancements. Historians and officials at the US FDA have concluded that, best case, some nostrums are not harmful, just not effective; worst case, some can kill you. The range of possibilities can confuse consumers. Sorting out information provided about these products, the intentions of their promoters, and the nature of their communications has to be part of any analysis of patent medicine advertising. Answering questions raised here provides additional insight into the role of misinformation and fake facts in American public life.

Purveyors of patent medicines were among the earliest and most aggressive users of advertising in North America. The most successful media mogul of the eighteenth century, Benjamin Franklin, routinely carried advertisements for these products in his newspapers, the *Pennsylvania Gazette* and the *Pennsylvania Chronicle*. With the massive expansion in the number of newspapers in the United States by the end of the 1820s, the amount of advertising for these products grew enormously. Watch a cable news program in the 2010s and you will still see these products advertised, even though the advertisements are misleading and despite a century of regulatory control over messaging and truth by the US FDA and Congress. Patent medicines have routinely constituted a highly profitable and often big business throughout American history. From 1810 to 1939, sales of patent medicines grew twenty-two times as much as the US economy overall, while the per capita GDP expenditure grew by a factor of five. Put another way, using the value of 2009 dollars, in 1810 a person spent 39 cents per year on patent medicines, by 1939 they spent $44.89. In 1909, the patent medicine industry ranked 38th out of 259 industries; it was the same size as the chemical industry.[64] A US Congressional committee concluded in 1984 that Americans annually spent $10 billion on these patent medicines; and although documenting the size of this business in the American economy is challenging, the size is no doubt far larger today.[65]

Textbox 7.1 provides a simple catalog of many types of patent medicines and cures available over the course of the past two centuries. Note the breadth of offerings, many of which were sold as cures for multiple ailments. This list does not include a range of electrical devices that appeared in the 1910s and 1920s, which were also sold as miracle cures. In 1929, federal officials began investigating questionable advertising concerning an even broader list of product offerings than those cataloged in the textbox. Patent medicines under investigation included those for many different ailments and purposes:

glands, asthma, piles, female weakness, bladder, fits, stomach troubles, colds, goiter, dropsy; and these kinds of "external health and beauty appliances": facial skin cures, bone straighteners, hair dyes, fat reducing, bust developers, baldness, rupture, deafness, hair removers, piles, eyelash growers, panaceas, leg sores, rheumatism, corns and bunions, optical.[66]

Both before and after the Second World War, cancer clinics in Mexico purported to have cures that were quicker to work and easier to endure than chemotherapy. Many patent remedies were targeted at ill-defined ailments, such as "tired blood," or at symptoms rather than illnesses, such as momentary pain or constipation, which nostrums could ameliorate or even alleviate without curing the underlying illness. Over the years, numerous patent remedies appeared for the common cold; but as today's medical professional will tell patients: "you can treat your cold for seven days and it will then go away, or you can not treat it for seven days and it will then go away."

Textbox 7.2 lists products still available that began as patent medicines. Over time, both their ingredients and their advertising evolved. Some other consumer products that began as patent medicines are no longer sold for medicinal purposes. The most famous of these is Coca-Cola, which was developed by a druggist in Atlanta. It contained cocaine in its original formulation. A number of soft drinks, foods, and snacks began their lives as patent medicines. These included 7-Up, Grape-Nuts, Hires Root Beer, Coca-Cola, Pepsi-Cola, Graham crackers, and tonic water.

Before moving on to a brief history of quack medicine and its information forms, let us consider homeopathy. It is often today identified as part of the patent medicine information ecosystem because its products and practices are widely dismissed by critics as useless or having only a placebo effect (at least in the Western world). It remains popular today as in the past. Sometimes known as "alternative medicine," homeopathy relies on the notion that a substance that causes symptoms of an illness can be used to cure those symptoms in the patient. Largely the creature of late eighteenth-century thinking, it spills over into what today is often referred to as the "wellness movement." But in its strict formulation, homeopathy called for a substance to be diluted with water or alcohol, based

Textbox 7.1. Sample Types of Patent Medicines, 1700s–2010s*

Types	*Examples*
Tired Blood	Geritol, Kickapoo Indian Sagwa Blood, Liver and Stomach Renovator
Pain reliever, fever reducer	Bayer aspirin
Arthritis	Zarumin, Dolcin tablets, Kordolin
Vitamins & Iron Pills	Multi-vitamins, energy & nutrition pills
Tonics	Lydia E. Pinkham's Vegetable Compound (women's complaints)
Tuberculosis Cures	Piso's Cure for Consumption, Tuberclecide
Cold Cures	Citroid, Vitamin C, Resistab, antihistamine
Tranquilizers	Happy pills, nerve pills, Miltown, Equanil
Laxatives & Antacids	Pepto-Bismol, Bromo-Quinine, Castoria, Swamp Root
Skin Cures	Livigen, creams, Dr. T. Felix Gourard's Oriental Magical Beautifier, hormones
Liver Pills	Carter's Little Liver Pills
Weight Reducers	Regimen, AYDS, R-D-X Plan, Hungrex,
Cancer Cures	Harry M. Hoxsey's clinics, carious roots, wood barks, potassium iodide, Radol
Diabetes Cures & Clinics	Kaadt's cures, saltpeter, vinegar
Male-Weakness & Sex Performance	Man Medicine, Sporty Days Invigorator, Organo Tablets, Enzyte
Animal bites, frost bites, etc.	Clark Stanley's Snake Oil Liniment
Nutritional & Food Supplements	Alfalfa, multi-vitamin mixtures, herbs
Aging	"Royal jelly" pills, Bee-Royale, Beauty for Life, Enerjol, Rojelan Formula 66
Venereal diseases	Mu-Wump Specific Preventive for all Venereal Diseases, Colloidal silver

* *Sources:* James Cook, *Remedies and Rackets: The Truth about Patent Medicines Today* (New York: W.W. Norton, 1958); James Harvey Young, *The Medical Messiahs: A Social History of Health Quackery in Twentieth-Century America* (Princeton, NJ: Princeton University Press, 1967).

Textbox 7.2. Some Products That Began as Patent Medicines and Are Still Employed Today for Medicinal Purposes*

Absorbine	Fletcher's Castoria
Bayer Aspirin	Luden's Throat Drops
BC Powder	Lydia E. Pinkham's Vegetable Compound
Bromo-Seltzer	Phillips' Milk of Magnesia
Carter's Little Pills	Smith Brothers Throat Drops
Doan's Pills	Vicks VapoRub

* *Sources:* James Cook, *Remedies and Rackets: The Truth about Patent Medicines Today* (New York: W.W. Norton, 1958); James Harvey Young, *The Medical Messiahs: A Social History of Health Quackery in Twentieth-Century America* (Princeton, NJ: Princeton University Press, 1967).

on formulas called *repertories*, its portions and proportions based on the specific symptoms, behavior, attitudes, and life history of the patient.[67]

Other forms of alternative medical practice and theory, such as acupuncture, chiropractic, eugenics, parapsychology, radionics (use of radioactive material), phrenology (studying bumps on one's head), and scientific racism could be regarded similarly to homeopathy for our purposes. The wide use of animal, plant (especially flowers), and mineral substances in these alternative medicine areas spilled over into patent medicines. All these fields—patent medicine included—relied heavily on aggressive advertising. Consider Zicam Cold Remedy, a twenty-first-century product, which included a variety of substances packaged together to serve as a cold remedy. Lawsuits against Zicam contended that the medication represented a dangerous mixture associated with some users losing their sense of smell.[68] Most patent medicines, in contrast, are harmless but ineffective at treating the causes of the illness.

In order to better understand our story about information and patent medicine, we need to give some brief background material about the history of medical practice. There was an inadequate supply of both doctors and effective medicines in sixteenth-, seventeenth-, and eighteenth-century England and North America. Modern medicine based on scientific research did not yet exist, especially in North America, where people had to rely on existing concoctions, recipes, and self-healing. That situation continued in England until after the Napoleonic Wars (1803–1815) and in the United States until the second half of the nineteenth century. Beginning in the nineteenth century, the medical profession expanded and brought in new medical practices, while at the same time science-based medications came on the scene. By 1920, many of the medical practices familiar today existed: formal training of doctors in medical schools, widespread belief in the germ-based theory of illnesses, sanitary hospitals, medical sub-specialties, a growing body of medicines to treat the underlying causes of diseases, clean urban water, and growing acceptance of hand washing and bathing.[69] While all of that was going on, purveyors of patent medicines continued to ply their trade, as demand for their goods and services never diminished.

Until 1860, patent medicines had no competition from science-based medicines that had been proven effective to cure medical ailments. Patent medicines filled the space. With the spread of newspapers across America during this period, announcements frequently appeared promoting the availability of various powders and tonics, many of them locally sourced and manufactured. Hardly any person who could read had not been inundated by advertisements concerning patent medicines by the 1850s.

In the decade following the Civil War, that is, during the late 1860s and early 1870s, patent medicines expanded dramatically in both number

and availability. A patent treatment was offered for almost every ailment. Many of these patent medicines contained alcohol, strengthened
with morphine, opium, or cocaine. Child mortality was common at this
time, and many patent medicines, targeted at colic and "fussiness," were
marketed as cures for children's ailments. Unfortunately, these patent
medicines led in some cases to childhood death. Another set of nostrums
focused on "female complaints."

Patent medicine became big business and, for most newspapers, advertising these products was the single largest source of advertising
revenue.[70] Where the advertising originally focused on the availability of
these products, over time the ads made increasingly extravagant claims
about the product's efficacy. Vendors launched "medicine shows" that
traveled throughout the nation hawking their products as "miracle medicines," while providing circus-like entertainment or educational lectures,
much along the lines of the contemporaneous educational Chautauqua
movement.[71] Daniel Pope, a historian of American advertising, described
what happened in the late nineteenth century:

> Simply put, in virtually all newspapers and most magazines of the Gilded
> Age, many advertisements were outright lies. Patent medicine ads promised
> to cure every disease known, and quite a few unknown, to medical science.
> Readers were informed that by becoming agents for this product or making
> that one in their spare time they could earn a secure and generous income
> with slight effort.[72]

Only at the turn of the twentieth century, as the Progressive Era came
to America, did newspapers begin to question these patent medicines and
the practices of their promoters.

Even during the Progressive Era of the early twentieth century and
even later, the business opportunity was too great to resist. One patent
medicine peddler proclaimed, "I can advertise *dish water* and sell it, just
as well as an article of merit. It is all in the advertising."[73] As Pope concluded, "nostrum peddlers were notoriously deceitful advertisers, for
honesty would usually have compelled them to admit that their drugs
lacked curative power."[74] People tried anything they thought provided
hope, and they were attracted by the products' alcoholic content. This
is not so different from more recent times: a survey conducted in 1972
reported that 75 percent of the respondents stated that, regardless of
the quality of their diets, taking vitamins would help them to achieve
"super health," including absence of illness, greater energy, reduced or
no anxiety, and freedom from depression—all leading to contentment.[75]
One observer put it cleverly: "The public wants magic, not science. . . . It
wants to hear about the latest magic cure, and doesn't want to know it's
just another 'snake oil' rip off."[76]

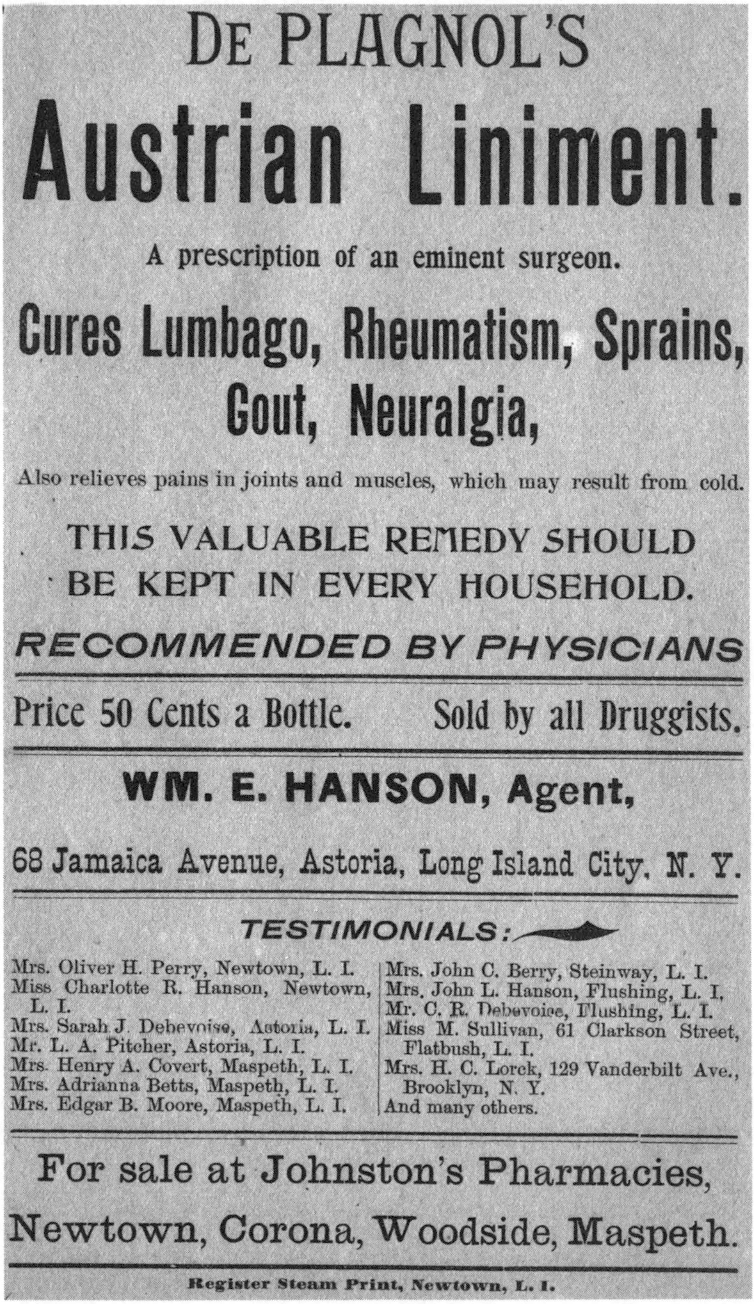

Figure 7.2.   Clark Stanley's Snake Oil Liniment, circa 1905. Note the wide range of illnesses it could cure. Courtesy Library of Congress.

While advertisers attempted to purge their profession of such practices toward the end of the nineteenth century, they were faced by the economic reality that of the 2,853 national and regional advertisers operating in 1898, 425 (approximately 15 percent) were patent medicine vendors.[77] This percentage was down from 50 percent of the newspaper advertising devoted to patent medicines earlier in the nineteenth century, but it was still hard for newspapers to turn away 15 percent of potential advertisers.[78] The situation became much more problematic for advertisers between 1899 and 1904—for in this five-year period, the value of patent medicine advertising rose by 128 percent.[79] While there was newfound understanding of the value of truth in advertising late in the nineteenth century, the economic incentives supported a different choice.

The rise in advertising of patent medicines happened at roughly the same time as another movement in the United States to regulate these medicines and foods more generally. The impulse to regulate took two forms during the twentieth century. The first involved having advertisers provide more accurate, truthful statements about what their products did, first calling for the reduction and later the elimination of falsehoods and exaggerations. The second thrust, appearing originally with food and later, increasingly, with medications, was to use government regulation to prevent dangerous products from coming to market. This second initiative resulted in waves of new laws and regulations, and increased staffing of the FDA, as the twentieth century unfolded.

Following the publication of Upton Sinclair's expose of the Chicago meatpacking houses in his 1906 book, *The Jungle*,[80] the United States passed the Pure Food and Drug Act of June 1906 and created an agency to enforce its terms, the FDA. This movement also led to more scrutiny of the patent medicine business. Nevertheless, the earlier practices of patent medicine vendors continued deep into the twentieth century—in part because the FDA had weak power and a tiny staff (often fewer than a dozen employees devoted to patrolling nostrums). Even the US Post Office Department, which had stronger regulatory power and a larger staff than the FDA to pursue fraudulent advertisers, was overwhelmed by the size of the patent medicine industry.[81] The advertising industry saw self-regulation of the patent medicine industry as its most important priority during the early years of the new century, and this concern became a central piece of the Truth in Advertising Movement of 1910–1920.[82] State and federal agencies began prosecuting mostly small-time suppliers of patent medicines. The government won most of the cases, but the fines and jail terms were typically so small as to be inconsequential. Real progress simply came slowly.[83] It did not help that the public was not discriminating in its assessment of advertisements. A public health doctor, M. W. Glover, groused in 1920: "Our experience has taught us that the appearance on the label of the name of a disease usually conveys to the user the impression that the preparation is all that he needs to get permanent relief from that trouble." In response to this sentiment, for the rest of this century federal regulators focused much of their attention on what vendors put on their labels.[84]

The American Medical Association (AMA) joined in the attack against patent medicines. However, the pro-business economic boom years of the 1920s and an expanding population provided fertile ground for the expansion of more patent medicines and, in particular, a rapid expansion in electronic medical devices that supposedly cured various ailments.

The ascendency of the New Deal Democrats to power in 1933, and the extent of the Great Depression, created new possibilities for regulatory reform. In 1938, Congress passed a comprehensive food and drug law that armed various government agencies with more tools with which to regulate patent medicines and their advertising. That signaled the birth of the third and most recent phase in the history of patent medicines. Known as the Food, Drug, and Cosmetic Act, this 1938 legislation introduced a set of laws that shaped the future of patent medicine information and advertising for decades. The legislation was stimulated by the deaths of over one hundred people in Oklahoma from a lethal mixture of sulfanilamide and diethylene glycol. The legislation authorized the FDA to regulate advertising, labeling, and content of food coloring and food additives, homeopathic medications, bottled water, cosmetics, dietary supplements, and medical devices. It allowed for both civil and criminal penalties. It also increased regulation of ethical drugs, not only quack medicines. The FDA and other agencies expanded to enforce the law. In almost every subsequent decade, Congress passed new laws building upon the 1938 legislation. Congress returned to the false labeling issue with passage of the Nutrition Labeling and Education Act in 1990 and the Dietary Supplement Health and Education Act in 1994; and then passing additional legislation to strengthen the authority of the FDA in 2007.[85]

Over the past century and a half, patent medicine vendors have extensively used every medium of information diffusion available to them. First there were the newspapers and magazines, then radio beginning in the 1920s, television beginning in the late 1940s, and the Internet beginning in the 1990s. These vendors expanded their use of bulk-mailed advertisements, particularly to rural communities, after rural mail delivery began at the dawn of the twentieth century. They rapidly adopted mail-order delivery in the 1930s and 1940s, and employed door-to-door salesmen from the 1920s through the 1960s.[86] Medicine shows, common in the late nineteenth century, were the only communication mechanism patent medicine vendors dropped, and only because they could reach the same markets more cost-effectively through radio.

What effect did the increased availability of effective, science-based (ethical) medicines beginning in the early 1900s have on quack medications? When ethical drugs appeared, they were marketed to doctors, not to patients. Doctors provided prescriptions, which drug stores filled. Not until the late twentieth century could pharmaceutical manufacturers advertise their products directly to potential patients; and when they did, they did so largely through television commercials. Expenditures on direct-consumer advertising by the pharmaceutical industry grew from $166 million in 1993 to $5.4 billion in 2005; patent manufacturers followed suit.[87]

Science-based medicine made impressive gains in the twentieth century. Penicillin effectively combatted infections. Chemotherapy helped to contain or eliminate various kinds of cancers. Vaccines became an effective tool at preventing people from contracting many kinds of disease, and a large group of drugs became available that could fight diseases after they were contracted. Certain nasty and widespread diseases, such as smallpox and cholera, were largely eliminated in the United States. The American public came to believe in the preventative and curative effects of medicine, although they may not have been so good at differentiating ethical medicines from quack medicines. As one historian explained, "John Doe did not possess the judgment to differentiate between a true miracle drug and a false article ordered offered with miraculous claims."[88] With the improved effectiveness of particular drugs for particular illnesses, officials increased enforcement of laws to protect people from underperforming or dangerous medications.

In this environment, what happened to quack medicines? They muted the claims for their products, but they did not disappear. Some quack medicines improved therapeutic abilities, and the makers of these drugs recommended using their products in conjunction with treatments that were still part art and not all science, such as chemotherapy treatments for cancer. By the late 1950s, Americans were still spending a billion dollars a year on nostrums.[89]

Consumer Reports and other media have reported on the problems of patent medicines regularly since the 1940s. They have attacked bromides, laxatives, and products including Citroid, Sleepeze, Sominex, and Geritol; nevertheless, these publications have had little impact on sales of these medications.[90] The American Cancer Society also published a steady stream of reports about fake treatments.[91]

Ironically, as the perception grew that medications were becoming more effective and that quackery was in decline, it became a more favorable climate in which quack medicine providers could operate. For example, in the 1880s, after Americans began hearing about germs, Radam's Microbe Killer could be more effectively marketed. It consisted of muriatic acid, wine, and water, and was sold as the cure to all diseases because it destroyed the germs that caused illnesses. Later, a competitive product, Liquozone, refined the argument by claiming to kill germs but without "killing the tissues too."[92] In the early 1900s, Hydrozone claimed to be a "scientific germicide" endorsed by doctors across the country, "killing the germs that cause these diseases, without injury to the tissue," medication that thus "cures the patient."[93] Not mentioned in this advertising, however, were other more effective underlying causes for improved health, notably the large impact that the availability of clean water supplies had on improved public health and significant reductions in death rates.

Over time, quack medicines began to shift emphasis by addressing now longer-living customers with chronic diseases, rather than treating acute infections that they advertised about during the nineteenth century.[94] There were more older customers with aches and pains and symptoms to care about as a percent of the total population, a circumstance that has continued to this day. Economists, who studied the increase in demand for nostrums after the arrival of effective—sometimes spectacularly effective—products as a result of true scientific progress, concluded that quack vendors were successful because they tied their products to innovations in science and that consumers assumed all products (both those that were science based and those that were not) were becoming more effective. As these economists noted, "consumers desperate to find a cure for what ails them might return to those manufacturers repeatedly in the withering though ever-present hope of finding an efficacious product."[95] Potential customers did not avoid nostrum manufacturers or challenge their claims. Challenges to patent medicines came instead from regulators, medical associations, and consumer advocacy groups—although these groups could never entirely keep up with the expansive patent medicine advertising.[96]

By the end of the nineteenth century a new illness—cancer—began catching the attention of nostrum manufacturers as a new business opportunity. Little was understood about cancer's complex characteristics until after the Second World War, so patent medicine manufacturers were not at a disadvantage to the science-based health industry. Indeed, the patent medicine manufacturers did address this new market. At the dawn of the twentieth century, one could open the newspaper and see an advertisement from the Dr. Johnson Remedy Company of Kansas City, Missouri, with the headline, "CANCER CURED AT HOME." Dr. Johnson promised to provide evidence that his cure works if a potential customer reached out to him.[97] One had no reason to trust Dr. Johnson any more than the ad that had appeared twenty-five years earlier: "Cancer Successfully Treated, without use of Knife or Caustics. . . . Send two postage stamps—Correspondence from Physicians solicited."[98] In fact, nostrums to cure cancer had been offered since the eighteenth century.

They shared common features in their use of misinformation or outright false facts. They scared potential customers with fearful language about the horrors of cancer and its pain—with great attention to the dangers of cutting, poisoning, burning, radiation, and dying. The nostrums always offered the promise of a painless cure that worked—"No knife or pain" said one 1912 advertisement. In the late twentieth century, the most pain one would experience, according to the most recent nostrum ads, was the pinprick of an injection. Many of these ads played upon a claim of some miraculous scientific breakthrough, such as a new ingredient, the "discovery" of an ancient cure known to a primitive tribe somewhere, or new insights from scientific research. The vendor commonly would commit to wiping out confusion and misunderstanding with clear statements about the causes of cancers and how the patient could be cured. As one advertisement stated: pick your cure and "it acts chemically to kill the cancer cell selectively without injury to the normal tissues of the body." When the nostrum makers received pushback from the medical establishment, they argued that they were "misunderstood" by professional doctors "blind" to possible cures. Sometimes, the advertiser would argue that they were subject to a conspiracy from the medical establishment (from pharmaceutical companies, the AMA, medical doctors, the FDA, and the National Cancer Institute) because an alternative cure would be threatening to these organizations. The story played out according to a similar pattern over two hundred years as each new disease became a market opportunity.[99]

The claims made by patent medicine advertisements reflected the style of language of their times. Just as claims were made that readers might consider outrageous by today's norms concerning President Andrew Jackson's family in the 1820s, the policies of the Spanish government in Cuba in the 1890s, or the more subdued, even politely worded accusations of papal interference in American political affairs in the 1960s, patent medicine advertisers adapted to changing standards of newspaper discourse as well as to the market opportunities that a newly discovered or newly widespread medical ailment created. Historians consider the period from the 1870s to the 1920s as the golden era of outlandish claims by patent medicine manufacturers.

Without much hope for relief from doctors throughout most of the 1800s, and often surviving while using nostrums often due to the body's natural healing properties, people paid attention to the details of advertising. People could afford nostrums and there was fierce competition for their business, with the competitive battles often occurring within the advertising. The hard sell proved essential and effective, accounting for much of the tone of language used and the kind of information proffered. Quantity of advertising, distinguishing one's product from a rival's, and communicating persuasively to customers became the three essential features of effective patent medicine information. Tactics included medicines coming from faraway places endorsed by ministers, personal testimonials about the patent medicine's effectiveness, and the appeal to exotic ingredients touted as being known to be effective.[100]

Sampling the texts for these patent medicines brings life to the role of fake facts and misinformation. Day's Kidney Pad (circa 1870s) would "cure by absorption all diseases of the kidneys, bladder, and urinary organs." Further, it was reportedly "the only true method of curing and controlling the most prevalent diseases that afflict mankind."[101] People bought it for over thirty years. The ability to cure many diseases with a single product was a standard declaration made by many patent medicines throughout the century. Kline's Painless Cancer Cure, applied to a tumor, made it "preeminently unrivalled in the treatment" of "the largest of cancers or tumors," importantly without using "a knife, caustics, loss of blood, or other fearful treatments." Who could resist such an offer? Kline's stayed on the market for more than twenty years.[102] Moxie Nerve Food (1880s) was advertised as "the successful enemy of the rum fiend" and the "finest nerve food" available. Mrs. Bulme testified that it cured her of "complete paralysis of both the motory and sensitive nerves" on her left side.[103] This Moxie product sold for some fifty years. If one had tuberculosis, that posed no problem because there was Saul's Catarrh Remedy, an inhalant, which appeared on the market for twenty years.[104] Swaim's Panacea was a cure-all that allegedly eliminated heart disease, leprosy, liver diseases, rheumatism, scurvy, myriad skin eruptions, and melancholia, staying on the market for nearly eighty years from its beginning in the 1820s. Swaim's was a concoction of herbs, dried flowers, and rhubarb.[105]

Tonics were widely distributed in the nineteenth and early twentieth centuries. The most famous was Lydia E. Pinkham's Vegetable Compound, first introduced in the 1870s, which she brewed with herbs in her basement in Lynn, Massachusetts. She aimed it at "women's weaknesses," such as menstrual cramps. Her tagline was, "Only a woman understands women's ills." She first advertised the product in 1876 in the *Boston Herald*, but the product soon went nationwide. In 1887, the advertising claimed that the product "offers the SUREST REMEDY for the PAINFULL ILLS AND DISORDERS SUFFERED BY WOMEN EVERYWHERE." "It relieves pain, promotes regular and healthy reoccurrence of periods and is a great help to young girls and women past maturity. It strengthens the back and the pelvic organs, bringing relief and comfort to tired women who stand all day in home, shop and factory." The ads carried a kindly picture of Pinkham; and those ads appeared everywhere—for example, on buildings, newspapers, fence posts, and trading cards.[106]

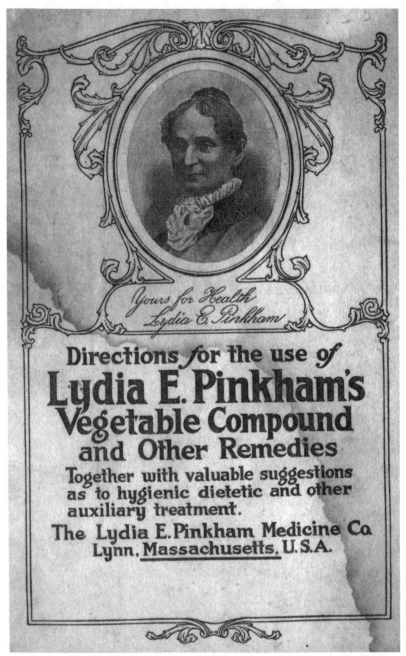

Yours for Health
Lydia E. Pinkham

Directions for the use of
Lydia E. Pinkham's
Vegetable Compound
and Other Remedies
Together with valuable suggestions
as to hygienic dietetic and other
auxiliary treatment.
The Lydia E. Pinkham Medicine Co.
Lynn, Massachusetts, U.S.A.

Figure 7.3. Lydia E. Pinkham's Herb Medicine was one of the most widely known in late nineteenth-century America and was sold to women, circa 1870s. Courtesy Library of Congress.

Pinkham was not alone. Kickapoo Indian Sagwa tonic sold at medicine shows and was unisex: it promised to cure "blood, liver and stomach" problems as a "renovator." "S. Andral Kilmer, MD" developed Swamp Root as "a diuretic to the kidneys and mild laxative." Another famous product, Clark Stanley's Snake Oil Liniment, claimed to be "the strongest and best liniment known for pain and lameness" and could also be used "for rheumatism, neuralgia, sciatica, lame back, lumbago, contracted cords, toothache, sprains, swellings, frost bites, bruises, sore throat, bites of animals, insects and reptiles," "good for man and beast," "it gives immediate relief," and "is good for everything a liniment ought to be good for." All this wondrous information appeared on the label.[107]

This was not only a late nineteenth-century phenomenon. Belle Dyspepsia Tablets came on the market in the early 1900s "for the relief of stomach distress due to indigestion or dyspepsia." Chewing a tablet provided instant relief for other ailments too:

> Flatulence "Gas," Nausea, Vertigo, Biliousness, Sour Stomach, Colic, Cramps, Palpitation, Pain, Weakness of Stomach, Acid Fermentation, Malassimilation of Food, Heartburn, Stomach Distress, Vomiting, Fullness of Stomach, Coated Tongue, Atonic Dyspepsia, Frog in Throat, Offensive Breath, Acid Stomach, Distress After Eating, Dizziness, Sick Headache, Bad Taste in Mouth, Bloating, Belching, Sour Risings, restless nights and other conditions caused by improper food or indigestion. Will normalize and cure indigestion, improve the appetite and if taken in time will instantly relieve a slight cold or attack of indigestion.[108]

Just before the First World War, with market segmentation in advertising becoming the norm, there was Burdock Blood Bitters for the ladies:

> It makes pure, healthy blood, and regulates all the organs to a proper action, cures constipation, liver and kidney complaint, female weakness, nervous and general debility, and all the distressing miseries from which two-thirds of all the women of America are suffering. ALL INVALID LADIES should send for our SPECIAL CIRCULAR addressed to LADIES ONLY, which treats on a subject of vital importance.[109]

Its customers were the "thousands of females in America who suffer untold miseries from chronic diseases common to their sex," with "their sufferings, most of which is endured in silence, unknown by even the family physician and most intimate friends."[110] In this advertisement we find an overt attack on doctors, generally regarded as enemies of patent medicine in the Progressive Era in America before the First World War.

Nostrum peddlers provided a remarkable amount of information in their advertising about the symptoms and diseases which they aimed their products at, the features of their cures, and the benefits one could expect from consuming them. This behavior went beyond simple testimonials from a wide range of "cured" patients and notables of society, such as ministers, doctors, and celebrities. A student of the history of nostrums concluded that "the practice of listing in advertising common symptoms like weariness, spots before the eyes, the blues, the blahs, as harbingers of dread diseases really persuaded the public." The placebo effect played into the hands of the nostrums, particularly in generating testimonials.[111] They could also be brief and to the point, as we see in figure 7.4 with Hamlin's Wizard Oil.

One feature widely used in communicating about the health benefits of nostrums was the alleged testimonials of users. Many of these testimonials came from ordinary citizens—housewives, gardeners, or day laborers—beginning in the 1700s. But people in more prestigious circumstances also participated, notably "doctors":

> I have within the last two years [in 1823] had an opportunity of seeing several cases of very inveterate ulcers, which, having resisted previously the regular modes of treatment, were healed by the use of Mr. Swaim's PANACEA; and I do believe, from what I have seen, that it will prove an important remedy in scrofulous, venereal, and mercurial diseases.[112]

Figure 7.4. Hamlin's Wizard Oil reflected the marketing style of the 1890s, linking the product to the popular practice of tent shows and circuses when such products would be sold. This one could cure "all pain in man or beast." Courtesy Library of Congress.

Even purveyors who openly sold alcoholic drinks, instead of disguising them as medications, relied on testimonials. Duffy's Pure Malt Whiskey was sold as "the comfort and support of the old," followed by an over-one-hundred-word explanation written in purposefully small typeface that would have been nearly impossible for the average person to read. In the advertisement is the picture of a very ugly, wrinkled faced woman, "A Dear Old Soul Active and Happy at 106, Mrs. Nancy Tigue of Lafayette, Ind." Tigue is quoted as saying: "I really don't feel like I'm a day over 60. Thanks to Duffy's Pure Malt Whiskey, which is the real secret of my great age, health, vigor and content." The reader is further informed that Mrs. Tigue is Blessed with All Her Faculties and Does Exquisite Fancy Work Without Glasses. She is as Spry as Many Women Half Her Age."[113] In another case, Mary Deemer of Allentown, Pennsylvania, offers a testimonial for a product called Natex, saying it gave her "relief." This testimonial was published in her hometown newspaper, the *Allentown Morning Call*, on May 27, 1935. Alas, Deemer died on May 25, and the newspaper carried both her testimonial and her death notice on the same page![114] One newspaper editor, frustrated by the proliferation of these sorts of testimonials at the end of the century, advised: "If your brains won't get you into the papers, sign a 'patent medicine' testimonial. Maybe your kidneys will."[115]

In his research on quack medicines, historian James H. Young found that producers liked to quote respected members of society, such as ministers and other notables. So did advertisers in the late twentieth century—ranging from NBA basketball players supporting Nike shoes to octogenarian Senator Bob Dole extoling the virtues of Viagra. As early as the 1700s, a generous donation to a church or religious school could result in a testimonial: "I have used the Tractors [a nostrum] with success in several other cases in my own family."[116] In 1906, another minister reflected on the results of eating a bowl of Grape-Nuts "after my Sabbath work is done," "my nerves are quieted and rest and refreshing sleep are ensured me." Catholic Nuns at the St. Mary's Infant Asylum in Massachusetts participated, touting the blessings of Ayer's Sarsaparilla. President Andrew Jackson complimented an ointment, while his vice president recommended a particular throat lozenge. Actor Edwin Booth did too.[117]

By 1910, the AMA files included copies of testimonials from thirteen thousand Americans and three thousand foreign doctors.[118] In the 1920s, testimonials were read over the radio, for instance the one from a man in Louisiana: "I no longer suffer from asthma." A woman wrote: "[in] crippling rheumatism for 10 years long . . . now I walk again." A man in New Orleans reported: "Was suffering terribly from disease of the blood . . . now back to work." A lady from Port Arthur, Texas, claimed: "I do not have heart trouble anymore." A man suffering from stomach ulcers, upon being told by a doctor that he had cancer, listened to his wife who recommended that he take Hadacol, and now he says "I can eat almost everything . . . even pork. In fact, I feel perfectly well. I work hard in the field with no ill effect."[119] A minister in his eighties also endorsed Hadacol, reporting he had experienced "a wonderful change" in his ability to eat and sleep as a result of taking this nostrum. Letters supposedly coming to the manufacturer of Hadacol spoke of women who had been "run down" now being full of energy, or a weak boy of thirteen now appearing as a star player on his baseball team. All these ads appeared in the 1950s![120]

Did the rhetoric in ad copy and testimonials evolve over time? A half-century later, in the 1950s, the tone had changed but not the misinformation. For example, Sentrol was advertised as follows: "Science has announced a remarkable new headache capsule specially developed for people who really suffer from headaches which aspirin does not seem to help" and "it does not cause stomach upsets the way aspirin often does," "a new formula never before available—*three times more effective than aspirin!*"[121] This product consisted of phenacetin, caffeine, and salicylamadine. These compounds acted like ordinary aspirin, but it had been known for years that they could also cause upset stomachs. In the same decade, arthritis sufferers were offered Zarumin, advertised as an "important new advance for the relief of common rheumatic and arthritic-like pains," now pushed as a relief but not as a permanent cure as earlier products were touted. Advertisements added that the advance offered by Zarumin was not due to any particular ingredient, but rather "in the structure of the pill, which is a timed-released 'pill-within-a-pill.'" AMA investigators acknowledged this feature might have some benefit.[122]

The health and wellness movement that surged at the end of the twentieth century led *Consumer Reports* to start warning people that "snake oil salesmen" were still around making "claims that are too good to be true."[123] But the cumulative effects of "truth in advertising" had also caught up with some of the messaging, and today one is more likely to find misinformation than outright lies. Even respected organizations continued marketing nostrums. Consider the case of Vital Proteins, which is stocked at Whole Foods.[124] Vital Proteins recommends that one boost of its "morning brew with the pure collagen nutrition of Vital Proteins . . . helps you stay energized and reduces hunger cravings, keeping you vibrant throughout the day"? Using this as a coffee creamer was also accompanied by images of beautiful, healthy-looking young men. Collagen is a gelatin protein (a peptide) and a good source of protein proven to break down amino acids and improve the look of aging skin, but nothing more. However, a brochure describing the product (available at Whole Foods in 2018) also promised to "encourage" hair and nail health, promote "overall gut health," and "support bones and joints, and aids in muscle recovery." Addressing the wellness customer: "The antioxidant power of coffee paired with Collagen, which is the building block of hair, skin, nails, bones and joints, makes for a well-rounded start to any day."[125] People still wanted medical magic.

At the same grocery store, one could pick up a fat brochure published by Boiron, which claims to be the "World Leader in Homeopathic Medicines." Its *Easy Guide* (catalog of its products) noted, like many advertisements of the previous century, that it was developed by qualified people, in this instance twin brothers who were pharmacists (in 1932). The company's general manager, Christian Boiron, declared that "the ability to maintain and restore our health is within each of us, and homeopathic medicines, rather than merely masking symptoms, help your body the natural way. More and more Americans are turning to these medicines as their first choice of treatment."[126] This brochure could have been published in 1900 or 1930. The regulatory environment, however, led Boiron to use qualifying language such as "rely on these medicines to help relieve symptoms" of [fill in your ailment, e.g., flu, teething, muscle pain, allergies, coughs, and so forth], which the firm acknowledges "are regulated as a homeopathic drug by the Food and Drug Administration." Other carefully crafted language included phrases such as "no known drug interactions," "low risk of side effects," and "improvement may occur more quickly when treatment is started at the onset of symptoms." This kind of advertisement spoke of "temporary relief" for some of its products, such as Children's Sabadil for allergies. A picture of the container's label and appealing contemporary illustrations accompanied each product.[127]

One final example of the nature of the information imparted today that is similar to that of earlier times comes from a magazine also available at Whole Foods. In the February 2018 issue of *What Doctors Don't Tell You* (launched in 2012), the two editors dispense advice on how to lower high blood pressure without recourse to medications that are currently routinely prescribed for this purpose and have been prescribed for more than a half century.[128] One editor, Lynne McTaggart, graduated from Bennington College with a degree in English literature and built a career in journalism; the other, Bryan Hubbard, earned a degree in philosophy from Birkbeck University of London and developed a career in marketing and journalism. Both have written extensively on alternative medicine; neither has a scientific or medical background. A fact-checker group, Quakometer, condemned them and their magazine for spreading inaccurate information. Another critique noted that some members of the editorial board had lost their licenses to practice medicine. Another objection was that, in the first issue of the magazine, the editors published an article stating that measles vaccines do not work, whereas the vaccine's efficacy has been established for decades.[129] In that article, the magazine sided with those who questioned the value of vaccines in general. This was a major issue debated in the 2010s, but, which almost all licensed doctors challenged because of overwhelming evidence collected over two hundred years demonstrating the efficacy of vaccines.[130]

"Disease mongering," as in examples of nineteenth-century advertising we have mentioned, continues today—with new versions created at the same time as the "health wellness movement." This term came into use in 1992 to describe efforts to make healthy people feel as though they were ill. Disease mongering was part of a strategy to create new customers for nostrums. But the approach dates to at least 1879 with the introduction of Listerine, sold as both a floor cleaner and a cure for gonorrhea. In 1895, Listerine began being sold to dentists for oral care, and in 1914 it became an over-the-counter mouthwash in the United States. The manufacturer, Lambert Pharmacal Company, needed an illness for which Listerine was a cure, and they invented it—*halitosis*. With such a condition, it would be impossible for people to succeed in romance, work, marriage, or other social situations. William James, the Harvard professor considered the father of American psychology, famously argued that the advertisers of Listerine "should be treated as public enemies and have no mercy shown."[131]

But this pattern of searching for illnesses to cure continues to the present day. Today's examples include erectile dysfunction, bipolar disorder, attention deficit hyperactivity (good for dealing with the children's market), social shyness (useful for reaching teenagers and young people), and balding (to reach both older men and women). These combine both perceived issues and real medical conditions—the latter being addressed by serious medical researchers and pharmaceutical companies, not just nostrum peddlers.

Nostrums continue to be big business. Americans spend $30 billion every year on dietary supplements—often with the intention of boosting one's immune system or fighting inflammation. No body of misinformation seems complete in American society without a dash of conspiracy added to the nostrum. Contemporary examples include the relation of vaccines to autism, the evils of water fluoridation, incorrect bra size causing breast cancer, and cell phone use causing brain cancer.[132] If this text sounds slightly sarcastic, it is not intended to be; it simply acknowledges that what existed in the United States a century or two ago with respect to fake facts and misleading information about medicines still exists.

The continuing belief of Americans in these folk stories and folk remedies seems incongruous with the fact that a higher percentage of Americans receive an education than in the nineteenth century, and that formal education is more extensive. But we see many examples, and various nonprofits are worried about how uncritical Americans are as consumers of information both online and in the real world.[133] The concerns seem similar to prior times.[134] Quackery survived the late twentieth century. Expenditures for quack treatments grew faster than the size of the population. The leading historian of medical quackery, James Harvey Young, reflecting on events of the late twentieth century, thought the young were more cynical and distrustful of modern institutions, "distrusted reason," and were willing "to flirt with wild varieties of unreason," reinforced by the negativism of the Vietnam War and Watergate, later by other scandals and national disappointments.[135] But consumer medical literacy, too, which had improved in the middle of the twentieth century, also entered a period of decline.[136] Young circled back, however, to an older notion that "whatever their capacity for being confused, Americans had entered upon a period of great preoccupation with keeping fit. Taking control of one's own health, in a variety of ways, amounted to a public passion," and the nostrum peddlers offered them products to support their newfound concerns.[137] In earlier times, the fact that "advertising ran rife in specialty catalogs, the magazines of unorthodoxy, and the scantily self-policed press," together with pyramid schemes and declining regulatory actions late in the century, all contributed to a renewal in medical quackery. Advertising "became increasingly sophisticated," with testimonials from trusted figures such as medical doctors, dentists, and PhDs, and with the products they introduced sounding like they had a scientific basis.[138]

Young reaffirmed a theme presented throughout this book, that the long existence of misinformation and falsehoods was carefully served up to the American public:

> Quackery has always been Pandora's box, constantly reopened with hope, never releasing a genuine benefit, although sometimes the opener is fooled into believing so. The box has an infinite capacity. Old cheats like before-and-after pictures and the fake diagnostic test come out wrapped in new tinsel.
>
> Pandora's box continues to be stuff with a variety of brazen health deceptions beyond recounting, perhaps beyond reckoning. Despite increased efforts at education, the perennial proneness seems not to have diminished perceptibly.[139]

So, the hope for a cure, the desire to fix an immediate problem without the complexity of engaging the health industry, and naiveté all played a role. Other critics pointed to a theme also permeating other facets of American life discussed in other chapters of this book—mobilization of political and social resources, and lobbyists and the media as major players.[140] Both hope and the inability to discern were behind this long history of patent medicines.

8

Information and Misinformation in the Tobacco Industry

Everyone knew but no one had proof.

—Robert N. Proctor[1]

In January 1954, Americans began to see in over four hundred newspapers a document titled "A Frank Statement to Cigarette Smokers," authored by an organization they had never heard of before, the Tobacco Industry Research Committee (TIRC). It began, "Recent reports on experiments with mice have given wide publicity to a theory that cigarette smoking is in some way linked with lung cancer in human beings. Although conducted by doctors of professional standing, these experiments are not regarded as conclusive in the field of cancer research." The statement went on to say that unnamed "distinguished authorities" have pointed out "that medical research of recent years indicates many possible causes of lung cancer, . . . that there is no agreement among the authorities regarding what the cause is, [and] . . . that there is no proof that cigarette smoking is one of the causes." The statement concludes, "we believe the products we make are not injurious to health." The TIRC pledged to assist in studying the issue, and "for this purpose we are establishing a joint industry group."[2]

With that statement, the leading American cigarette manufacturers publicly took on the growing swell of scientific evidence and public concern that smoking causes lung cancer. The industry made public its intent to operate a coordinated initiative to combat what its members saw as an existential threat to their multimillion-dollar business. From the first day, they had formed a strategy, written a playbook on how to proceed, and used it for decades with minimal revision. The initiative was less about developing good science than about executing excellent marketing and effective lobbying. In a 1984 version of the playbook, those in the industry were coached to argue that "there is disagreement among medical experts as to whether the reported associations between smoking and various diseases are causal," thus calling for more research to be done. Further claims were made that "tobacco smoke has not been proven hazardous to the health of nonsmokers"—a slight modification from the original statement since passive breathing of someone else's smoke had become a public issue. The playbook argued that opponents to smoking "frequently resort to scare tactics to make nonsmokers believe their health is being harmed by tobacco smoke," and "against this background of misinformation, public bodies are making rules about public smoking that intrude into personal liberty."[3] The briefing packet ran to ninety-nine single-spaced, typed pages, supplying evidence and counterarguments. The war against the industry's critics is still being waged today. In the past half century, the industry spent millions of dollars each year fighting the notion that smoking causes cancer.

The history of this battle for the survival of the industry was fought over whose information to believe. It was the first large example of an entire industry coming together to embrace a line of thinking and a set of facts that were known to its members to be false or at least misleading. This case is important because it became the model used in challenging climate change, health care insurance, mortgages and student loans, immigration restriction, gun control resistance led by the National Rifle Association, pro-voter ID law advocates, and those wanting to prohibit abortions, gay marriages, transgenders in the military, and child immunizations.[4] The same advertising agency was hired in a number of these cases.[5] In the next chapter, we review similar tactics employed by the fossil fuel industries, with some participants operating in both the tobacco and fuel industries. The tobacco industry's methods were applied by both industries and political parties. Similar methods were applied in US elections in 2016 and 2018.

The tobacco industry's activities are among the best documented misuses of information in American history, because nearly 5.5 million documents from various trial exhibits were ordered to be made public by a US Federal Court in 1998. Today, ninety million pages are available in an online searchable file known as the Tobacco Industry Documents through the University of California at San Francisco.[6] The case has spawned a rapidly growing body of literature.[7] We discuss the story by introducing the cigarette cancer issue, describing what the industry did to counter emerging research results harmful to its business interests, then exploring the kind of information it used and the arguments in which these techniques were embedded. We conclude by summarizing the evolution of contrary evidence from non-tobacco industry experts, covering that evolution in medical findings up to the end of the twentieth century. As with other case studies, understanding context is crucial in order to understand what constituted truth, misinformation, fake facts, and outright lies. In the particular cases of tobacco and climate change, we encounter highly educated protagonists who are not only experts in their fields but also capable of dueling intellectually with each other at a level of sophistication surpassing what was evident, say, with Lincoln's assassination or the sinking of the USS *Maine*.

SELLING "CIGS" AS BIG BUSINESS

Cigarettes were an invention of the nineteenth century, a mundane product that began as tissue paper and pulverized tobacco that one could roll up into a form that could be smoked. By the late 1800s, cigarette manufacturers appeared and quickly learned how to sell their otherwise similar products with aggressive brand-defining advertising. By the mid-1920s, and extending until the end of the twentieth century, large manufacturing firms appeared and made smoking fashionable through aggressive advertising and marketing. The flapper girls of the 1920s were seen as fashionable, socially edgy, and smokers; that image continued through movies and television shows for decades.[8] Packaging of cigarettes added to the mystique. For example, one brand was called *Kool*. The Marlboro Man who appeared in the Marlboro cigarette ads became recognizable to the vast majority of adults in post–Second World War America. During both world wars, American armed services personnel were given free cigarettes. Nearly half of all men smoked by the start of the Second World War.[9] Per capita cigarette smoking among those over the age of eighteen quadrupled between 1900 and 1940, while consumption among children and teenagers grew as well.[10] Cigarette manufacturers consolidated into ever-larger corporations in the early 1900s, as did firms in dozens of other industries in this era of conglomerate formation. Cigarettes had become Big Business by the 1930s, and cigarette consumption expanded rapidly into the post–Second World War era.[11]

Looming quietly in the background was an economic and social cancer that would infect the industry starting in the late 1920s. It became critical by the early 1950s and a chronic condition afflicting the industry for the rest of the century. The finding that emerged from the scientific evidence was that smoking cigarettes was unhealthy and that it killed smokers. It was a situation in which scientific facts clashed with misinformation, false facts, and massive advertising, marketing, and lobbying. It was an information-driven crisis, and we begin this story with the evidence that started it all.

THE CIGARETTE CANCER ISSUE, 1910s–1960s

Cancer had been recognized as a disease in the nineteenth century; and many of its variants were identified by the First World War, although it remained a rare medical condition. Medical research advanced rapidly in quantity, quality, and approach between 1870 and the First World War, and the United States became a leader in this kind of investigation.[12] As cigarette smoking became more widespread in the early 1900s, incidents of lung cancer rose and often proved deadly. Deaths per one hundred thousand males reached ten by the 1930s and increased by 50 percent during the next decade. In the early 1900s, it was not yet known what causes accounted for these deaths; the connection to cigarettes would begin to become evident by the 1920s. The death rate continued to climb, approaching fifty deaths per one hundred thousand men by 1960. Women contracted lung cancer at much lower rates because fewer smoked. Per capita smoking paralleled these cancer rates. Americans (mostly men) on average smoked 54 cigarettes per year in 1900, but by the early 1960s the number had skyrocketed to 4,300 cigarettes per year—and now women were also well represented in the smoking population. By the early 1950s, lung cancer had become the most commonly diagnosed form of cancer in men.[13] Before that, men had died in larger proportions from cancers of the stomach, colon, and liver.[14]

In 1912, Dr. Isaac Adler suggested a link between lung cancer and smoking.[15] Others pursued that link, and in 1939 Franz Hermann Müller at the Cologne Hospital concluded that lung cancer patients "were far more likely than non-cancer controls to have smoked." By the end of 1943, other research confirmed the link.[16] After the Second World War, further research reaffirmed the connection, permanently shifting the discussion from possible connections and coincidences to direct causes.[17] The apex came in 1950, when four studies appeared adding evidence of the link—two of them appearing in the prestigious *Journal of the American Medical Association*, which guaranteed these findings would receive public attention.[18]

Meanwhile, in the early 1950s, the results of a large longitudinal study circulated in the medical community and reached the cigarette industry, confirming that deaths rates for lung cancer patients increased by the amount they smoked. This was the study that finally caused actionable alarm in the cigarette industry. Conducted by E. Cyler Hammond and Daniel Horn, this study also appeared in the *Journal of American Medi-*

cal Association, where it received general media attention. The authors followed 188,000 men over the age of fifty, continuing their study until 1955. Hammond and Horn were emphatic: "The death rate from lung cancer was much higher among men with a history of regular cigarette smoking than among men who never smoked regularly."[19] This was what we might today call "Big Science" at work. Given how large the data set was, the findings were compelling to both the scientific community and the general public. Gone were the days when reports about the links included in their titles such tentative words as "Preliminary Report." Now, as the Hammond and Horn paper described, the subject was "The Relationship between Human Smoking Habits and Death Rates." Similar scientific findings appeared throughout the remainder of the century. It did not help cigarette manufacturers that, in early December 1953, Dr. Ernest Wynder at the Sloan Kettering Institute for Cancer Research published a report linking cancer and cigarette tar in mice. That story received widespread media coverage, including in the *New York Times*, *Life Magazine*, and *Reader's Digest*. *Reader's Digest* titled its story "Cancer by the Carton."[20]

During the 1950s, 1960s, and 1970s, the medical establishment came out clearly linking cigarette smoking to cancer. In 1957, the US Public Health Service supported the scientific evidence linking lung cancer to smoking. In 1962, the Royal College of Physicians of London declared that smoking caused lung cancer, leaving scientists and the public little room to argue that increased rates of lung cancer were only coincidental to the increased consumption of cigarettes. The American Surgeon General commissioned studies that took place in the 1960s and 1970s.[21] But the event that directly led to the regulations of the tobacco industry was the publication of a 1964 report by the US Surgeon General. This report ended with the statement, "Cigarette smoking is a health hazard of sufficient importance in the United States to warrant appropriate remedial action." The public paid greater attention to this than to other pronouncements by the health establishment, possibly because of the continuous press coverage of the problem over the previous decade. Over the next half century, smoking by Americans declined by 50 percent.[22]

RESPONSE OF THE TOBACCO INDUSTRY, 1950s–1990s

It was not the warnings of these public health organization, but instead the earlier Wynder study, that caused the tobacco industry to first take notice. Within two weeks of the Wynder report, the tobacco industry's CEOs met to discuss how best to deal with the existential threat that scientific evidence now posed to their business. On December 15, 1953, the

SMOKING *and* HEALTH

REPORT OF THE ADVISORY COMMITTEE
TO THE SURGEON GENERAL
OF THE PUBLIC HEALTH SERVICE

U.S. DEPARTMENT OF HEALTH, EDUCATION, AND WELFARE
Public Health Service

Figure 8.1. This is the cover of the landmark study published by the US Surgeon General on January 11, 1964, that became the most famous public statement by an American government official that smoking cigarettes caused cancer. Courtesy National Institute of Health.

presidents of six tobacco companies met in New York City to discuss how to counter the rising tide of evidence against their product triggered by Wynder's report. They were joined by John Hill, founder of Hill & Knowlton, one of the most successful public relations firms in the United States. Like the CEOs from American Tobacco, Benson & Hedges, Philip Morris, US Tobacco, R. J. Reynolds, and Brown & Williamson who attended the meeting, Hill was critical of government regulation of the industry.[23] He proposed that the tobacco industry collectively launch an information counterattack against the science being reported to the public. This industry had a long history of shaping public opinion about cigarettes, so his proposal could leverage well-honed skills.

Hill proposed to the tobacco executives that they create new scientific information to counter growing evidence that cigarettes killed people. He recommended an extensive and carefully coordinated campaign. Rather than turn to advertising, Hill argued that the industry must dominate the scientific conversation and not simply deny the validity of the growing evidence against tobacco. He proposed these firms embrace scientific research, fund more of it, and skew the evidence away from the negative. His aim was to promote skepticism and, hence, the call for additional research (buying the industry time), which would cast doubt on the certainty of prior evidence and build scientific controversy. The tactic Hill recommended was not for the companies to hire their own scientists, but instead to find academics who were already skeptical about past findings linking tobacco and cancer and fund them. The ultimate objective was to create in the public's mind the notion that the evidence of the dangers of smoking remained an open scientific question and was not settled. Hill believed the public would buy the argument, especially if the industry was seen as supporting further research.[24] The CEOs hired him to manage the process.

Hill immediately developed a plan that cautioned the industry "to exercise great care not to add fuel to the flames."[25] He urged these companies to establish the TIRC to communicate to the public "the facts" of smoking. In his words to the CEOs, "it is important that the public recognize the existence of weighty scientific views which hold there is no proof that cigarette smoking is a cause of lung cancer."[26] The companies immediately agreed to his plan. So Hill went about identifying skeptics in academia and elsewhere who could be recruited to stimulate scientific controversy. His agency moved quickly over the next several weeks to collect articles and citations of statements challenging the rising swell of anti-smoking sentiment and research. As one student of the process and of the committee concluded, "the call for new research implied that existing studies were inadequate or flawed. It made clear that there was more to know, and it made the industry seem a committed participant in the scientific enterprise rather than a self-interested critic."[27]

The committee worked in a suite of offices located one floor above Hill & Knowlton, with an initial budget of $1.2 million. It introduced itself to the public on January 4, 1954, only two weeks after the CEOs had met with Hill in New York. The message the committee delivered remained essentially unchanged for decades. With Hill & Knowlton's guidance, the committee established and closely followed for many years a set of talking points:

Research suggests there are multiple causes of lung cancer
Experts do not agree on the cause
Proof of smoking causing cancer does not exist
Statistics linking smoking to lung cancer could be applied to other facets of life, so the numbers are not trustworthy / accurate

The advertising that announced the establishment of the Committee explained the Committee's role as one of "pledging aid and assistance to the research effort into all phases of tobacco use and health." They gave this the trappings of scientific professionalism: "In charge of the research activities of the Committee will be a scientist of unimpeachable integrity and national repute," together with "an Advisory Board of scientists disinterested in the cigarette industry."[28]

Some forty-three million Americans, or nearly 27 percent of the US population, were exposed to this announcement. Hill recognized that by funding select scientists and shaping their research agenda, the industry could control the messaging and make these researchers dependent on the committee to continue their work. The industry was also instructed to proclaim its commitment to "public well-being," rather than degenerate into competitive rivalries over the quality of their products. The companies demonstrated strong discipline over the next half century. They cooperated with one another, maintained a unified front, and colluded. Ideas introduced in the "Frank Statement" remained the core message for decades.

For the next half century, the industry funded studies and reports intended to cast doubt and confusion regarding the safety issue of smoking. What made the industry's work notorious in the history of science, advertising, and corporate irresponsibility was the fact that it knew in 1953, and probably even before, that smoking was lethal. The industry succeeded in staving off government regulations that limited smoking, delayed warning the public of its hazards for a decade, and slowed subsequent efforts into the twenty-first century. The tobacco industry's lobbying efforts in Washington, DC, set standards for promoting special interests that were followed by other industries for the next half century. Court cases, and access to evidence made public in the late 1990s, laid bare this cynical use of scientific misinformation and confusion. Never before had an industry colluded to undermine scientific research on such a spectacular scale.[29] Even the highly successful marketing efforts and lack of verifiable results of the patent medicine movement of the nineteenth century had not coordinated efforts to this extent.[30]

Hill & Knowlton prepared for the committee its first major publication, released in May 1954, titled *A Scientific Perspective on the Cigarette Controversy*. It mailed the document to 176,000 doctors and thousands of reporters, with an initial print run of 200,000 copies. Its dissemination was a massive effort, unprecedented in scope in modern times by any industry.[31] Beginning in 1954, the committee hired doctors and scientists to add credibility to its messaging.[32] The committee, continuing to work with Hill & Knowlton, seeded large media outlets with articles and advertisements for years. Congressional investigators discovered that the committee and Hill & Knowlton even infiltrated antismoking organizations to uncover information to target.[33] Distinguished journalists were also recruited to the cause, most notably media giant CBS's Edward R. Murrow, himself a smoker.[34]

A parallel lobbying organization was established in 1958 to isolate the committee from charges of being biased. Called the Tobacco Institute, it quickly became one of the best funded and most influential lobbying organizations in Washington. It managed to slow and shape regulations despite the rising tide of evidence against tobacco. Every time regulators proposed or announced new restrictions, the Tobacco Institute flooded the halls of government with its staff, then funded massive advertising campaigns. The Tobacco Institute's mandate was to take the fight to the new battleground of politics as the old wars over scientific evidence were being lost.[35]

But the evidence against smoking proved to be strong, and by 1964 that fact was clear to both the public and government regulators. In 1958, a Gallup poll had reported that 44 percent of Americans were convinced that smoking caused cancer; by 1968, that number had grown to 78 percent. There was a rapid increase in public support for regulation. The US Surgeon General, Leroy E. Burney, issued a report warning of the dangers of tobacco that resulted in a 1965 law requiring warning labels on all cigarette packages.[36] The committee rebranded itself as the Council for Tobacco Research, operating until it was forced to close in 1998.[37] The industry kept pushing contrarian evidence throughout the 1960s, 1970s, and 1980s; and by 1990 its annual expenditures reached $20 million.[38]

Hill's efforts changed how one went about conducting public relations in many industries, including concern over the role of asbestos in causing cancer deaths in the 1960s and the role of chlorofluorocarbons (CFCs) in harming the ozone layer of Earth's atmosphere in the 1970s. In the latter case, scientists casting doubt on the dangers of CFCs even won a Nobel Prize![39] The value of scientific truth in American society had taken a great fall, thanks to the tobacco industry. As one student of the industry's tactics summarized its attraction: "Why correct bad behavior when you can simply deny the facts? Just cast doubt upon science and smear the reputations of your critics."[40]

In addition to the battlegrounds of science and research (addressed by the committee) and lobbying over politics and regulations (handled by the institute), the courts constituted a third front for the information battle over tobacco. Regulatory restraints on the tobacco industry did not come fast enough for individuals who believed their families had been harmed by cigarettes. As scientific evidence mounted on the deleterious effects of tobacco in the 1950s, so too did the number of lawsuits against the manufacturers. By 1964—the year the US Surgeon General finally took a firm stance against the industry—there were approximately thirty cases working their way through the courts. The litigants accused the industry of "negligence" and "malfeasance." The industry succeeded in winning many of these cases or having them dismissed, largely through heavy legal fire power and by demonstrating doubts about the certainty of scientific evidence. The potentially catastrophic impact of losing one of these court cases caused the industry to devote considerable attention to its legal exposure. Committee experts were brought to court as witnesses on behalf of the industry, arguing there was "no proof" that cigarettes caused deadly lung cancer. Even after 1964, the industry maintained its legal vigilance and stance right into the twenty-first century. Lawyers defending the industry warned cigarette manufacturers, their lobbyists, and the Committee not to shift away from their hard stance established in 1954, otherwise the courts might rule that the industry had made an "implied admission" that it knew of the dangers of cigarettes.[41] Moreover, there was concern that a softening of the industry's position would simply encourage a flood of new lawsuits.

What were some of the consequences of the misinformation campaign? Per capita consumption of cigarettes peaked in the United States in 1964, then declined precipitously. By 2010, cigarette consumption was down to levels not seen since the early 1930s. Lung deaths in men peaked in 1990, followed by a sharp decline. Deaths of women smokers peaked in the early 2000s and slowly began to decline.[42] As of 2015, some 15.1 percent of all adults in the United States still smoked (16.7 percent of men, 13.6 percent of women). As late as 2005, the overall percentage of smokers in the US population had been nearly 21 percent. That year 36.5 million people smoked every day (80.8 percent of all smokers), while the other 20 percent smoked less often. Level of education was inversely proportional to the percentage of people who smoked.[43] Considering that nearly half of all adults smoked after the Second World War, the percent decline was substantial, even if achieved slowly. The total US population increased after 1945, and while the percentage of smokers decreased, the actual number of smokers increased for a while.[44]

One industry goal was to replace lost smokers—lost to death or smoking cessation—by attracting new smokers; hence, the industry created a campaign targeting high school students. This is a story that parallels the discussion in this chapter about general population messaging, advertising, and use of misinformation. While the long-term trend of adult smoking declined from roughly 42 percent to nearly 17 percent by 2014, according to the Center for Disease Control and Prevention (CDC), the tobacco industry was having some success with this new campaign. As late as 1993, for example, a third of all high school students smoked, but only 25 percent of the adult population. Eventually, students also began to avoid smoking, and by 2014 only 15.7 percent of teenagers smoked as compared to 17.8 percent of the adult population.[45] These statistics suggest that the industry's strategy, while successful for a half century, was experiencing a long decline (with the exception of e-cigarettes, which is a story that is still unfolding).[46] As social media became prominent beginning in the 1990s, the tobacco industry ported over many of its methods and messages used earlier in print media and in TV and radio advertising.[47]

THE INDUSTRY'S ARGUMENTS AND INFORMATION

What did the industry tell the American public? What were its words, its language? Unlike other cases in American history where the messages— the stated facts—kept changing, as occurred with the assassinations of Presidents Abraham Lincoln and John F. Kennedy, the tobacco industry remained faithful to both its message and its language for decades. As new issues arose, the industry adapted its time-tested strategy and language to slow regulatory restraints on use of tobacco products, recruited new customers, resisted new evidence of the dangers of smoking, and added new arguments. Examining the text produced by the tobacco industry shows how it used facts and misinformation.

The appointment in 1954 of Timothy Hartnett, retired CEO of Brown & Williamson, as chairman of the committee resulted in a new press release:

> It is the obligation of the Tobacco Industry Research Committee at this time to remind the public of these essential points: There is no conclusive scientific proof of a link between smoking and cancer. Medical research points to many possible causes of cancer. . . . The millions of people who derive pleasure and satisfaction from smoking can be reassured that every scientific means will be used to get all the facts as soon as possible.[48]

In 1969, the chairman of the Committee, Joseph Cullman, argued that the "introduction of polluted air into the lungs, including cigarette smoke, is injurious to health" but added, "I don't think people really know" if smoking is harmful.[49] While the industry took the position in the 1970s that children should not smoke, it hedged its language. With respect to nicotine, which by then had been linked to cancer, one committee doctor, Robert Hockett, mildly argued that nicotine "and perhaps other ingredients in smoke reduced somewhat the efficiency of the production of muscle and other body tissues" in children.[50] As new objections appeared, the industry returned to its line of argument that it had relied upon since the 1950s. When in the 1970s it was suspected that smoking caused allergic reactions, the industry argued that "it has not been clearly established that allergens for man are present in tobacco smoke." Yet an internal committee report from 1965 had already reported that "certain tobacco effects . . . may be due to specific allergic susceptibility of particular individuals." In testimony before a Congressional committee in 1972, another industry representative admitted "there may be people who have an unusual hypersensitivity to tobacco smoke."[51]

The industry told the public that its members would modify their products should it ever be found that compounds in cigarettes "can be proved harmful, modern technology certainly would be applied in efforts to modify the product accordingly." In 1981, that seemed a reasonable position to take. In the late 1970s, however, in a short film the committee circulated, titled *The Answers We Seek*, the commentator argued that perhaps the personality of the smoker was the source of cancer: "it may be the smoker rather than the smoking that should be investigated."[52] Another industry publication, *The Smoking Controversy: A Perspective* (1978), argued that smoking was beneficial, particularly for those individuals who suffer from "critical levels of hypertension." The industry proffered other arguments during the 1970s and 1980s, including that smoking helped digestion, reduced anxiety and tension, and provided treatment for Parkinson's disease and aphthous ulcers. One industry doctor, Sheldon Sommers, stated in 1982 that smoking helped those with "severe psychic or psychologic[al] problems."[53]

When secondhand smoke began to be linked to lung cancer, the arguments made by the industry had a similar refrain: "It has not been scientifically established that smoking causes disease in nonsmokers" and when pressed by Congressional investigators, an industry spokesman acknowledged that a "statistical relationship" existed between smoking and health problems, but that questions on causation "remained open."[54]

Thirty years after the establishment of the committee, the industry continued to assert doubt and denials of the facts that now existed linking smoking to lung cancer. R. J. Reynolds Tobacco Company circulated a position paper on "Smoking and Health" in 1984, which neatly summarized the industry's arguments and use of information:

The fact is . . . smoking has not been scientifically established as the cause of any human disease. Scientists simply do not know the cause or causes of the diseases claimed to be associated with smoking. Nor do they understand the mechanism or mechanisms whereby these diseases develop. [Therefore,] R.J. Reynolds Tobacco Company has deliberately set out to put the controversy into perspective by setting forth evidence contrary to what has unfortunately become the conventional wisdom.

The position paper continued for forty pages, with more than two hundred citations of scientific studies, arguing for the harmlessness of smoking (see textbox 8.1). Each statement came with citations from scientific journals, US government publications, or other books and pamphlets—some of which were sponsored by the industry. The document presented similar facts and arguments regarding cardiovascular disease and chronic obstructive pulmonary disease. All these declarations were used in public presentations, Congressional hearings, publications, lobbying, and legal testimony. The consistency and discipline with which the industry stuck to these messages were reinforced by the kinds of detailed position papers prepared, such as the R. J. Reynolds brief.

But the industry's messaging was aimed not only at lawyers, Congressmen, and regulators, but also at the public at large (through advertisements). In a content analysis of cigarette advertisements from 1929 to 1984, Kenneth E. Warner of the Department of Health Planning and Administration at the University of Michigan concluded that the industry had responded directly to all the health concerns leveled at it by emphasizing health themes, which "tend to emphasize the 'technological fix,' such as the scientifically designed filter and the low-tar cigarette. Subtle changes in cigarette advertising include the elimination of visible smoke from ads."[55] The advertisements implemented three tactics: (1) "Focusing on nonhealth attributes of smoking," such as "flavor" and "satisfaction"; (2) promoting "less hazardous" cigarettes with less tar, so as one ad put it, "If you smoke and are concerned about your health, switch to Vantage"; and (3) "promoting smoking among women and children" because the number of men and boys not smoking had to be replaced.[56] The largest number of advertisements appeared in the 1970s, in an attempt to counteract the rising tide of evidence against smoking and the effects of the warning labels that had now (and for the past decade) appeared on every package of cigarettes.[57] The industry used rich visual images to support its three messages. These included models and beautiful scenery and, of course, most famous of all, the vigorous Marlboro Man, who drew upon the American admiration of cowboys and their association with "rugged individualism."[58]

The advertising worked, slowing the negative effects of the rising tide of evidence against the cigarette industry. For example, promotion of low-

---

Textbox 8.1. Tobacco Industry Talking Points, Examples from 1984*

- "Those who claim that smoking causes disease rely primarily on the statistical associations that have been reported between smoking and these various diseases. But they ignore the differences between statistical association and cause, calling instead for further research."
- "Those who assert claims against smoking also ignore the fact that the genetic or constitutional make up of the smoker, rather than smoking itself, could well be a better explanation for the reported statistical association than the smoking causation hypothesis."**

Regarding lung cancer:

- "recent studies have found that among workers exposed to various chemicals, the smokers had a lower incidence of lung cancer than the non-smokers."
- "Many investigators have found that cigarette consumption data in various countries do not correlate with lung cancer death rates in those countries."
- "A study published in 1979 in the *Journal of the U.S. National Cancer Institute* found a significant increase in lung cancer among non-smokers, both males and females."
- "Despite the claims, there are well-known scientists who maintain the view that smoking has not been scientifically established as a cause of lung cancer."
- "Researchers report many factors in addition to smoking to be statistically associated with the disease. These factors include personality, hormone levels, ethnicity, socio-economic status, diet and occupational exposures. However, which—if any—of these factors plays a causal role in the development of lung cancer is as yet undetermined."***

---

   * Source: R. J. Reynolds Tobacco Company, "Smoking and Health" (1984).
  ** R. J. Reynolds Tobacco Co., "Position on Smoking and Health," August 6, 1984, 2–3, Tobacco Industry Documents.
*** Ibid., 5–7.

---

tar products, which had generated 5 percent of all cigarette sales in the early 1970s, increased to 60 percent a decade later. Reluctant government endorsement of their use by smokers who simply could not give up their addiction helped as well. However, low-tar smokers often smoked more to compensate for the reduced levels of nicotine in the new cigarettes.[59] The public began to think these products were "safe." As one industry-sponsored survey in 1980 bluntly stated: "it has not been proven that smoking low-tar, low-nicotine cigarettes does not significantly increase a person's risk of disease over that of a nonsmoker."[60] One-third of the respondents reported not knowing if this was a true statement. In the 1980s, it seemed the industry had won its campaign; its advertisements brought back glamour, beautiful women and handsome men, success, sexual attraction, and sociability. Success was measured in an increasing number of smokers, even if the proportion of Americans who smoked was dropping.[61]

The battle continues today between government regulators and advocacy groups who want to limit smoking and restrict the tobacco industry's tactics of sowing doubts about the scientific basis for tobacco products being harmful, sponsored research, advertisements, and lobbying. One team of researchers exploring how the industry used information and arguments in the period 1990 through 2013 observed several behaviors: "The tobacco industry frequently claims that the proposed policy will have negative unintended consequences, that there are legal barriers to regulation, and that the regulation is unnecessary because, for example, industry does not market to youth or adhere to a voluntary code."[62] With respect to what the industry did with its information, several behaviors were evident to a far greater extent than, for example, when recommending an alternative strategy, litigating, destabilizing enemy constituencies, offering financial incentives, or forming alliances. Yet even these others strategies were deployed since the 1940s.

So what has the industry done with information since the 1990s? By then, the industry had a worldwide problem inasmuch as information about the negative effects of smoking had spread. The global response was essentially the same, relying on the playbook developed in the United States. The tobacco industry took on scientists, legislators, regulators, and advocacy groups and their lawyers around the world, often bringing to the fight more resources than academic scientists or non-profit advocacy groups could offer. The industry behaved in four ways in how it used information. (1) It conducted direct lobbying and correspondence with regulators and legislators. That involved producing white papers, publishing reports, presentations, testimony, and distributing alternative published points of view. (2) It deployed alternative lobbying methods, and by that means directed third parties and front groups to carry out the same tasks as the industry's own lobbyists. (3) As in the period from the 1940s to the 1980s, the industry shaped the body of evidence. It commissioned independent writers as well as ghostwriters as advocates of tobacco use and helped to disseminate their writings. (4) Increasingly after the 1980s, the industry established industry and policymaking collaborative initiatives, advisory councils, and other work groups, to work—"collaborate"—with regulators to formulate "sensible" policies.[63]

As in earlier decades, industry spokesmen did not hesitate to state as absolute fact that there was insufficient evidence to support a negative stance. Lobbyists argued that there was insufficient evidence to support behavioral changes intended by a proposed new regulation. Or, that restricting a marketing initiative would have no effect, because it was used only to differentiate brands and capture market share. This last argument was an old one used in the 1950s, when US regulators wanted to eliminate advertisements on radio and television (eventually they succeeded) and in more recent times, use of smoking in movies.[64]

9

Misinformation, Politics, and Climate Change

The underlying reality is that we are colliding with the planet's ecological system, and its most vulnerable components are crumbling as a result.

—Al Gore[1]

Hyped as an environmental nightmare, global warming hysteria is truly the environmentalist's dream come true.

—Christopher C. Horner[2]

If one believes that how information about the effects of tobacco use has been presented, misrepresented, and used to serve political and industry-specific agendas is complicated, that subject is diminished by the discussions concerning climate change and global warming. Our description of the tobacco controversy demonstrated that alternative points of view were buttressed by the use of true facts, selective data, misinformation, and lies, all embedded within strongly worded points-of-view publications, speeches, and legal testimony—many by organizations more keen on promoting a point-of-view than in sharing accurate scientific information. Between the 1950s and the 1990s, the tobacco war raged, but it is over, with only lingering guerrilla operations on the periphery of new technologies such as e-cigarettes and proposed narrow changes to governmental regulations. In contrast, the information battle over climate change lives on.[3]

The United States is currently in the thick of the global warming debate, but not the rest of the world. This debate began later than the tobacco controversy—in the 1980s in the United States—and it only shows a few

signs of closure. Many of the practices on display in handling information with tobacco have reappeared in the climate-change controversy. But
with climate change, the debate is at least one order of magnitude larger,
as measured by the number of think tanks involved, individual experts
and advocates, and number of publications. Instead of hundreds of scientists and doctors discussing the evils of smoking, we have thousands of
scientists conducting research on climate change. It is a global as well as
a national issue. The United States led the world in resolving the dangers
of tobacco, but it is not at the forefront of the effort to mitigate the human
effect on the Earth's environment. Americans are essentially at the same
point today with climate change as they were with the question of cigarette dangers in the 1960s.

The complexity of the topic, the number of people engaged with it,
and the fact that it continues today complicate the story of how climate
change information has been created and used. The scientific community
has overwhelmingly believed since the early 1990s that humans have
negatively affected the climate, and additional evidence accumulates each
passing year. By 2010, many large corporations had also concluded there
are economic advantages to supporting changes in products and behaviors to mitigate these environmental dangers. Meanwhile, cities, counties,
and states—but less so the federal government—have pushed ahead with
their own laws and regulations to address the concerns of scientists. The
debate has extended far beyond the keepers of truth and scientific evidence to involve politicians and their benefactors. For example, on March
9, 2018, the *New York Times* ran a story about the Trump administration
wanting to introduce the same kind of fear, uncertainty, and doubt that
mimicked the tobacco industry's playbook:

> The tension between the White House and the E.P.A. . . . . reflects a broader
> rift within the administration over whether and how directly to attack cli-
> mate change science itself. While the words "climate change" have been
> removed from many federal websites, and Mr. Trump has mocked global
> warming in tweets, the administration has stopped short of using the power
> of the federal government to attack the science.[4]

Nine months earlier Scott Pruitt, head of the Environmental Protection
Agency (EPA), announced that he planned to convene scientists to, in the
words of the *New York Times*, "test the scientific premise of human-caused
climate change." Reporters said this initiative was the latest of several
taken by the Trump administration to undermine academic research
at the EPA. One scientist at Texas A&M University thought reopening
the debate on climate warming was "like a red team–blue team exercise
about whether gravity exits."[5] By then, many surveys of the scientific
community had reported that over 97 percent of all climate scientists

believed in human-directed climate change was not only underway but also in advanced stages of destruction. In 2018, the United Nations issued a warning captured in a headline, "We Have 12 Years to Limit Climate Change Catastrophe."[6]

The topic is so partisan that, by writing this chapter, we may be accused of taking one side or another.[7] However, our goal is simply to place this debate in the long-standing patterns of the use and misuse of information evident throughout American history. While the topic is alive, active, and contentious, it is also a familiar story that shares many similarities with the other case studies in this book involving multiple constituencies who create and use truth, lies, selective facts, and misinformation. Context and motives shape the "truthiness" of facts, and climate change has proved no different.[8] To explain these points, we describe the global warming issue and its history, identify key actors, delve into their "facts" and how they are presented, and conclude with a summary of the characteristics of the information involved in climate change.

Climate change is a widely discussed topic, affecting large numbers of people in their daily lives. A few recent accounts make this obvious. *The Guardian* reported on March 20, 2018, that some of Britain's favorite dishes, "including fish and chips and chicken tikka masala could be under threat as a result of climate change, environmentalists warn in a new report on Tuesday." Warmer seas would affect the supply of cod that is essential to fish and chips. Earth Hour, "the world's largest event to protect the planet," reported other favorite dishes would taste different and argued people should "eat more sustainably." Weeks earlier, there was a press report with the headline, "Resigned Climate Scientists Say to Just Enjoy Next 20 Years as Much as You Can." A meeting in Geneva, "to discuss alarming new data on rising sea levels, a weary group of top climatologists suddenly halted their presentation Friday . . . and stated that the best thing anyone can do at this point is just try to enjoy the next couple of decades."

Climate change deniers, too, were in the news, presenting at another conference held in Washington, DC, what they believed would convince these committed foes of the existence of climate change. Quoting one of the deniers, "For us to accept that the average surface temperatures of the Earth has risen to critical levels due to mankind's production of greenhouse gases, we'll need to see some actual visible evidence, including a global death toll of no less than 500 million people within a single year." The spokesman, William Davis, added that sufficient data might be having 70 percent of all islands submerged and supercoil "tornadoes of category F4 or higher ripping through Oklahoma at least three times a day." Almost in response, the UN Intergovernmental Panel on Climate Change (UNIPCC) released its annual report in September 2017, listing every nation on Earth and the year in which it would become uninhabitable. Algeria, for example, would reach that point in 2027, American Samoa in 2024. The United States would face that reality in 2033. The UN agency hoped governments would start making "forward-thinking, evidence-based decisions about how and when to euthanize their populations."[9]

By the last line of the previous paragraph, it should have become obvious that something was not quite right, but the other stories appeared dead-on, at least until one reads more closely in these narratives—because all of these reports are fake. All were published by the satirical American online magazine, *The Onion*. All began with credible headlines and first paragraphs, and depending on whether one was a believer or denier of climate change, there seemed something credible in each story. The fish and chips story was accompanied by a photograph of this dish; the resigned climate scientists were pictured as a panel at a conference, complete with a vanity drape on their table, each with a microphone and a tent card with their names; while at the denier's conference, a photograph showed a large image of a dried up lake from a PowerPoint presentation. Each story paid homage to scientific facts, presented the story in an appropriate manner in which to display their evidence and point of view, and the last one even tapped into drought as a widely believed factor influencing climate change.

The satirical writers at *The Onion* are not climate change experts or even professional reporters. The point of this discussion about *The Onion* is that the topic of climate change is not subject to obvious understanding; truth, veracity, empirical evidence, and scientific findings are difficult to identify, authenticate, and even understand. Thus, misinformation, semi-truths (rising oceans will probably affect fish supplies), and outright falsehoods (the Geneva conference) are difficult to spot and often appear adjacent to real facts. That is one reason why the important topic of climate change has drawn the attention of so many advocates for and against it and why it also lends itself to a dissemination of a vast body of suspicious data, misinformed points of view, and political beliefs that have become signature earmarks of one's true allegiance to political parties on the right or the left, independent of the scientific realities of climate change. This has happened nowhere more so than in the United States, which, as of this writing in 2019, is the only nation to officially not embrace global initiatives to mitigate climate change.

WHAT IS CLIMATE CHANGE?

Even definitions are partisan, contentious, and have their own history. In the 1950s, scientists began observing increasing temperatures around the world, and early press reports spoke of "climate change." By the late 1950s, the latter label was increasingly being applied to the idea that CO_2 emissions were driving up temperatures and that humans were creating all this extra carbon dioxide, resulting in a "greenhouse effect." Documentation on temperature changes and the speculation of its impact led quickly to the idea that a large worldwide "global warming" event was in the offing. Then, in 1975, a scientist specializing in climatology at Columbia University, Wallace Smith Broeker, published an academic paper, "Climate Change: Are We on the Brink of a Pronounced Global Warming?" He presented evidence that "a strong case can be made that the present cooling trend will, within a decade or so, give way to a pronounced warming induced by carbon dioxide." Earlier cooling trends gave way to warming ones, resulting in "the exponential rise in the atmospheric carbon dioxide content" that "by early in the next century will have driven the mean planetary temperature beyond the limits experienced during the last 1000 years."[10] Because this prediction was made by an acknowledged expert in a leading scientific journal (*Science*), it caught the attention of academics and the national media. In 1979, the National Academy of Sciences used Broeker's phrase, "global warming" to describe the rise in surface temperatures and "climate change" to explain the effects of increased CO_2.[11]

This differentiation in the meanings is important. To be specific, *global warming* means the increase in Earth's average temperature due to rising levels of greenhouse gases, while *climate change* refers to a long-term change in the Earth's climate, sometimes of a particular region on the planet rather than the entire planet. In the 1980s, a third term entered the conversation, *global change*, which was increasingly used by the scientific community, blending together the two earlier terms. But it did not attract media acceptance, while "global warming" did. We use the two terms interchangeably in this chapter because that is the way partisans of the broader issue of climate change often do.

Meanwhile, scientists continued their research, uncovering additional and more varied evidence of climate change: changing patterns of precipitation, melting glaciers leading to rising levels of oceans, and changing patterns of drought (and the concomitant implications for feeding humans). The growing understanding led scientists and later protagonists of various points of view to refer to the entire subject as "climate change." Non-scientists also embraced the term, but for different reasons. If a lobbyist or proponent wanted to discuss global warming in the media, say, in February in Minneapolis or Boston, it would be challenging to get the public to focus on that issue: "What global warming? It's really cold outside today." So, those interested in sustaining interest in the topic found that "climate change" provided a more compelling tagline. We deal with critics of the science next, but they, as well, purposefully chose their labels, usually challenging "climate change" as speculation or inadequately linked to CO_2 levels, preferring "global warming" to the more ominous "climate change."

EMERGENCE OF THE CLIMATE CHANGE ISSUE, 1960s–1980s

In the 1950s and 1960s, environmentalists, which included scientists, concerned citizens, and public officials, focused primarily on short-term, local, narrowly defined issues such as pollution caused by oil spills, wastes dumped into rivers and oceans, and the threat of nuclear contamination. Nevertheless, there were also earth scientists working in both academic and government settings who were studying the Earth's atmosphere, changes in surface temperatures, levels of oceans, earthquakes, volcanoes, deforestation, droughts, and changing weather patterns.

Another stakeholder in the climate change debates were the fossil fuel companies, which began receiving reports in the 1970s that use of their products was introducing so much carbon dioxide into the atmosphere that the world's climate was beginning to be affected.[12] Exxon's senior management, in particular, received briefings during that period from its own scientists that the scientific community was rapidly coming to consensus on the dangers of CO_2. In 1978, one Exxon scientist reported to his management that "man has a time window of five to ten years before the need for hard decisions regarding changes in energy strategies might become critical."[13] This became a major management issue for Exxon in 1981, when the company was exploring the development of an oil field off Indonesia, which management knew within seven years would produce so much oil that the resulting CO_2 would lead directly to global warming. Like the tobacco industry, in the 1990s Exxon and other petroleum companies established an industry organization (the Global Climate Coalition) to resist the increasing alarms being sounded by scientists.[14] Exxon CEO Lee Raymond proclaimed at the 1997 World Petroleum Congress that scientific and environmental claims that CO_2 was damaging the environment "defies common sense and lacks foundation in our current understanding of the climate system."[15] ExxonMobil has continued to fight regulation and climate management up to the present, but by the early 2000s many other fossil fuel companies had figured out that resistance was useless and instead began to consider how they could benefit economically from the changed mood about global warming.[16]

The unfolding of climate change as both a political and business issue took time. Scientists first had to identify the problem. Between the 1950s and 1970s, scientific knowledge of the atmosphere and weather patterns expanded. It took from the mid-1960s until the early 1980s for scientific evidence and consensus on the effects of CO_2 on the atmosphere to attract attention of the petroleum industry and government officials.[17] As late as 1979, when organizers of the First World Climate Conference were extending invitations to participate, public officials showed no interest. A decade later, however, the US Congress was holding hearings on global warming, the UN General Assembly had taken up the issue, and some national leaders attended the Second World Climate Conference held in 1990.

One of the points of debate in global warming was the use of computer modeling. At MIT during the Second World War, Jay W. Forrester and a staff of some one hundred scientists and engineers began developing control equipment that evolved into flight simulators, and later in the 1950s into computers, which were used as national defense networks monitoring incoming enemy aircraft. In 1956, Forrester created the field of system dynamics and showed how computer modeling could be used to study the world's problems. In 1957–1958, sixty-seven countries participated in scientific projects intended to foster international collaboration, called the International Geophysical Year. It provided a model of how to deal with worldwide issues, presaging coordination over climate change for the rest of the century. The combination of increasing computer monitoring and modeling, coupled with the growing willingness of national governments to collaborate on scientific issues, gained focus when the Earth Day movement began in the United States in 1970 and spread around the world. The movement called for humans to protect the Earth's environment, steward its plants and animals, reduce pollution, and keep the air clean.

During the 1970s and 1980s, researchers began increasingly to use computer modeling to understand climate change. By this time, computers were fast and reliable enough, and memory devices were much more able to handle the massive climate data that was being collected. Based on the results of these climate models, scientists predicted global warming with increased confidence. (Beginning in the 1990s, however, these models became a point of debate for skeptics of global warming, who questioned their validity and accuracy.) Over time, the models became more sophisticated, leading scientists to increase their confidence in their results.

In 1979, the US National Academy of Sciences published a report arguing that if CO_2 levels continued to rise, there would "be no reason to doubt that climate change will result and no reason to believe that these changes will be negligible."[18] The United Nations engaged in promoting this point of view as well. The 1979 reporting became the first major statement that signaled consensus among the researchers. By the mid-1980s, scientists had documented other human (anthropogenic) behavior contributing to the greenhouse effect, such as the release of methane and nitrous oxides. Critical to the story in the 1980s was the accumulation of historical temperature records that made clear to scientists that the Earth's average temperature had increased since mid-century and showed no signs of reversing. These new data were presented at a half dozen worldwide scientific conferences between the mid-1980s and the early 1990s, with increasing coverage by the media.[19]

Between 1985 and 1988, scientists generated enough information about the subject to attract the interests of the public, government officials, and the petroleum industry around the world. Scientists in the United States and in Western Europe in particular persisted in bringing attention to the issue, translating their findings into nontechnical language circulated through general publications such as *Scientific American*, testimony at Congressional hearings, and calls on public officials. Scientific reporting, in a series of reports in the early 1980s, on the emergence of the Antarctic ozone hole caused by too much emission of fluorocarbons (CFCs), drew considerable public attention because it was tangible proof of how people were negatively affecting the environment. A heat wave in North America during the summer of 1988 added urgency to the issue. The three activities—activism by scientists, ozone hole, and hot weather—gave believability to those early scientists who were raising the alarm about CO_2 emissions.

Public awareness had increased so much that *Time* magazine labeled Earth "Planet of the Year" in January 1989. Scientists began using quantitative rather than qualitative measures and establishing timetables—calling for global emissions of CO_2 to be cut back 20 percent by 2005. They also called for an international treaty to enforce the altered behavior they were calling for, and advocated for the coal and oil industries to fund repair work on the environment. For those skeptical of the science or who felt threatened by it, 1988 was the turning point, much as 1953 had been for the tobacco industry. An existential threat to the planet had emerged, driven by rapidly emerging bodies of new scientific information.[20]

RESPONSE OF CLIMATE CHANGE DENIERS AND THE PETROLEUM INDUSTRY, 1988–1997

Until 1988, scientists were the main participants in climate change discussions. Then government officials increasingly became involved on both sides of the Atlantic. The United Nations and the World Meteorological Organization (WMO) established the Intergovernmental Panel on Climate Change (IPCC) in 1988. Two years later, the IPCC published a landmark report on what established science had to say about global warming. It reported that 170 scientists from twenty-five countries were "certain"

Figure 9.1.   This is the first worldwide report published reporting on climate change, 1979. This document launched a global initiative to address the problem. Subsequent reports of this kind continued to appear from scientific bodies over the next four decades. Courtesy United Nations.

that "emissions resulting from human activities are substantially increasing the atmospheric concentrations of the greenhouse gases carbon dioxide, methane, chlorofluorocarbons (CFCs) and nitrous oxide." The report predicted that global warming would increase: "we calculate with confidence that . . . carbon dioxide has been responsible for over half the enhanced greenhouse effect in the past, and is likely to remain so in the future." The report's key line, however, was that "the long-lived gases would require immediate reductions in emissions from human activities of over 60% to stabilize their concentrations at today's levels, methane would require a 15–20% reduction." If nothing changed, the temperature would rise by 3 degrees Celsius in the next century—more temperature change than had occurred over the previous ten thousand years.[21] The report called for additional measurements and studies of climate change.

The report received worldwide attention from scientists, the media, government officials, and skeptics. European governments as well as those of Canada, Australia, and New Zealand wanted to take action along the lines that had been used in dealing successfully with the ozone depletion issue. That included taking measurements and establishing numerical targets and timetables for remediation. The United States, by contrast, argued for additional research and establishment of national rather than international targets and mandates. The Republican Reagan administration focused on the perceived uncertainties of the scientific findings and the economic costs of addressing the warming problem. Public officials in many countries began proposing international laws for climate change and pondered what to do next. Governments moved toward agreement on collective action—other than the oil-producing nations, which objected to any international convention. The United States aligned with the oil-producing countries. The world pushed ahead, and the first important global convention to mitigate global warming went into effect on March 21, 1994. This included the subsequent negotiation of a global treaty (the Kyoto Protocol of 1997).[22] The Kyoto agreement articulated specific actions industrialized countries needed to implement in order to limit and then reduce their contributions to worldwide greenhouse gas emissions. As one student of the process noted, "linguistic debates became a proxy for political confrontations."[23] Considerable activity and debate occurred within the United States, and the nation often was an outlier in the international move to address climate change in the new century. With various points of view held in the United States, multiple constituencies chose as their weapons of choice scientific data, editorializing, political lobbying, and sometimes falsehoods and lies.[24]

ENTER THE LOBBYISTS, THINK TANKS, AND THE TWO NATIONAL POLITICAL PARTIES, 1990s–2010s

With scientists continuing to publish their mounting evidence of climate change and national governments around the world embracing these findings and negotiating international policies to address the issue, parties in the United States hostile to those developments swung into action. The earliest critics were fossil fuel companies; they funded a coordinated attack on the facts presented by scientists and opposed the Kyoto Protocol. Exxon and others sought out scientists who did not agree with the general scientific opinion about climate change and global warming, and the oil companies encouraged these scientists to provide alternative facts. The industry offered training to some of these researchers on how to deal with the media. The strategy was to persuade the media that climate science remained "uncertain" so that the public, too, would be uncertain and conflicted about climate change. This, in turn, would lead American government officials to resist enacting their own restrictions or approving international regulations. One observer of the process, Ari Rabin-Havt, noted that "the lessons learned from the decades-long fight waged . . . on behalf of tobacco companies were applied to the fight over climate change. The parallels between the two campaign efforts could not be more striking."[25]

Indeed, some of the participants appeared in both the tobacco and climate change debates. For example, Dr. Frederick Seitz, who had managed the distribution of $145 million in grants by tobacco companies to advocates of their cause, now supported the same process for the petroleum firms, despite the fact that by 2001 he was, in the words of one pro-petroleum supporter, "quite elderly and not sufficiently rational to offer advice."[26] This remark was made by a representative of the Heartland Institute, one of the leading think tanks supporting the industry. Fred Singer also worked with both the tobacco industry and the petroleum industry. Like a number of tobacco industry advocates, he was driven by ideological considerations, including repugnance of regulatory constraints. These industry advocates aligned naturally with conservative political beliefs in the United States. In the 1990s and early 2000s, scientific points of view became politically partisan, with each side using scientific data to defend their positions. The organizations that supported distribution of misinformation against climate change included the Edison Electric Institute, the National Coal Association, the Western Fuels Association, and the Information Council on the Environment (ICE). All of them were funded by corporations in their respective industries. They and their allies became known as "deniers"; their purpose was to confuse the public and cause people and politicians to question what was now overwhelmingly incontrovertible scientific evidence of climate change. The deniers collectively ran public relations campaigns, even commissioning advertisements, such as one by ICE: "If the Earth is getting warmer, why is Minneapolis getting colder?"[27] This was pure obfuscation, since local fluctuations in temperature did not contradict global warming trends.

Over the course of the 1990s and through the Bush administration of the early 2000s, the climate denial movement evolved from a goal of industry lobbyists and think tanks to being a core value of conservative politics, including of the Republican Party and later the Tea Party movement in particular. Facts no longer mattered, ideology did. Individual members of Congress became involved. For example, Senator James Inhofe (R-OK) ridiculed the scientists, even publishing a book titled *The Greatest Hoax: How the Global Warming Conspiracy Threatens Your Future.*[28] Inhofe was chairman of the Senate Committee on Environmental and Public Works. One of his staff members, Marc Morano, went on to establish a denial website, called Climate Depot. When *Rolling Stone* magazine broke the news of who was behind this website, it called Morano the "Matt Drudge of Climate Denial," named after the political commentator and news aggregator.[29] Morano advocated that one should "keep it simple, people will fill in the blank [with], I hate to say biases, but with their own perspective in many cases."[30] He and the deniers were effective, as he explains, because "you go up against a scientist, most of them are going to be in their own policy wonk world or area of expertise . . . very arcane, very hard to understand, hard to explain, and very boorrring."[31]

Morano had a point. Consider one example from the scientists intended for regulators, legislators and the public:

> To evaluate the magnitude and feasibility of needed changes in all these areas, we examined the result of a recent NRC study . . . which estimated the technical potential for aggressive near-term (i.e., 2020 and 2035) deployment of key technologies for energy efficiency and low-carbon energy production. We compared this to estimates of the technology deployment levels that might be needed to meet the representative emissions budget. This analysis suggests that limiting domestic GHG emissions to 170 Gt CO_2-eq by 2050 by relying only on those near-term opportunities may be technically possible but will be very difficult.[32]

Now compare that to the simpler version of a point-of-view advocated by the deniers aimed at the same audiences:

Yet, despite all this evidence [of global warming routine over the millennia] millions of well-educated people, many scientists, many respected organizations . . . are telling us that the Earth's current warming is caused by human-emitted CO_2 and deadly dangerous. They ask society to renounce most of its use of fossil fuel-generated energy and accept radical reductions in food production, health technologies, and standards of living to "save the planet."[33]

The volume of contrasting discussions increased in the United States and became increasingly vitriolic in the mid-1990s, peaking in 1997 when other nations around the world signed onto the Kyoto Protocol's guidelines for countering CO_2 and other emissions. The Democratic Clinton administration signed the agreement, but the Republican Senate did not ratify the treaty.[34]

The quantity of material circulating in American society on the topic of global warming also increased, with much of it skeptical of climate change. One study surveyed 141 books promoting environmental skepticism. One hundred one of them were published in the United States, mostly written by conservative think tanks and associations. Five were published in the 1970s, thirteen in the 1980s, fifty-six in the 1990s, and the rest between 2000 and 2005.[35] Scientists overwhelmingly carried on their conversations in peer-reviewed scientific journals, which were read primarily by their scientific colleagues, not by policy makers or the public. By the early 2000s, there were over fifty American think tanks engaged in discussing environmental issues, of which forty-five promoted skepticism on their websites; eight were completely devoted to the topic. Many of these sites also criticized other scientific studies, calling them "junk science," especially projects funded by the US Environmental Protection Agency (EPA). For example,

The *New England Journal of Medicine* now vacillates, becoming a propaganda rag on political issues but a scientific paragon when there are no political agendas to consider—lurching from outrageous dust and air pollution junk science to multivariate regression analysis of alternative causes of cerebral edema in diabetics with ketoacidosis. Which will it be?[36]

The anti-global warming think tanks were well funded and prolifically active. Many of them were devoted solely to the subject of climate change. Others represented conservative political organizations and, for them, climate change was only one of several issues they addressed. Doubter organizations included the American Policy Center, Institute for Contemporary Studies, National Legal Center for the Public Interest, Weidenbaum Center, American Council on Science and Health, Reason Foundation,

Pacific Research Institute for Public Policy, National Center for Policy Analysis, Competitive Enterprise Institute, George C. Marshall Institute, Junkscience.com, Frontiers of Freedom Foundation, Small Business and Entrepreneurship Council, and the Committee for a Constructive Tomorrow. Note that the majority of these organizations had bland titles that gave little indication of their purpose. There were a few more obvious ones, however. These included the Foundation for Research on Economics and the Environment, the Greening Earth Society, PERC—Property and Environmental Research Center, the Science and Environmental Policy Project, and the Institute for Study of Economics and the Environment.[37] Note their link to a fundamental argument of resistors: that government intrusion into economic affairs to restrict use of fossil fuels would harm the economy, the nation's prosperity, and personal liberties.

How did the American public view these think tanks, skeptics, and scientists describing global warming? Surveying the public about its opinions on global warming and climate change did not begin until the end of the 1980s. As the topic increased in public importance, the number of surveys did too; in fact, over seventy surveys were conducted between 2002 and 2013.[38] One common finding is that scientists had less influence on the public than did political and fuel industry advocates. The public expressed greater concern about climate change in the early 1990s than in the 2000s. Social scientists have explained these changing views in three ways. First, politically conservative Americans increasingly dismissed concerns about climate change as the amount of political negative media and activism increased over time. Second, how the media covered the topic affected public opinion. Mainstream media aspired to present a balanced view of an issue and so, when reporting on the topic, would present the consensus view of the scientific community that climate change was real, serious, and dangerous; but to appear unbiased and balanced, they would also present the perspective of a denier or skeptic. That practice made it appear to many media consumers that perhaps the science was still "unsettled," even though the hostile view represented only a very small contingent. Third, the views of well-known elites influenced people's thinking. These included Vice President Al Gore supporting the scientific view and President George W. Bush playing the skeptic.[39]

Some students of the issue also point out that the lack of public concern is explained in part by lack of public scientific literacy on environmental issues. The arguments of scientists are often not only jargon-filled but subtle; whereas the public often understands ecological issues instead in terms of their personal experience. An individual citizen may have experienced a drought and could relate personally to it, but understanding the complex long-term global aspects of global warming lie typically beyond the ken of firsthand experiences.[40] Also, individual experience with extreme weather remained mixed, as people had long understood that tornadoes, hurricanes, flash floods, and other severe phenomenon are "normal."[41]

Political beliefs and how the press covers them has had an effect on an individual's belief about climate change. Generally speaking, if someone is a Republican, they tend to dismiss or minimize the problem of global warming; and that has been the case since the mid-1990s. Similarly, Democrats, especially left-leaning ones, believe in and worry about global warming. Evidence for or against climate change was and is filtered through these political frames.[42] One scholar stated in 2016, "there is no dispute that over the past four decades, the major political parties have gone from consensus to polarization on the issue of climate change."[43] Members of Congress and advocacy groups have been particularly influential on public opinion, and media served as a link between events and collective perceptions.[44] As two media scholars observed, "the frequency of coverage and a story's placement within newspapers mattered more than the actual content of reporting in conveying the importance of the issue."[45] Economic factors also influenced people's opinions inasmuch as they were linked to political belief by liberal or conservative views of the economy.[46]

Public interest ebbed and flowed. In the early 1990s, the public generally thought there was a problem, that global warming was real. As the fossil fuel industry, its lobbying think tanks, and conservative politicians increased their rhetoric in the mid-1990s out of concern that the American government would embrace the Kyoto Protocol, the public began aligning their opinions along party lines. Since then, public opinions about the threat of climate change has remained fairly steady, when public concern increased. Both political parties developed actions on climate change. Al Gore released his widely read report, *An Inconvenient Truth*, in 2006 and the following year the IPCC released a document declaring that scientists overwhelmingly believed climate change was occurring and was caused by human activity.[47]

Public concern about climate change decreased after 2007, and it took a short-term nose-dive after a minor scandal known as Climategate (discussed in detail later in this chapter), in which some hacked e-mails by climate change scientists were released that questioned their objectivity, although these e-mails were later seen to have been quoted out of context.[48] For example, students of polling results concluded that promulgation of scientific information about climate change did not significantly effect public concern or levels of media coverage, even though how media covered an issue was profoundly influential on the public. The public read more about unemployment, economic prosperity, and America's wars. Heightened political polarization led to shifting political regimes with a nearly evenly divided base of voters. Recall that the Clinton administration, which defended climate change, was in power from 1993 to 2001; then the George W. Bush administration, which was hostile to climate change claims, served from 2001 to 2009; and then came another Democratic administration with President Barack Obama from 2009 to 2017, which supported taking action on global warming; followed by the Republican Trump administration, beginning in 2017, which has proven more hostile to implementing any mitigation of climate change than all prior administrations.[49]

Gallup polls usefully have used the same questions about climate change over time.[50] They confirm political polarization on the issue of climate change within the Congress. Party operatives strongly influenced public opinion about global warming. Scientific facts were of minimal influence.[51] The opinion gap increased after 2000, with Democrats more concerned, Republicans less so. The messages delivered by both sides were viewed through media trusted by the public, with less regard for its accuracy and more for its source. Liberals paid attention to what was discussed by the *New York Times*, MSNBC, and PBS TV, while conservatives listened to the *Wall Street Journal* and FOX News—both sides creating an "echo chamber" effect in which one's preconceived notions of the issue were constantly reinforced. The public rejected facts that ran contrary to their prior notions, while accepting those that fit their preexisting worldviews. Scientific facts did not usually matter, but when they did, it was with Democrats and other liberal thinking Americans and not with Republicans or other conservative-thinking individuals.[52] This behavior occurred despite the scientific community becoming more definitive in stating the case for climate change, as their data and research results cumulatively added evidence of the growing problem.[53] Gallup polls demonstrated that, if anything, the public generally believed climate change was probably real by the middle of the second decade of the new century but remained divided and conflicted on such issues as to what extent, how much humans played a role, and what to do about it.[54]

Harking back to the tobacco industry's strategy, the fossil fuel industry and its political allies sowed misinformation, distrust of the data, and outright lies concerning climate change to confuse large swaths of the public. The history of how the various protagonists interacted is a long and complex story for which we have only been able to give a summary here. Exploring the information and arguments used by all sides helps to explain how the public embraced facts, misinformation, and false facts. As had happened so many times in American history, opinions and arguments buttressed by selective use of data and other facts shaped what people believed to be true and how they used those findings, framing, and filtering evidence through their worldviews.[55]

THE SCIENTIFIC CASE FOR CLIMATE CHANGE

To understand the central role of information in the controversy of climate change, it is helpful to reflect on differences in this case from others in this book. While similarities with the tobacco industry's campaign may appear obvious, there are also differences. With climate change, differences of opinion among experts regarding phenomena and causes of climate change existed from the 1950s through the 1970s. Only with the accumulation of evidence from various lines of research did it become possible for scientists to reach consensus that the Earth's climate was altering due to increasing emissions of CO_2 into the atmosphere by humans and that the Earth was warming as a consequence. These various lines of research often involved scientists who normally did not interact with one another. For example, three distinct set of scientists examined ice samples going back thousands of years, studied tree rings, and documented weather patterns and atmospheric conditions. As their findings reinforced one another's work, a worldwide scientific consensus on the realities of climate change became sufficiently persuasive to motivate government officials, entire industries and companies, and individuals to either accept the reality of the situation and act on it, or instead to launch serious assaults on those who wished to mitigate this environmental problem. All factions weaponized their findings and points of view with numerically measurable data, extensive use of computer models, numerous publications, funding campaigns, and lobbying. Scientific data remained the foundation for this climate change controversy, not conspiratorial speculation or the highly selective use of facts, as had occurred around the Kennedy assassination or with the tobacco lobbyists.

The most distinguishing feature of climate change information was its scientific nature. During the twentieth century, Americans had come to respect the value of scientific facts. They had learned about how this kind of information came to be. People trained in science learned how to observe nature, describe what was occurring, and identify causes of natural events. They brought into play rational thinking, increased use of mathematics, massive collection of data, expanded analysis of this data thanks to more powerful computers, and acceptance of the scientific method of verification through replication of experiments. Although the scientific method was a creation of the seventeenth century, it had come into play in the United States to any great extent only beginning in the 1870s with the professionalization of science; while the application of a scientific approach to climate change and global warming had occurred only since the Second World War. Scientists worked out their methods and protocols. They created channels of distribution of scientific information through peer-reviewed academic specialty journals, formal training programs for undergraduate and graduate students, professional scientific associations and conferences, and conversations with many stakeholders: legislators and their staffs, government regulators, and fellow scientists in senior management positions in corporations, including those in the fossil fuel industries.[56]

Scientific findings emerged out of this information ecosystem. In order to appreciate the role of misinformation, fake facts, or outright lies, we first need to understand the kinds of scientific information that began emerging and how it was made public because "alternative facts" appeared in response to these scientific findings. Scientists were not shy about writing in support of the human role in climate change. Between 1993 and 2003, approximately 75 percent of all papers on the subject offered evidence of human involvement. While the skeptics dramatically increased their printed output, scientists contributed roughly 45 percent of all publications between 2004 and 2008.[57] Lianne M. Lefsrud and Renate E. Meyer, experts on the media of climate change, have suggested using framing as a way to define information on the topic. We apply their approach in the next several pages.[58] Framing is a method used to analyze information by topic and by its receptivity; it is another way of saying that people filter information through the lens of their prior beliefs and knowledge.[59]

Lefsrud and Meyer surveyed more than a thousand scientists and identified several categories of issues and roles. Much of their discussion centered on *diagnostic themes*, most notably identifying scientific evidence and human impact, with human contingency not widely regarded as having a major role in the way the Earth operated. They also considered *prognostic themes*, that is to say, arguments presented of greater impact of human activity with short-term effects, possibly risks to the public and personal life. This category included scientists' solutions to embrace the Kyoto Protocol and implement regulations. A third theme, which Lefsrud and Meyer labeled *action mobilization*, was an extension of the Kyoto argument, calling upon a range of engagements from the individual level to the international level to mitigate the effects of CO_2 and other emissions. Scientists were certain of their understanding of climate change; for them, the debate was over, climate change was real and it was time to get on with its remediation. As Lefsrud and Meyer noted, scientists viewed their work through the lens of their professional associations and the need for collaboration. They and others had to take responsibility for the problem, find answers, and take action. Experts were seen as being factual and unemotional about the matter. Their sense of professional identity was a compelling frame: they were expected to personally conduct research and report results. They expected other scientists to do the same, following the norms of science.[60]

In Lefsraud and Meyer's analysis, 36 percent of the interviewees supported complying with the Kyoto treaty and implementing changes in line with it; many publications endorsed this position, most famously those of Vice President Gore.[61] A second frame, embraced largely by the skeptics, was that nature is overwhelming and that climate change is a normal course of events.[62] Typical of this group is the quotation, "if you think about it, global warming is what brought us out of the Ice Age."[63] A third frame involved economic responsibility, of which 10 percent of those surveyed said they had not completely bought into the climate change argument, that it may not yet be fully understood, and so one should be careful not to do anything that harms the nation's economy. In a fourth frame, 17 percent argued that climate change was both human and naturally caused—the fatalist's thinking—and while these people were not fully convinced that scientific research had completely resolved the issue, they wanted to press on with additional study. In a fifth frame, scientists viewed the world through active regulation, arguing that the risks of climate change to humans was moderate, even less so personally to themselves. Thus, even among scientists, there was a range of perspectives underlining their research, publications, and use of information in public.[64]

A central tenet of those who acknowledged the existence of climate change was that humans were damaging the climate and the world should take immediate action to fix the problem. For example, in 2011 the National Research Council published a report for the general public, written in nontechnical language. It reported that "scientists have been taking widespread measurements of Earth's surface temperature since around 1880. These data have steadily improved and, today, temperatures are recorded by thermometers at many thousands of locations, both on the land and over the oceans." The report went on to note that many scientific groups were working together "carefully to make sure the data aren't skewed by such things as changes in the instruments taking the measurements or by other factors that affect local temperature."[65] The resulting data and analysis, it was reported:

> All show that Earth's average surface temperature has increased by more than 1.4°F (0.8°C) over the past 100 years, with much of this increase taking place over the past 35 years. A temperature change of 1.4°F may not seem like much if you're thinking about a daily or seasonal fluctuation, but it is a significant change when you think about a permanent increase averaged across the entire planet. Consider, for example, that 1.4°F is greater than the average temperature difference between Washington, D.C., and Charleston, South Carolina, which is more than 450 miles farther south. Consider, too, that a decrease of only 9°F (5°C) in global average temperatures is the estimated difference between today's climate and an ice age.[66]

Beginning in the 1970s, satellites helped scientists to create a global picture of changes in temperatures of water and land surfaces, as well as shifts in precipitation and land cover.[67]

In response to the question of how scientists knew that it was the greenhouse gases that led to warming, the scientists responded:

> As early as the 1820s, scientists began to appreciate the importance of certain gases in regulating the temperature of the Earth. Greenhouse gases—which include carbon dioxide (CO_2), methane, nitrous oxide, and water vapor—act like a blanket in the atmosphere, keeping heat in the lower atmosphere. Although greenhouse gases comprise only a tiny fraction of Earth's atmosphere, they are critical for keeping the planet warm enough to support life as we know it.
>
> Here is how the "greenhouse effect" works: as the Sun's energy hits Earth, some of it is reflected back to space, but most of it is absorbed by the land and oceans. This absorbed energy is then radiated upward from Earth's surface in the form of heat. In the absence of greenhouse gases, this heat would simply escape to space, and the planet's average surface temperature would be well below freezing. But greenhouse gases absorb and reflect some of this energy downward, keeping heat near Earth's surface. As concentrations of heat-trapping greenhouse gases increase in the atmosphere, Earth's natural greenhouse effect is enhanced (like a thicker blanket), causing surface temperatures to rise. Reducing the levels of greenhouse gases in the atmosphere would cause a decrease in surface temperatures.[68]

On the question of how scientists knew it was human action that was causing greenhouse gas concentrations to increase, their answer was, "once humans began digging up long-buried forms of carbon such as coal and oil and burning them for energy, additional CO_2 began to be released into the atmosphere much more rapidly than in the natural carbon cycle."[69] Other human activities, such as burning wood, also contributed. In the 1950s, scientists began to notice that the oceans were not absorbing this excess CO_2, hence measurements taken in the next half-century resulted in hundreds of reports about rising levels of carbon monoxide. The story was similar with methane and nitrous oxide. Measurements indicating "that about 45% of the CO_2 emitted by human activities remains in the atmosphere . . . outstripping the Earth's natural ability to remove it from the air. As a result, atmospheric CO_2 levels are increasing and will remain elevated for many centuries." Much of that CO_2 was found to have come from fossil fuels.[70] "Together these lines of evidence prove conclusively that the elevated CO_2 concentration in the atmosphere is the result of human activities."[71] All of these quotes were accompanied by tables and charts in a nearly fifty-page document.

The scientific community wanted to share its findings with government leaders in order to determine and implement a plan of action. Scientists ran computerized models of what would happen to the climate if temperatures rose at various rates for varying periods of time. Hundreds of these models were created in the early 2000s, with some variation in the results, but the consensus point-of-view was that ice would melt, sea levels would rise, coastlines would sink, coastal communities would flood, droughts would increase, violent storms would become more severe, and food crops would be threatened.[72] The National Research Council listed four consensus recommendations from the scientific community:

> Reduce underlying demand for goods and services that require energy
> Improve the efficiency with which energy is used
> Expand use of low- and zero-carbon energy sources
> Capture and sequester CO_2 directly from the atmosphere.[73]

Implementing these recommendations would "depend to a large degree on private sector investments and on the behavioral and consumer choices of individual households. Governments at federal, state, and local levels have a large role to play in influencing these key stakeholders through effective policies and incentives."[74] From those recommendations one could see how skeptics, deniers, and fossil fuel companies would be driven to band together to protect their economic interests and political beliefs. As the report noted, "robust scientific knowledge and analyses are a crucial foundation for informing choices."[75]

Writing from the political side, one major voice was that of Al Gore, the Senator from Tennessee who later became vice president of the United States and unsuccessful Democratic candidate for president. Gore had strong writing and political skills but no scientific background. Here is how he explained the scientific findings about climate change:

> The relationship between human civilization and the Earth has been utterly transformed by a combination of factors, including the population explosion, the technological revolution, and a willingness to ignore the future consequences of our present actions. The underlying reality is that we are colliding with the planet's ecological system, and its most vulnerable components are crumbling as a result.
>
> Not only does human-caused global warming exist, but it is also growing more and more dangerous, and at a pace that has now made it a planetary emergency.
>
> I [t] became clear that the Bush-Cheney administration was determined to block any policies designed to help limit global-warming pollution. They launched an all-out effort to roll back, weaken, and—wherever possible—completely eliminate existing laws and regulations.
>
> Two thousand scientists, in a hundred countries, working for more than 20 years in the most elaborate and well-organized scientific collaboration in

the history of humankind have forged an exceptionally strong consensus that all the nations on Earth must work together to solve the crisis of global warming. The voluminous evidence now strongly suggests that unless we act boldly and quickly to deal with the underlying causes of global warming our world will undergo a string of terrible catastrophes, including more and stronger storms like Hurricane Katrina, in both the Atlantic and the Pacific.

We are dumping so much carbon dioxide into the Earth's environment that we have literally changed the relationship between the Earth and the Sun.

The atmosphere is thin enough that we are capable of changing its composition.[76]

The message is unmistakably clear. This crisis means "danger!"[77]

Gore's admonition was the same as the one delivered by scientists, but he wrote in more apocalyptic language. He became one of the most widely read authors on the subject. His three-hundred-plus page book included photographs taken both on the surface of the planet and from space, as well as beautiful color charts and graphs of temperature changes. The battle lines were drawn, with the war on what to do fought on a battlefield of scientific evidence and hyped rhetoric.[78] Climate scientists and their allies realized that the opposition had numerous writers similar to Gore, and they worried. As two observers noted:

Not least important is how scientists communicate—or fail to do so. Reasons for that failure include what scientists talk about as well as how they talk about it. Narrative skills help reach people. Effective communication is usually not a lecture but a conversation that involves what people really care about. People generally care less about basic science than about how climate change will affect them and what can be done about it.

They observed that "climate change is often framed as an environmental issue, when it should more appropriately be framed as an issue threatening the economy and affecting humanity's most basic needs: food, water, safety, and security," with "a disturbingly large gulf between the research community's knowledge and the general public's perception."[79]

The language used by scientists often did not resonate with politicians, regulators, and the public, who were all less trained in scientific norms and idioms to appreciate the data the researchers wished to present. Scientists wanted to "enhance" while the public thinks they mean to "improve." Scientists spoke about "aerosol," while "the public believes these people are discussing spray cans." "Positive feedback" was a fine scientific phrase, but the public translated that to mean "good responses" or "praise." To them "theory" was fuzzy, connotating a hunch or speculation, while the scientific use of "uncertainty" meant ignorance and "bias" meant distortion or political motive. Scientists spoke of "values," which did not mean the same to the public because the latter viewed the word as meaning ethics or monetary worth. "Schemes," which had a very precise meaning to scientists, was translated by the public as a devious plot.[80]

The more media-savvy opposition, while its scientists were just as guilty of poor communications, used language more clearly understood by the general public. "Enhance," could be replaced with "increase," "aerosol" with "tiny atmospheric particles," "positive trend" with "upward trend," "theory" with "scientific understanding," "uncertainty" with "range," "sign" with "plus" or "minus," and "values" with "numbers" or "quantity." Words perfectly clear to scientists had to be replaced with less sinister meaning terms, such as "manipulation"—a scientific term—with "scientific data processing," or "schemes" with "systematic plans." Even "climate change" was often replaced with "global warming" (the original phrase for the problem), because it could be attacked in winter in a city such as Minneapolis or Boston. How protagonists used language helped to shape whether data (facts) were fake, misrepresentations, misinformation, or alternatives to what scientists offered. Truth became difficult to identify, as people filtered it through their political and ideological frameworks.

THE SKEPTICS' CASE DENYING GLOBAL WARMING AND THEIR EVIDENCE

During the 1990s, coal and oil companies, and their allies, fought back with a variety of tactics. An early tactic that later proved less effective was to criticize the scientists, inasmuch as mounting evidence of climate change led to wide consensus among them that the problem was exacerbated by humans. Skeptics and deniers were blunt and sometimes even rude in their language. For example, in a speech on October 30, 1997, David Ridenour, the vice president of the National Center for Public Policy Research, criticized the scientists: "The balance of evidence—to use the UN's lingo—now suggests that some scientists will do anything to ensure that their access to federal grants for global warming research continues."[81] Another climate change doubter tactic was to attack the peer-reviewed academic literature. For example, the conservative online magazine, *American Thinker*, reported that "*Science* magazine is run by a True Believer in global warming. . . . So you have to assume that in reaching [sic] *Science* magazine you're always reading the *New York Times*, and you always have to read for spin and bias. It's a breakdown of normal science, and it is potentially a disaster."[82] This prolific blogger had attacked what was arguably the most highly regarded scientific journal in the world.

Casting doubt about the scientists' findings in measured language also continued as a tactic of climate change doubters in the 1990s and early 2000s. A briefing document prepared in 2002 for Republican political candidates by Frank Luntz, a Republican strategist, provided the following talking points:

> The scientific debate remains open. Voters believe there is no consensus about global warming within the scientific community. . . . Therefore, you need to continue to make the lack of scientific certainty a primary issue in the debate, and defer to scientists and other experts in the field.
>
> We must not rush to judgment before all the facts are in. We need to ask more questions. We deserve more answers. And until we learn more, we should not commit America to any international document that handcuffs us either now or into the future.[83]

However, at the time in 2002 when these talking points were written, consensus in the scientific community across multiple academic disciplines already existed.

If one steps forward to the period 2005–2009, by which time much of the antiglobal warming rhetoric had been polished and codified for over a decade, we can see clearly the skeptical arguments on full display, particularly the use of misinformation and frontal attacks. Consider an example from Christopher C. Horner, who was a Senior Fellow at the Competitive Enterprise Institute, a conservative Republican foundation established to provide "pro-business" policy statements.[84] His attack on the environmentalists went as follows:

> Al Gore and his friends . . . declare "global warming" an unprecedented global crisis. Hyped as an environmental nightmare, global warming hysteria is truly the environmentalist's dream come true. It is the perfect storm of demons and perils, and the ideal scare campaign for those who would establish "global governance" . . . with strict control over corporate actions and individual behavior.
>
> Environmentalism has served for decades as the best excuse to increase government control over your actions, in ways both large and small: It's for Mother Earth! It's for the whales! But standard, run-of-the mill environmental scares of the past proved to be of finite utility. Most pollution issues are relatively local—confined to individual sites or even regions. The bigger-ticket items—acid rain, the ozone hole—had been addressed and simply weren't ripe for revisiting until the next generation.
>
> Global warming possesses no such weaknesses. Not only is planetary existence on the line, but with global warming, the greens can argue that greenhouse gas emissions in Ohio threaten people in Paris. Global problems demand global solutions, they argue, thus helping to bypass the irritating obstacles by sovereignty and democratic decision-making.
>
> Upon review, however, it turns out that if global warming were as bad as they say then no policy imaginable . . . could "solve" it. According to the greens' own numbers, worldwide deindustrialization is absolutely critical—given available and even foreseeable energy technologies—if we are to save the planet. This explains the mantra honed during prior alarms, that "we

must act now!" Indeed, with "global warming," no matter how much we sacrificed there would still be more to do. It is the bottomless well of excuses for governmental intervention and authority.[85]

After criticizing Gore for his prescriptions (and lack thereof), this anti–climate change partisan continues, "expert opinion remains clear: at the least we'll see massively higher costs and direct or indirect energy rationing." Then turning to attack the scientific community, "they declare there is 'consensus,' a political concept generally alien to the scientific method. They liken skeptics to Holocaust deniers and demand "Nuremberg-style" trials of the disbelievers. They want to control our lifestyles—and they don't want you to question their cause."[86] The "Greens" were now the new Communists in the post–Cold War Era: "When communism didn't work out, environmentalism became the anti-capitalist vehicle of choice, drawing cash and adoration from business, Hollywood, media, and social elites. Environmental pressure groups have boomed into a $2 billion industry."[87] The attacks on the messengers of global warming had a striking similarity to the attacks used by tobacco industry lobbyists on the role of cigarettes in causing cancer.

Another tactic involved challenging the "alarmist" view of climate change. Skeptics quoted many types of evidence to deny the severity of the problem, such as American government statistics that air pollution had been declining for years while the number of miles driven by citizens had increased.[88] Alarmists were accused of "cherry-picking data," arguing that "the EPA now brazenly and routinely selects [*sic*] the interpretation . . . of a set of data that can justify its power grab."[89] Critics accused the EPA of manipulating evidence in various ways, "for example by simply funding huge numbers of scientifically shoddy studies," many of which were observational rather than experimental: "these studies try to find a correlation between some sort of malady and a particular pollutant or emission. Showing a correlation, however, is hardly a proof of causation."[90] Linking bad method to people with an agenda helped shape the narrative critical of global warming evidence.

Critics of the global warming argument characterized its key tenets as "myths." These included:

pro–climate change lists about rising temperatures that the 1990s were the "hottest" decade on record
the science is "settled" with CO_2 causing the warming
the climate was stable until humans walked the Earth
glaciers were melting
sea levels were rising
the weather change represented the greatest threat to the poor
there would be more violent storms

In each instance, scientific evidence had, in fact, demonstrated these were not myths. But in each case, enemies offered counterarguments. Two examples illustrate how they marshaled information to offer alternative perspectives.

In the case of rising temperatures, critics argued that it matters which baseline you choose. While the temperatures in the early 2000s were warmer than in the 1970s, they were cooler than in the 1930s or even in the year 1000 A.D.[91]

What did the skeptics say about the role of CO_2 as a cause of global warming?

Historically, atmospheric CO_2 typically increases *after* warming begins, not *before*. The most common effort to dodge an actual debate over the causes of global warming is to claim that we had the debate, it is over, and there is "consensus" (about *what* is left unspoken). If it is really settled, why don't the scientists forgo the $5 billion in taxpayer money they get every year to research climate? What scientists *do* agree on is little and says nothing about Manmade global warming. Namely, they agree that (1) global average temperature is probably 0.6° Celsius—or 1° Fahrenheit—higher than a century ago; (2) atmospheric levels of carbon dioxide (CO_2) have risen by about 30 percent over the past two hundred years; (3) CO_2 is a greenhouse gas, and greenhouse gases should have a warming effect, all else being equal (which it demonstrably is not). Regardless, "consensus" is the stuff of politics. It means ending debate in order to "move on." Stifling debate is inherently antiscientific.[92]

The climate change skeptics marshalled numerous arguments that ranged from questions about whether there was global warming, to the economic costs of rectification, to the causes of global warming, to the validity of computer modeling. See textbox 9.1 for some of their most common arguments.

Another important line of reasoning put forth by the Deniers is that the Earth routinely cools and heats and that today's rise in temperatures is more a product of that process than of human activities. Two leading lights of the Denier movement wrote and spoke frequently on this topic: S. Fred Singer, a professor at George Mason University, and Dennis T. Avery, a senior fellow at the Hudson Institute. Their basic argument held that "the Earth is warming but physical evidence from around the world tells us that human-emitted CO_2 (carbon dioxide) has played only a minor role in warming. Instead, the mild warming seems to be part of a natural 1,500-year climate cycle ($\pm$500 years) that goes back at least one million years."[93] They cited various climate studies to defend that chronology. They argued further that the Earth's climate will remain moderate for decades to come, consistent with ancient patterns of temperature modulation. So, asking people to give up energy to alter the world's temperature—to "save the planet"—makes no sense. Why should people give up

---

Textbox 9.1. Common Argument of Climate Change Skeptics
- The science remained unsettled.
- Warming occurred in parts of the world, not all over the planet.
- This pattern of warming in select places has been going on for thousands of years.
- The extent of the warming remains uncertain.
- Some glaciers are increasing in size.
- Adoption of the Kyoto protocols would cost the average American family between \$1,300 and \$3,000 each year [citing MIT studies that the MIT authors countered were misquoted, as these costs would be closer to \$13].*
- Humans were not the only creators of greenhouse gases, and scientists left out of their considerations (not true), other sources such as the large number of cattle, plants, and even humans ("typically after a meal of Mexican food") that exude methane gas—in short, arguing that most CO_2 emissions are natural.**
- Computer models are suspect—"as with any model, [these climate models] can be designed to produce whatever outcome is desired." In particular, these models were dismissed as inaccurate because they forecasted linear growth in CO_2 emissions.***

---

* Aaron M. McCright and Riley E. Dunlap, "Challenging Global Warming as a Social Problem: An Analysis of the Conservative Movement's Counter-Claims," *Social Problems* 47, no. 4 (November 2000): 515–17; Horner, *The Politically Incorrect Guide™ to Global Warming and Environmentalism*, 245–70.
** Horner, *The Politically Incorrect Guide™ to Global Warming and Environmentalism*, 68.
*** A point of clarification: models have relied extensively on being able to document the timing of when the Earth's temperature rose, and by how much, to the amount of CO_2 in the air over the past 800,000 years. Air bubbles for each year going back that far were trapped in ice, which have been measured, quantified, and compared to evidence of temperature changes. Patterns—correlations—between the two were consistent for the entire period, that is to say, if CO_2 increased in the atmosphere, so too did temperatures at consistently predictable rates over the entire period, making it possible to project out a mere fifty to one hundred years with confidence what one could expect. Further, CO_2 generated from fossil fuels has a different fingerprint than other natural forms, and samples of both were also trapped in ice and snow, providing evidence that manmade CO_2 emissions had occurred at sharply rising rates since the 1700s.

---

their improved quality of life, the benefits of scientific and technological creations, and their economic fruits? "Massive human sacrifices would be required to meet the CO_2 stabilization goals of the Kyoto Protocol."[94]

They relied on fear, uncertainty, and doubt to buttress their argument:

> Suppose the world went all-organic in its farming, gave up the man-made fertilizer, and cleared half of the world's remaining forests for more low-yield crops. It's reasonable to expect that half the world's wildlife species would be lost in the land clearing and one-fourth of the world's people would succumb to malnutrition. What if research then confirmed that the climate was warming due to the natural cycle instead of CO_2? Is that a no-regrets climate insurance policy?

> What if the Kyoto treaty or some similar arrangement prevented the Third World from moving away from using wood for heating and cooking? How much additional forest would then be sacrificed for firewood in the developing countries over the next fifty years?

The stakes in the global warming debate are huge. Humanity and wildlife may both be losing the debate.[95]

Singer and Avery cited the comments of others willing to engage with the pro-global warming scientists:

The study, appearing in the March 21 issue of the journal *Science*, analyzed ancient tree rings from 14 sites on three continents in the northern hemisphere and concluded that temperatures in an era known as the Medieval Warm Period some 800 to 1,000 years ago closely matched the warming trend of the 20th century.

Hurricanes, brutal cold fronts and heat waves, ice storms and tornadoes, cycles of flood and drought, and earthquakes and volcanic eruptions are not unforeseeable interruptions of normality. Rather, these extremes are the way that the planet we live on does its business. . . . What we call "climate" is really an average of extremes of heat and cold, precipitation and drought . . . .

[T]he number of major [Chinese] floods averaged fewer than four per century in the warm period of the ninth through eleventh centuries, while the average number was more than double that figure in the fourteenth through seventeenth centuries of the Mini Ice Age.[96]

Deniers felt comfortable challenging hard scientific evidence by engaging in a discussion of both historical and scientific evidence as the data on global warming increased. As an example of working with temperature data, consider this reasoning (presented in 2006) by Singer and Avery:

The Earth has recently been warming. This is beyond doubt. It has warmed slowly and erratically—for a total of about 0.8 degrees Celsius—since 1850. It had one surge of warming from 1850 to 1870 and another from 1920 to 1940. However, when we correct the thermometer records for the effects of growing urban heat islands and widespread intensification of land use, and for the recently documented cooling of the Antarctic continent over the past thirty years, overall world temperatures today are only mostly warmer than they were in 1940, despite a major increase in human CO_2 emissions.[97]

The same authors argued that the "Alarmists":

Don't have much evidence to support their position—only (1) the fact that the Earth is warming, (2) a theory that doesn't explain the warming of the past 150 years very well, and (3) some unverified computer models. Moreover, their credibility is seriously weakened by the fact that many of them have long believed modern technology should be discarded whether the Earth is warming too fast or not at all.[98]

Adding to this logic, critics claimed that "polls of climate-qualified scientists show that many doubt the scary predictions of the global computer models"—in short, that "there is no scientific consensus."[99] "Why have humans chosen to panic about the planet returning to what is very probably the finest climate the planet has known in all its millions of years? Is it simply guilt because climate alarmists told us we humans were causing the change?"[100]

An economic argument *in favor* of global warming emerged as early as 2000. In testimony before a Senate committee, Yale Economist Robert Mendelson argued, "Climate change is likely to result in small net benefits for the United States over the next century. The primary sector that will benefit is agriculture. The large gains in this sector will more than compensate for damages expected in the coastal, energy, and water sectors, unless warming is unexpectedly severe."[101]

When Skeptics attacked the "consensus" argument, they accused its defenders of being dependent on "discredited reports, character assassinations, and fake experts." Their literature, texts of speeches, and testimony to Congressional committees over the past four decades is voluminous. See textbox 9.2.

Historian of science Naomi Oreskes, who was an accepted source for the case of consensus, became a target of criticism from the political right, Skeptics, and Deniers. She had reported being unable to find any refutations of global warming. Her critics responded:

> She didn't really look that hard, though. She conducted a computer search for articles in peer-reviewed scientific journals that contained the phrase "global climate change." She found 928 since 1993. None challenged the

---

Textbox 9.2.   Message to Congress of Climate-Change Skeptics

- "research. . . that a few, typically, quite narrow, areas of general agreement do exist regarding climate change"
- many websites demonstrate the debate is diverse and unsettled
- "most areas of scientific agreement are trivial and uncontroversial"
- implementing the Kyoto Protocol will be expensive and disruptive and not result in much improvement
- consensus is "wishful thinking cut from whole cloth, or mischaracterize the scientific research incorporated in reports by the United Nations Intergovernmental Panel on Climate Change (IPCC) or U.S. National Academy of Sciences (NAS)"*
- The NAS report's arguments of consensus were portrayed as representing, "a consensus of government representatives . . . rather than of scientists. The resulting document has a strong tendency to disguise uncertainty, and conjures up some scary scenarios for which there is no evidence."**

---

* Christopher C. Horner, *The Politically Incorrect Guide to Global Warming and Environmentalism* (Washington, DC: Regnery Publishing, 2007), 82–83.
** "The Press Gets It Wrong: Our Report Doesn't Support the Kyoto Treaty," *Wall Street Journal*, June 11, 2001.

scientific consensus on global warming. She claimed to have searched for all articles using the phrase "climate change"—a search that would have yielded about 10,000 more articles.[102]

Criticism of her work continued:

> In reality most of the 928 papers do not even mention anthropogenic global warming, let alone confirm alarmism in their conclusions. Her search parameters limited the universe of literature to 928 papers. Furthermore, some papers merely assumed for their purposes that rising CO_2 levels from burning hydrocarbons will affect the climate, as opposed to having research findings establishing this. Most didn't present any analysis or conclusions at all about it.[103]

Skeptics and Deniers argued that the facts that Oreskes was a historian and had no environmental policy experience compromised her credibility. They further argued that if she had conducted a "proper" search, she would have reached a different conclusion. She was portrayed as part of a larger group of "false experts" on climatology:

> The experts invoked to proclaim alarm often are merely experts in that which purportedly would be impacted by the outcome the alarmists predict. That is, the alarmists tell us that the planet will heat up, and then they bring out an owl specialist to say what a hot planet would do to owls. Voters get an earful of scary stories about the extinctions, migration, and so on in the event the alarmists are right.[104]

Continuing this argument, the Skeptics posited, "when it suits the alarmists' needs, a geologist suffices as a 'climate scientist.'"[105]

Just as the pro-climate change community criticized the media for giving the skeptics too much attention in order to provide what appeared to be balanced reporting, the opposition also found fault with the press. For example, "The need to sell copy or attract viewers, together with the general government-as-savior leanings and resentment of real businessmen, drive the media to embrace—in fact *drive*—environmental and climate alarmism."[106] Joel Schwartz at the American Enterprise Institute complained, "through exaggeration, omission of contrary evidence, and lack of context, regulators, activists and even many health scientists misrepresent the results of air pollution health studies and the overall weight of the evidence from research literature."[107] Critics linked air pollution to CO_2 emission discussions beginning in the 1990s. Stories about the environment were labeled "science-by-anecdote." The *New York Times* came in for ongoing criticism for exaggerating global warming.[108] The Skeptics complained that the press exaggerated, often through their headlines. One example from *ABC News* illustrates their point: "Will the

Earth Become Too Hot? Are Our Children in Danger?"[109] Gore's video about global warming led the political right to complain that "the press embarrassingly fawns over" his movie. "Ratings-starved cable news and entertainment industries pile on, with even FOX News Channel and HBO presenting alarmist specials." In 2006 the Weather Channel began broadcasting "alarmist" stories and entire programs, such as "The Climate Code," and "It Could Happen Tomorrow." The political left routinely linked cyclical solar activity to global warming, while the right reminded its supporters that such activity was normal and had been for eons.[110]

The most extensive conversation generated by the right in the first decade of the new century centered on Gore's *An Inconvenient Truth.* It is useful to summarize key criticisms of his presentation within the context of factual misrepresentations and falsehoods, often the two combined. These criticisms largely centered around what his critics believed he left out, his sins of omission. See textbox 9.3. As one critic put it, "Gore uses apocalyptic rhetoric to make the case for global warming as a colossal threat."[111]

Gore was only one target of the Right's ire. Two other issues particularly attracted their attention: the Kyoto Protocol, because it called for more regulations to reduce use of energy with its negative economic impact on companies, individuals, and the economy, not to mention the right of people to thrive without regulatory constraints; and a controversy known as Climategate. The latter is worth exploring briefly as another ex-

---

Textbox 9.3. Criticisms of Al Gore's *An Inconvenient Truth*

- Scientific evidence that was not settled
- Methods—proxies—used to estimate weather in earlier eras
- Reduced energy consumption that would make people safer from hurricanes
- Ignoring the costs of policies, such as the Kyoto agreement
- Ignoring other causes of weather-related damages, such as people living increasingly in flood plains and along ocean coastlines
- Ignoring recent warming trends that were milder than the models showed
- Relying on climate models that predict the most extreme scenarios
- Omitting to mention that Greenland was equally warm in the 1920s as today, heating up faster at that time than during the 1990s and early 2000s
- Ignoring that the Artic was warmer in the early phase of the Holocene Epoch of today
- Accepting that CO_2 patterns links to the Earth's temperature rises and falls (evidence that the Skeptics reject)
- Ignoring that ice sample evidence shows other times with higher temperatures
- Misrepresenting how CO_2 contributes to greenhouse effects*

---

* Christopher C. Horner, *The Politically Incorrect Guide to Global Warming and Environmentalism* (Washington, DC: Regnery Publishing, 2007), 214–17.

ample of how the political left and climate scientists thought the Deniers and their confederates manipulated information and misinformation to their advantage. In 2009, the American presidency and both houses of Congress were in Democratic control, that is to say in the control of the pro-climate change politicians. The Obama administration wanted to regulate energy use and the Kyoto Protocol beckoned. The Tea Party movement on the far political right emerged as part of a broad campaign of resistance to the Democrats, and to President Obama in particular; and its members generally thought that global warming was a "hoax." This far right contingent of the Republican Party was on its way to dominating conservative politics. A climate bill working its way through Congress ultimately failed to pass, but in the process lobbyists on both ends of the political spectrum advocated their points of view. World leaders were also gathering to discuss a global climate treaty.

As the conference in Copenhagen was about to convene, word surfaced of a cache of hacked e-mails from the University of East Anglia in England. These were thousands of e-mails sent back and forth among climate scientists concerning their work. Excerpts from these e-mails quickly made it into the blogs of skeptics, who claimed that these e-mails showed that scientists had manipulated data to demonstrate that the Earth was warming thanks to human activity.[112] While this claim of data manipulation was eventually shown to be false, the skeptics relished the e-mail excerpts they published. The episode was quickly dubbed Climategate.[113] As the creator of the term wrote, "The conspiracy behind the Anthropogenic Global Warming myth . . . has been suddenly, brutally and quite deliciously exposed," drawn from the university's Climate Research Unit, involving some sixty-two megabytes of files.[114] The term "Climategate" spread widely through the Internet in a matter of days. As one student of the controversy later noted, "Those skeptical of climate change viewed the scandal as definitive proof of their wildest fantasy—that scientists around the world had concocted a global warming hoax."[115] Public belief in climate change declined, skepticism rose, and trust in scientists eroded over the next year, largely driven by attacks from individuals with conservative political views. Fox News mentioned Climategate almost every time its reporters ran a story about the climate. As its managing editor in Washington instructed his staff, "Given the controversy over the veracity of climate change data, we should refrain from asserting that the planet has warmed (or cooled) in any given period without IMMEDIATELY pointing out that such theories are based upon data that critics have called into question."[116]

What was in the scientists' e-mails? The first batch comprised over one thousand messages written between 1996 and 2009. A curated selection of those were distributed through various websites, with phrases taken out of context or offered such as to obfuscate their intended messages. For example, one scientist summarizing a complex piece of research wrote, "We can't account for the lack of warming at the moment, and it is a travesty that we can't."[117] Skeptics pointed out that if even experts cannot account for global warming, it probably is not occurring. A high-profile politically conservative TV host, Glenn Beck, commented: "What are these guys saying behind closed doors about their so-called bulletproof consensus?" Quoting the researcher who was having difficulty with the data, Beck reacted: "Incorrect data? Inadequate systems? Yeah. Travesty, pretty good word for it."[118]

The author of the e-mail, Kevin Trenberth, who worked at the National Center for Atmospheric Research, later explained that his use of the word "travesty" meant that "we don't have an observing system adequate to track" global warming but that "there are all kinds of signs aside from global mean temperatures, including melting of Arctic sea ice and rising sea levels and a lot of other indicators, that global warming is continuing." Trenberth added that people "can cherry-pick and take things out of context."[119]

Even more controversial than Trenberth's e-mail was the work of Michael Mann of the University of Virginia, who had created what came to be known as the "Hockey Stick" graph used by Al Gore and many other pro-climate change advocates. The simple graph showed the trend in global temperatures over the previous two thousand years. The temperatures had been consistent since the time of Jesus Christ, then in the twentieth century rose (as represented by the short piece of the hockey stick). That uptick coincided with human use of coal and oil. Mann was collaborating with a scientist at the University of East Anglia. A thousand years of their hockey stick graph had to be based on data prior to the invention of thermometers, so they needed other ways to collect that early data. They used other sources such as tree rings and core samples from coral reefs. But these methods left his graph open to critique. One of the hacked e-mails from a colleague stated, "I've just completed Mike's *Nature* trick of adding in the real temps to each series for the last 20 years (i.e., from 1981 onwards) and from 1961 for Keith's to hide the decline."[120]

Mann's work had already been under attack from climate Deniers so this quotation invigorated them. They believed that Mann was untruthful and the hockey stick a smoking gun. In his defense, colleagues noted that he was using a "trick" to report out his temperature data. As one defender noted, "they mean it [trick] as a clever way of doing something—a shortcut can be a trick"; they did not mean deceit.[121] Vulgar criticisms challenged the veracity of Mann's work and that of all like-minded climate change researchers. Both his employer and the National Science Foundation conducted an audit of his work and cleared him of falsifying or producing fake data. They did not uncover evidence of "research mis-conduct."[122] Candidates running for state government in Virginia in 2010 on the Republican side wanted to pursue punishing him and made it a local political issue. He fought back, to little avail. Anti–climate change think tanks, such as the Cato Institute and the Competitive Enterprise Institute, continued to criticize his work. The latter referred to Mann's work and exoneration as a "cover-up and whitewash."[123]

Calmer critics hostile to Mann had argued long before the hockey stick controversy that his work in general had "contradicted hundreds of historical sources on the Medieval Warming and Little Ice Age, as well as hundreds of previous scientific papers with evidence of those major past changes in the Earth's climate."[124] Nevertheless, both before and after the hockey stick brouhaha, scores of other scientists demonstrated the accuracy of the hockey stick graph.[125]

The intensity of the attacks on this and other climate change advocates came at a period of heightened tension for the fossil fuel industry, which became more active in fighting potential regulatory and legal threats. President Obama had announced that climate change remediation would be a central theme of his administration. During the summer of 2009, a bill was working its way through Congress to establish a cap-and-trade system for carbon emissions. As proposed, the legislation would set limits (a *cap*) on how much CO_2 could be released into the atmosphere. Companies would be allowed to buy federal permits to emit gas and to *trade* those with other firms. The idea was to monetize carbon in the atmosphere, hence motivate firms to reduce the release of CO_2 into the atmosphere. Those companies that had not used up their quotas could sell the remaining portion to other companies that were exceeding their quota. Both coal and oil companies would have to buy these, which would raise their cost of doing business.

The coal and oil industries increased their resources to fight this bill. One of the largest fronts in this operation was the Coalition for Clean Coal Electricity (ACCCE), which in 2009 alone spent $28 million lobbying against cap-and-trade legislation. Democratic Congressmen in Virginia and Pennsylvania began receiving letters in opposition to this legislation, ostensibly from local civil rights organizations, including the NAACP chapter in Charlottesville, Virginia. A letter from this chapter, under the signature of its president, William Ernst, asked the local Congressman, Tom Perriello, to "use your position to help protect minorities and other consumers in your district from higher electric bills" and not to "vote to force cost increases on us, especially in this volatile economy."[126] He received similar letters from the American Association of University Women and the Jefferson Board for the Aging. The problem was that all these letters turned out to be forgeries, written by the public relations firm of Bonner & Associates, under contract to the ACCCE. When it all came out in the open, Bonner & Associates fired a supposed "rogue employee" and kept lobbying for the coal and fuel industries.[127] It was during this period that another lie was floating around about how much it would cost the average household should cap-and-trade legislation become law.[128] One observer of the information flows from the Skeptics and Deniers, some of their many front organizations, and the blatant lies and forgeries that appeared concluded that "their combined efforts form one of the largest attempts at mass deception in human history."[129] While historians of twentieth-century European history might challenge such an assertion with Hitler and Stalin in mind, the behavior of the fossil fuel industries was perhaps the most extensive in American history.

In November 2016, just after the US national elections in which Republican candidate Donald Trump was elected president, ExxonMobil was back in the news about climate change. This time, company officials were accusing the Rockefeller family of "masterminding a conspiracy against it," of using their foundation to attack the company. The oil company had been accused of paying surrogates to deny the dangers of climate change and was fighting state attorneys general, journalists, and environmentalist organizations over this charge. Ironically, the founder of the company that became Exxon was John D. Rockefeller, who in 1870 created Standard Oil and from whose wealth the Rockefeller Foundation came into being. The *New York Times* reported, "journalists have published exposés of the company's research into climate change, including actions it took to incorporate climate projections into its exploration plans while playing down the threat." ExxonMobil, "in public statements, court filings and thick dossiers on the company's opponents, says it is the target of a well-funded and politically motivated conspiracy to harm its core business." Yet the Rockefeller family wanted to use the wealth created by fossil fuels "to combat the damage done by" these fuels and so went public with its criticisms of ExxonMobil.[130] In one report of this contretemps:

> Industry-backed policy groups like Energy in Depth generate stories that attack the family and its philanthropy. Their charges are echoed in conservative news outlets like the *Wall Street Journal*'s opinion page and *The Daily Caller*. Breitbart News has called the collaboration among environmental groups to urge the investigation of Exxon a "RICO conspiracy," using the acronym for the federal racketeering law.[131]

Two years later, it was ExxonMobil's turn to be sued, this time by cities and counties in California and Colorado, as well as by New York City, which alleged that ExxonMobil's products contributed to climate change, thereby exacerbating various types of natural disaster, such as droughts, wildfires, and severe storms—all of which were affecting adversely agriculture and tourism. Such events, the litigants claimed, "place a burden on local governments." In short, "Our communities and our taxpayers should not shoulder the cost of climate change adaption alone. . . . These companies need to pay their fair share."[132] In Texas, ExxonMobil announced it would countersue.

In the decade since the mid-2000s, much had changed. ExxonMobil finally conformed to the position taken a few years earlier by its competitors, publicly acknowledging the reality of climate change and supporting the Paris climate agreement, even a carbon tax. But it was too late, and what some lawyers labeled "nuisance suits" against the company were moving ahead, as they had in an earlier time against the tobacco companies. As one critic of ExxonMobil stated: "If ExxonMobil spent as much time cleaning up their operations as they do fighting people who are trying to protect the planet, we'd be a lot better off."[133]

Finally, what about the Internet? Have false facts and misinformation become part of that world? While the subject has yet to be explored in detail, the evidence suggests that the story that played out in the traditional media of newspapers and television is being repeated on the Internet. For example, Americans for Prosperity (AFP) is a skeptic group with an online presence. It created a number of social media platforms to increase the illusion of a large community of skeptics, as a means to resist implementation of policies favored by pro-climate change constituencies. However, the pro-climate change groups also did this, making it difficult to determine which claims were valid and which organizations were responsible and knowledgeable spokesmen for the issues.[134] It was the same problem that had existed long before the arrival of the Internet; and the types of participants remained the same: lobbyists, representatives of industries and firms, academics, journalists, think tank "senior research fellows," and politicians. Students of the AFP experience and other issue-based Internet activities noted that controversial issues aired on the Internet "can lead to perceptions of a highly divided public even when that is not the case."[135] This is important because, by 2013–2014, over 70 percent of adults in the United States accessed the Internet, doing so in greater numbers than those who read newspapers and magazines. Only radio and television experience higher levels of use today.[136] Internet experts watching how Americans responded to climate change issues over the Internet were finding, "that people can indeed by influenced by informational cues in social media environments," regardless of the veracity of the information they were viewing.[137]

10

Conclusions

When the fake news moniker has faded, the problem will still exist, and eventually reemerge with a new name.

—Nicole A. Cooke[1]

L ibrary and information studies scholar Nicole Cooke has to deal with the issue of fake versus real facts in her job of training future librarians, who need to help students and adults find factual information. But, then, don't all of us have to do the same? Ultimately, the value of exploring the history of fake facts turns on the notion of information literacy. This book has demonstrated that lies and misinformation have been spread across the nation in every decade of its history. The ability to disseminate misinformation and fake facts, stir up rumors and conspiracies, and encourage bad decision-making and malicious behavior is enabled in part by targeting those less able to discern truth from lies.

President Thomas Jefferson, in a foul mood early during his second term in the first decade of the nineteenth century, grumbled that the press "live by the zeal they can kindle, and the schisms they can create."[2] Over two hundred years later, opinion writer for the *New York Times*, Frank Bruni, echoed the same concerns about the Internet: "What a glittering dream of expanded knowledge and enhanced connection it was at the start. What a nightmare of manipulated biases and metastasized hate it had turned into."[3] Cooke, Jefferson, and Bruni all wrestled with the same problem—the use of information in ways contrary to the central belief that truth is nobler and wiser to embrace than fake facts.

As this book has demonstrated, bad information works. Its dissemination makes it possible for its creators to accomplish their objectives: to deride a presidential candidate, to push America into a war, to promote smoking, to prevent Congress from restraining carbon monoxide pollution, or to get Americans to buy patent medicines that do not work. We learned through this book that information—both fake and real—was created and spread for a purpose, and was often weaponized to make the technique more effective, whether it was with good or evil intent. "Trusted sources" could be created or manipulated, too, as Russian trolls did on Facebook during the US national elections of 2016. All these cases raise a question: what are the implications for modern society? We argued at the start of this book that people lie, that trusted institutions of the past are questioned, and that individuals have difficulty distinguishing between truth and lies.

So, we begin our discussion in this chapter with a summation of why people lied in our case studies. The answer is complicated, but ultimately obvious. Next, we summarize cross-cutting patterns we have identified as having occurred many times over the past two centuries. Our hope is that, by recognizing these patterns, readers will be more readily able to distinguish between facts and falsehoods. Part of this story is about trusted sources and media and delivery mechanisms, so we look briefly at the activities of media, presaging the situation Bruni complained about. While historians shy away from drawing "lessons from history," the problem of falsehoods is too great to ignore, so we briefly discuss differentiating truth from lies—including their motives, phrasing, and delivery—as a way of suggesting how people can work with information based on historical perspectives.

WHY AND HOW LIES AND MISREPRESENTATIONS FUNCTIONED IN AMERICAN LIFE

The presidential elections of the 1820s were dramatic because so many more people could vote for the first time; also because the earlier divide of New England versus the South was shifting to a divide between the East and the rapidly expanding West, making it possible for a westerner (Jackson) to challenge a New Englander (Adams). Campaigning styles differed from East to West, with the westerners being more blunt and crude, and with greater concern about Indian problems than those living in New England had. Not surprisingly, false information and misinformation was mixed with purposeful lying to win important elections in early nineteenth-century America. It was at this time that political parties learned with certainty that massive character assassinations, combined with outright falsehoods and insults, could sway public opinion.

Newspapers and pamphlets, the media of politics of the early nineteenth century, continued to be effective continuously until at least the 1960s national elections. Television became an effective new medium for American politics in the 1960s, supplementing rather than supplanting the other media. Television enabled politicos to offer up new forms of misinformation, such as a positive image of a candidate's physical appearance when the candidate was actually in poor health. Television also enabled the transmission of less factual traits about candidates, such as charisma. Kennedy came off better than Nixon in the televised debates. Over a century earlier, nobody would have been able to notice; most citizens did not even know what presidential candidates looked like, at least until the 1860 campaign, when political advocates played upon Lincoln's gaunt figure. To win the close-fought presidential election of 1960, multiple forms of information were gainfully employed, including the candidate's looks and personality. Because these techniques were effective, today we see political candidates routinely worrying as much about their image in photographs, video, and commentary as they do about the substance of their positions on national issues. Balding politicians get hair transplants or comb their manes to make it appear fuller.

The case studies in this book illustrate more than a half dozen general purposes for lies and misinformation in American public life: to gain a political advantage (elections, for example), foment fear (assassinations, war), stir up anti-business attitudes (tobacco, climate change), fight competitors (business advertising), protect one's business (tobacco and climate change from government regulators), foster beliefs in conspiracies (Kennedy assassination, tobacco, climate change), start a war (1898), and position one ethnic or political group against another (East vs. West in 1828, Catholics vs. Protestants in 1960). There are additional reasons that our limited number of case studies did not adequately cover, such as religious issues (covered only briefly in the election of 1960), or the role of misinformation to encourage US entry into both world wars, or rumors and gossip used for entertainment purposes.

Providing confusion about facts sways how people approach issues and their stances on them. Historical evidence teaches us that conspiracies motivate the use of misinformation; they cause people to link together disparate facts and misinformation in unreasonable ways and guess when there are no hard facts at hand. People want to understand why events occur, how circumstances can affect them, and how best to respond to perceived dangers or opportunities. So, most people will fill gaps in their understanding with whatever information is available, regardless of its quality. This is a harsh finding of history, but one known to those who trade in misinformation. Presidential assassinations provide an excellent example of the dynamics involved. People in the 1860s were cognitively similar to those of the 1960s in that they sought to understand the events of Lincoln's assassination and make sense of why things happened, and so they reasoned based on what they knew, coupled to their prior experiences, beliefs, and prejudices.

Every one of our case studies pointed to conspiracies in one way or another. These cases illustrate that, even if someone did not know of the actual existence of a plot, they assumed conspiracies existed; and sometimes these suspicions were right to some degree. Conspiracy theories developed almost instantly and spread quickly. They could survive for over a century, as happened with the Lincoln assassination. Even "settled facts" could continue to be disputed—no matter how massive the evidence—as our cases about climate change, tobacco, and the Kennedy assassination show.

We learned from the Spanish-American War (but it was also true about the First and Second World Wars) that editors and reporters could influence events and opinions. We also learned that their influence could just as easily occur with false facts as with truth, with misunderstandings and lazy reporting as much as with rigorous research and analysis. This was possible because the public did little critical thinking about facts and were swept up by impressions, prior perspectives, and emotions. In 1898, Americans were ready to go to war with Spain before the US Navy had completed its factual and reasoned analysis of the destruction of the USS *Maine*. Congress, however, showed more restraint and waited until the official report came in (and only declared war the following month).[4]

Lying was not limited to politics and public administration. We saw cases involving small companies (e.g., patent medicine firms in the 1800s), larger corporations (e.g., tobacco companies), and entire industries (e.g., tobacco and energy) by the second half of the twentieth century. Clearly, the motives and techniques of misinformation pioneered in the political arena applied just as effectively in the private sector. Businesses could be even more extreme in this behavior, such as the patent medicine vendors who promoted outrageously exaggerated lies in large quantities. Businesses, including their industries and trade associations, were often better funded than politicians and staffed with more skilled purveyors of false facts. It was the private sector that invented the profession of public relations and its body of best practices known as advertising. In fact, they were so good at it that politicians and public officials today rely on those two sets of skills as they go about their work. One slight difference existed between the public and private sectors, however: in our case studies, rumors seemed to play a greater role in the private sector, such as snakes in blouses or dead mice in soft drinks. Rumors—today sometimes called "buzz" by PR professionals on the Internet—were sometimes spread by individuals rather than institutions. But institutions are also involved. Think, for example, of President Trump speaking on behalf of the Republican Party when he says that "People are talking," as a way to raise doubts and suspicions about an issue, or to support a specific rumor.

The case studies demonstrate that when a political position or other issues were contested, especially across multiple sectors of the society, partisans had long been willing to employ misleading or false facts to achieve their objectives. This phenomenon existed long before the Internet, even though its early history has received only limited historical attention, so far. In the tobacco industry, for example, companies and industry spokesmen aimed their messages at multiple targets—some at government regulators and legislators, others at potential customers. We learned that public officials were significantly influenced by arguments from industry casting doubts and uncertainties regarding scientific facts linking smoking and lung cancer. In this case, we saw consumers (voters), public officials, and corporate management intertwined in the milieu of facts and fakes. The climate change case demonstrated there were no territorial or intellectual limits to that mixture of facts and fakes, as the debate quickly went global and misinformation tactics that had proved effective in the United States were plied around the world. The outcomes were not always the same, however. The United States stands alone among major nations in its doubts and policy mitigation efforts concerning global warming.[5]

The climate change controversy also points out that Americans have much to learn about how science works and how to discriminate between bad research and valid scientific results. The merchandizing of doubt, in particular, has proved effective in dealing with scientific evidence. Americans do not generally understand that it is a legitimate scientific practice for "settled facts" to continue to evolve as more evidence comes to light; or that, when in doubt about a scientific issue, taking no action based on what is regard as an unsettled issue is often the proper step (rather than taking action knowing that may be based on false assumptions, bad information, or simply unknown possibilities).[6]

Historian Michael Kammen, in a study of American culture and tastes, pointed out a feature of American behavior that clearly was in evidence in the complex scientific discourses regarding the effectiveness of patent medicines, tobacco, and climate change; although he presented his insights in a different context based on how people viewed history and disliked revisionist interpretations of what they considered settled facts. He commented: "I believe that it is a curious obsession with perceptions of *authenticity*, a desire that dates back at least a century and a half."[7] Other historians have made similar comments.[8] Kammen noted in his exploration of how the public has viewed art and culture is similar to what we have observed in this book. In particular, he points to behavior that "arises from the brevity of the public's attention span," a variation of the habit of people skim-reading their newspapers in earlier times.[9] In the era of the Internet, fact purveyors and opinion writers count on people's unwillingness to work through lengthy messages. It is an era of blogs, sound bites, and slogans. All sides in the climate change debate could be confident that the American public would not read the many hundreds of pages of testimony presented by scientists demonstrating the veracity of climate change research. However, this interest in brevity and instant gratification was not a product of the late twentieth century. It arose in an earlier era, from the actions of both advertisers and politicians.

Several times we reported that a particular method of fake fact dissemination worked; in fact, all of these efforts worked to some degree. The length of time to debunk these falsehoods gives an indication of their effectiveness. Just how long did this process of debunking take? Establishing who blew up the USS *Maine* took seventy-five years; settling the facts of Lincoln's assassination, eighty-five years; the number of shooters in Kennedy's death remains an open issue, and we are fifty years on with that case. Tobacco's case took one decade to debunk and communicate to the public; while climate change remains an open issue, despite the fact that scientists are over 95 percent in agreement on the basics of global warming and its causes. The charges against Andrew Jackson were resolved in approximately fifteen years; the truth about Kennedy's health and religious views was resolved approximately five years after the 1960 campaign. The most effective and thorough debunking of fake facts among our case studies occurred with Lincoln's assassination, the Spanish-American War, the tobacco conspiracy, and environmental change. It is clear that fake facts can linger for a very long time.

CROSS-CURRENTS IN AMERICAN FAKE FACTS AND MISINFORMATION

Recall that the first chapter introduced five cross-cutting themes in evidence in all the case studies. They are:

all participants in these case studies used information and misinformation as a primary tool for accomplishing specific goals

information of all types and degrees of accuracy was presented in the literary and rhetorical style of their day

people and organizations weaponized information to accomplish their objectives more effectively as ever-larger organizations formed, they too (and not just individuals) used misinformation

over time, the impact of individuals declined, although never disappeared, while the importance of institutions grew

These five behaviors can be viewed as central findings of our study. In one form or another, they have existed at least since the late eighteenth century.

These five cross-currents have continued to apply in the time of the public Internet, which began in 1993. At the birth of the United States in the late eighteenth century, the largest diffusers of misinformation were individuals and small groups. Even the great media mogul of the time, Benjamin Franklin, was a small operator with a tiny staff, and he controlled only a few media outlets. He gained wide attention through the mechanism that many other individuals, such as editors of small newspapers across the country, and other small groups spread his messages. Not until after the Civil War did organizations become large enough that they could diffuse their messages directly to mass audiences.[10] By the early 1900s, organizations became the principal medium through which voices were heard. Individuals got their point across working through institutions such as newspapers, book publishers, business firms, government agencies, and universities; it was difficult for a person to operate otherwise. Even the letter to the editor, a mainstay for voicing individual opinion, required the existence of the institution of newspapers.

With the arrival of the Internet, individuals became newly empowered (or perhaps more accurately, re-empowered) to communicate true and fake facts directly. Using blogs or social media platforms, they could even compete for attention against large institutions. YouTube, Facebook, Snapchat, Instagram, Twitter, and numerous websites empowered individuals. And there is wide use of these communication technologies. In 2018, 73 percent of all adults reported using YouTube, 68 percent Facebook, and 35 percent Instagram. The numbers are even more striking among young people. The same survey reported that 94 percent of eighteen- to twenty-four-year-olds use YouTube, 80 percent Facebook, 78 percent, Snapchat 78 percent, Instagram 71 percent, and 45 percent Twitter.[11] Considering all adults, on average an American in 2018 was routinely using three media platforms. Pew Foundation Internet surveys over the previous two decades have made it clear that using social media has become deeply engrained in the information-handling habits of Americans, and this is hardly expected to change in any fundamental way in the years to come.[12] In other words, the five cross-currents identified in the case studies of earlier times can be expected to remain evident in the decades to come and thus can serve as crude guideposts with which to study future information-handling practices, although prudence is recommended when taking guidance from historical precedent.

HOW MEDIA HELPED SPREAD FAKE FACTS, MISINFORMATION, AND RUMORS

The authors of the American constitution and the earliest members of the US Congress had it in mind to encourage freedom of speech and to facilitate the communication of ideas. To implement those twin goals, the Post Office was immediately established with guidelines to deliver newspapers for free, later for low prices. Mail a book or other printed matter today, and you still get a discount on the mailing charge. The first amendment to the Constitution laid down the fundamental rule still in force that "Congress shall make no law . . . abridging the freedom of speech, or of the press, or of the right of people peaceably to assemble, and to petition the Government for a redress of grievances." Subsequent laws and endless rounds of federal and state-level lawsuits have largely supported the freedom of speech proviso. As the nation expanded in the nineteenth century, the information infrastructure expanded, often triggered by the establishment of a new town on the frontier. The largest building in the new town, such as a store or hotel, would double as the post office, since no town felt it was an urban center without postal service. Soon after came the local newspaper. By the end of Jackson's two terms as president, in 1837, the nation had a thick network of newspapers able to reprint content from other newspapers, ensuring that debates occurring in other parts of the nation were aired locally. Both accurate and inaccurate information moved about the country through this newspaper network. One main reason for inaccurate information was that early newspapers were the chosen instruments of political parties and even of individual politicians for promoting their informational goals.

During the first 150 years of the United States, newspapers served as the primary instrument for the delivery of misinformation to the public, just as it served similarly to deliver accurate facts. Pamphlets played a decreasing role over time, while magazines throughout this period remained a secondary, less effective tool for such purposes. Newspapers were effective because most adults were exposed to them. One did not need even to be literate because the post office would deliver newspapers to a general store, where one person would read it aloud to a room full of people. Pages of newspapers would commonly be posted on walls of stores and hotels; that is how many people learned during the Civil War if one of their family members had been killed in a recent battle, as their names would be printed in the local newspaper. The newspapers remained the most widely used vehicle for disseminating fake facts until the 1970s, although radio had also become a force in the 1920s and television in the 1950s.

Television, with its ability to present images with voices, began to grab people's attention. From the 1960s to the present, television advertising by candidates or organizations promoting a point of view served as the most effective medium for shaping public opinion. Cable television became an important part of the information ecology; it has seen a record number of viewers in the 2010s. "Talking heads" on MSNBC, CNN, and FOX "spinning" their points of view on political matters pushed conspiracy theories, interpreted facts, and shaped opinions. These shows have largely filled the role played by nineteenth-century partisan newspapers, but reaching millions of people in an instant. Meanwhile, the newspaper business became less biased, more balanced in its coverage, and one of the strongest advocates for truthful reporting. Radio has had talk programs since the mid-twentieth century, often broadcasting during those times of the day when rush-hour traffic gave drivers something to listen to in their cars and trucks.

Americans deployed almost immediately every new form of communications technology and format for presenting both true and false information. The list is impressive: telegraph, telephone, radio, television, and the Internet among electronic tools, earlier the penny press, books, paperbacks, later cheap paperbacks, slick magazines with photographs, even blending newspapers and telegraphic communications to speed up the presentation of information. During most of American history, there were between one thousand and two thousand local newspapers; and almost every occupied part of the United States could be reached by radio and television. Today, the Internet is available in all cities and towns, and is spreading increasingly into rural areas. However, contrary to public perception, the Internet has had the slowest diffusion of any of the major information communications technologies available to the nation.[13]

With such a thick information infrastructure, it has been easy and cost-effective for individuals, political parties, businesses, corporations, associations, and various government agencies to spread both truth and lies. Messaging has been a creative process that included use of billboards in the twentieth century along highways and, even before that, massive quantities of signs and advertisements plastered to the sides of buildings. It was nearly impossible to escape messaging, as we have seen in our studies of patent medicines and political campaigns. So, it is no mystery that misinformation would be used to fulfill an individual's or an organization's objectives. By the late 1800s, a resident in the United States would have been simultaneously deluged with fake facts (accurate ones, too) from multiple media. That became even more common as the twentieth century unfolded, making it possible for purveyors of false information to create multi-platform communications strategies. For example, tobacco companies and political candidates advertised in magazines and newspapers, while delivering the same messages at the same time over radio and television. Later, they added websites and social networking sites. Repetition and frequency of messaging were well-understood ways of increasing believability and acceptance of a point of view by the 1880s. These attributes of how humans process information explains, for example, why one might see the same automobile advertisement two or three times in a half hour while watching a television program. It is why a politician might repeat the same message over and over again for months on end. It works.

One might wonder, did a person have a choice whether to be exposed to fake facts? The answer is no, or at best only to a limited extent. How does one avoid reading a billboard along the highway, a screaming headline in their local or national newspaper, or advertisements broadcast while watching television dramas or the news and weather reports? Flyers stuffed into front doors, neighbors and friends conversing about topics spreading fake facts and rumors either intentionally or out of ignorance of the truth all made it impossible to avoid exposure to fake facts. As we explained in several chapters, social scientists have shown that it is easier to believe a fake fact one is exposed to if it is consistent with what one knew before. Recall our discussion about the role of rumors? If an employer routinely lays off workers, then remaining employees will believe further layoffs are coming and will accept as true rumors of impending layoffs without benefit of knowing from the executive making that decision whether the rumor has any basis in truth. Ultimately, people in an information-rich society will be exposed to both fake and accurate facts. People who are literate, educated, and prosperous enough to acquire multiple forms of media are exposed to larger quantities of fake facts. Their ability to discern truth from falsehoods is complicated by the diversity of what is pushed at them: about food, politics, health, product characteristics, science, religion, and hobbies and sports, for example. Media remains a central feature of any discussion of fake facts.

EMERGING ISSUES IN THE INTERNET ERA

We now turn to the central communications phenomenon of our time—the Internet. "Phenomenon" is the correct word to use to describe the Internet's influence on today's Americans. Its power and pervasiveness are extraordinary. Over half of the adults living in the United States used at least one social media site by 2010; today, that figure approaches 70 percent. While the youngest adults were the earliest and are currently the heaviest users, reaching 50 percent use by 2006 and hovering at 90 percent in 2018, even the demographic category with the least social media penetration (people over the age of sixty-five), stands at 25 percent since 2015.[14]

There has been a revolution in the means to access information on the Internet. When the Internet went public in the 1990s, one had access only through devices that were not very portable (clunky desktop computers or heavy laptops—one of the early laptops weighing twenty-four pounds). Late in the first decade of the twenty-first century, portability has become both possible and affordable—first with lightweight laptops and tablets, then with smartphones. Credit for the surge in the use of more portable technology can be laid at the feet of Steve Jobs and his employees at Apple Computer, especially for the tablet and the smartphone. Over the next decade, Apple products and those of its competitors resulted in more people walking around with a computer in their pocket than there were personal computers and laptops. A few numbers suggest why "phenomenon" is the right word to use. By 2010, there were some 232 million mobile phone users in the United States; that number grew to over 260 million by the end of 2016.[15] Today, 95 percent of adults have a cell phone—of which 77 percent are smartphones, up from 35 percent in 2011.[16] Those statistics now parallel the number of people who have access to television and radio, and surpass those who read newspapers and books.

How much do Americans use these devices? Many surveys have been done since 2008 to answer that question. By 2017–2018, the data suggested that users spent an *average* of over seventy hours per month on apps; that is, two hours and thirty minutes a day.[17] Teenagers are the heaviest users, but older Americans also use smartphones extensively. These numbers compel us to consider the Internet as a new, yet in many ways continuous, stage in the history of misinformation. Historians of information have demonstrated how acceptance and use of both good and bad information has remained relatively constant from one decade to the next.[18] For example, people have been "googling" since the eighteenth century—if we mean by that neologism searching for information. Studies of how people use the Internet, increasingly with their smartphones, reaffirm that observation.[19] So, lessons learned from earlier times could just as easily be ripped off the headlines of today's media. Nowhere does this seem so central to the discussion of fake news as the concern consumers of information have about how to distinguish fake facts from truthful facts. Similar concerns have been raised over the past two centuries, but here we focus on the contemporary situation.

There has long been a concern on the part of Americans that fake news and fake facts were circulating and too influential. The case studies in this book exhibit examples of these concerns, but the issues are magnified by the Internet and particularly by social media, which has removed almost all barriers for anyone to post whatever they want to say. There are few if any safeguards, such as print media had through its editorial practices or academic journals and government agencies had through the peer review process. The "like" system employed on many social media sites does not contribute much in the way of safeguards about the accuracy of information found online. In fact, the "like" system often reflects group bias.

In a Pew Foundation survey conducted in December 2016—the season of the presidential election, which for most Americans launched the era of fake facts—two-thirds reported that fabricated news stories confused voters about issues and recent events. Pew reported that "this sense is shared widely across incomes, education levels, partisan affiliations and most other demographic characteristics."[20] Yet, at that point, 40 percent of respondents felt they could differentiate between truth and falsehoods. Their confidence level would be challenged over the next two years as it became apparent that the new president told many lies and that these lies were repeated by numerous followers on the Internet. A third of the people reported they routinely saw fake facts on the Internet. Nearly 25 percent of people engaging in political discussion admitted to sharing fake news; 16 percent reported that they later realized that they had done so. Nearly half the respondents expected politicians, governments, and other institutions to curb the spread of fake facts; but that did not happen.[21] Librarians suspected that Internet users were less able to discern truth from falsehoods, realizing also that, with the push to get news content out to the public quickly as a source of advertising revenue, news outlets were contributing to the problem by being perceived as trusted sources but pushing material out before properly vetting it.[22]

The issue of distinguishing factual and opinionated statements in the news is not going away. In another study that your authors are conducting, we are finding the debate and the responses to the issue of falsehoods on the Internet has ballooned far more than was the case as late as 2010.[23] Kammen's comment about shorter attention spans and the inability to distinguish facts from fiction as purveyors of falsehoods accentuates the problem for today's users of information. Because of the increased turbulence of American politics since 2015, much of the focus on fake facts centers on political issues and the media's role. For many, the term "media" encompasses the participants/users—people, parties, politicos, policy advocates—requiring a combination of political awareness, Internet savviness, and trust in sources to navigate around untruths.

Tests run by the Pew Foundation to measure how well people distinguish truth from mistruth do not generate confidence in the public's abilities in this area. The Pew study revealed "that even this basic task presents a challenge," because "a majority of Americans correctly identified at least three of the five statements in each set. But this result is only a little better than random guesses. Far fewer Americans got all five correct, and roughly a quarter got most or all wrong."[24] The more successful test takers displayed the three required skills just listed; the implication for readers of the report being that, if Americans were to improve in their ability to discern truth from falsehoods in political discussions, they needed to be politically aware, technically savvy, and rely on trusted sources.

The results of this survey suggest a variety of issues that all users of the Internet will need to confront. First, there is the problem of organizations facilitating the diffusion of fake facts, using social media platforms, especially Facebook; political outlets, such as think tanks, partisan newspapers, and cable TV, and fronts for lobbyists, which we saw in abundance in the tobacco and climate change debates; government agencies misleading the public, as happened, for example, in the state government of Georgia in its attempts to discourage voting by African Americans in the midterm elections of 2018, and probably as well in the Johnson administration's treatment of the Tonkin incident during the Vietnam War. American government regulators may eventually enact rules to mitigate problems created by social media firms, as the European Union is already pioneering. Remember that a substantial amount of false information online comes from a few sources, which are then widely disseminated by many people, groups, and organizations.[25] The media oligarchies, such as Viacom, CBS, Time Warner, Hearst, and Comcast, are today among the largest generators of content. But media oligarchies have been a reality in the United States for nearly a century.[26] Blogs are perhaps the greatest consumer of content from media sources, which is then repackaged to reflect an author's point of view before posting to the Internet for others to consume and diffuse.

Second, some news outlets are fighting the epidemic of fake facts by exposing lies as they surface. This includes major newspapers, notably the *New York Times*, *Washington Post*, and *LA Times*. It also includes political fact-checking organizations such as PolitiFact, FactCheck.org, and snopes.[27]

Third is the problem of adults and teenagers not understanding how to differentiate truth from falsehoods or misleading information. This problem strikes at the heart of what education is all about and ultimately it is the individual, not institutions, who may have to take responsibility for his or her own use of information. Even though public relations experts, political operatives, psychologists, psychiatrists, and advertisers have believed for many decades that public opinion can be manipulated, the structure of American life is predicated on individuals being responsible for their behavior and to inform their own opinions. That the greatest battleground for ideas and fake facts is the political life of the nation, with commerce a very close second, the problem of discerning truth remains a chronic condition that regulators have only partially mitigated, for example, as the FDA has done with patent medicines. Educators' ability to teach critical thinking has always been an uneven venture compounded by their slow embrace of personal computing and the Internet in their teaching.[28] Two hundred years of experience suggests that institutions have less incentive to address these issues, while individuals have long sought to be better educated and informed, even if they often failed to progress, as witnessed by how they responded to patent medicines for two centuries and more recently to virulent partisan politics.

There is a need for critical thinking skills, equally relevant to students and adults, similar to the ability to read or perform basic mathematics skills. Being skeptical about what one reads is an important learned attitude, but this also needs to be accompanied by the ability to discriminate based on sources, language, argumentation, and content. Too many readers on the Internet accept at face value what they read; the Pew surveys provide strong evidence of that behavior. Already some organizations, such as the MacArthur Foundation, and some professions, such as librarians, are beginning to prescribe solutions. History teaches that we should listen to them.[29] One particular skill people could learn is how to distinguish between information from a source they are associated with (e.g., a political party) from other sources. That requires more than viewing FOX News (politically conservative) or reading the *New York Times* (politically left of center). Besides such general skills and habits, much needs to be done to learn digital literacy, similar to how people in the nineteenth century learned how to read books and newspapers.[30]

Librarians are beginning to suggest a variant of digital literacy that can help in recognizing fake facts, but at the same time what they are teaching is a skill that could be used to distribute fake facts, too. Called *metaliteracy*, it merges knowledge of emerging information technologies with other types of literacy skills:

> Metaliteracy asks us to understand the format type and delivery mode of information; evaluate dynamic content critically; evaluate user feedback of information; produce original content in multiple media formats; create a context for user-generated information; understand personal privacy, information ethics, and intellectual property issues; and share information in participatory environments."[31]

It calls for people to think more broadly and contextually about what they are reading, lessons handed down for generations but not including information presented on the digital platter of the Internet.[32]

We are then left with the question of the ethics of promoting the use of fake facts, a topic that takes us beyond the scope of this book, but which can be evaluated within the historical framework of American values of the past and how they were applied largely in the diffusion of information. The historical record presented in this book suggests there were always individuals prepared to lie and misinform and spread rumors to achieve personal and institutional objectives. This behavior is not original to today's political operators. Both Thomas Jefferson and Andrew Jackson were slandered about their sexual behavior at a time when people simply did not discuss such things in public, nor even within the confines of their own homes.

FAKE FACTS, MISINFORMATION, CONSPIRACIES, AND RUMORS IN AMERICAN LIFE

Americans have always lived in a parallel information-rich universe consisting of a great deal of accurate, truthful information and also a massive quantity of falsehoods. In this book, we focused on the dark side of the subject—fake facts—but its history reflected patterns of information use that mimicked what Americans did with truthful practical information and data with which to inform their decisions.[33] It cannot be overstated how vibrant and energetically falsehoods were injected into society and so willingly accepted. People were prepared to go to war, to kill off native tribes, elect unqualified inexperienced politicians, smoke until they died of cancer, and risk the extinction of the human race. Yet, we know too little about fake facts and what little we understand remains fragmented. That is why this book is a collection of case studies used to test the historical evidence for the story.

We learned that fake facts could be flushed out of the historical experience of Americans, but also that the topic is widespread across American society and not limited to the political, business, and scientific examples presented here. What the American government told generations of American Indians, what charismatic ministers and priests preached in the 1920s and 1930s, what advertisers proclaimed in every industry over two centuries, or what children were taught are examples. Some falsehoods were innocent enough—"you look very nice in that dress" or, "I am fine," when you are not—because banter and gossip—little white lies—can be socially reinforcing, as some parents would argue about Santa Claus or the Easter Bunny, or when Americans told each other before the Vietnam War that the United States never lost a war, or to echo President Ronald Reagan and other leaders who spoke of the United States as the "last great hope" of mankind. But, as the Pew Foundation surveys suggest, Americans cling to an old belief that truth and honesty are better than lies and deceit as guiding lights in their lives. That they were either duped or embraced the opposite of true facts spoke more to human frailties or to one's focus on the "means justify the end." However, one views the matter, the ultimate truth is that fake facts has a long and varied history.

Notes

PREFACE

1. If you came to this note you did what he and we suggest—check out the sources of information. For his quote, see Mike Allen, "Axios AM: Mike's Big 6—Four Ways to Fix 'Fake News,' October 21, 2018, https://mail.google.com/mail/u/0/#inbox/FMfcgxvzLFFTBzGTpgsZFrcCnd WnFvkB (last accessed October 21, 2018).

CHAPTER 1

1. Joseph Rain, *The Unfinished Book about Who We Are* (Amazon Kindle/ Lucita Publishing, 2018).

2. Alexandre Koyre, *Reflexions sur le mensonge* (1943; Reprinted in Paris: les editions Allia, 1966).

3. Bella DePaulo, "I Study Liars. I've Never Seen One Like Donald Trump." *Chicago Tribune*, December 8, 2017, http://www.chicagotribune .com/news/opinion/commentary/ct-donald-trump-liar-20171208-story .html (accessed August 14, 2018).

4. James W. Cortada, *All the Facts: A History of Information in the United States since 1870* (New York: Oxford University Press, 2016).

5. For a philosophical investigation of what a lie is, see the discussion of information scientist Don Fallis, "What Is Lying?" *The Journal of Philosophy* 106 (2009): 29–56. On lying and deception, see Don Fallis, "Lying and Deception," *Philosopher's Imprint* 10 (November 11, 2010): 1–22. On disinfor-

mation, see Fallis, "Floridi on Disinformation," *Etica & Politica* 13 (2) 2011: 201–214; Fallis, "A Functional Analysis of Disinformation" in *iConference 2014 Proceedings*, 621–627; Fallis, "What Is Disinformation?" *Library Trends* 63 no. 3 (2015): 401–26; and Fallis, "Disinformation, Deception, and Politics," in *American Political Culture*, ed. Michael Shally-Jensen (Santa Barbara, CA: ABC-CLIO, 2015), 334–40. On bullshitting, see Fallis, "Frankfurt Wasn't Bullshitting!" *Southwest Philosophical Studies* (2015).

6. Studied by distinguished moral philosopher Harry G. Frankfurt, *On Bullshit* (Princeton, NJ: Princeton University Press, 2005).

7. https://www.snopes.com/glossary/ (accessed August 23, 2018).

8. Ibid.

9. Ion Mihai Pacepa and Ronald J. Rychlak, *Disinformation: Former Spy Chief Reveals Secret Strategies for Undermining Freedom, Attacking Religion, and Promoting Terrorism* (New York: WND Books, 2013).

10. Ibid.

11. Mike Wendling, "The (Almost) Complete History of 'Fake News,'" BBC Trending, January 22, 2018, https://www.bbc.com/news/blogs -trending-42724320 (accessed August 23, 2018).

12. Koyre, *Reflexions sur le mensonge*.

13. Friedrich Nietzsche, *On the Genealogy of Morals* (1887) (London: T.N. Foulis, 1913).

14. Friedrich Nietzsche, *On Truth and Lies in the Nonmoral Sense* (1873). Reprinted online at http://nietzsche.holtof.com/Nietzsche_various/ on_truth_and_lies.htm (accessed August 30, 2018).

15. Austin Cline, "Nietzsche, Truth, and Untruth," July 24, 2018, ThoughtCo, https://www.thoughtco.com/nietzsche-truth-and-un truth-250548 (accessed August 27, 2018).

16. Friedrich Nietzsche, *Beyond Good and Evil* (1886). English translation by Helen Zimmern, 2009. https://www.gutenberg.org/ files/4363/4363-h/4363-h.htm (accessed August 30, 2018).

17. Nietzsche, *On Truth and Lies in the Nonmoral Sense*.

18. Emile Durkheim (1895), *The Rules of Sociological Method* (English edition, New York: Free Press, 1982).

19. On Durkheim's sociology of knowledge, see Warren Schmaus, *Durkheim's Philosophy of Science and the Sociology of Knowledge: Creating an Intellectual Niche* (Chicago: University of Chicago Press, 1994).

20. Cheng Wen, "What exactly did Nietzsche and Foucault mean when they declared: 'There are no facts, only interpretations'? And what is the use in thinking this way?" *Quora*, March 2, 2017, https://www .quora.com/What-exactly-did-Nietzsche-and-Foucault-mean-when-they -declared-There-are-no-facts-only-interpretations-And-what-is-the-use -in-thinking-this-way (accessed August 28, 2018).

21. Thomas Kuhn, *The Structure of Scientific Revolutions* (Chicago: University of Chicago Press, 1962).

22. Bruno Latour and Steve Woolga, *Laboratory Life: The Construction of Scientific Facts* (Princeton, NJ: Princeton University Press, 1986).

23. Alvin Goldman and Thomas Blanchard, "Social Epistemology," *Stanford Encyclopedia of Philosophy*, April 28, 2015, https://plato.stanford .edu/entries/epistemology-social/ (accessed August 27, 2018).

24. *Oxford English Living Dictionary*'s definition of "post-truth"; see also Lee McIntyre, *Post-Truth* (Cambridge, MA: MIT Press, 2018).

25. Friedrich Nietzsche, *The Will to Power* (1901) (New York: Vintage, 1968); also see Alexis Papazoglou, "The Post-Truth Era of Trump Is Just What Nietzsche Predicted," *The Conversation*, December 14, 2016, http:// theconversation.com/the-post-truth-era-of-trump-is-just-what-nietzsche -predicted-69093 (accessed August 28, 2018); and Maria Popova, "Nietzsche on Truth, Lies, the Power and Peril of Metaphor, and How We Use Language to Reveal and Conceal Reality," https://www.brainpic kings.org/2018/03/26/nietzsche-on-truth-and-lies-in-a-nonmoral -sense/ (accessed August 28, 2018).

26. Cortada, *All the Facts*.

CHAPTER 2

1. Richard Hofstadter, "The Paranoid Style in American Politics," *Harper's Magazine* (November 1964), 77.

2. Ibid.

3. Ibid., 86.

4. The Times Editorial Board, "Why We Took a Stand on Trump," *Los Angeles Times*, April 9, 2017, http://www.latimes.com/projects/la-ed -trump-series/ (accessed July 12, 2018).

5. Although when looked at in detail across the post–Second World War period, comparing one decade to another in that postwar period, many phases and issues become evident, as discussed in more detail in the next chapter. See Jay G. Blumler and Dennis Kavanagh, "The Third Age of Political Communication: Influences and Features," *Political Communication* 16, no. 3 (1999): 209–30.

6. Jennifer Kavanagh and Michael D. Rich, *Truth Decay: An Initial Exploration of the Diminishing Role of Facts and Analysis in American Public Life* (Santa Monica, CA: RAND Corporation, 2018), 27–78.

7. Murray Edelman, *Political Language: Words That Succeed and Policies That Fail* (New York: Academic Press, 1977), 37.

8. Ibid.

9. Edmund F. Kallina Jr., *Kennedy v. Nixon: The Presidential Election of 1960* (Gainesville: University Press of Florida, 2010), 201–14.

10. H. W. Brands, *Andrew Jackson: His Life and Times* (New York: Doubleday, 2005), 553–60.

11. Murray Edelman, *Politics as Symbolic Action: Mass Arousal and Quiescence* (Chicago: Markham, 1971), 31.

12. Ibid.

13. Edelman, *Politics as Symbolic Action*, 46–48.

14. Hahn, *Political Communication*, 210–11.

15. Edelman, *The Symbolic Uses of Politics*, 114–51, 172–87.

16. James W. Cortada, *All the Facts: A History of Information in the United States since 1870* (New York: Oxford University Press, 2016), 132–88, 236–80; Robert A. Dahl, *Democracy and Its Critics* (New Haven, CT: Yale University Press, 1989), 338.

17. Bruce Bimber, *Information and American Democracy: Technology and the Evolution of Political Power* (Cambridge: Cambridge University Press, 2003), 17.

18. Ibid., 18.

19. Blumler and Kavanagh, "The Third Age of Political Communications."

20. C. Wardle, "Fake News. It's Complicated," February 16, 2017, https://medium.com/1st-draft/fake-news-its-complicated-d0f773766c79.

21. D. Jackson, "Issue Brief: Distinguishing Disinformation from Propaganda, Misinformation and 'Fake News,' National Endowment for Democracy, October 17, 2017, https://www.ned.org/issue-brief-distinguishing-disinformation-from-propaganda-misinformation-and-fake-news/.

22. See, for example, Aaron Smith, "The Internet and Campaign 2010," Pew Research Center: Internet and Technology, March 17, 2011, http://www.pewinternet.org/2011/03/17/the-internet-and-campaign-2010/ (accessed July 14, 2018).

23. J. Weedon, W. Nuland, and A. Stamos, "Information Operations and Facebook," April 27, 2017, https://fbnewsroomus.files.wordpress.com/2017/04/facebook-and-information-operations-v1.pdf, pp. 1–13.

24. On the study of misinformation by communications researchers, see L. Bode and U. K. Vraga, "In Related News, That Was Wrong: The Correction of Misinformation through Related Stories Functionality in Social Media," *Journal of Communication* 65, no. 4 (2015), 619–38. On the role of disinformation in politics, see A. Marwick and R. Lewis, "Media Manipulation and Disinformation Online," (2017) Data and Society Research Institute, from https://datasociety.net/output/media-manipulation-and-disinfo-online/, pp. 1–104.

25. Jacob E. Cook, ed., *The Federalist* (Middletown, CT: Wesleyan University Press, 1961); Bimber, *Information and American Democracy*, 35.

26. Ibid., 34–35.

27. Quoted in Ibid., 43.

28. Cortada, *All the Facts.*

29. Irving Fang, *A History of Mass Communication: Six Information Revolutions* (Boston, MA: Focal Press, 1997), 52.

30. Robert J. Rayback, *Millard Fillmore: Biography of a President* (Newtown, CT: American Political Biography Press, 1992), 375–414; Paul Finkelman, *Millard Fillmore* (New York: Times Books, 2011), 72–100; and for comparison to President Trump, Jude Sheerin, "Is This the US President Most Like Trump?" BBC News, July 6, 2018, https://www.bbc.com/news/world-us-canada-44688337 (accessed July 14, 2018).

31. Annette Gordon-Reed, *Thomas Jefferson and Sally Hemings: An American Controversy* (Charlottesville: University of Virginia Press, 1997); Jan Ellen Taylor and Peter S. Onuf, eds., *Sally Hemings and Thomas Jefferson: History, Memory, and Civic Culture* (Charlottesville: University of Virginia Press, 1999).

32. Quoted in Michael John Burton and Daniel M. Shea, *Campaign Craft: The Strategies, Tactics, and Art of Political Campaign Management* (Santa Barbara, CA: Praeger, 2010), 55.

33. Quoted in F. I. Luntz, *Candidates, Consultants, and Campaigns: The Style and Substance of American Electioneering* (Oxford: Blackwood, 1988), 72.

34. Burton and Shea, Campaign Craft, 56.

35. Ibid., 59–60.

36. William J. Bryan, *Speeches of William Jennings Bryan* (New York: Funk & Wagnalls, 1913), 249.

37. William T. Horner, *Ohio's Kingmaker: Mark Hanna, Man and Myth* (Athens: Ohio University Press, 2010), 176–212.

38. Some Democratic Party campaign offices distributed flat metal ephemera with a picture of Nixon and the phrase "Tricky Dick" imprinted on it that, when squeezed, made a "click" sound. One of your author's had one.

39. Hunt Allcott and Matthew Gentzkow, "Social Media and Fake News in the 2016 Election," NBER Working Paper 23089, April 2017, National Bureau of Economic Research, http://www/nber.org/papers/w23089 (accessed July 14, 2018).

40. H. W. Brands, *Andrew Jackson: His Life and Times* (New York: Doubleday, 2005), 414.

41. John Lewis Gaddis, *On Grand Strategy* (New York: Penguin, 2018), 218.

42. Sean Wilentz, *The Rise of American Democracy: Jefferson to Lincoln* (New York: W.W. Norton, 2005), 255.

43. Lynn Hudson Parsons, *The Birth of Modern Politics: Andrew Jackson, John Quincy Adams, and the Election of 1828* (New York: Oxford University Press, 2009), 160.

44. Parsons, *The Birth of Modern Politics*, 160.

45. Quoted in Brands, *Andrew Jackson*, 63.

46. Ibid. Another, Robert V. Remini, arguably the most highly regarded biographer of Jackson, did too: "Technical adultery and bigamy had been committed, although Rachel and Andrew were guiltless of intentional wrongdoing," *The Election of Andrew Jackson* (Philadelphia, PA: J.B. Lippincott, 1963), 152. For his account of the scandal, Ibid., 151–53.

47. Quoted by Pessen, *Jacksonian America*, 173.

48. Norma Basch, "Marriage, Morals, and Politics in the Election of 1828," *Journal of American History* 80, no. 3 (December 1993): 890–918.

49. Ibid., 892.

50. Ibid., 893.

51. Brands, *Andrew Jackson*, 397–402.

52. Quoted in Basch, "Marriage, Morals, and the Election of 1828," 897. Quotes below from contemporary pamphlets and newspapers are from her article.

53. Quoted in Ibid., 897.

54. Ibid.

55. Ibid., 897–900.

56. All quotes in Ibid., 900–901.

57. In addition to the Virginia legislation there was the equally damaging text of the divorce papers themselves issued by the Court of Quarter Sessions in Mercer County, Kentucky, a public record.

58. Quoted in Basch, "Marriage, Morals, and Politics in the Election of 1828," 903.

59. Quoted in Ibid.

60. Quoted in Ibid., 904.

61. All quoted in Parsons, *The Birth of Modern Politics*, 143–44.

62. Ibid., 906.

63. Brands, *Andrew Jackson*, 398.

64. *Supplemental Account of Some of the Bloody Deeds of General Jackson, Being a Supplement to the 'Coffin Handbill,'* " US Library of Congress, available at https://campaignrhetoric.files.wordpress.com/2014/01/1828 -supplemental-account-text.pdf (accessed July 30, 2018).

65. Ibid.

66. Remini, *The Election of Andrew Jackson*, 189–91.

67. Pessen, *Jacksonian America*, 178.

68. Ibid., 179.

69. A number of historians looking at this election commented about the rhetoric and charges exchanged, including Robert V. Remini, *The Elec-*

tion of Andrew Jackson (Philadelphia, PA: Lippincott, 1963); Robert Gray Gunderson, *The Log-Cabin Campaign* (Lexington: University of Kentucky Press, 1957); Pessen, *Jacksonian America*; Lynn Hudson Parsons, *The Birth of Modern Politics: Andrew Jackson, John Quincy Adams and the Election of 1828* (New York: Oxford University Press, 2009); Donald B. Cole, *Vindicating Andrew Jackson: The 1828 Election and the Rise of the Two-Party System* (Lawrence: University Press of Kansas, 2009),

70. Remini, *The Election of Andrew Jackson*, 76–80.

CHAPTER 3

1. Richard Hofstadter, "The Paranoid Style in American Politics," *Harper's Magazine*, November 1964, 77.

2. For decades a pro-Kennedy book defined what Americans knew about the election, Theodor H. White, *The Making of the President 1960* (New York: Atheneum, 1961).

3. Kallina Jr., *Kennedy v. Nixon*, 1–2.

4. Ibid., 2.

5. A subject studied almost from the beginning, James G. Powell, "An Analytical and Comparative Study of the Persuasion of Kennedy and Nixon in the 1960 Campaign." PhD dissertation, University of Wisconsin, 1963; Vito N. Silvestri, "John F. Kennedy: His Speaking in the Wisconsin and West Virginia Primaries in 1960." PhD dissertation, Indiana University, 1966.

6. White, *The Making of the President 1960*, 232.

7. Ibid.

8. Quoted in David Pietrusza, *1960 LBJ vs. JFK vs. Nixon: The Epic Campaign That Forged Three Presidencies* (New York: Union Square Press, 2008), 167.

9. *New York Times*, July 5, 1960, 1, 18.

10. Quoted in Pietrusza, *1960 LBJ vs. JFK vs. Nixon*, 169. During Donald Trump's run for the presidency in 2016, he, too, had his doctor release a similar letter that also proved to be less than truthful.

11. Discussed in considerable detail by David L. Robb, *The Gumshoe and the Shrink: Guenther Reinhardt, Dr. Arnold Hutschnecker, and The Secret History of the 1960 Kennedy/Nixon Election* (Solana Beach, CA: Santa Monica Press, 2012). Copies of Nixon's records were put into the hands of the Democratic campaign staff, Ibid., 192.

12. Quoted in Ibid., 194.

13. Kallina Jr., *Kennedy vs. Nixon*, 31.

14. Quoted in Ibid., 32, and his footnote 19, 223, citing various contemporary figures who heard the same denials.

15. Pietrusza, *1960 LBJ vs. JFK vs. Nixon*, 247.

16. *Look*, March 3, 1959, 13–17.

17. Pietrusza, *1960 LBJ vs. JFK vs. Nixon*, 247–49.

18. Quoted in Ibid., 248.

19. Gary A. Donaldson, *The First Modern Campaign: Kennedy, Nixon, and the Election of 1960* (Lanham, MD: Rowman & Littlefield, 2007), 57–60.

20. Pietrusza, *1960 LBJ vs. JFK vs. Nixon*, 250; Donaldson, *The First Modern Campaign*, 39–42.

21. Summarized in Pietrusza, *1960 LBJ vs. JFK vs. Nixon*, 250.

22. Joseph P. Lash, *Eleanor: The Years Alone* (New York: W.W. Norton, 1972), 282.

23. Quoted in Pietrusza, *1960 LBJ vs. JFK vs. Nixon*, 252.

24. Quoted in Ibid., 251.

25. Quoted in Ibid., 252.

26. Quoted in Ibid.

27. Ibid.; Mark S. Massa, "A Catholic for President? John F. Kennedy and the "Secular" Theology of the Houston Speech, 1960," *Church and State* 39 (1997): 297–317.

28. For a larger set of quotes from that speech, see White, *The Making of the President 1960*, 285.

29. For a history of the Houston event, see Diane A. Kemper, "John F. Kennedy before the Greater Houston Ministerial Association, September 12, 1960: The Religious Issue." PhD dissertation, Michigan State University, 1968.

30. *Milwaukee Journal* published on April 3 an analysis of the religious factor in voting, which added attention on top of the mailings. For analysis, see Kallina, *Kennedy vs. Nixon*, 57–58.

31. Ibid.

32. But analysis of the election results of November demonstrated that religious views definitely affected voter behavior, Andrew R. Baggaley, "Religious Influence on Wisconsin Voting, 1928–1960," *American Political Science Review* 56, no. 1 (March 1962): 66–70.

33. Kallina, *Kennedy vs. Nixon*, 58–59.

34. Ibid., 60.

35. William F. Thompson, *The History of Wisconsin: Continuity and Change, 1940–1965* (Madison: State Historical Society of Wisconsin, 1988), 686–92.

36. Kallina, *Kennedy vs. Nixon*, 61.

37. Ibid., 65.

38. Ibid.; Seymour Hersh, *The Dark Side of Camelot* (Boston: Little, Brown, 1997), 90, 101; White, *The Making of the President 1960*, 104–25.

39. For a detailed discussion, quotes of complaints, and analysis, see Kallina, *Courthouse over White House*, 99–144.

40. *Chicago Tribune*, November 24, 1960.

41. *New York Herald Tribune*, December 4–7, 1960; Edmund F. Kallina, "Was the 1960 Presidential Election Stolen? The Case of Illinois," *Presidential Studies Quarterly* 15, no. 1 (Winter 1985): 113–18. These were four of a planned twelve articles; the last eight were not published because Nixon had asked the newspaper not to do so to avoid creating a constitutional crisis. The reported repeatedly confirmed Nixon's action for the rest of his life.

42. Quoted in Kallina, *Kennedy v. Nixon*, 201.

43. Ibid., 206.

44. Ibid., 207.

45. Ibid., 209, and for evidence of fraud, 209–14.

46. Ibid., 212.

47. White, *The Making of the President 1960*, 366–69. White was the creator of the Camelot myth about Kennedy, which first appeared in a *Life* magazine article shortly after Kennedy's assassination.

48. Ibid., 333.

49. Pietrusza, *1960 LBJ vs. JFK vs. Nixon*, 342–53; Donaldson, *The First Modern Campaign*, 118; even the vice president acknowledged this fact, Richard Nixon, *Six Crises* (Garden City, NY: Doubleday, 1962), 325.

50. Quoted in Anthony Summers, *The Arrogance of Power: The Secret World of Richard Nixon* (New York: Viking, 2000), 208.

51. Kallina, *Kennedy v. Nixon*, 116–31.

52. For a video of the fifty-eight-minute debate, see https://www.youtube.com/watch?v=gbrcRKqLSRw (accessed July 18, 2018).

53. Alan Schroeder, *Presidential Debates: Fifty Years of High-Risk TV* (New York: Columbia University Press, 2008), 282, 285, 292–94, 297, 304.

54. Kallina, *Kennedy v. Nixon*, 124.

55. All quotes from Jay G. Blumler and Dennis Kavanagh, "The Third Age of Political Communication: Influences and Features," *Political Communication* 16 (1999): 1; on the idea of a Golden Age, see K. Janda and T. Colman, "Effects of Party Organization on Performance During the 'Golden Age' of Parties," *Political Studies* 46 (1998): 611–32; on the idea of consensus in this period, see D. C. Hallin, "The Passing of the 'High Modernism' in American Journalism," *Journal of Communication* 42, no. 3 (1992): 14–25.

56. Blumler and Kavanagh, "The Third Age of Political Communication: Influences and Features," 219; on the role of political misinformation, see L. Boda and E. K. Vraga, "In Related News, That Was Wrong: The Correction of Misinformation through Related Stories Functionality in Social Media," *Journal of Communication* 65, no. 4 (2015): 619–38.

CHAPTER 4

1. Philip Shenon, *A Cruel and Shocking Act: The Secret History of the Kennedy Assassination* (New York: Henry Holt, 2013), 525.

2. A recent example of continuing interest in presidential assassinations are two best-selling books *Killing Lincoln: The Shocking Assassination That Changed America Forever* (New York: Henry Holt, 2011), and *Killing Kennedy: The End of Camelot* (New York: Henry Holt, 2012)—and a less popular volume perhaps because the president did not die—*Killing Reagan: The Violent Assault That Changed a Presidency* (New York: Henry Holt, 2015). All three were written by Bill O'Reilly and Martin Dugard.

3. One professional historian who braved the risk and emerged with his reputation intact and with an outstanding book on Lincoln's assassination was William Hanchett, professor of history at San Diego State University and author of *The Lincoln Murder Conspiracies* (Urbana: University of Illinois Press, 1983).

4. The study of conspiracies has become a virtual growth industry among political scientists, sociologists, media experts, and historians, Joseph E. Uscinski, "The Study of Conspiracy Theories," *Arguments* 3, no. 2 (2018): 233–45.

5. Gabor Borritt, *The Lincoln Enigma: The Changing Faces of an American Icon* (New York: Oxford University Press, 2001); Philip B. Kunhardt III, Peter W. Kunhardt, and Peter W. Kunhardt Jr., *Looking for Lincoln: The Making of an American Icon* (New York: Alfred A. Knopf, 2008); Merrill D. Peterson, *Lincoln in American Memory* (New York: Oxford University Press, 1994).

6. Printed (no city or date) in *Stern Broadside*, vol. 4, no. 53, Rare Books and Special Collections Division, US Library of Congress.

7. For example, see, "Washington, Top the List of Favorite Presidents," February 17, 2014, Rasmussenreports.com (accessed February 16, 2018). This report is based on public polling. Historians and other experts on the presidency have also been polled for decades, and they too place Lincoln high on their lists, but not so frequently as being first or second in rank; Brandon Rottinghaus and Justin S. Vaughn, "How Does Trump Stack Up against the Best—and Worst—Presidents?" *New York Times*, February 19, 2018, 1. Being assassinated does not help one's rankings, as William McKenley, shot in 1901, ranked nineteenth in the 2018 survey indicates; meanwhile, FDR always came in about third in all rankings, and he was never shot.

8. Philip B. Kunhardt III, "Lincoln's Contested Legacy," *Smithsonian* 39, no. 11 (2009): 34–35.

9. Quoted in Harold Holzer, ed., *President Lincoln Assassinated: The Firsthand Story of the Murder, Manhunt, Trial, and Mourning* (New York: Library of America, 2014), 153, 154.

10. Quoted in Ibid., 160.

11. Quoted in Ibid., 182.

12. Quoted in Ibid., 169.

13. Quoted in Ibid., 257.

14. Quoted in Ibid., 354.

15. William Hanchett, *The Lincoln Murder Conspiracies* (Urbana: University of Illinois Press, 1986), 1.

16. As quoted in Dorothy Meserve Kunhardt and Philip B. Kunhardt, *Twenty Days* (New York: Harper & Row, 1965), foreword.

17. Hanchett, *The Lincoln Murder Conspiracies*, 1–2.

18. Edward Steers Jr., *Lincoln's Assassination* (Carbondale: Southern Illinois University Press, 2014), 3.

19. Ibid., 245.

20. See, for example, the anti-Booth tome, Michael W. Kauffman, *American Brutus: John Wilkes Booth and the Lincoln Conspiracies* (New York: Random House, 2004). For a friendlier, more complete treatment, see Terry Alford, *Fortune's Fool: The Life of John Wilkes Booth* (New York: Oxford University Press, 2015).

21. Walter Stahr, *Stanton: Lincoln's Secretary of War* (New York: Simon & Schuster, 2007).

22. Elizabeth D. Leonard, *Lincoln's Forgotten Ally: Judge Advocate General Joseph Holt* (Chapel Hill: University of North Carolina Press, 2011).

23. As an example of a possible several hundred by a distinguished Civil War historian relying largely on the president's papers, see David Herbert Donald, *Lincoln* (New York: Simon & Schuster, 1995).

24. Christopher A. Thomas, *The Lincoln Memorial and American Life* (Princeton, NJ: Princeton University Press, 2002), 144–68.

25. See, for example, Hanchett, *The Lincoln Murder Conspiracies*; Harold Holzer and Frank J. Williams, *The Lincoln Assassination: Crime and Punishment, Myth and Memory* (New York: Fordham University Press, 2010); Edward Steers, *Blood on the Moon* (Lexington: University of Kentucky Press, 2001).

26. Bill O'Reilly and Martin Dugard, *Killing Lincoln: The Shocking Assassination That Changed America Forever* (New York: Henry Holt, 2011).

27. John Rhodehamel and Louise Taper, eds., *"Right or Wrong, God Judge Me"* (Urbana: University of Illinois Press, 2001); Hamilton Howard, *Civil War Echoes: Character Sketches and State Secrets* (1907).

28. Clara Laughlin, *The Death of Lincoln: The Story of Booth's Plot, His Deed, and the Penalty* (New York: Doubleday, Page and Co., 1909); Kauffman, *American Brutus*.

29. William A. Tidwell, James O. Hall, and David Winfred Gaddy, *Come Retribution: The Confederate Secret Service and the Assassination of Lincoln* (New York: Barnes & Noble, 1988); Charles Higham, *Murdering Mr. Lincoln: A New Detection of the 19th Century's Most Famous Crime* (Beverley Hills, CA: New Millennium Press, 2004); William Hanchett, *The Lincoln Murder Conspiracies* (Urbana: University of Illinois Press, 1986), 59–89.

30. Of the advocates of his role, the most influential was Otto Eisenschiml, *Why Was Lincoln Murdered?* (New York: Grosset & Dunlap, 1937); for a detailed analysis of his claims that are debunked, see Hanchett, *The Lincoln Murder Conspiracies*, 158–209, 214–33.

31. Most recently argued by Higham, *Murdering Mr. Lincoln.*

32. All of the *Herald's* issues of April 15 are on exhibit at the Newseum in Washington, DC.

33. Quoted in Elahe Izadi, "How Newspapers Covered Abraham Lincoln's Assassination 150 Years Ago," *Washington Post*, April 14, 2015. See also, James R. Carroll, "Abraham Lincoln Assassination Coverage Revisited," Louisville, Kentucky, *Courier-Journal*, April 14, 2015, reprinted in *USA Today*, April 14, 2015.

34. Press reported reproduced in Harold Holzer, "The Assassination of Abraham Lincoln: What the Newspapers Said When Lincoln Was Killed," Smithsonian.com and also in *Smithsonian Magazine* (March 2015).

35. Harold Holzer, *Lincoln and the Power of the Press: The War for Public Opinion* (New York: Simon & Schuster, 2014).

36. "Assassination of President Lincoln!" *Richmond Whig*, April 17, 1865, 4.

37. Washington *Evening Star*, May 15, 1865, 1, US Library of Congress.

38. Ibid.

39. *Cleveland Leader*, June 30, 1865, 1, U.S Library of Congress.

40. Quoted in Hanchett, *The Lincoln Murder Conspiracies*, 11–12.

41. Quoted in Ibid., 18.

42. Ibid., 25.

43. Quoted in Thomas Reed Turner, *Beware the People Weeping: Public Opinion and the Assassination of Abraham Lincoln* (Baton Rouge: Louisiana State University Press, 1982), 46.

44. Quoted in Hanchett, *The Lincoln Murder Conspiracies*, 59.

45. Quoted in Ibid., 59.

46. Ibid., 75, 85–86.

47. Ibid., 158, although Alford in *Fortune's Fool*, has made the most concerted effort so far to resolve that issue.

48. For an excellent rebuttal, see Hanchett, *The Lincoln Conspiracies*, 158–84.

49. Ibid., 181.

50. Hanchett, *The Lincoln Conspiracies*, 183.

51. Eisenchiml, *Why Was Lincoln Murdered?* 17–18.

52. "Abraham Lincoln," *TV Guide*, http://www.tvguide. com/celebri ties/abraham-lincoln/credits/217924/ (accessed May 22, 2018).

53. Hanchett, *The Lincoln Conspiracies*, 214, and the case for false evidence, 185–244.

54. Ibid., 244.

55. On the difficulty of changing people's minds set within a political context, see Brendan Nyham, "Fake News and Bots May Be Worrisome, but Their Political Power Is Overblown," *New York Times*, February 13, 2018.

56. Washington, DC, *Evening Star*, May 15, 1865, 1.

57. https://www.nps.gov/moru/learn/management/statistics.htm.

58. Bernard Barber, *The Logic and Limits of Trust* (New Brunswick, NJ: Rutgers University Press, 1983); Vivien Hart, *Distrust and Democracy: Political Distrust in Britain and America* (New York: Cambridge University Press, 1978).

59. Cass Sunstein and Adrian Vermeule, "Conspiracy Theories: Causes and Cures," *Journal of Political Philosophy* 17, no. 2 (2009): 202–27; Uscinski, "The Study of Conspiracy Theories," 233–34.

60. J. Eric Oliver and Thomas J. Wood, "Conspiracy Theories and the Paranoid Style(s) of Mass Opinion," *American Journal of Political Science* 58, no. 4 (October 2014): 953.

61. Ibid., 952–66.

62. Michael Barkun, *A Culture of Conspiracy: Apocalyptic Visions in Contemporary America* (Berkeley: University of California Press, 2003); Mark Fenster, *Conspiracy Theories: Secrecy and Power in American Culture* (Minneapolis: University of Minnesota Press, 2008); and the founding father of such observations, Richard Hofstadter, *The Paranoid Style in American Politics* (New York: Knopf, 1964), especially 29. On the role narratives, see also Molly Patterson and Kristen Renwick Monroe, "Narrative in Political Science," *Annual Review of Political Science* 1 (1998): 315–31.

63. For the theoretical underpinnings of this observation, see Marc Hetherington, "The Political Relevance of Political Trust," *American Political Science Review* 92, no. 4 (1998): 791–808.

64. Oliver and Wood, "Conspiracy Theories and the Paranoid Style(s) of Mass Opinion," 964.

65. See, for example, Erving Goffman, *Interaction Ritual* (New York: Pantheon, 1967); Peter M. Hall, "The Quasi-Theory of Communication and the Management of Dissent," *Social Problems* 18 (1970): 18–27. For context and history of conspiracies as strategy by two sociologists, see Ginna Husting and Martin Orr, "Dangerous Machinery: 'Conspiracy Theorist' as a Transpersonal Strategy of Exclusion," *Symbolic Interaction* 30, no. 2 (2007): 127–50.

66. Eleanor Heartney, "The Sinister Beauty of Global Conspiracies," *New York Times*, October 16, 2003, 31.

67. David Altheide, *Creating Fear: News and the Construction of Crisis* (New York: Aldine de Gruyter, 2002), but see also his, "Notes toward a Politics of Fear," *Journal for Crime, Conflict, and the Media* 1, no. 1 (2003): 37–54; Barry Glassner, *The Culture of Fear: Why Americans Are Afraid of the Wrong Things* (New York: Basic Books, 1999).

CHAPTER 5

1. David Talbot, *Brothers: The Hidden History of the Kennedy Years* (New York: Free Press, 2007), 10.

2. Assassination Records Review Board, *Final Report of the Assassination Records Review Board* (September 1998), https://fas.org/sgp/adv isory/arrb98/index.html (accessed February 24, 2018); John R. Tunheim, "The Assassination Records Review Board: Unlocking the Government's Secret Files on the Murder of a President," *The Public Lawyer* 8, no. 1 (Winter, 2000), reprinted at http://mcadams.posc.mu.edu/arrb/tunheim.htm (accessed February 24, 2018).

3. In addition to these materials, publications appeared—so many, in fact, that one historian was able to publish a bibliography on the subject just nine years later, David R. Wrone, "The Assassination of John Fitzgerald Kennedy: An Annotated Bibliography," *The Wisconsin Magazine of History* 56, no. 1 (Autumn 1972): 21–36.

4. https://en.wikipedia.org/wiki/Assassination_of_John_F._Ken nedy. The entry is frequently updated (accessed February 24, 2018).

5. https://en.wikipedia.org/wiki/John_F._Kennedy_assassination _conspiracy_theories. This entry is frequently updated (accessed February 24, 2018).

6. One of the authors of this book (Cortada) was in a high school typing class, when another student burst in and said, "The president's been shot." Our all-boys school was located one block from the White House at 1736 G Street, so this was personal. Two hundred students poured out of their classes and rushed into a large assembly hall to see events on TV. High school boys don't cry, but this day they did.

7. As one example, *New York Times* best-seller, Philip Shenon, *A Cruel and Shocking Act: The Secret History of the Kennedy Assassination* (New York: Henry Holt, 2015); so too the Kennedy family "approved" version by William Manchester, *The Death of a President: November 20–November 25 1963* (New York: Harper & Row, 1967).

8. For example, Gallup Poll, November 21, 2003, www.gallup.com/poll/9751/americans-kennedy-assassination-conspiracy.aspx (accessed February 24, 2018).

9. "One JFK Conspiracy That Could Be True," *CNN*, November 18, 2013.

10. Manchester, *The Death of a President.*

11. *Report of the President's Commission on the Assassination of President John F. Kennedy* (Washington, DC: US Government Printing Office, 1964); 95th Congress, 2d Session, House Report No. 95-1828, Part 2, *Report of the Select Committee on Assassinations, U.S. House of Representatives Ninety-Fifth Congress* (Washington, DC: US Government Printing Office, 1979).

12. Walter Cronkite, *Who Shot President Kennedy?* (Public Television Stations and NOVA, 1988), available at https://www.youtube.com/watch?v=GpXN4ISn0zE (accessed February 28, 2018).

13. One of the most thorough investigations along this line of thinking is Joseph McBride, *Into the Nightmare: My Search for the Killers of President John F. Kennedy and Officer J. D. Tippit* (Berkeley, CA: Hightower Press, 2013).

14. https://www.archives.gov/press/press-releases/nr18-05 (accessed February 27, 2018).

15. See, for example, a survey from 1997 taken thirty-four years after the assassination, Karlyn Bowman, "Most Americans Don't Know Much about Fast-Track," *American Enterprise Institute for Public Policy Research*, September 4, 1997.

16. Lydia Saad, "Americans: Kennedy Assassination a Conspiracy," November 21, 2003, Gallup, gallup.com; Garry Langer, "John F. Kennedy's Assassination Leaves a Legacy of Suspicion," *ABC News*, November 16, 2003, http://abcnews.go.com/images/pdf/937a1JFKAssassination.pdf (accessed February 28, 2018).

17. Dana Blanton, "Poll: Most Believe 'Cover-Up' of JFK Assassination Facts," foxnews.com, http://www.foxnews.com/story/2004/06/18/poll-most-believe-cover-up-jfk-assassination-facts.html (accessed February 28, 2018).

18. "Majority in U.S. Still Believe JFK Killed in a Conspiracy: Mafia, Federal Government Top List of Potential Conspirators," Gallup, Inc., November 15, 2013, http://news.gallup.com/poll/165893/majority-believe-jfk-killed-conspiracy.aspx (accessed February 28, 2018).

19. Robert A. Caro, *The Passage of Power: The Years of Lyndon Johnson* (New York: Alfred A. Knopf, 2012), 450.

20. Vincent Bugliosi, *Reclaiming History: The Assassination of President John F. Kennedy* (Self-published in 2007; New York: W.W. Norton, 2008), 1273; James F. Broderick, *Web of Conspiracy: A Guide to Conspiracy Theory Sites on the Internet* (Medford, NJ: CyberAge Books, 2008), 208–209.

21. Shenon, *A Cruel and Shocking Act*, 11.

22. James D. Perry, ed., *Conspiracy Theories in American History: An Encyclopedia* (Santa Barbara, CA: ABC-CLIO, 2003), 383.

23. Quoted in Shenon, *A Cruel and Shocking Act*, 134.

24. Quoted in Ibid., 135.

25. Ibid., 135–38; but see as a widely circulated example, Mark Lane, *Rush to Judgment* (New York: Holt, Rinehart & Winston, 1966) and his sequel, *A Citizen's Dissent: Mark Lane Replies* (New York: Holt, Rinehart & Winston, 1968).

26. Shenon, *A Cruel and Shocking Act*, 13.

27. Ibid., 533.

28. Ibid., 535.

29. Ibid., 539.

30. Clarence M. Kelley and James Kirkpatrick Davis, *Kelley: The Story of an FBI Director* (Kansas City, MO: Andrews McMeel Publishing, 1987), 249.

31. Ibid.

32. Shenon, *A Cruel and Shocking Act*, 538–42.

33. Quoted in William Sullivan and Bill Brown, *The Bureau: My Thirty Years in Hoover's FBI* (New York: W.W. Norton, 1979), 51.

34. Shenon, *A Cruel and Shocking Act*, 548.

35. Ibid.

36. Ibid., 549.

37. Ibid., 550 cited articles in the *Dallas Morning News*, January 13, 2013; *Washington Post*, January 13, 2013.

38. Quotes in Shenon, *A Cruel and Shocking Act*, 558, 561.

39. Warren Commission Report, chapter 3, "The Shots from the Texas School Book Depository."

40. *Report of the Select Committee on Assassinations of the U.S. House of Representatives*, 44.

41. Ibid., Appendix VI; "3 Gunmen Involved in JFK's Slaying; 4 Bullets Fired," *St. Joseph Gazette*, November 16, 1967, 1A–2A, https://news.google.com/newspapers?id=4xNdAAAAIBAJ&sjid=MVoNAAAAIBAJ&pg=1431%2C2577977 (accessed March 9, 2018).

42. *Warren Report*.

43. Frequently reported in histories of the assassination, for example, Shenon, *A Cruel and Shocking Act*, 180, 196, 249–50, 252, 402, 447, 525; Jim Marrs, *Crossfire: The Plot That Killed Kennedy* (New York: Basic Books, 2013), 13–18, 20, 23, 39, 79–80, 82–88, 293–302.

44. Shenon, *A Cruel and Shocking Act*, 260–62.

45. Marrs, *Crossfire*, 550. Oswald stated on Friday afternoon that he was set up, using the word "patsy" to describe his role.

46. His main thesis, McBride, *Into the Nightmare.* It has been suggested that he had a different weapon for the shooting that was later swapped out for a regular police handgun by a confederate or at the site of his killing two hours later. Other reports of a rifle being used at that site and then hidden in a gutter drain also circulated.

47. Sylvan Fox, *The Unanswered Questions about President Kennedy's Assassination* (New York: Award Books, 1965), 84.

48. Ibid., 91.

49. Ibid., 97–98.

50. Jean Stafford, *A Mother in History: Marguerite Oswald, The Mother of the Man Who Killed Kennedy* (New York: Bantam Books, 1966), 14–15.

51. For example, McBride, *Into the Nightmare*; Marrs, *Crossfire.*

52. Shenon, *A Cruel and Shocking Act*, 451.

53. For an analysis of that concept, relying on the Lincoln funeral which was less designed to create myth than Kennedy's, but had that effect, see, B. Schwartz, "Mourning and the Making of a Sacred Symbol: Durkheim and the Lincoln Assassination," *Social Forces* 70, no. 2 (December 1991): 343–64.

54. 88th Congress, 1st Session, *John Fitzgerald Kennedy: Eulogies to the Late President Delivered in the Rotunda of the United States Capitol, November 24, 1963*, Senate Document No. 46 (Washington, DC: US Government Printing Office, 1963), 1.

55. Ibid., 3.

56. Ibid., 5.

57. Ibid., 6.

58. Larry J. Sabato, "Five Myths about John F. Kennedy," *Washington Post*, November 13, 2013, https://www.washingtonpost.com/opinions/five-myths-about-john-f-kennedy/2013/11/13/bf1d1442-4b1a-11e3-be6b-d3d28122e6d4_story.html?utm_term=.123ffb786bf5 (accessed March 9, 2018).

59. Peter Foster, "JFK: The Myth That Will Never Die," *Telegraph*, November 16, 2013, https://www.telegraph.co.uk/news/worldnews/northamerica/usa/johnfkennedy/10454024/JFK-the-myth-that-will-never-die.html (accessed March 9, 2018).

60. Larry J. Sabato, *The Kennedy Half-Century: The Presidency, Assassination, and Lasting Legacy of John F. Kennedy* (New York: Bloomsbury USA, 2013).

61. In fact, he wore a hat to his inauguration, taking it off only when delivering his speech, "John F. Kennedy's Hat: Did John F. Kennedy Appear Hatless as His Inauguration?" snopes.com, https://www.snopes.com/history/american/jfkhat.asp (accessed March 8, 2018). However, even snopes got it partially wrong, because Kennedy did not normally wear a

hat in his daily comings and goings, and increasingly other younger men did not either in the 1960s when dressed in suits.

62. Sabato, *The Kennedy Half-Century*, 424. See Ibid., 424–25, for a useful discussion of why President Kennedy remained so attractive to Americans, even a half century after his death, even with his widow's creation of Camelot, which Sabato called "brilliant fiction" that Americans were prepared to believe, Ibid., 425.

63. Stephanie Kelley-Romano, "Trust No One: The Conspiracy Genre on American Television," *Southern Communication Journal* 73, no. 2 (2008), 105–21; Jill Edy and Erin Baird, "The Persistence of Rumor Communities: Public Resistance to Official Debunking in the Internet Age," *APSA 2012 Annual Meeting Paper*, July 15, 2012, https://papers.ssrn.com/sol3/papers.cfm?abstract_id=2108292.

64. Shanto Iyengar, *Is Anyone Responsible? How Television Frames Political Issues* (Chicago: University of Chicago Press, 1991), 11–16, 82–102.

65. Robert A. Caro, *The Passage of Power: The Years of Lyndon Johnson* (New York: Knopf, 2012), 437–51.

CHAPTER 6

1. J. B. Crabtree, *The Passing of Spain and the Ascendency of America* (Springfield, MA: King-Richardson Publishing, 1898), 422.

2. George Bronson Rea, *Facts and Fakes about Cuba* (New York: George Munro's Sons, 1897).

3. The historical literature is substantial. Some good examples include Walter LaFeber, *The New Empire: An Interpretation of American Expansion, 1860–1898* (Ithaca, NY: Cornell University Press, 1963); G. J. A. O'Toole, *The Spanish War: An American Epic 1898* (New York: W.W. Norton, 1984); and Joyce Milton, *The Yellow Kids: Foreign Correspondence in the Heyday of Yellow Journalism* (New York: Harper & Row, 1989). For a US Navy reassessment of the fate of the USS *Maine*, see H. G. Rickover, *How the Battleship Maine Was Destroyed* (Washington, DC: Department of the Navy, 1976).

4. Thirty-five years after the end of the war, the volume of analytical and academic literature on the topic was substantial, see the citations in Joseph E. Wisan, *The Cuban Crisis as Reflected in the New York Press (1895–1898)* (New York: Columbia University Press, 1934), 461–66; and for a more recent bibliography, see Michael Blow, *A Ship to Remember: The Maine and the Spanish-American War* (New York: William Morrow, 1992), 465–77. For the most comprehensive history of the war, see Ivan

Musicant, *Empire by Default: The Spanish-American War and the Dawn of the American Century* (New York: Henry Holt, 1998).

5. LaFeber, *The New Empire*, 285–62; Luis Martínez-Fernández, *Torn between Empires: Economy, Society, and Patterns of Political Thought in the Hispanic Caribbean, 1840–1878* (Athens: University of Georgia Press, 1994), but see two older studies more focused on Cuba, Basil Rauch, *American Interest in Cuba, 1848–1855* (New York: Columbia University Press, 1948) and James W. Cortada, *Spain and the American Civil War: Relations at Mid-Century, 1855–1868* (Philadelphia, PA: American Philosophical Society, 1980), 10–29, 83–92.

6. The phrase "yellow journalism," also called "yellow press," refers to journalism that published sensational stories with few or no validated facts in order to promote the sale of newspapers. Yellow journalists exaggerated events, made up or promoted scandals, sensationalized stories, and employed other unprofessional journalistic practices in their coverage of the Cuba situation. See Joseph W. Campbell, *Yellow Journalism: Puncturing the Myths, Defining the Legacies* (Westport, CT: Greenwood Press, 2001); and Mark. M. Welter, "The 1895–1898 Cuban Crisis in Minnesota Newspapers: Testing the 'Yellow Journalism' Theory," *Journalism Quarterly* 47 (Winter 1970): 719–24.

7. Marcus M. Wilkerson, *Public Opinion and the Spanish-American War: A Study in War Propaganda* (Baton Rouge: Louisiana State University Press, 1932); Joseph E. Wisan, *The Cuban Crisis as Reflected in the New York Press, 1895–1898* (New York: Columbia University Press, 1934).

8. Musicant, *Empire by Default*; Milton, *The Yellow Kids*; James W. Cortada, *Two Nations over Time: Spain and the United States, 1776–1977* (Westport, CT: Greenwood Press, 1978), 89–129. There is a robust and growing body of historical research written in Spanish not yet reflected in American historical analyses of the Spanish-American War. See, for example, Cristobal Robles Muñoz, *1898: Diplomacia y Opinion* (Madrid: Consejo Superior de Investigaciones Cientificas, 1991), 31–86; Javier Rubio, *El Final de la Era de Cánovas: Los Preliminares del "Desastre" de 1898*, 2 vols. (Madrid: Ministerio de Asuntos Exteriores, 2004); Julián Companys Monclús, *España en 1898: Entre la Diplomacia y la Guerra* (Madrid: Ministerio de Asuntos Exteriores, 1991), 309–17; and José Manuel Allendesalazar, *El 98 de los Amercianos* (Madrid: Ministerio de Asuntos Exteriores, 1997), 39–116. Perhaps the most useful study of American opinions regarding Cuba and Spain in this period has been written by Jaime de Ojeda Eiseley, *El 98 en el Congreso y en la Prensa de los Estados Unidos* (Madrid: Ministerio de Asuntos Exteriores, 1999), see especially 41–104, on the period up to the declaration of war. During the centennial decade of the war in the 1990s some forty scholarly books were published in Spain, only five in the United States.

9. The most thorough treatment is by Musicant, *Empire by Default*.

10. While Congressmen railed against Spain on the floor of the US Congress, behind the scenes for decades they sought, collected, and published detailed, fact-based collections of studies and diplomatic correspondence related to the Cuban question. On the *Black Warrior* incident of 1854, see, for example, "Message from the President of the United States, A Report in Regard to Spanish Violations of the Rights of American Citizens," 33rd Congress, 1st Session, 1854, which extended to 378 pages; on additional ship seizures in the early days of the Ten Years War (1868–1878), see *Correspondence of the Department of State in Relation to the Seizure of American Vessels and Injuries to American Citizens* (Washington, DC: Government Printing Office, 1870), a 246-page document; and on the explosion of the USS *Maine* see the sober and thorough analysis conducted by the US Navy, *Message from the President of the United States, Transmitting the Report of the Naval Court of Inquiry upon the Destruction of the United States Battle Ship Maine in Havana Harbor, February 15, 1989, Together with the Testimony Taken before the Court* (Washington, DC: Government Printing Office, 1898). More than forty reports and documents were published about Cuba as part of Congressional proceedings between 1819 and the mid-1890s.

11. The spread of stories was facilitated by the wire services of the Associated Press (AP, founded 1846), headquartered in New York. Most regional newspapers belonged to AP. Between development of new printing techniques that facilitated publication of multiple daily editions of a newspapers—hence invention of what later would be called the "news cycle" and extensive use of the telegraph (later telephone) to transmit information to subscribers, newspapers all over the United States could repeat stories, rumors, and the like, published by members of the network. See Richard Allen Schwarzlose, *The Nation's Newsbrokers*, vol. 2, *The Rush to Institution: From 1865 to 1920* (Chicago: Northwestern University Press, 1990), 10–38.

12. On the rumors and legends surrounding the 9/11 terrorist attacks, see the authors' forthcoming book, *From Urban Legends to Political Fact-Checking: Online Scrutiny in America, 1990–2015*.

13. See our coverage of the 9/11 terrorist attacks in our *From Urban Legends to Political Fact-Checking*.

14. "The Spanish Butchery," *Harper's Weekly*, November 29, 1873, 6. At the time of the Spanish-American War, earlier incidents with Spain were brought up again—with illustrations. With this case, there was the publication of an etching showing a Spanish Army execution squad lined up as the captain of the ship says his final farewell before being shot along with a line of other crew members. See James W. Buel, *Hero Tales of the*

American Soldier and Sailor as Told by Heroes Themselves and Their Comrades: The Unwritten History of American Chivalry (Century 1899), 141.

15. Cortada, *Two Nations over Time*, 52–109; Musicant, *Empire by Default*, 38–78; Ojeda Eiseley, *El 98 en el Congreso y en la Prensa de los Estados Unidos*, 12–36; Gerald E. Poyo, *"With All, and for the Good of All": The Emergence of Popular Nationalism in the Cuban Communities of the United States, 1848–1898* (Durham, NC: Duke University Press, 1989), 20–94.

16. The standard work is by Tom Chaffin, *Fatal Glory: Narcisco López and the First Clandestine US War against Cuba* (Charlottesville: University of Virginia Press, 1996); see also, Rodrigo Lazo, *Writing to Cuba: Filibustering and Cuban Exiles in the United States* (Chapel Hill: University of North Carolina Press, 2005); two important studies by Robert E. May, *Manifest Destiny's Underworld: Filibustering in Antebellum America* (Chapel Hill: University of North Carolina Press, 2002) and *The Southern Dream of a Caribbean Empire* (Gainesville: University of Florida Press, 2002). Even the earliest history of the expeditions discussed the inaccurate news coverage and its politicization, for example, Anderson G. Quisenberry, *Lopez's Expeditions to Cuba, 1850 and 1851* (Louisville, KY: Louisville University Press, 1906).

17. Chaffin, *Fatal Glory*, quoted, 59.

18. Ibid., 144.

19. Ibid., for quote.

20. Ibid., for quote.

21. Ibid., for quote.

22. Ibid., for quote, 196. "Lexington" was a reference to the first battle of the American Revolution on April 19, 1775, and was seen as the first military step leading to the establishment of the United States independent from the British. Every child attending school in the nineteenth century would have understood the reference.

23. Ibid., for quote, 218.

24. Ibid., for quote, 219.

25. Ibid., for quotes, 218–19.

26. The subject of much important historical analysis, of which the most useful include Gavin B. Henderson, "Southern Designs on Cuba, 1854–1857 and Some European Opinions," *Journal of Southern History* 5, no. 3 (1939): 371–85; Lester D. Langley, "Slavery, Reform, and American Policy in Cuba, 1823–1889," *Revista de Historia de America* (1968): 71–84; J. Preston Moore, "Pierre Soulé: Southern Expansionist and Promoter," *Journal of Southern History* 21, no. 2 (May 1955): 203–23; Lars Shoultz, *Beneath the United States: A History of US Policy toward Latin America* (Cambridge, MA: Harvard University Press, 1998), 39–58.

27. "Message from the President of the United States, A Report in Regard to Spanish Violations of the Rights of American Citizens," 33rd

Congress, 1st Session, 1854. An authoritative discussion of the role of the *Black Warrior* affair can be found in Amos Aschbach Ettinger, *The Mission to Spain of Pierre Soulé: A Study in the Cuban Diplomacy of the United States* (New Haven, CT: Yale University Press, 1932), 250–90.

28. The standard work is by Richard H. Bradford, *The Virginius Affair* (Boulder: Colorado Associated University Press, 1980).

29. Quoted in James Morton Callahan, *Cuba and International Relations: A Historical Study in American Diplomacy* (Baltimore, MD: Johns Hopkins University Press, 1899), 402.

30. *New York Times*, November 18, 1873.

31. First quote, *New York Post*, November 13, 1873, second quote, *New York Times*, November 13, 1873.

32. Quoted in Stephen McCullough, *The Caribbean Policy of the Ulysses S. Grant Administration: Foreshadowing an Informal Empire* (Lanham, MD: Lexington Books, 2018): 154.

33. Ibid., quoted in, 173.

34. Ibid., quoted in, 65; see also, Wilkerson, *Public Opinion and the Spanish-American War*, 24–25.

35. Bradford, *The Virginius Affair*, 66.

36. The press even accused each other of falsification of news, see, for example, *New York Times*, November 28, 1873, which attacked the *Herald*, accusing it of "bogus" news; Bradford concluded the press had acted moderately in general, *The Virginius Affair*, 131.

37. George W. Auxier, "The Propaganda Activities of the Cuban Junta in Precipitating the Spanish-American War, 1895–1898," *Hispanic American Historical Review* 19, no. 3 (August 1939): 286–305; Poyo, "With All, and for the Good of All," 120–25; Toole, *The Spanish War*, 39–40, 59–64.

38. Milton, *The Yellow Kids*.

39. Ibid.; see, too, Wisan, *The Cuban Crisis as Reflected in the New York Press*, and Wilkerson, *Public Opinion and the Spanish-American War*.

40. Gabriel Cardona and Juan Carlos Losada, *Weyler: Nuestro Hombre en La Habana* (Barcelona: Planeta, 1997), 34–59.

41. Quoted in Musicant, *Empire by Default*, 67.

42. Cardona and Losada, *Weyler*, 154–241.

43. Andreas Stucki, *Las Guerras de Cuba: Violencia y campos de concentración (1868–1898)* (Madrid: Laesfera de los libros, 2017), 10. In 2013, he published the original German edition of his study, *Aufstand und Zwangsumsiedlung. Die Kubanischen Unabhängigkeitkriege (1868–1898)* (Hamburg: Hamburger Edition, 2012).

44. Their role is the central topic of discussion by Milton, *The Yellow Kids*.

45. Auxier, "The Propaganda Activities of the Cuban Junta in Precipitating the Spanish-American War, 1895–1898," 288.

46. Ibid., 291–92.

47. Claude Mathews, *The Cuban Cause Is Just: The Right Shall Prevail, and in God's Own Time Cuba Shall Be Free* (Philadelphia, PA: Hoes Collection, US Library of Congress, 1895).

48. Auxier, "The Propaganda Activities of the Cuban Junta in Precipitating the Spanish-American War, 1895–1898," 299–300.

49. Musicant, *Empire by Default*, 83–85.

50. Ibid., 132.

51. *Chicago Times-Herald*, January 26, 1896, 6.

52. Quoted in Wilkerson, *Public Opinion and the Spanish-American War*, 29.

53. Quoted in Ibid., 32.

54. Quotes in Ibid., 33.

55. Quoted in Ibid., 34.

56. Quoted in Ibid., 35.

57. Ibid.

58. Quoted in Ibid., 37.

59. Stucki, *Las Guerras de Cuba*; but see also, Wilkerson, *Public Opinion and the Spanish-American War*, 39–40.

60. Wilkerson, *Public Opinion and the Spanish-American War*, 46.

61. *World*, February 13, 1897, 6.

62. Wilkerson, *Public Opinion and the Spanish-American War*, 45.

63. Two examples from a larger body of numerous reports are "Affairs in Cuba: Message of the President of the United States on the Relations of the United States to Spain," and "Report of the Committee on Foreign Relations, United States Senate, Relative to the Affairs in Cuba," published together (Washington, DC: Government Printing Office, 1898) in 636 pages, complete with photographs and maps. For a review of Congressional behavior, see Ojeda Eiseley, *El 98 en el Congreso y en la Prensa de los Estados Unidos*, 39–72.

64. Wisan, *The Cuban Crisis as Reflected in the New York Press*, 65–66; Ojeda Eiseley, *El 98 en el Congreso y en la Prensa de los Estados Unidos*, 68–70.

65. Wilkerson, *Public Opinion and the Spanish-American War*, 52.

66. Wisan, *The Cuban Crisis as Reflected in the New York Press*, 47–48, 94–98.

67. Ibid., 61; but for details of the incident, see Rea, *Facts and Fakes about Cuba*, 151.

68. The most current and useful account can be found in Musicant, *Empire by Default*, 126–44, 147–49, 150–57, 169–70.

69. George W. Auxier, "Middle Western Newspapers and the Spanish American War, 1895–1898," *The Mississippi Valley Historical Review* 26, no. 4 (March 1940): 523–34; Harold Sylwester, "The Kansas Press and the Coming of the Spanish-American War," *Historian* 31, no. 2 (February

1969): 251–67; Carmen González López-Briones, "The Indiana Press and the Coming of the Spanish-American War, 1895–1898," *Atlantis* 12, no. 1 (June 1990): 165–76.

70. The principal board of inquiry was the one convened in 1898, as reported in *Message of the President of the United States Transmitting the Report of the Naval Court of Inquiry upon the Destruction of the United States Battle Ship Maine in Havana Harbor, February 15, 1898, Together with the Testimony Taken before the Court* (Washington, DC: Government Printing Office, 1898). It was a thorough, detailed analysis of approximately three hundred pages. Additional important sources on the subject include: Thomas B. Allen, "What Really Sank the Maine?" *Naval History* 11 (March–April 1998): 30–39; Michael Blow, *A Ship to Remember: The Maine and the Spanish-American War* (New York: William Morrow, 1992); Philip S. Foner, *The Spanish-Cuban-American War and the Birth of American Imperialism, 1895–1902*, 2 vols., but especially vol. 1 (New York: Monthly Review Press, 1972); John Edward Weems, *The Fate of the Maine* (College Station: Texas A&M University Press, 1992).

71. Thomas B. Allen, "Remember The Maine?," *National Geographic* 193, no. 2 (February 1998): 92–111.

72. Musicant, *Empire by Default*, 147–49, 166–70; Blow, *A Ship to Remember*, 422–41.

73. Louis A. Pérez Jr., "The Meaning of the Maine: Causation and the Historiography of the Spanish-American War," *Pacific Historical Review* 58, no. 3 (August 1989): 36. For a diverse set of historical interpretations based on the use of this incident, see Ibid., 315–19.

74. For example, Edward J. Marolda, *Theodore Roosevelt, the US Navy and the Spanish-American War* (London: Palgrave Macmillan, 2001).

75. Musicant, *Empire by Default*, 143–44.

76. Quoted in Ibid., 144.

77. Wisan, *The Cuban Crisis as Reflected in the New York Press*, 391–92.

78. Quotes from Musicant, *Empire by Default*, 144.

79. Quotes from Ibid.

80. Wilkerson, *Public Opinion and the Spanish-American War*, 100–107.

81. Ibid., 102.

82. Quoted in Ibid., 104.

83. Sylwester, "The Kansas Press and the Coming of the Spanish-American War"; López-Briones, "The Indiana Press and the Coming of the Spanish-American War, 1895–1898."

84. Quotes in Wilkerson, *Public Opinion and the Spanish-American War*, 106.

85. Ibid., 107.

86. For example, see Wisan, *The Cuban Crisis as Reflected in the New York Press*, 400–421.

87. Ibid., 459.

88. John Maxwell Hamilton, Renita Coleman, Bettye Grable, and Jaci Cole, "An Enabling Environment: A Reconsideration of the Press and the Spanish-American War," *Journalism Studies* 7, no. 1 (2006): 78.

89. Wisan, *The Cuban Crisis as Reflected in the New York Press*, 459.

90. Ibid., 460.

91. Ibid.

92. López-Briones, "The Indiana Press and the Coming of the Spanish-American War, 1895–1898," 165–76.

93. Once the war began, American reporters in the field partially reversed course and became more careful not to report on matters that compromised military security; they competed instead for stories that did not put soldiers at risk. Military censors on both sides looked to reporters for information—intelligence—that they could use inasmuch as their own reconnoitering and scouting efforts often proved less effective. For details on self-censorship, see Randall S. Sumpter, "'Censorship Liberally Administered': Press, US Military Relations in the Spanish-American War," *Communication Law and Policy* 4, no. 4 (1999): 463–81.

94. Christopher B. Daly, *Covering America: A Narrative History of a Nation's Journalism* (Amherst: University of Massachusetts Press, 2012), 151–84; David T. Z. Mindich, *Just the Facts: How "Objectivity" Came to Define American Journalism* (New York: New York University Press, 1998).

95. His flagship at the battle was the USS *Olympia*, a close copy of the USS *Maine*, preserved in the Philadelphia harbor and available for visits by tourists.

96. Musicant, *Empire by Default*, 375–89.

97. Ibid., 410–25.

98. Theodore Roosevelt, *The Rough Riders* (New York: Collier, 1899) in a 319-page edition. It went through numerous editions and remains in print.

99. Such as the excellent history of the war by Musicant, *Empire by Default*; but see also, for example, Graham A. Cosmas, *An Army for Empire: The United States Army in the Spanish-American War* (Columbia: University of Missouri Press, 1971).

100. Christine Bold, "The Rough Riders at Home and Abroad: Cody, Roosevelt, and Remington and the Imperialist Hero," *Canadian Review of American Studies* 18, no. 3 (1987): 322; full article, 321–50.

101. Ibid., 322.

102. Ibid., 322.

103. Ibid., for history of the Rough Rider image, 325–38.

104. Peggy and Harold Samuels, *Frederick Remington: A Biography* (Garden City, NY: Doubleday, 1982), 196; also Edmund Morris, *The Rise of Theodore Roosevelt* (New York: Ballantine Books, 1980), especially 460.

105. G. Edward White, *The Eastern Establishment and the Western Experience: The West of Fredric Remington, Theodore Roosevelt, and Owen Wister* (New Haven, CT: Yale University Press, 1968).

106. Quoted in Virgil Carrington Jones, *Roosevelt's Rough Riders* (Garden City, NY: Doubleday, 1971), 213.

107. Bold, "The Rough Riders at Home and Abroad: Cody, Roosevelt, Remington Rand and the Imperialist Hero," 331–32.

108. Quoted in Ibid., 332.

109. Ibid.

110. Jones, *Roosevelt's Rough Riders*, 265.

111. Quoted in Bold, "The Rough Riders at Home and Abroad: Cody, Roosevelt, Remington Rand and the Imperialist Hero," 332.

112. Quoted in White, *The Eastern Establishment and the Western Experience*, 169.

113. Jerome B. Crabtree, *The Passing of Spain and the Ascendency of America* (Springfield, MA: King-Richardson Publishing, 1898).

114. Quoted and discussed in Morris, *The Rise of Theodore Roosevelt*, 729.

115. Quoted in Bold, "The Rough Riders at Home and Abroad: Cody, Roosevelt, Remington Rand and the Imperialist Hero," 334.

116. Ibid., 347.

117. J. Hampton Moore, *Reminiscences and Thrilling Stories of the War by Returned Heroes Containing Vivid Accounts of Personal Experiences by Officers and Men,* and the title continues for many lines, such as *Daring Deeds of Our Brave Regulars and Volunteers at the Battles of La Quasina, El Caney and San Juan . . . Exciting Experiences in Porto Rico and at the Capture of Manila* (Chicago: H.J. Smith Publishing, 1898).

118. Joseph L. Stickney, *Life and Glorious Deeds of Admiral Dewey Including a Thrilling Account of Our Conflicts with the Spaniards and Filipinos in the Orient* (Philadelphia, PA: P.W. Ziegler, 1899).

119. Gonzalo de Quesada and Henry Davenport Northrop, *America's Battle for Cuba's Freedom Containing a Complete Record of Spanish Tyranny and Oppression Scenes of Violence and Bloodshed; Daring Deeds of Cuban Heroes and Patriots, Thrilling Incidents of the Conflict . . . Secret Expeditions; Inside Facts of the War* (Chicago: The Dominion Company, 1898).

120. Bold, "The Rough Riders at Home and Abroad: Cody, Roosevelt, Remington and the Imperialist Hero," 336–38.

121. G. J. Meyer, *The World Remade: America in World War I* (New York: Bantam, 2017), 27–43, 171–76.

122. Alan Axelrod, *Selling the Great War: The Making of American Propaganda* (New York: Palgrave Macmillan, 2009), 97–188; Elmer E. Cornwall, "Wilson, Creel and the Presidency," *Public Opinion Quarterly* 23, no. 2 (1959): 189–202.

123. James W. Cortada, *All the Facts: A History of Information in the United States Since 1870* (New York: Oxford University Press, 2016), 164–67.

124. For a more complete list with circulation statistics, see Ibid., 165.

125. Ibid., 230–33.

126. James W. Cortada, ed., *Modern Warfare in Spain: American Military Observations on the Spanish Civil War, 1936–1939* (Washington, DC: Potomac Books, 2012), xxii–xxv.

127. Parallel to military uses of information and misinformation was the more shadowy world of spies in evidence in American wars since the 1700s. Beginning in the Second World War and extending down to the present, the American government created a large collection of intelligence gathering agencies that also planted fake facts, lies, and misinformation within enemy organizations. The story of American warfare is thus much larger than what we are telling here, such as the activities of the OSS, CIA, NSA, and military intelligence agencies. The literature on this subject is vast. For introductions to this side of America's use of misinformation in warfare, see, G. J. A. O'Toole, *Honorable Treachery: A History of US Intelligence, Espionage, and Covert Action from the American Revolution to the CIA* (New York: Atlantic Monthly Press, 1991); Michael J. Sulick, *Spying in America: Espionage from the Revolutionary War to the Dawn of the Cold War* (Washington, DC: Georgetown University Press, 2012); R. Harris Smith, *OSS: The Secret History of America's First Central Intelligence Agency* (Berkeley: University of California Press, 1972); Patrick K. O'Donnell, *Operatives, Spies, and Saboteurs: The Unknown Story of the Men and Women of WWII's OSS* (New York: Free Press, 2004); on the CIA, see, David F. Rudgers, *Creating the Secret State: The Origins of the Central Intelligence Agency, 1943–1947* (Lawrence: University Press of Kansas, 2000), 149–81; Steve Coll, *Directorate S: The C.I.A. and America's Secret Wars in Afghanistan and Pakistan* (New York: Penguin Press, 2018); on the NSA, Fred Kaplan, *Dark Territory: The Secret History of Cyber War* (New York: Simon & Schuster, 2016); James Bamford, *The Puzzle Palace* (Boston: Houghton Mifflin Harcourt, 1984); Christopher Andrew, *The Secret World: A History of Intelligence* (New Haven, CT: Yale University Press, 2018), which includes a detailed bibliography; and Stephen F. Knott, *Secret and Sanctioned: Covert Operations and the American Presidency* (New York: Oxford University Press, 1996), which is especially useful in discussing the planting of misinformation in the American and foreign press, using techniques similar to those of the tobacco industry in the 1950s–2000s.

128. Michael Beschloss, *Presidents of War: The Epic Story, from 1807 to Modern Times* (New York: Crown, 2018), 492–95, 507–20, 541–43.

129. "Gulf of Tonkin Resolution Is Repealed," *New York Times*, January 14, 1971, https://www.nytimes.com/1971/01/14/archives/gulf-of-tonkin-resolution-is-repealed-without-furor.html.

130. Tom Gaskin, "The Lies and Legacy of LBJ's Gulf of Tonkin Resolution," HeraldNet, August 8, 2014, https://www.heraldnet.com/opinion/the-lies-and-legacy-of-lbjs-gulf-of-tonkin-resolution/.

CHAPTER 7

1. James Fenimore Cooper, *Miles Wallingford: Sequel to Afloat and Ashore* (New York: James G. Gregory, 1863 edition), 425.
2. Stuart Ewen, *PR! A Social History of Spin* (New York: Basic Books, 1996), 380.
3. Gary Alan Fine, "The Third Force in American Folklore: Folk Narratives and Social Structures," *Fabula* 29 (1988): 342–53; Prashant Bordia and Nicholas DiFonzo, "When Social Psychology Became Less Social: Prassad and the History of Rumor Research," *Asian Journal of Social Psychology* 5 (2002): 49–61; Roland Marchand, *Creating the Corporate Soul: The Rise of Public Relations and Corporate Imagery in American Big Business* (Berkeley: University of California Press, 1998); Ewen, *PR!*
4. Consumer beliefs in truthfulness of advertising has been in decline since the 1990s, with less than half confident in what they see, Judann Pollack, "Hey Brands: Almost Half of Americans Don't Find You Honest," *AdAge*, April 3, 2017, http://adage.com/article/special-report-4as-conference/mccann-survey-finds-half-america-trust-brand/308544/ (accessed July 30, 2018); for similar findings, "Under the Influence: Consumer Trust in Advertising," *Nielsen.com*, September 17, 2013, http://www.nielsen.com/us/en/insights/news/2013/under-the-influence-consumer-trust-in-advertising.html (accessed July 30, 2018).
5. Allan J. Kimmel, *Rumors and Rumor Control: A Manager's Guide to Understanding and Combatting Rumors* (Mahway, NJ: Lawrence Erlbaum Associates, 2004), 123–202.
6. This is not to be confused with the concept of *mercantilism*, which is an economic theory that postulates that trade generates wealth and that it is fostered by conducting profitable business supported by government policies that maximizes its national trade and economy. This term is still used by economists and historians.
7. William James, *Pragmatism and the Meaning of Truth* (Cambridge, MA: Harvard University Press, 1978)—combined edition of two books published in 1907 and 1909, respectively.
8. Ewen, *PR!* 40.
9. Ibid.

10. On new ways to acquire information that could only be partially derived from statistics but now can be acquired through other methods, see Judea Pearl, *The Book of Why: The New Science of Cause and Effect* (New York: Basic Books, 2018), 23–51, 109–10.

11. Lee McIntyre, *Post-Truth* (Cambridge, MA: MIT Press, 2018), 105.

12. James W. Cortada, *All the Facts: A History of Information in the United States since 1870* (New York: Oxford University Press, 2016), 64, 112–13, 166–185. We might add, secularization of society pushed aside some, but not all assessments of the veracity of facts through religious and folkloric lenses.

13. Quoted in Ewen, *PR!* 81.

14. Harry Overstreet, *Influencing Human Behavior* (New York: W.W. Norton, 1925), 34.

15. Marchand, *Creating the Corporate Soul*, 7–47.

16. G. W. Allport and L. J. Postman, *The Psychology of Rumor* (New York: Holt, Rinehart and Winston, 1947); Kimmel, *Rumors and Rumor Control*, 20–22, 30.

17. Kimmel, *Rumors and Rumor Control*, 25–28, and for types, 47.

18. On the differences between gossip and rumors, Ralph L. Rosnow and Gary Alan Fine, *Rumor and Gossp: The Social Psychology of Hearsay* (New York: Elsevier, 1976), 81–93.

19. S. Anthony, "Anxiety and Rumor," *Journal of Social Psychology* 89 (1973): 91–98.

20. Tamotsu Shibutani, *Improved News: A Sociological Study of Rumor* (Indianapolis, IN: Bobbs-Merrill, 1966).

21. Bordia and DiFanzo, "When Social Psychology Became Less Social: Prasad and the History of Rumor Research," 53.

22. Ibid., 54.

23. A long-understood behavior, Allport and Postman, *The Psychology of Rumor*.

24. Pew Foundation surveys on how Americans use the Internet conflate rumors and fake facts together. For recent patterns of behavior with respect to rumors see, Joanna Anderson and Lee Rainie, "The Future of Truth and Misinformation Online," Pew Research Center, October 19, 2017, http://assets.pewresearch.org/wp-content/uploads/sites/14/2017/10/19095643/PI_2017.10.19_Future-of-Truth-and-Misinformation_FINAL.pdf (accessed July 30, 2018).

25. Fine, "The Third Force in American Folklore," 345.

26. Ibid.

27. Ibid., 347.

28. Ibid., 348.

29. Kimmel, *Rumors and Rumor Control*, 4–14.

30. Ibid., 14–15.

31. Gary Alan Fine, "Redemption Rumors: Mercantile Legends and Corporate Beneficence," *Journal of American Folklore* 99 (1986): 208–22.

32. Fine, "The Third Force in American Folklore," 348.

33. Marchand, *Creating the Corporate Soul*; Ewen, *PR!*; Fred Koenig, *Rumors in the Marketplace: The Social Psychology of Commercial Hearsay* (New York: Praeger, 1985).

34. Fine, "The Third Force in American Folklore," 350.

35. Fine, "Mercantile Legends and the World Economy," 154.

36. Ibid.

37. Jan H. Brunvand, *The Vanishing Hitchhiker* (New York: W.W. Norton, 1981), 161.

38. "Snake in Coat Pocket," *Snopes*, https://www.snopes.com/fact -check/coat-of-armed/ (accessed July 31, 2018).

39. Brett M. Christensen, "Bananas Injected with HIV Hoax Warning," *Hoax-Slayer*, February 11, 2016, https://www.hoax-slayer.net/bananas -injected-with-hiv-hoax-warning/ (accessed July 30, 2018).

40. Véronique Campion-Vincent, "Complots et Avertissements: Légendes Urbaines dans la Ville," *Revue Français de Sociologie* 30 (1989): 91–105.

41. Quoted by Fine from a source published in 1989, Fine, "Mercantile Legends and the World Economy," 157.

42. Ibid., 158; Gary Alan Fine, *Manufacturing Tales: Sex and Money in Contemporary Legends* (Knoxville: University of Tennessee Press, 1992), 168–69.

43. For a summary of his use of that and other similar terms, see Kaitlyu D'Onofrio, "Trump Again Dehumanizes—Calls Them Vermin That Will 'Infest' America," June 20, 2018, *Diverstylnc*, https://www.diversi tyinc.com/news/trump-dehumanizes-immigrants-again-calls-them-ver min-that-will-infest-america.

44. Fine, "Mercantile Legends and the World Economy," 159.

45. Ibid.

46. Nicholas DiFonzo and Prashant Bordia, "How Top PR Professionals Handle Hearsay: Corporate Rumors, Their Effects, and Strategies to Manage Them," *Public Relations Review* 26, no. 2 (2000): 173–90 and by the same authors, "Corporate Rumor Activity, Belief and Accuracy," *Public Relations Review* 28, no. 1 (2002): 1–19 and the same authors with Ralph L. Rosnow, "Reining in Rumors," *Organizational Dynamics* 23 (1994): 47–62.

47. Kimmel, *Rumors and Rumor Control*, 36–37, 40.

48. DiFonzo, Bordia, and Rosnow, "Reining in Rumors," 49.

49. Kimmel, *Rumors and Rumor Control*.

50. James W. Cortada, *IBM: The Rise and Fall and Reinvention of an Iconic Corporation* (Cambridge, MA: MIT Press, 2019), 542–43, 566–70.

51. Gary Alan Fine, "Among Those Dark Satanic Mills: Rumors of Kooks, Cults, and Corporations," *Southern Folklore* 47 (October 1990): 133.

52. Kimmel, *Rumors and Rumor Control*, 4–14, 65–67, 93–94.

53. Ibid., for McDonald's 14–15, 57–58, 77–78, 178–79, 182–84, 62–65, for KFC, 36–37, 44–45, 72.

54. The Catholic Church prohibited people from loaning money at interest in the Middle Ages; so, credit was offered by Jewish bankers. They dominated banking into the twentieth century, but by the nineteenth century Christian bankers were active on both sides of the Atlantic. In the United States, Jewish film moguls were said to dominate Hollywood, although as in banking that perception was only partially correct, Neal Gabler, *An Empire of Their Own: How the Jews Invented Hollywood* (New York: Doubleday, 1988), 387–432.

55. Fine, "Among Those Dark Satanic Mills," 137.

56. Ibid., 133–46.

57. Ibid., 141; "Coors Beer: What Hit Us?" *Forbes* October 16, 1978, 71–73. Even this distinguished business magazine was suspected of nefarious connections since it too was a privately owned enterprise; Julie Solomon, "Procter & Gamble Fights New Rumors of Link to Satanism," *Wall Street Journal*, November 8, 1984.

58. Fine, *Manufacturing Tales*, 80.

59. James W. Cortada collected hundreds of these humorous ephemera between 1974 and 2013. Many were rumors, others cartoons and sayings that poked fun at IBM's culture and image in a good-hearted manner.

60. Quoted in Young, *The Medical Messiahs*, 260.

61. All quoted in Ibid., 269.

62. Werner Troesken, "The Elasticity of Demand with Respect to Product Failures; Or Why the Market for Quack Medicines Flourished for More Than 150 years," NBER Working Papers 15699 (Washington, DC: National Bureau of Economic Research, January 2010), 1–2.

63. Key studies include Stuart H. Holbrook, *The Golden Age*; James Harvey Young, *The Toadstool Millionaires: A Social History of Patent Medicines in America Before Federal Regulation* (Princeton, NJ: Princeton University Press, 1961) and his sequel, *The Medical Messiahs: A Social History of Health Quackery in Twentieth-Century America* (Princeton, NJ: Princeton University Press, 1967); Ann Anderson, *Snake Oil, Hustlers and Hambones: The American Medicine Show* (Jefferson, NC: McFarland, 2000).

64. Troesken, "The Elasticity of Demand with Respect to Product Failures; Or Why the Market for Quack Medicines Flourished for More Than 150 years," 1.

65. US House of Representatives, *A$10 billion scandal: Hearing before the Subcommittee on Health and Long-Term Care of the Select Committee on Aging, House of Representatives, Ninety-eighth Congress, second session, May 31, 1984* (Washington, DC: US Government Printing Office, 1984).

66. Quoted in Young, *The Medical Messiahs*, footnote 16, 121.

67. Consumer Reports, "Homeopathic Drugs: No Better Than Placebos?" *Washington Post*, December 21, 2015.

68. Clare Dyer, "Shareholders Are to Sue Drug Firm for Not Disclosing Adverse Reactions Even though Number Wasn't Significant," *British Medical Journal* 342 (March 29, 2011), https://search.proquest.com/openview/37870390d8dfd55d637b6be8389ca70c/1?pq-origsite=gscholar&cbl=2040978; Gardiner Harris, "F.D.A. Warns Against Use of Popular Cold Remedy," *New York Times*, June 16, 2009, https://www.klinespecter.com/sites/www.klinespecter.com/files/Zicam-FDA.pdf; Amy Gaither, "Over the Counter, Under the Radar: How the Zicam Incident Came About Under FDA's Historic Homeopathic Exception," *Administrative Law Review* 62, no. 2 (2010): 488–510.

69. Paul Starr, *The Social Transformation of American Medicine: The Rise of a Sovereign Profession and the Making of a Vast Industry* (New York: Basic Books, 1982), but see also his *Remedy and Reaction: The Peculiar American Struggle over Health Care Reform* (New Haven, CT: Yale University Press, 2013).

70. For several collections of advertising literature and labels, see the collection at the Hagley Museum and Library, https://findingaids.hagley.org/xtf/search?keyword=patent+medicines.

71. Anderson, *Snake Oil, Hustlers and Hambones*, 48–73, 103–25.

72. Daniel Pope, *The Making of Modern Advertising* (New York: Basic Books, 1983), 185.

73. Quoted in Ibid., 186.

74. Ibid., 187.

75. Reported in Young, *American Health Quackery*, 71.

76. Victor Herbert, *Nutrition Cultism: Facts and Fictions* (Philadelphia, PA: George F. Stickley, 1980), 14.

77. Ibid., 193.

78. Young, *The Toadstool Millionaires*.

79. Pope, *The Making of Modern Advertising*, 197.

80. Upton Sinclair, *The Jungle* (New York: Doubleday, Jabbar, 1906).

81. Young, *The Medical Messiahs*, 29–40.

82. Ibid., 113–28.

83. Ibid., 52–56.

84. Ibid., 63–64.

85. Ibid.

86. Door-to-door salesmen represented a notorious channel to distribute fake news and exaggerations that could not be documented or easily regulated of enormous concern to regulators, Young, *The Medical Messiahs*, 282–95.

87. IMS Health, "Top Line Industry Data: Total U.S. Promotional Spend by Type, 2005," http//www.imshealth.com/ims/portal/front/article/0.27777,2777.659978084568_78152318.00.html.

88. Young, *The Medical Messiahs*, 391.

89. Ibid.

90. James Cook, *Remedies and Rackets* (New York: W.W. Norton, 1958), 219–37.

91. For examples, see Young, *The Medical Messiahs*, footnote 13, 398.

92. Troesken, "The Elasticity of Demand with Respect to Product Failures," 48.

93. Ibid.

94. Barry Smith, "Guillible's Travails: Tuberculosis and Quackery, 1890–1930," *Journal of Contemporary History* 20 (1985): 733–56.

95. Troesken, "The Elasticity of Demand with Respect to Product Failures," 55.

96. Julie Donohue, "A History of Drug Advertising: The Evolving Roles of Consumers and Consumer Protection," *Milibank Quarterly* 84, no. 4 (December 2006): 659–99.

97. From advertisement replicated in Young, *American Health Quackery*, 96.

98. Ibid., 92.

99. Young, *American Health Quackery*, 234–39.

100. James Harvey Young, "Patent Medicines: An Early Example of Competitive Marketing," *The Journal of Economic History* 20, no. 4 (December 1960): 648–56.

101. Quoted in Troesken, "The Elasticity of Demand with Respect to Product Failures," 21.

102. Quoted in Ibid., 21.

103. Quoted in Ibid., 22.

104. Ibid.

105. Young, *The Toadstool Millionaires*, 58–59, 61–65, 137.

106. Peter Conrad and Valerie Leiter, "From Lydia Pinkham to Queen Levitra: Direct to Customer Advertising and Medicalism," *Sociology of Health & Illness* 30, no. 6 (2008): 825–38.

107. Copy on bottle at the Hagley Museum and Library.

108. From advertisement displayed in Anderson, *Snake Oil, Hustlers and Hambones*, 33.

109. From advertisement displayed in Ibid., 46.

110. Ibid.

111. His conclusion after studying patent medicines for over forty years, Young, *American Health Quackery*, 93.

112. Quoted in Young, *The Toadstool Millionaires*, 60.

113. Advertisement reproduced in Young, *American Health Quackery*, 36.

114. For illustrations of the advertisement and death notice, Ibid., 37.

115. Ibid., 188.

116. Ibid., 26.

117. Ibid., 186–87.

118. Ibid., Young, *The Medical Messiahs*, 132.

119. All quotes from Ibid., 319–20.

120. Ibid., 322.

121. Quoted in Cook, *Remedies and Rackets*, 51.

122. Ibid., 57.

123. "Snake Oil for the 21st Century," *Consumer Reports*, September 2013.

124. Although we choose our contemporary examples all from Whole Foods, one can find similar products at many other groceries and pharmacies today.

125. *Collagen + Coffee = A Perfect Match* (No City: Vital Proteins, circa 2018), unpaginated.

126. *Easy Guide to Homeopathic Medicines* (Newtown Square, PA: Boiron, 2017), unpaginated.

127. Ibid.

128. Lynne McTaggart and Bryan Hubbard, "Lower Your Blood Pressure without Drugs," *What Doctors Don't Tell You* (February 2018): 28–30, 33, 35, 37.

129. Margaret McCartney, "What a New Consumer Health Magazine Doesn't Tell You," *British Medical Association Journal*, October 10, 2012, https://www.bmj.com/content/345/bmj.e6817.

130. Guy Chapman, "What Doctors Don't Tell You—Dangerous Advice," *James Randi Educational Foundation*, November 23, 2014, https://web.randi.org/swift/what-doctors-dont-tell-you-dangerous-advice.

131. Young, *The Medical Messiahs*, 147–48.

132. Jen Gunter, "Worshipping the False Idols of Wellness," *New York Times*, August 1, 2018. The author is an obstetrician and gynecologist medical doctor; Young, *American Health Quackery*, 256–85.

133. Andrew J. Flanagin and Miriam J. Metzger, et al., *Kids and Credibility: An Empirical Examination of Youth, Digital Media Use, and Information Credibility (John D. and Catherine T. MacArthur Foundation Reports on Digital Media and Learning)* (Cambridge, MA: MIT Press, 2010), 31–72.

134. James Harvey Young, "The Persistence of Medical Quackery in America," *American Scientist* 10 (1972): 318–26.

135. James Harvey Young, "Afterward," *Quackwatch*, 2002, http://www.quackwatch.org/13Hx/MM/21.html.

136. John Allen Paulos, *Innumeracy: Mathematical Illiteracy and Its Consequences* (New York; Hill & Wang, 1988).

137. Young, "Afterward," *Quackwatch.*

138. Ibid.

139. Ibid.

140. Ibid.

CHAPTER 8

1. Robert N. Proctor, "'Everyone Knew but No One Had Proof': Tobacco Industry Use of Medical History Expertise in US Courts, 1990–2002," www.tobaccocontrol.com.

2. "Tobacco Industry Research Committee A Frank Statement to Cigarette Smokers," Tobacco Industry Documents, Lorillard. Bates No. 86017454. Available at http://legacy.library.ucsf.edu/tid/qxp91e00 (accessed March 22, 2018).

3. "Public Smoking Position Paper," October 2, 1984, Tobacco Industry Documents, https://www.industrydocumentslibrary.ucsf.edu/tobacco/docs/#id=fshf0003 (accessed March 22, 2018).

4. Ari Rabin-Havt and Media Matters for America, *Lies, Incorporated: The World of Post-Truth Politics* (New York: Anchor Books, 2016).

5. For specific examples and case studies, Ibid.

6. https://features.propublica.org/ibm/ibm-age-discrimination-american-workers/(accessed March 22, 2018).

7. See, for example, Richard Kluger, *Ashes to Ashes: America's Hundred-Year Cigarette War, the Public health, and the Unabashed Triumph of Philip Morris* (New York: Knopf, 1996); Philip J. Hilts, *Smoke Screen: The Truth behind the Tobacco Industry Cover-Up* (Boston: Addison-Wesley, 1996); David Kessler, *A Question of Intent: A Great American Battle with a Deadly Industry* (New York: Public Affairs, 2001); Allan Brandt, *The Cigarette Century: The Rise, Fall, and Deadly Persistence of the Product That Defined America* (New York: Basic Books, 2007); and Naomi Oreskes and Erik M. Conway, *Merchants of Doubt: How a Handful of Scientists Obscured the Truth on Issues from Tobacco Smoke to Global Warming* (New York: Bloomsbury, 2010).

8. C. Mekemson and S. A. Glantz, "How the Tobacco Industry Built Its Relationship with Hollywood," *Tobacco Control* 11 (Suppl. I) (2002): i81–i91; see also on imaging, M. Wakefield, C. Morley, J. K. Horan, and K. M. Cummings, "The Cigarette Pack as Image: New Evidence From Tobacco Industry Documents," *Tobacco Control* 11 (Suppl. I) (2002): i73–i80.

9. "How the 'Marlborough Man' Flexed His Muscles and Became No. 1," *Advertising Age*, April 30, 1980, 12.

10. US Department of Agriculture.

11. Centers for Disease Control and Prevention, "Trends in Current Cigarette Smoking among High School Students and Adults, United States, 1965–2014," http://www.cdc.gov/ (accessed March 22, 2018).

12. As part of a broad range of new and often large scientific research projects across many disciplines, see James W. Cortada, *All the Facts: A History of Information in the United States Since 1870* (New York: Oxford University Press, 2016), 179–86.

13. Elizabeth Mendes, "The Study That Helped Spur U.S. Stop-Smoking Movement," American Cancer Society, January 9, 2014, https://www.cancer.org/latest-news/the-study-that-helped-spur-the-us-stop-smoking-movement.html (accessed March 22, 2018).

14. Phyllis A. Wingo et al., "Long-Term Trends in Cancer Mortality in the United States, 1930–1998," Supplement, *Cancer* 97, no. 2 (June 15, 2003): 3133–275.

15. For the story of this research, see Robert N. Proctor, "The History of the Discovery of the Cigarette-Lung Cancer Link: Evidentiary Traditions, Corporate Denial, Global Toll," *Tobacco Control* 21 (2012): 87–91.

16. For quote and story, Ibid.

17. C. White, "Research on Smoking and Lung Cancer: A Landmark in the History of Chronic Disease Epidemiology," *Yale Journal Biology Medicine* 63 (1990): 29–46.

18. R. Doll and A. B. Hill, "Smoking and Carcinoma of the Lung: Preliminary Report," *BMJ* 2 (1950): 739–48; M. L. Levin, H. Goldstein, and P. R. Gerhardt, "Cancer and Tobacco Smoking: A Preliminary Report," *Journal of the American Medical Association* 143 (1950): 336–38; R. Schrek, L. A. Baker, G. P. Ballard, and S. Dolgoff, "Tobacco Smoking as an Etiological Factor in Disease. I. Cancer," *Cancer Research* 10 (1950): 49–58; E. L. Wynder and E. A. Graham, "Tobacco Smoking as a Possible Etiological Factor in Bronchogenic Carcinoma: A Study in Six Hundred and Eighty Four Proved Cases," *Journal of the American Medical Association* 143 (1950): 329–36.

19. E. C. Hammond and D. Horn, "The Relationship between Human Smoking Habits and Death Rates," *Journal of the American Medical Association* 155 (1954): 1316–28.

20. Naomi Oreskes and Erik M. Conway, *Merchants of Doubt: How a Handful of Scientists Obscured the Truth on Issues from Tobacco Smoke to Global Warming* (New York: Bloomsbury Press, 2010), 10–15.

21. For an account of events from the 1950s to the end of the century, see Arthur William Musk and Nicholas Hubert Dee Klerk, "History of Tobacco and Health," *Respitology* 8 (2003): 286–90.

22. Elizabeth Mendes, "The Study That Helped Spur the U.S. Stop-Smoking Campaign," *American Cancer Society*, January 9, 2014, https://

www.cancer.org/latest news/the-study-that-helped-spur-the-us-stop
-smoking-movement.html (accessed March 22, 2018).

23. Oreskes and Conway, *Merchants of Doubt*, 10–35; Kevin Moloney, *Rethinking Public Relations: PR Propaganda and Democracy* (London: Routledge, 2006), 89; Rabin-Havt and Media Matters, *Lies, Incorporated*, 23–26.

24. Mendes, "The Study That Helped Spur the U.S. Stop-Smoking Movement."

25. Documentation from this meeting is available at the Tobacco Archives. The quote is from Hill's report to the CEOs, December 24, 1953, http://www.archive.tobacco.org/Documents/531224hill&knowlton.html (accessed March 23, 2018). Note the date of the report—Christmas Eve—suggesting that even at the start of a major holiday, addressing the crisis was too urgent to put off even for a couple of days.

26. Ibid.

27. Allan M. Brandt, "Inventing Conflicts of Interest: A History of Tobacco Industry Tactics," *American Journal of Public Health* 102, no. 1 (2012): 63–71.

28. For the full text, see "A Frank Statement to Cigarette Smokers," Tobacco Archive, http://www.archive.tobacco.org/History/540104frank.html (accessed March 23, 2018).

29. Wendy A. Ritch and Michael E. Begay, "Strange Bedfellows: The History of Collaboration between the Massachusetts Restaurant Association and the Tobacco Industry," *American Journal of Public Health* 91, no. 4 (April 2001): 598–603; J. Drope, S. A. Bialous, and S. A. Glantz, "Tobacco Industry Efforts to Present Ventilation as an Alternative to Smoke-Free Environments in North America," *Tobacco Control* 13 (Suppl. I): i41–i47; Lisa A. Bero, "Tobacco Industry Manipulation of Research," *Public Health Reports* 120 (March–April 2005): 200–208; Kelly D. Brownell and Kenneth E. Warner, "The Perils of Ignoring History: Big Tobacco Played Dirty and Millions Died. How Similar Is Big Food?" *The Milbank Quarterly* 87, no. 1 (2009): 259–94; Robert N. Proctor, "The History of the Discovery of the Cigarette-Lung Cancer Link: Evidentiary Traditions, Corporate Denial, Global Toll," *Tobacco Control* 21 (2012). 87–91.

30. Werner Troesken, "The Elasticity of Demand with Respect to Product Failures; Or Why the Market for Quack Medicines Flourished for More Than 150 Years," *National Bureau of Economic Research*, January 10, 2010, http://www.nber.org/papers/w15699 (accessed March 12, 2018).

31. Earlier examples included various US government propaganda publications during the First and Second World Wars and before that to various Bible societies distributing this and other religious tracks in the three decades prior to the American Civil War. For details on each of these initiatives, see Cortada, *All the Facts*.

32. David D. Rutstein, "An Open Letter to Dr. Clarence Cook Little," *The Atlantic* (October 1957); Christopher Zbrozek, "The Strange Career of C. C. Little," *The Michigan Daily*, September 26, 2006; Rabin-Havt and Media Matters, *Lies, Incorporated*, 27–30; Robert N. Proctor, "'Everyone Knew but No One Had Proof': Tobacco Industry Use of Medical History Expertise in US Courts, 1990–2002," *Tobacco Control* 15 (Suppl. IV): iv117–iv125; Brandt, *The Cigarette Century*, 167–72, 331–34; Kessler, *A Question of Intent*, 165–394.

33. Kessler, *A Question of Intent*, 46–48, 160–64, 234–50.

34. Rabin-Havt and Media Matters, *Lies, Incorporated*, 30–31.

35. Brandt, *The Cigarette Century*, 5–6, 250–51, 255–56, 273–74, 276–77, 301, 205, 308. But see also, on activities in the 1980s and 1990s, J. V. Dearlove, S. A. Bialous, and S. A. Glantz, "Tobacco Industry Manipulation of the Hospitality Industry to Maintain Smoking in Public Places," *Tobacco Control* 11 (2002): 94–104; examples from the 1990s, Dorie E. Apollonio and Lisa A. Bero, "The Creation of Industry Front Groups: The Tobacco Industry and 'Get Government Off Our Back,'" *American Journal of Public Health* 97, no. 3 (March 2007): 419–27; and industry lobbying in the 1990s and early 2000s, Katherine Bryan-Jones and Lisa A. Bero, "Tobacco Industry Efforts to Defeat the Occupational Safety and Health Administration Indoor Air Quality Rule," *American Journal of Public Health* 93, no. 4 (April 2003): 585–92.

36. "History of the Surgeon General's Reports on Smoking and Health," Centers for Disease Control, http://www.cdc.gov/tobacco/data_statistics/sgr/history/ (accessed March 23, 2018).

37. Brandt, *The Cigarette Century*, 188, 232–36, 294, 333–34.

38. Rabin-Havt and Media Matters, *Lies, Incorporated*, 32.

39. Ibid., 32.

40. Ibid.

41. Brandt, "Inventing Conflicts of Interest: A History of Tobacco Industry Conflicts," 69; L. M. Kyriakoudes, "Historians' Testimony on 'Common Knowledge' of the Risks of Tobacco Use: A Review and Analysis of Experts Testifying on Behalf of Cigarette Manufacturers in Civil Litigation," *Tobacco Control* 15 (2006): (Suppl. 4): iv107–iv116.

42. Statistics tracked by the US Department of Agriculture since the 1930s.

43. "Smoking and Tobacco Use Fact Sheet," Centers for Disease Control and Prevention, https://www.cdc.gov/tobacco/data_statistics/fact_sheets/index.htm?s_cid=osh-stu-home-spotlight-001 (accessed March 23, 2018).

44. It is difficult to break out US spending on cigarettes since the industry increasing exports its products. Nonetheless, between 2002 and 2017, annual shipments usually exceeded $30 billion, The Statistics Portal,

https://www.statista.com/statistics/187428/us-cigarette-product-ship ment-value-since-2002/ (accessed March 23, 2018).

45. Data from the Centers for Disease Control and Prevention; however, for a more detailed analysis of trends and events, see John P. Pierce et al., "Tobacco Industry Promotion of Cigarettes and Adolescent Smoking," *Journal of the American Medical Association* 279, no. 7 (February 18, 1998): 511–15; Cheryl L. Perry, "The Tobacco Industry and Underage Youth Smoking: Tobacco Industry Documents from the Minnesota Litigation," *Archives of Pediatric Adolescent Medicine* 153 (September 1999): 935–41; Pamela M. Ling and Stanton A. Giantz, "Tobacco Industry Research on Smoking Cessation: Recapturing Young Adults and Other Recent Quit- ters," *Journal of General Internal Medicine* 19 (May 2004): Part 1, 419–26.

46. Editorial Board, "Big Tobacco Attacks Sensible F.D.A. Rules on Vaping," *New York Times*, April 19, 2017, https://www.nytimes .com/2017/04/19/opinion/big-tobacco-attacks-sensible-fda-rules-on -vaping.html (accessed March 23, 2018); "Tobacco Companies Taking over the E-Cigarette Industry," *Huffpost*, February 27, 2017, https:// www.huffingtonpost.com/entry/tobacco-companies-taking-over-the-e -cigarette-industry_us_58b48e02e4b0658fc20f98d0 (accessed March 23, 2018).

47. Yunji Liang et al., "Exploring How the Tobacco Industry Pre- sents and Promotes Itself in Social Media," *Journal of Medical Internet Research* 17, no. 1 (January 2015), published online, https://www.jmir .org/2015/1/e24/ (accessed March 23, 2018).

48. Quoted in Brandt, "Inventing Conflicts of Interest: A History of Tobacco Industry Tactics," 66.

49. "Tobacco Industry Positions on Smoking and Health," May 24, 1988, 5.

50. Ibid.

51. Ibid., 5–6.

52. Both quotes in Ibid., 7.

53. Ibid., 7–8.

54. Ibid., 37.

55. Emily Savell, Anna B. Gilmore, and Gary Fooks, "How Does the Tobacco Industry Attempt to Influence Marketing Regulations? A Sys- tematic Review," *PLOS ONE* 9, no. 2 (February 2014): 115.

56. Ibid., 116.

57. The US National Library of Medicine contains much information on this topic, https://profiles.nlm.nih.gov/ps/retrieve/Narrative/NN/p -nid/60 (accessed April 20, 2018). The text appearing on packages: "Cau- tion: cigarette smoking may be hazardous to your health."

58. Ibid., 124. Eric Lawson, the fourth individual to serve in that role, appeared in print advertisements from 1978 to 1981. He died of respira-

tory failure resulting from chronic obstructive pulmonary disease at the age of seventy-two in 2014.

59. D. R. Gerstein and P. K. Leavison, eds., *Reduced Tar and Nicotine Cigarettes: Smoking Behavior and Health* (Washington, DC: National Academy Press, 1982).

60. Kenneth F. Warner, "Tobacco Industry Response to Public Health Concern: A Content Analysis of Cigarette Ads," *Health Education Quarterly* 12, no. 2 (Summer 1985): 115–27, quote p. 124.

61. Pamela M. Ling and Stanton A. Glantz, "Using Tobacco-Industry Marketing Research to Design More Effective Tobacco-Control Campaigns," *Journal of the American Medical Association* 287, no. 22 (June 12, 2002): 2983–89.

62. Savell, Gilmore, and Fooks, "How Does the Tobacco Industry Attempt to Influence Marketing Regulations? A Systematic Review," 1.

63. Ibid., 4.

64. Peter S. Arno et al., "Tobacco Industry Strategies to Oppose Federal Regulation," *Journal of the American Medical Association* 275, no. 16 (1996): 1258–62.

CHAPTER 9

1. Al Gore, *An Inconvenient Truth: The Planetary Emergency of Global Warming and What We Can Do about It* (Emmaus, PA: Rodale, 2006).

2. Christopher C. Horner, *The Politically Incorrect Guide to Global Warming (and Environmentalism)* (Washington, DC: Regnery Publishing, 2007).

3. Lisa Bero, "Implications of the Tobacco Industry Documents for Public Health and Policy," *Annual Review of Public Health* 24 (2003): 267–88.

4. Lisa Friedman and Julie Hirschfeld Davis, "The E.P.A. Chief Wanted a Climate Science Debate, Trump's Chief of Staff Stopped Him," *New York Times*, March 9, 2018, https://www.nytimes.com/2018/03/09/climate/pruitt-red-team-climate-debate-kelly.html (accessed April 9, 2018).

5. Brad Plumer and Coral Davenport, "E.P.A. to Give Dissenters a Voice on Climate, No Matter the Consensus," *New York Times*, June 30, 2017, https://www.nytimes.com/2017/06/30/climate/scott-pruitt-climate-change-red-team.html?action=click&contentCollection=Climate&module=RelatedCoverage&region=Marginalia&pgtype=article (accessed April 9, 2018).

6. "We Have 12 Years to Limit Climate Change Catastrophe," *Guardian*, October 8, 2018, https://www.theguardian.com/environment/2018/oct/08/global-warming-must-not-exceed-15c-warns-landmark-un-report (accessed October 18, 2018).

7. Some scholars sidestep the issue. For example, in his magisterial history of energy, historian Vaclav Smil avoided the topic entirely, *Energy and Civilization: A History* (Cambridge, MA: MIT Press, 2017).

8. The term "truthiness" means that a statement of fact is truthful because it seemed intuitively or reasonably accurate to someone or some group. One did not have to rely on evidence, logic, proven facts, or scrutiny. Ignorant assertions, propaganda, or outright falsehoods can possess truthiness. Stephen Colbert, an American comedian coined the word, introducing it on his television program *The Colbert Report* on October 17, 2005. It quickly entered the English language, particularly with respect to discussing the veracity of statements made by the political right in the United States, "Truthiness," *Wikipedia*, https://en.wikipedia.org/wiki/Truthiness (accessed April 4, 2018).

9. Rebecca Smithers, "Fish and Chips to Curry: UK's Favorite Dishes at Risk from Climate Change, Research Shows," *The Onion*, March 20, 2018; "Sighing, Resigned Climate Scientists Say to Just Enjoy Next 20 Years as Much as You Can," *The Onion*, February 23, 2018; "Climate Change Deniers Present Graphic Description of What Earth Must Look Like for Them to Believe," *The Onion*, August 19, 2015; "Climate Change Report Just List of Years Each Country Becomes Uninhabitable," September 21, 2017, *The Onion*, all available at https://www.theonion.com (accessed April 16, 2018).

10. Wallace S. Broeker, "Climate Change: Are We on the Brink of a Pronounced Global Warming?" *Science* 189, no. 4201 (August 8, 1975): 460–63.

11. For further discussion of the name differences, see Erik Conway, "What's in a Name? Global Warming vs. Climate Change," *National Aeronautics and Space Administration (NASA) Internet Resource, News Topics*, December 5, 2008, https://www.nasa.gov/topics/earth/features/climate_by_any_other_name.html (accessed April 8, 2018).

12. Quoted in Ari Rabin-Havt and Media Matters, *Lies, Incorporated: The World of Post-Truth Politics* (New York: Anchor Books, 2016), 35.

13. Ibid.

14. Suzanne Goldenberg, "Exxon Knew of Climate Change in 1981, Email Says—But It Funded Deniers for 27 More Years," *Guardian*, July 8, 2015, https://www.theguardian.com/environment/2015/jul/08/exxon-climate-change-1981-climate-denier-funding (accessed April 18, 2018). Exxon's counterargument was that "the science in 1981 on this subject was in the very, very early days and there was considerable division of opinion," Ibid.

15. Quoted in Havt and Media Matters, *Lies, Incorporated*, 36.

16. Ans Kolk and David Levy, "Winds of Change: Corporate Strategy, Climate Change and Oil Multinationals," *European Management Journal* 19, no. 5 (October 2001): 501–9.

17. Daniel Bodansky, "The History of the Global Climate Change Regime," in *International Relations and Global Climate Change*, Urs Luterbacher and Detlef F. Sprinz, eds. (Cambridge, MA: MIT Press, 2001), 23–40.

18. National Research Council, *Carbon Dioxide and Climate: A Scientific Assessment* (Washington, DC: National Academy Press, 1979), viii.

19. Bodansky, "The History of the Global Climate Change Regime," 24–26.

20. Ibid., 26–27; Havt and Media Matters, *Lies, Incorporated*, 37–39.

21. J. T. Houghton, G. J. Jenkins, and J. J. Ephraums, eds., *Climate Change: The IPCC Scientific Assessment* (Cambridge: Cambridge University Press, 1990), vi.

22. Michael Grubb, Christiaan Vrolijk, and Duncan Brack, *The Kyoto Protocol: A Guide and Assessment* (London: Royal Institute for International Affairs/Chatham House, 1999).

23. Bodansky, "The History of the Global Climate Change Regime," 38.

24. The most useful overview is Havt and Media Matters, *Lies, Incorporated*, 34–57.

25. Both quotes in Havt and Media Matters, *Lies, Incorporated*, 42.

26. Ibid., 37.

27. Ibid., 42.

28. James Inhofe, *The Greatest Hoax: How the Global Warming Conspiracy Threatens Your Future* (Washington, DC: WND Books, 2012).

29. Jeff Godell, "As the World Burns: How Big Oil and Big Coal Mounted One of the Most Aggressive Lobbying Campaigns in History to Block Progress on Global Warming," *Rolling Stone*, January 6, 2010, https://www.rollingstone.com/politics/news/as-the-world -burns-20100106 (accessed April 18, 2018).

30. Quoted in Havt and Media Matters, *Lies, Incorporated*, 43.

31. Ibid., 44. Morano's spelling of the word "boring."

32. America's Climate Choices Panel on Limiting the Magnitude of Climate Changes, Board on Atmospheric Sciences and Climate, Division on Earth and Life Sciences, and National Research Council, *Limiting the Magnitude of Future Climate Change* (Washington, DC: National Academic Press, 2010), 4.

33. S. Fred Singer and Dennis T. Avery, *Unstoppable Global Warming: Every 1,500 Years* (Lanham, MD: Rowman & Littlefield, 2007), 3.

34. Myanna Lahsen, "Technocracy, Democracy, and U.S. Climate Politics: The Need for Demarcations," *Science, Technology, & Human Values* 30, no. 1 (Winter 2005): 137–69; Peter J. Jacques, Riley E. Dunlap, and Mark Freeman, "The Organization of Denial: Conservative Think Tanks and Environmental Skepticism," *Environmental Politics* 17, no. 3 (2008): 349–85; Riley E. Dunlap and Aaron M. McCright, "A Widening Gap: Republican and Democratic Views on Climate Change," *Environment* 50,

no. 5 (September/October 2008): 26–35; Aaron M. McCright and Riley E. Dunlap, "The Politicization of Climate Change and Polarization in the American Public's Views of Global Warming, 2001–2010," *The Sociology Quarterly* 52 (2011): 155–94; Andrew J. Hoffman, "The Growing Climate Divide," *Nature Climate Change* 1, no. 4 (2011): 195–96; Nicholas Smith and Anthony Leiserowitz, "The Rise of Global Warming Skepticism: Exploring Affective Image Associations in the United States over Time," *Risk Analysis* (2012): 1–12; Carmichael and Brulle, "Elite Cues, Media Coverage, and Public Concern: An Integrated Path Analysis of Public Opinion on Climate Change, 2001–2013"; Jason T. Carmichael, Robert J. Bruelle, and Joanna K. Huxster, "The Great Divide: Understanding the Role of Media and Other Drivers of the Partisan Divide in Public Concern Over Climate Change in the USA, 2001–2014," *Climate Change* 141, no. 4 (April 2017): 599–612.

35. Jacques, Dunlap, and Freeman, "The Organization of Denial," 360–61.

36. Quoted in Ibid., 364.

37. Ibid., 384–385.

38. Carmichael and Brulle, "Elite Cues, Media Coverage, and Public Concern," 1.

39. See, for example, K. Andrew and N. Caren, "Making the News: Movement Organizations, Media Attention, and the Public Agenda," *American Sociological Review* 75, no. 6 (2010): 841–66; R. Bord, R. E. O'Connor, and A. Fisher, "In What Sense Does the Public Need to Understand Global Climate Change?" *Public Understanding of Science* 9 (2000): 205–28; C. Borick and B. Rabe, "A Reason to Believe: Examining the Factors That Determine Individual Views on Global Warming," *Social Science Quarterly* 91, no. 3 (2010): 777–800; R. Bruelle, J. Carm, and J. C. Jenkins, "Shifting Public Opinion on Climate Change: An Empirical Assessment of Factors Influencing Concern over Climate Change in the US, 2002–2010," *Climate Change* 114, no. 2 (2012): 169–88; D. Darmofal, "Elite Cues and Citizen Disagreement with Expert Opinion," *Political Research Quarterly* 58, no. 3 (2009): 381–95; S. Donner and J. McDaniels, "The Influence of National Temperature Fluctuations on Opinions about Global Warming," *Climate Change* 118 (2013): 537–50; P. Habel, "Following the Opinion Leaders? The Dynamics of Influence among Media Opinion, the Public, and Politicians," *Political Communications* 29 (2012): 257–77; L. Hamilton, "Education, Politics and Opinions about Climate Change: Evidence for Interaction Effects," *Climate Change* 104, no. 2 (2010): 231–42; A. Malka, J. A. Krosnick, and G. Langer, "The Association of Knowledge with Concern about Global Warming: Trusted Information Sources Shape Public Thinking," *Risk Analysis* 29, no. 5 (2009): 633–47; M. McCombs, *Setting the Agenda: The Mass Media and Public Opinion* (Malden, MA: Polity,

2004); L. Scruggs and S. Benegal, "Declining Public Concern about Climate Change: Can We Blame the Great Recession?" *Global Environmental Change* 22, no. 2 (2012): 505–15; Y. Tan and D. Weaver, "Local Media, Public Opinion and State Legislative Policies: Agenda Setting at the State Level," *International Journal of Press/Politics* 14, no. 4 (2009): 454–76; E. Weber and P. Stern, "Public Understanding of Climate Change in the United States," *American Psychologist* 66, no. 4 (2011): 315–28; J. Yin, "Elite Opinion and Media Diffusion: Exploring Environmental Attitudes," *Harvard International Journal of Press/Politics* 4 (1999): 62–86.

40. J. Brooks et al., "Abnormal Daily Temperature and Concern about Climate Change Across the United States," *Review of Policy Research* 31, no. 3 (2014): 199–217; P. Egan and M. Mullin, "Turning Personal Experience into Political Attitudes: The Effect of Local Weather on Americans' Perceptions about Global Warming," *Journal of Politics* 74, no. 3 (2012): 796–809; Y. Li, E. Johnson, and L. Zaval, "Local Warming: Daily Temperature Change Influences Belief in Global Warming," *Psychological Science* 22, no. 4 (2011): 454–59.

41. Carmichael and Brulle, "Elite Cues, Media Coverage, and Public Concern," 4.

42. Lawrence C. Hamilton, "Education, Politics and Opinions about Climate Change: Evidence for Interaction Effects," *Climate Change* 104 (2011): 231–42.

43. C. R. Shipan and W. R. Lowry, "Environmental Policy and Party Divergence in Congress," *Political Research Quarterly* 54, no. 2 (2001): 245–63.

44. Ibid.

45. Ibid., 6.

46. M. E. Kahn and Matthew J. Kotchen, "Environmental Concern and the Business Cycle: The Chilling Effect of Recession," *NEBR Working Paper No. 16241,* July 2010, http://www.nber.org/papers/w16241.pdf (accessed April 18, 2018).

47. Al Gore's report received enormous coverage. See, for the report, Al Gore, *An Inconvenient Truth*, and his video under the same title (New York: Melcher Media, 2006).

48. For a summary of Climategate, see Anthony A. Leiserowitz et al., "Climategate, Public Opinion, and the Loss of Trust," *American Behavioral Scientist* 57, no. 6 (2013): 818–37; Brigitte Nerlich, "'Climategate': Paradoxical Metaphors and Political Paralysis," *Environmental Values* 19, no. 4 (November 2010): 419–42.

49. See, for example, Alexander C. Kaufman, "Leaked Memo: EPA Show Workers How to Downplay Climate Change," *Mother Jones*, March 28, 2018, https://www.motherjones.com/environment/2018/03/leaked -memo-epa-gives-its-employees-talking-points-on-how-to-downplay-cli mate-science/ (accessed April 18, 2018).

50. For all its surveys, with trend charts dating to 1987 are available at http://www.gallup.com/home.aspx (accessed April 18, 2018).

51. Carmichael, Brulle, and Huxter, "The Great Divide," 3; on earlier periods, see R. E. Dunlap, "Climate Change Skepticism and Denial: An Introduction," *American Behavioral Science* 57 (2013): 691–98; D. L. Guber, "A Cooling Climate for Change? Party Polarization and the Politics of Global Warming," *American Behavioral Science* 57 (2013): 93–115; and the various Gallup polls.

52. Dunlap and McCright, "A Widening Gap"; Cary Funk, "How Much Does Science Knowledge Influence People's Views on Climate Change and Energy Issues?" *Pew Research Center*, March 22, 2017; Bruce Stokes, "Global Concern about Climate Change, Broad Support for Limiting Emissions," *Pew Research Center*, November 5, 2015, both available at www.pewresearch.org (accessed April 18, 2018); Maxwell T. Boykoff and Jules M. Boykoff, "Climate Change and Journalistic Norms: A Case-Study of US Mass-Media Coverage," *Geoforum* (2007), available at www.scien cedirect.com (accessed April 18, 2018); Maxwell T. Boykoff, "Flogging a Dead Norm? Newspaper Coverage of Anthropogenic Climate Change in the United States and United Kingdom from 2003 to 2006," *Area* 39, no. 4 (December 2007): 470–81; Douglas Blanks Hindman, "Mass Media Flow and Differential Distribution of Politically Disputed Beliefs: The Belief Gap Hypothesis," *Journalism & Mass Communication Quarterly* 86, no. 4 (Winter 2009): 790–808; Maxwell T. Boykoff, "Lost in Translation? United States Television News Coverage of Anthropogenic Climate Change, 1995–2004," *Climate Change* 86 (2008): 1–11; Lisa Antilla, "Climate of Skepticism: US Newspaper Coverage of the Science of Climate Change," *Global Environmental Change* 15 (2005): 338–52.

53. Amanda C. Staudt, "Recent Evolution of the Climate Change Dialogue in the United States," *BAMS* (July 2008): 979.

54. "Environment," Gallup Inc., 2016, available at http://www.gal lup.com/poll/1615/environment.aspx (accessed April 18, 2018).

55. On framing, see Andrew J. Hoffman, "Talking Past Each Other? Cultural Framing of Skeptical and Convinced Logics in the Climate Change Debate," *Organization & Environment* 24, no. 1 (2011): 3–33; Ariel Malka, Jon Krosnick, and Gary Langer, "The Association of Knowledge with Concern about Global Warming: Trusted Information Sources Shape Public Thinking," *Risk Analysis* 29, no. 5 (2009): 633–47.

56. Emily S. Rosenberg, "Transnational Currents in a Shrinking World," in *A World Connecting*, Emily S. Rosenberg, ed. (Cambridge, MA: Harvard University Press, 2012), 919–59; Steven Pinker, *Enlightenment Now: The Case for Reason, Science, Humanism, and Progress* (New York: Viking, 2018), 64, 385–93, 409; James W. Cortada, *All the Facts: A History of Information in the United States Since 1870* (New York: Oxford University Press, 2016), 183–84.

57. Naomi Oreskes, "The Scientific Consensus on Climate Change," *Science* 306, no. 5702 (2004): 1686; Klaus-Martin Schulte, "Scientific Consensus on Climate Change?" *Energy & Environment* 19 (2008): 281–86; Lianne M. Lefsrud and Renate E. Meyer, "Science or Science Fiction? Professionals' Discursive Construction of Climate Change," *Organization Studies* 33, no. 11 (2012): 1478.

58. Lefsrud and Meyer, "Science or Science Fiction? Professionals' Discursive Construction of Climate Change," 1477–506.

59. Ibid., 1480–81; Craig Trumbo, "Constructing Climate Change: Claims and Frames in US News Coverage of an Environmental Issue," *Public Understanding of Science* 5 (1996): 269–83.

60. Lefsrud and Meyer, "Science or Science Fiction?" 1489–90.

61. Gore, *An Inconvenient Truth*.

62. Among the few skeptics with scientific experience, see Singer and Avery, *Unstoppable Global Warming*.

63. Lefsrud and Meyer, "Science or Science Fiction?" 1493.

64. Ibid.

65. National Research Council, *Climate Change: Evidence, Impacts, and Choices* (Washington, DC: National Research Council, 2011), 3.

66. Ibid., 3–4.

67. Ibid., 4.

68. Ibid.

69. Ibid., 6.

70. Quote and data, Ibid., 8.

71. Ibid.

72. For a large bibliography of this literature, National Research Council, *Limiting the Magnitude of Future Climate Change*, 225–37, and Lefrud and Meyer, "Science or Science Fiction?" 1502–506.

73. National Research Council, *Climate Change*, 32–33.

74. Ibid., 33.

75. Ibid., 36.

76. Gore, *An Inconvenient Truth*, all quotes from unpaginated pages, except last one, p. 24.

77. Ibid., unpaginated.

78. Naomi Oreskes and Erik M. Conway, *Merchants of Doubt: How a Handful of Scientists Obscured the Truth on Issues from Tobacco Smoke to Global Warming* (New York: Bloomsbury, 2010); Rabin-Havt and Media Matters, *Lies, Incorporated*, 34–57; Horner, *The Politically Incorrect Guide to Global Warming and Environmentalism*; James Howard Kunstler, *The Long Emergency: Surviving the End of Oil, Climate Change, and Other Converging Catastrophes of the Twenty-first Century* (New York: Grove Press, 2006); Luke W. Cole and Sheila R. Foster, *From the Ground Up: Environmental Racism and the Rise of the Environmental Justice Movement* (New York: Uni-

versity of New York Press, 2001); Singer and Avery, *Unstoppable Global Warming*; Peter Senge, *The Necessary Revolution: How Individuals and Organizations Are Working Together to Create a Sustainable World* (New York: Doubleday, 2008).

79. Both quotes in Richard C. Somerville and Joy Hassol, "Communicating the Science of Climate Change," *Physics Today* 64, no. 10 (2011): 49.

80. Ibid., 51.

81. Quoted in Aaron M. McCright and Riley E. Dunlap, "Defeating Kyoto: The Conservative Movement's Impact on U.S. Climate Change Policy," *Social Problems* 50, no. 3 (August 2003): 357.

82. James Lewis, "Making It Up in Global Warming Theory," *American Thinker*, September 6, 2009, https://www.americanthinker.com/articles/2009/09/making_it_up_in_global_warming.html (accessed April 19, 2018).

83. David Michaels, *Doubt Is Their Product: How Industry's Assault on Science Threatens Your Health* (New York: Oxford University Press, 2008), 198.

84. On the Institute's origins, see Naomi Oreskes and Erik M. Conway, *Merchants of Doubt: How a Handful of Scientists Obscured the Truth on Issues from Tobacco Smoke to Global Warming* (New York: Bloomsbury, 2010), 125.

85. Horner, *The Politically Incorrect Guide to Global Warming and Environmentalism*, xiii–xiv.

86. Ibid., xiv–xv.

87. Ibid., 3.

88. Ibid., 37; *2000 EPA Annual Report: Performance Results* (Washington, DC: US Government Printing Office, 2000); Joel Schwartz, "No Smog for the Fear Factory," May 3, 2006, *TCS Daily*, May 3, 2006, http://www.ideasinactiontv.com/tcs_daily/2006/05/no-smog-for-the-fear-factory.html (accessed April 19, 2018).

89. Horner, *The Politically Incorrect Guide™ to Global Warming and Environmentalism*, 42–43.

90. Ibid., 43.

91. Ibid., 62.

92. Ibid., 62–63.

93. Singer and Avery, *Unstoppable Global Warming*, 3.

94. Ibid.

95. Ibid., 3–4.

96. All quoted in Ibid., 4–5.

97. Ibid., 5.

98. Ibid., 6.

99. Ibid.

100. Ibid., 18.

101. Quoted in Horner, *The Politically Incorrect Guide to Global Warming*, 314. Word of caution, some of Horner's sources cited in his endnotes are not accurate or are sloppy, such as for this commentary at a Senate committee hearing.

102. Ibid., 91; Naomi Oreskes, "The Scientific Consensus on Climate Change: How Do We Know We're Not Wrong?" in Joseph F. C. DiMento and Pamela Doughman, *Climate Change: What It Means for Us, Our Children, and Our Grandchildren* (Cambridge, MA: MIT Press, 2007), 65–99.

103. Horner, *The Politically Incorrect Guide™ to Global Warming*, 92.

104. Ibid., 106.

105. Ibid., 107.

106. Ibid., 169.

107. Joel M. Schwartz, "Air Pollution and Health: Do Popular Portrayals Reflect the Scientific Evidence?" *Environmental Policy Outlook* (January 2006), https://www.researchgate.net/publication/237267069 _Air_Pollution_and_Health_Do_Popular_Portrayals_Reflect_the_Sci entific_Evidence?enrichId=rgreq-77516d9e51e9d0786dda848c7f b551ea-XXX&enrichSource=Y292ZXJQYWdlOzIzNzI2NzA2OTtBUzoxM DEzOTU3MTc5NTU1ODVAMTQwMTE4NjAzMTM3Nw%3D%3D&el= 1_x_2&_esc=publicationCoverPdf (accessed April 20, 2018).

108. Horner, *The Politically Incorrect Guide to Global Warming*, 174–76.

109. Cited in Ibid., 179.

110. Ibid., 178–82.

111. Ibid., 240.

112. "Climategate," *FactCheck.org*, December 10, 2009, https://www .factcheck.org/2009/12/climategate/ (accessed April 20/2018).

113. Christopher Booker, "Climate Change: This Is the Worst Scientific Scandal of Our Generation," *The Telegraph*, November 28, 2009, https://www.telegraph.co.uk/comment/columnists/christopher booker/6679082/Climate-change-this-is-the-worst-scientific-scandal-of -our-generation.html (accessed April 20, 2018).

114. James Delingpole, "Climategate: The Final Nail in the Coffin of 'Anthropogenic Global Warning'?" Ibid., November 21, 2009, http:// www.globalclimatescam.com/causeeffect/climategate-the-final-nail-in -the-coffin-of-anthropogenic-global-warming/ (accessed April 20, 2018).

115. Rabin-Havt and Media Matters, *Lies, Incorporated*, 49.

116. Quoted in Ibid., 50.

117. Quoted in Ibid., 50–51.

118. Quoted in Ibid., 51.

119. Quoted in Ibid.

120. Quoted in Ibid. 52.

121. Quoted in Ibid., 54.

122. Jim Efstathiou Jr. "No 'Research Misconduct' by Climate-Change Scientist, U.S. Says," *Bloomberg,* April 22, 2011, https://www.bloomberg.com/news/articles/2011-08-22/climate-change-scientist-cleared-in-u-s-data-altering-inquiry (accessed April 20, 2018).

123. Quoted in Rabin-Havt and Media Matters, *Lies, Incorporated,* 56.

124. Singer and Avery, *Unstoppable Global Warming,* 68–69.

125. Anne-Marie Blackburn and Dana Nuccitelli, "Hockey Stick Scores Another Point in Climate Study: Op-Ed," *Live Science,* April 25, 2013, https://www.livescience.com/29068-hockey-stick-climate.html (accessed April 20, 2018).

126. Quoted in Rabin-Havt and Media Matters, *Lies, Incorporated,* 46.

127. Ibid. 46–47.

128. Ibid., 47–48.

129. Ibid., 44.

130. John Schwartz, "Exxon Mobil Accuses the Rockefellers of a Climate Conspiracy," *New York Times,* November 21, 2016.

131. Ibid.

132. John Schwartz, "Climate Lawsuits, Once Limited to the Coasts, Jump Inland," *New York Times,* April 18, 2018.

133. Ibid.

134. James T. Spartz, Leona Yi-Fan Su, Robert Griffin, Dominique Brossard, and Sharon Dunwoody, "YouTube, Social Norms and Perceived Salience of Climate Change in the American Mind," *Environmental Communication* 11, no. 1 (2017): 5.

135. Ibid., 5; but see also, A. C. Gunther, C. T. Christen, J. L. Liebhart, and S. C. Y. Chia, "Congenial Public, Contrary Press, and Biased Estimates of the Climate of Opinion," *Public Opinion Quarterly* 65 (2001): 295–320.

136. Cortada, *All the Facts,* 426–40.

137. Spartz, Yi-Fan Su, Griffin, Brossard, and Dunwoody, "YouTube, Social Norms and Perceived Salience of Climate Change in the American Mind," 11.

CHAPTER 10

1. Nicole A. Cooke, *Fake News and Alternative Facts: Information Literacy in a Post-Truth Era* (Chicago: ALA Editions, 2018), 20.

2. Quoted in Jill Lepore, *These Truths: A History of the United States* (New York: W.W. Norton, 2018), 174.

3. Frank Bruni, "The Internet Will Be the Death of Us," *New York Times,* October 31, 2018, https://www.nytimes.com/2018/10/30/opinion/internet-violence-hate-prejudice.html?action=click&module=Opinion&pgtype=Homepage.

4. The report was formally delivered to Congress on March 28, 1898, the war declared on April 25th, 55th Congress, 2d Session, Senate, *Message from the President of the United States Transmitting the Report of the Naval Court of Inquiry Upon the Destruction of the United States Battle Ship Maine in Havana Harbor, February 15, 1898, Together with the Testimony Taken before the Court*, Document No. 207 (Washington, DC: US Government Printing Office, 1898), a report consisting of over three hundred pages.

5. To place a fine point on the issue, however, individual states and cities have publicly stated that they would adhere to the standards and actions called for by the Kyoto and Paris accords and have taken action, often in collaboration with companies accused in earlier decades of polluting, such as automotive manufacturers and energy companies.

6. Naomi Oreskes and Erik M. Conway, *Merchants of Doubt: How a Handful of Scientists Obscured the Truth on Issues from Tobacco Smoke to Global Warming* (New York: Bloomsbury Press, 2010), 266–74.

7. Michael Kammen, *American Culture American Tastes: Social Change and the 20th Century* (New York: Knopf, 1999), 238.

8. Lawrence W. Levine, *Highbrow/Lowbrow: The Emergence of Cultural Hierarchy in America* (Cambridge, MA: Harvard University Press, 1988); Miles Orvell, *The Real Thing: Imitation and Authenticity in American Culture, 1880–1940* (Chapel Hill: University North Carolina Press, 1989).

9. Kammen, *American Culture American Tastes*, 240. Decades earlier Walter Lippmann made the observation about skim-reading newspapers, *Public Opinion* (New York: Harcourt, Brace, 1922), 59.

10. One major exception to this statement was the bible societies of pre–Civil War era that mailed tens of thousands of publications all over the United States.

11. All survey data derived from Aaron Smith, "Social Media Use in 2018," March 1, 2018, Pew Research Center.

12. A key finding in James W. Cortada, *All the Facts: A History of Information in the United States Since 1870* (New York: Oxford University Press, 2016), 426–39; presaged in a collection of case studies on the early uses of the Internet, William Aspray and Barbara M. Hayes, eds., *Everyday Information: The Evolution of Information Seeking in America* (Cambridge, MA: MIT Press, 2011), especially 329–39.

13. A reviewer of our manuscript questioned this assertion. One needs to differentiate between speed of diffusion to privileged users and speed of diffusion to the totality of geographical regions. While the Internet diffused rapidly to people in cities and suburbs, there are portions of Arkansas, Mississippi, Wyoming, New Mexico, and Montana, for example, that still do not have Internet coverage twenty-five years after the creation of the Internet. Newspapers, by contrast, achieved widely dispersed geographic coverage very quickly. See "Internet Access Rankings,"

U.S. News, https://www.usnews.com/news/best-states/rankings/infr astructure/Internet-access (accessed March 13, 2019).

14. All survey data derived from "Social Media Fact Sheet," February 5, 2018, Pew Research Center.

15. Statista, "Number of Mobile Phone Users in the U.S. from 2012 to 2020," https://www.statista.com/statistics/222306/forecast-of-smart phone-users-in-the-us/.

16. Ibid.

17. "How Much Time Do People Spend on Their Mobile Phones in 2017?," May 9, 2017, *Hackernoon*, https://hackernoon.com/how-much -time-do-people-spend-on-their-mobile-phones-in-2017-e5f90a0b10a6.

18. James W. Cortada, *All the Facts: A History of Information In the United States since 1870* (New York: Oxford University Press, 2016); Naomi Oreskes and Erik M. Conway, *Merchants of Doubt: How a Handful of Scientists Obscured the Truth on Issues from Tobacco Smoke to Global Warming* (New York: Bloomsbury Press, 2010); James Harvey Young, *American Health Quackery* (Princeton, NJ: Princeton University Press, 1992); Kevin Young, *Bunk: The Rise of Hoaxes, Humbug, Plagiarists, Phonies, Post-Facts, and Fake News* (Minneapolis, MN: Graywolf Press, 2017); Julia Abramson, *Learning from Lying: Paradoxes of the Literary Mystification* (Newark: University of Delaware Press, 2005); Michael Farquhar, *A Treasury of Deception: Liars, Misleaders, Hoodwinkers, and the Extraordinary True Stories of History's Greatest Hoaxes, Fakes, and Frauds* (New York: Penguin, 2005); Jaap Kooijman, *Fabricating the Absolute Fake: America in Contemporary Pop Culture* (Amsterdam: Amsterdam University Press, 2008); and a classic on propaganda by Jacques Ellul, *Propaganda: The Formation of Men's Attitudes* (New York: Knopf, 1965) and the classic study on public relations, Edward L. Bernays, *Public Relations* (New York, 1928, but available in more recent editions, Norman, OK: University of Oklahoma Press, 2013).

19. See, for example, studies from the Pew Research Center, John B. Horrigan, "Internet and Cell Phone Facts," July 6, 2005, "Cell Phone Activities over Time," November 25, 2012, and Paul Hitlin, "Internet, Social Media Use and Device Ownership in U.S. Have Plateaued after Years of Growth," September 28, 2018.

20. Michael Barthel, Amy Mitchell, and Jesse Holcomb, "Many Americans Believe Fake News Is Sowing Confusion," December 16, 2016, Pew Research Center, 3.

21. Ibid., 3–4.

22. Cooke, *Fake News and Alternative Facts*, 10–11.

23. Aspray and Cortada, *From Urban Legends to Political Fact-Checking: Online Scrutiny in America, 1990–2015* (forthcoming).

24. Amy Mitchell, Jeffrey Gottfried, Michael Barthel, and Nami Sumida, "Distinguishing Between Factual and Opinion Statements in the News," June 18, 2018, Pew Research Center, unpaginated.

25. Stephanie Craft and Charles N. Davis, *Principles of American Journalism: An Introduction* (New York: Routledge, 2016), 87–96; Cooke, *Fake News and Alternative Facts*, 11; Kate Vinton, "These 15 Billionaires Own America's News Media Companies," *Forbes*, June 1, 2016, https://www .forbes.com/sites/katevinton/2016/06/01/these-15-billionaires-own -americas-news-media-companies/#59e32de0660a.

26. Michael J. Wolf, *The Entertainment Economy: How Mega-Media Forces Are Transforming Our Lives* (New York: Times Books, 1999); Benjamin M. Compaine and Douglas Gomory, *Who Owns the Media? Competition and Concentration in the Mass Media Industry* (Mahwah, NJ: Lawrence Erlbaum Associates, 1979, 1982, 2000); Robert G. Picard, *The Economics and Financing of Media Companies* (New York: Fordham University Press, 2002); James W. Cortada, *The Digital Hand: How Computers Changed the Work of American Financial, Telecommunications, Media, and Entertainment Industries* (New York: Oxford University Press, 2006), 263–77.

27. See Aspray and Cortada, *From Urban Legends to Political Fact-Checking*.

28. Particularly in secondary education. For details, see James W. Cortada, *The Digital Hand*, volume 3, *How Computers Changed the Work of American Public Sector Industries* (New York: Oxford University Press, 2008), 251–83, 446–49.

29. For example, Daniel J. Levitin, *A Field Guide to Lies: Critical Thinking in the Information Age* (New York: Dutton, 2016).

30. Michael B. Eisenberg, Carrie A. Lowe, and Kathleen L. Spitzer, *Information Literacy: Essential Skills for the Information Age* (Westport, CT: Greenwood Press, 2004); David Bawden, "Origins and Concepts of Digital Literacy," in Colin Lankshear and Michele Knobel, eds., *Digital Literacies: Concepts, Policies and Practices* (New York: Peter Lang, 2008), 17–32; David Bawden and Lyn Robinson, "Promoting Literacy in a Digital Age: Approaches to Training for Information Literacy," *Learned Publishing* 15, no. 4 (2002), 297–301.

31. Cooke, *Fake News and Alternative Facts*, 18.

32. For the most detailed conversation about the concept, see Thomas P. Mackey, *Metaliteracy: Reinventing Information Literacy to Empower Learners* (Chicago: American Library Association, 2014).

33. For a detailed account of that more positive use, see Cortada, *All the Facts*.

Bibliographic Essay

Recent political events in the United States have supercharged interest in such topics as fake news, fake facts, alternative facts, and various kinds of lies, misrepresentations, and rumors in American public life. While these various kinds of misinformation and questionable information have been part of the American experience for centuries, when historians have looked at this issue, they have seen it not as a coherent story in and of itself, but rather as a feature of many other stories in American history.

Misinformation is beginning to emerge as a topic in its own right. The political scientists have done the most to understand the presentation or manipulation of truth and facts for immediate political purposes, such as to win elections. In the past two decades, experts on media and advertising have contributed to a more theoretically based understanding of the role of information and misinformation. Historians are just beginning to weigh in on the matter, and this book represents an early example of that initiative. But historians still lack a comprehensive overview of the role of the range of misinformation in the United States. While our book does not completely fill that gap, it takes us down that path by exploring obvious—often notorious—cases, and by identifying some themes that cut across our many case studies. To a large extent, we rely on the work of experts looking at different facets of information within their disciplines positioned against what scholars are learning about the broader role of information and misinformation. This short bibliographic essay highlights the scholarship we have principally relied upon to write this book. We focus here on the key books, for the most part leaving to endnotes the citations of specific articles and narrow monographs. Our intention is to offer suggestions of where future scholars and interested readers can begin to explore this relatively new subfield of information history. This essay follows the organization of the chapters.

Chapters 2 and 3 consider the 1828 and 1960 US presidential elections. It is the nature of these two—and all presidential—elections to present information about candidates in ways that make the candidates attractive to voters or that misrepresent the positions and biographies of opponents in unfavorable ways. These efforts are extensive and are often crafted according to polling results and experience with past elections. Negative representation of opponents is a strategy of choice for most presidential candidates.

The two case studies—1828 and 1960—can be documented through both traditional political science analyses and historical studies. To understand the language of the politician, a useful place to begin is with Murray Edelman's *Political Language: Words That Succeed and Politics That Fail* (New York: Academic Press, 1977). Edelman is a senior political scientist who has written several books on American political behavior that are central to understanding the role of information in national elections; one of the most useful of which is his *Politics as Symbolic Action: Mass Arousal and Quiescence* (Chicago: Markham, 1971), but also see his *The Symbolic Uses of Politics* (Urbana: University of Illinois Press, 1985). A related study worthy of examination is Dan F. Hahn's *Political Communication: Rhetoric, Government, and Citizens* (State College, PA: Strata Publishing, 1998). On the tactical uses of information in campaigns, two studies are particularly useful: Michael John Burton and Daniel M. Shea's *Campaign Craft: The Strategies, Tactics, and Art of Political Campaign Management* (Santa Barbara, CA: Praeger, 2010; especially the fourth edition) and Bruce Bimber's *Information and American Democracy: Technology in the Evolution of Political Power* (Cambridge: Cambridge University Press, 2003). Both books have extensive bibliographies.

The election of 1828 has been well studied. Begin with biographies of Andrew Jackson, notably H. W. Brands's *Andrew Jackson: His Life and Times* (New York: Doubleday, 2005) and Robert V. Remini's *The Life of Andrew Jackson* (New York: Harper Perennial Modern Classic, 2010; originally published in 1984). Historians of the election have commented extensively on the rhetoric as well as the distortion of facts by the candidates. Key works include: Robert V. Remini, *The Election of Andrew Jackson* (Philadelphia, PA: Lippincott, 1963); Robert Gray Gunderson, *The Log-Cabin Campaign* (Lexington: University of Kentucky Press, 1957); Lynn Hudson Parsons, *The Birth of Modern Politics: Andrew Jackson, John Quincy Adams and the Election of 1828* (New York: Oxford University Press, 2009); and Donald B. Cole, *Vindicating Andrew Jackson: The 1828 Election and the Rise of the Two-Party System* (Lawrence: University Press of Kansas, 2009).

The election of 1960 has a much larger, but more recent literature that includes substantial material focusing on the uses of information and misinformation. The author of the Camelot theme, Theodor H. White, began the discussion in *The Making of the President 1960* (New York: Atheneum, 1961). Any study of this election should begin with two well-researched books by Edmund K. Kallina Jr.: *Courthouse over White House: Chicago and the Presidential Election of 1960* (Orlando: University of Central Florida Press, 1988) and *Kennedy v. Nixon: The Presidential Election of 1960* (Gainesville: University Press of Florida, 2010). One expert on the entire Kennedy presidency, W. J. Rorabaugh, has described many of the information "dirty tricks" of the election in *The Real Making of the President: Kennedy, Nixon, and the 1960 Election* (Lawrence: University Press of Kansas, 2009). For the most comprehensive study of the election, consult David Pietrusza, *1960 LBJ vs. JFK vs. Nixon: The Epic Campaign That Forged Three Presidencies* (New York: Union Square Press, 2008). Also useful is a short book by Gary A. Donaldson, *The First Modern Campaign: Kennedy, Nixon, and the Election of 1960* (Lanham, MD: Rowman & Littlefield, 2007). For an almost spy-novel discussion of secret and misused information, see David L. Robb, *The Gumshoe and the Shrink: Guenther Reinhardt, Dr. Arnold Hutschnecker, and the Secret History of the 1960 Kennedy/Nixon Election* (Solana Beach, CA: Santa Monica Press, 2012). On the televised debates, the key work is Alan Schroeder, *Presidential Debates: Fifty Years of High-Risk TV* (New York: Columbia University Press, 2008).

Chapters 4 and 5 concern the assassinations of Abraham Lincoln and John F. Kennedy. Of particular importance to our theme is the role of conspiracies and the attendant handling of facts, misinformation, and rumors. Presidential assassinations may generate more controversy and misinformation than any other activity in American society. The literature spun off by these two events is colossal, with the Kennedy assassination literature being more extensive because it involved far more suspicious participants than in the case of Lincoln. Although many books accounting for these two events continue to appear, not all of them add to our understanding. A few, however, are particularly useful for understanding the various conspiracy theories and information swirling around these assassinations.

The most useful academic study of the Lincoln conspiracies is William Hanchett's *The Lincoln Murder Conspiracies* (Urbana: University of Illinois Press, 1983). While published many years ago, it remains the single most useful starting point for the study of this assassination. Closely linked to the issue of conspiracies is the mythologizing of Lincoln. Three key studies explore this issue: Gabor Borritt, *The Lincoln Enigma: The Changing Faces of an American Icon* (New York: Oxford University Press, 2001); Philip B. Kunhardt III, Peter W. Kunhardt, and Peter W. Kunhardt Jr., *Looking for Lincoln: The Making of an American Icon* (New York: Alfred A. Knopf, 2008); and Merrill D. Peterson, *Lincoln in American Memory* (New York: Oxford University Press, 1994). While many histories of Lincoln's assassination have been published, for a straightforward historical account consult Edward Steers Jr., *Lincoln's Assassination* (Carbondale: Southern Illinois University Press, 2014). For the context of Lincoln's administration with emphasis on rhetoric and political discourse, the standard work is now Harold Holzer's *Lincoln and the Power of the Press: The War for Public Opinion* (New York: Simon & Schuster, 2014). Also useful is Thomas Reed Turner's *Beware the People Weeping: Public Opinion and the Assassination of Abraham Lincoln* (Baton Rouge: Louisiana State University Press, 1982).

It is a mark of the public's interest in the Kennedy assassination that books on the subject are routinely best sellers. The first major study, published with the blessing of the Kennedy family, was William Manchester's *The Death of a President: November 20–November 25, 1963* (New York: Harper & Row, 1967), which instantly triggered vehement criticisms from conspiracy theorists. Even the official government report on the assassination became a best seller and the basis for considerable controversy over the next half century: *Report of the President's Commission on the Assassination of President John. F. Kennedy* (Washington, DC: US Government Printing Office, 1964). This report appeared in multiple printings from various publishers. A subsequent government report added to the controversy about what information was available and how it was used: *Report of the Select Committee on Assassinations, U.S. House of Representatives Ninety-Fifth Congress* (Washington, DC: US Government Printing Office, 1979). For a detailed history by an amateur historian demonstrating the nature of the information and theories about the assassination, see Joseph McBride's *Into the Nightmare: My Search for the Killers of President John F. Kennedy and Officer J. D. Tippit* (Berkeley, CA: Hightower Press, 2013). But also see Jim Marrs's *Crossfire: The Plot That Killed Kennedy* (New York: Basic Books, 2013). Currently, the best researched study that includes significant information about the surrounding information handling and dissemination is Philip Shenon's *A Cruel and Shocking Act: The Secret History of the Kennedy Assassination* (New York: Henry Holt, 2013).

Chapter 6 discusses the Spanish-American War of 1898. This event stimulated the earliest studies on how people and organizations used information to promote a point of view designed to sway national opinions and affect public policies. Historians noted the profound influence of newspapers in causing the United States to go to war with Spain. The manipulation of information was even addressed at the time, by George Bronson Rea in his *Facts and Fakes About Cuba* (New York: George Munro's Sons, 1897). For a useful general overview of the war, consult G. J. A. O'Toole, *The Spanish War: An American Epic 1898* (New York: W.W.

Norton, 1984). For the most definitive history currently available, see Ivan Musicant's *Empire by Default: The Spanish-American War and the Dawn of the American Century* (New York: Henry Holt, 1998). Joyce Milton's *The Yellow Kids: Foreign Correspondents in the Heyday of Yellow Journalism* (New York: Harper & Row, 1989) describes the adventures of various reporters, but unfortunately it falls short in describing the manipulation of information.

Some of the earliest studies on the role of information in this war began appearing within a generation. The key early work was Joseph E. Wisan's *The Cuban Crisis as Reflected in the New York Press (1895–1898)* (New York: Columbia University Press, 1934). A more recent study covering the topic more broadly is Joseph W. Campbell's *Yellow Journalism: Puncturing the Myths, Defining the Legacies* (Westport, CT: Greenwood Press, 2001). The importance of public opinion is a major element of this study. The earliest is by Marcus M. Wilkerson, *Public Opinion and the Spanish-American War: A Study in War Propaganda* (Baton Rouge: Louisiana State University Press, 1932). It should be read in tandem with Wisan's book (mentioned earlier). Perhaps the most thorough study of the effects of public opinion on the US Congress was Jaime de Ojeda Eiseley's *El 98 en el Congreso y en la Prensa de los Estados Unidos* (Madrid: Ministerio de Asuntos Exteriores, 1999). There is no substitute, however, for reading contemporary polemical literature to see how misinformation and other facts were used. For a good example of such issue-oriented literature, see Claude Mathews, *The Cuban Cause Is Just: The Right Shall Prevail and in God's Own Time Cuba Shall Be Free* (Philadelphia, PA: no publisher, 1895). For other polemical literature consult the Hoes Collection at the US Library of Congress.

Chapter 7 covers advertising, business rumors, and the marketing of patent medicines. The central information issues in business include the role of advertising and the public relations issues of countering negative press, rumors, and conspiratorial theories. Patent medicine represents an extreme case, lasting more than two centuries, rife with misinformation, rumors, and conspiracy theories. The professionalization of public relations and advertising in the second half of the nineteenth century resulted in the continuous and professionalized management of information. For a useful introduction to this topic see Stuart Ewen's *PR! A Social History of Spin* (New York: Basic Books, 1996) as well as Roland Marchand's *Creating the Corporate Soul: The Rise of Public Relations and Corporate Imagery in American Big Business* (Berkeley: University of California Press, 1998).

For a guide to how public relations and advertising people respond to rumors and other fake facts about a corporation, see Allan J. Kimmel's *Rumors and Rumor Control: A Manager's Guide to Understanding and Combatting Rumors* (Mahwah, NJ: Lawrence Erlbaum Associates, 2004), which includes case studies and examples. Also consult Fred Koenig's *Rumors in the Marketplace: The Social Psychology of Commercial Hearsay* (New York:

Praeger, 1985) and folklorist Gary Alan Fine's *Manufacturing Tales: Sex and Money in Contemporary Legends* (Knoxville: University of Tennessee Press, 1992). For a useful introduction to the history of advertising, see Daniel Pope, *The Making of Modern Advertising* (New York: Basic Books, 1983).

The literature on patent medicines is rich and detailed. The dominant scholar of its history, James Harvey Young, published three major studies emphasizing the role of misinformation and false facts: *The Toadstool Millionaires: A Social History of Patent Medicines in America before Federal Regulation* (Princeton, NJ: Princeton University Press, 1961), *The Medical Messiahs: A Social History of Health Quackery in Twentieth-Century America* (Princeton, NJ: Princeton University Press, 1967), and *American Health Quackery* (Princeton, NJ: Princeton University Press, 1992). For an earlier study that includes additional material not covered by Young, see James Cook's *Remedies and Rackets: The Truth about Patent Medicines Today* (New York: W.W. Norton, 1958). The delivery of misinformation through medicine shows and lectures is documented by Ann Anderson in *Snake Oil, Hustlers and Hambones: The American Medicine Show* (Jefferson, NC: McFarland, 2000). For a study of nutrition and wellness information, see the early study by Victor Herbert, *Nutrition Cultism: Facts and Fictions* (Philadelphia, PA: George F. Stickley, 1980).

Chapter 8 covers the health impacts of smoking and the tobacco industry. A key issue tied to this case study is how companies and an entire industry misinformed—indeed lied—to the American public (and others overseas) for a half century. It is possible to study this case study because court rulings made vast quantities of internal memoranda and other documents available to the public and, subsequently, to students of misinformation and faulty data and arguments. A useful source to consult on various modern conspiracies, including a chapter on smoking and tobacco, is Ari Rabin-Havt and Media Matters for America, *Lies, Incorporated: The World of Post-Truth Politics* (New York: Anchor Books, 2016). Several histories and exposés serve as useful reviews of the events and information involved in this case. These include Richard Kluger, *Ashes to Ashes: America's Hundred-Year Cigarette War, the Public Health, and the Unabashed Triumph of Philip Morris* (New York: Knopf, 1996); Philip J. Hilts, *Smoke Screen: The Truth behind the Tobacco Industry Cover-Up* (Boston: Addison-Wesley, 1996); David Kessler, *A Question of Intent: A Great American Battle with a Deadly Industry* (New York: Public Affairs, 2001); Allan Brandt, *The Cigarette Century: The Rise, Fall and Deadly Persistence of the Product That Defined America* (New York: Basic Books, 2007); and Naomi Oreskes and Erick M. Conway, *Merchants of Doubt: How a Handful of Scientists Obscured the Truth on Issues from Tobacco Smoke to Global Warming* (New York: Bloomsbury, 2010). This last book is the most authoritative study currently available based on the massive cache of industry documents.

Chapter 9 covers global warming and environmental change. This case study demonstrates the interaction among misinformation, politics, and science—across the globe, but especially in the United States. While the subject has more than a half century of history, it remains a current issue, resulting in a continuous, almost daily discussion and monthly production of books and scholarly publications. The National Research Council, *Carbon Dioxide and Climate: A Scientific Assessment* (Washington, DC: National Academy Press, 1979), produced an important study of the negative effects of human behavior on the environment. It stirred both scholars and advocates on all sides of the issue. The worldwide discussion of this issue, which has affected relations among nations, is presented in Urs Luterbacher and Detlef F. Sprinz, eds., *International Relations and Global Climate Change* (Cambridge, MA: MIT Press, 2001). The views of the scientific community are reported in J. T. Houghton, G. J. Jenkins, and J. J. Ephraums, eds., *Climate Change: The IPCC Scientific Assessment* (Cambridge: Cambridge University Press, 1990), which extended a study originally published by the National Research Council in 1979. National governments came together to establish a global strategy, reported on by Michael Grubb, Christiaan Vrolijk, and Duncan Brack in *The Kyoto Protocol: A Guide and Assessment* (London: Royal Institute for International Affairs/Chatham House, 1999).

For a useful example of the use of information in a polemical setting, see James Inhofe's *The Greatest Hoax: How the Global Warming Conspiracy Threatens Your Future* (Washington, DC: WND Books, 2012). For an alternative view, see the National Research Council, *Limiting the Magnitude of Future Climate Change* (Washington, DC: National Academic Press, 2010). Historical perspective, combined with the use of a growing body of scientific evidence of the Earth's evolving climate over the millennium can be found in S. Fred Singer and Dennis T. Avery's *Unstoppable Global Warming: Every 1,500 Years* (Lanham, MD: Rowman & Littlefield, 2007). The most widely available discussion of the issues, demonstrating alternative uses of similar data, rhetoric, and opinions can be found in Al Gore's *An Inconvenient Truth: The Planetary Emergency of Global Warming and What We Can Do about It* (Emmaus, PA: Rodale, 2006) and a video he produced under the same title (New York: Melcher Media, 2006). For a more academic discussion along similar lines as Gore's, see the National Research Council's *Climate Change: Evidence, Impacts, and Choices* (Washington, DC: National Research Council, 2011).

More polemical literature that reflects various forms of misinformation, factual scientific data, and various perspectives on plots and controversies include Christopher C. Horner, *The Politically Incorrect Guide to Global Warming and Environmentalism* (Washington, DC: Regnery Publishing, 2007); James Howard Kunstler, *The Long Emergency: Surviving the End of*

Oil, Climate Change, and Other Converging Catastrophes of the Twenty-first Century (New York: Grove Press, 2006); and Luke W. Cole and Sheila R. Foster, *From the Ground Up: Environmental Racism and the Rise of the Environmental Justice Movement* (New York: University of New York Press, 2001). Do not overlook a book by Peter Senge, who is best known for his work on how organizations work: *The Necessary Revolution: How Individuals and Organizations Are Working Together to Create a Sustainable World* (New York: Doubleday, 2008). A useful study devoted to the manipulation of information crucial to the topic of environmental change is David Michaels, *Doubt Is Their Product: How Industry's Assault on Science Threatens Your Health* (New York: Oxford University Press, 2008).

There is also a growing number of websites where one can read about the themes discussed in this book, but we mention here only a single printed source, James F. Broderick and Darren W. Miller, *Web of Conspiracy: A Guide to Conspiracy Theory Sites on the Internet* (Medford, NJ: Information Today, 2008), which is organized by case studies such as Roswell, AIDS, and the Moon Landing.

Index

ABC News, 204
ACCCE. *See* Coalition for Clean Coal
   Electricity
action mobilization, 192
activists role, 12
Adams, John Quincy, 10, 31–32
Addison's disease, 41
Adler, Isaac, 162
Adolph Coors Company, 134
adultery, 32–34
advertising: of corporations, 123–24;
   customers persuaded by, 124;
   information provided in, 151–52;
   in newspapers, 138; of patent
   medicines, 136–57; rumors and,
   125–26; testimonials in, 157; of
   tobacco industry, 161–62, 171–72
advocacy groups, 92
aerosol cans, 196
AFP. *See* Americans for Prosperity
African Americans, 223
Age of Information, 125
air pollution, 199
alcohol content, 142
Alexander I (Czar), 34
Algeria, 178

*All the Facts: A History of Information
   in the United States Since 1870*
   (Cortada), 2
alternative facts, 192
alternative medicine, 139–41, 155
AMA. *See* American Medical
   Association
ambiguous language, 22–23, 24, 127
American Health Quackery (Young), 284
American Medical Association (AMA),
   145
American Revolution, 247n22
Americans for Prosperity (AFP), 210
American Surgeon General, 163
Anderson, Ann, 284
Andrew Jackson: His Life and Times
   (Brand), 280
The Answers We Seek (film), 170
antioxidant power, 155
AP. *See* Associated Press
Apple Computer, 221
arrest, of Oswald, 76
*Ashes to Ashes: America's Hundred-Year
   Cigarette War, the Public Health,
   and the Unabashed Triumph of Philip
   Morris* (Kluger), 284

The Assassination of Abraham Lincoln (PBS), 68
Assassination Records Review Board, U.S., 73
assassinations, 214; character, 3; conspiracy theories on, 59–60, 64–65; Lincoln, A., image transformed by, 57, *57*, 66; media coverage of, 54; misinformation about, 67; preexisting knowledge of, 70; presidential ranking and, 236n7. *See also* Kennedy, John F., assassination; Lincoln assassination
Associated Press (AP), 246n11
Atzerodt, George, 55, 64–65
audience identity, 128
authenticity, 215
autopsy reports, 83–84
Avery, Dennis T., 200, 202, 285
Ayer's Sarsaparilla, 153

back-room deals, 31
ballot box corruption, 46
Bancroft, George, 58
Basch, Norma, 33–34
Bates, Edward, 66
Battles: of Gettysburg, 54; of Horseshoe Bend, 37; of Las Guasimas, 110; Lexington, 247n22; of Little Big Horn, 93; of Manila, 109; of New Orleans, 32, 37, *38*; of San Juan Hill, 90, 111–12, *113*
Beck, Glenn, 207
believability, 127
Belle Dyspepsia Tablets, 151
Beware the People Weeping: Public Opinion and the Assassination of Abraham Lincoln (Turner), 282
Beyond Good and Evil (Nietzsche), 7
bible societies, 276n10
Bimber, Bruce, 280
Binns, John, 37
biography, of Johnson, L., 79
The Birth of Modern Politics: Andrew Jackson, John Quincy Adams and the Election of 1828 (Parsons), 280
Black Warrior (U.S. vessel), 95

Blaine, James G., 28
blogs, 223
Blumler, Jay G., 26, 51
Boiron, Christian, 155
Bold, Christine, 111, 115, 117
Bonner & Associates, 209
Booth, Edwin, 153
Booth, John Wilkes, 14–15, 53, 55, 61–62, 67
Borritt, Gabor, 281
Brack, Duncan, 285
Brand, H. W., 280
Brandt, Allan, 284
bravery, of Roosevelt, T., 110–11
Broderick, James F., 286
Brown & Williamson, 169
Bruni, Frank, 211–12
Bryan, William Jennings, 29
Buffalo Bill's Wild West Show, 112
bullshitting, 3
Burdock Blood Bitters, 151
Burney, Leroy E., 167
Burton, Michael John, 280
Bush, George W., 188, 190
Bush, Herbert W., 118

Campaign Craft: The Strategies, Tactics, and Art of Political Campaign Management (Burton and Shea), 280
campaigning styles, 212–13
campaigns, 28, 31, 40, 98
Campbell, Joseph W., 283
cancer, 147, 159, 162–71
candidates, 16–17, 20, 24–25, 27–29
cannibalism, 37
cap-and-trade system, 208–9
Carbon Dioxide and Climate: A Scientific Assessment (National Research Council), 285
carbon dioxide emissions (CO_2), 179, 191, 194; greenhouse gases and, 200; research consensus on, 181–82; in U.S., 13–14. *See also* fossil fuel companies
Caribbean colonies, 89–90
Caro, Robert, 79
Carter, Jimmy, 49

case studies, 9; cross-cutting themes in, 14–18, 216–17; of fake facts, 221–22; of lies and misrepresentation, *10*; political and commercial, 13; truth vetted in, 16

Castro, Fidel, 81

Catholicism, 14, 42–44, 48, 257n54

Catton, Bruce, 59

cautionary tales, 4

Center for Disease Control and Prevention (CDC), 169

CFCs. *See* chlorofluorocarbons

Chaffin, Tom, 95

Chapman Hall canker and dyspepsia cure, *137*

character assassination, 3

chemotherapy, 146

Chicago Tribune, 107

chlorofluorocarbons (CFCs), 167, 182, 184

church and state separation, 45

Churchill, Winston, 86

Church of Satan, 133

CIA, 81

The Cigarette Century: The Rise, Fall and Deadly Persistence of the Product That Defined America (Brandt), 284

cigarette manufacturing, 163

cigarette smoking, 159, 162–63, *164*, 165–68; nicotine in, 170, 172; secondhand smoke from, 170–71

citizens, 194, 196–97, 201

Civil War, 56–57

Clark Stanley's Snake Oil Liniment, *143*, 151

Clay, Henry, 31, 33

Cleveland, Grover, 28

climate change, 124; cap-and-trade system and, 208–9; catastrophes from, 196–97; climate cycles and, 200–201; computer models of, 181, 195; defining, 178–80; deindustrialization and, 198; deniers of, 182–84, 186, 197–210, *203*; droughts from, 178; Earth's average temperature and, 193–94; emerging issues of, 180–82; false

experts on, 204; First World Climate Conference and, 181; Global Climate Coalition and, 180; global warming and, 175, 177, 179–80; Gore's comments on, 195–96; greenhouse effect and, 186; human's basic needs and, 196–97; misinformation about, 185–86, 215; nuisance suits and, 210; oceans warming from, 177; Paris climate agreement, 210, 276n5; political parties on, 189; public opinion on, 188, 216; scientific community on, 176–77, 190–97, 202–3; think tanks on, 187–88; United Nations warning on, 177; U.S. debates on, 13–14, 175–76, 184; worldwide report on, *183*. *See also* carbon dioxide emissions; global warming

Climate Change: Evidence, Impacts, and Choices (National Research Council), 285

Climate Change: The IPCC Scientific Assessment (Houghton, Jenkins and Ephraums), 285

Climategate, 189, 205–7

Clinton, Bill, 190

Clinton, Hillary, 17, 31

CO_2. *See* carbon dioxide emissions

Coalition for Clean Coal Electricity (ACCCE), 208

Coca-Cola, 134

Cody, William "Buffalo Bill," 110, 112, 115

coffin handbill, 35, *36*

Colbert, Stephen, 267n8

Cole, Donald B., 280

Cole, Luke W., 286

collagen, 154–55

college students, 1–2, 16

colonialism, Spanish, 90–92

Committee on Public Information (CPI), 118

communications, 20–21, 26

computer models, of climate change, 181, 195

computers, 26

Confederate officials, 14, 62, 67
Congress, 13, 82–83, 102, 145, 190
Connally, John, 76–77, 84
Connally, Nellie, 76
conspiracy theories: on assassinations,
    59–60, 64–65; facts and, 53,
    214; grand conspiracy in, 67;
    information manipulation and, 71;
    on Kennedy, John, assassination,
    11, 53–54, 74–75; on Lincoln
    assassination, 11, 53–55, 62–69;
    in presidential assassinations,
    11; about Stanton, 62; Warren
    Commission types of, 84–85
consumer products, 130–31, 139–41,
    140
Consumer Reports, 146, 154
consumers, formal education of,
    156–57
Conway, Erick M., 284
Cook, James, 284
Cooke, Nicole, 211
Coors, Joe, 134
corporations: advertising of, 123–24;
    environmental issues facing, 176;
    IBM, 133–34; information use and,
    12–13; misinformation from, 17–18;
    P&G, 133–34; public relations
    of, 126; R. J. Reynolds Tobacco
    Company, 170–71; rumors about,
    132
corruption charges, 31, 33, 46
Cortada, J. W., 2
Council for Tobacco Research, 167
countries, rumors involving, 131–32
*Courthouse over White House: Chicago
    and the Presidential Election of 1960*
    (Kallina), 281
CPI. *See* Committee on Public
    Information
Crabtree, Jerome B., 114–15
*Creating the Corporate Soul: The Rise
    of Public Relations and Corporate
    Imagery in American Big Business*
    (Marchand), 283
Creelman, James, 100
crew members, USS *Maine*, 96–97

critical thinking, 214, 224
Cronkite, Walter, 45, 76
cross-cutting themes, 14–18, 216–17
Crossfire: The Plot That Killed Kennedy
    (Marrs), 282
*A Cruel and Shocking Act: The Secret
    History of the Kennedy Assassination*
    (Shenon), 282
Cuba: fake facts about, 90, 94;
    newspapers sending reporters to,
    99; revolution of, 90; Roosevelt,
    T., exploits in, 110; ships with
    contraband and, 93–94; Spain revolt
    and, 95–96, 101–2; U.S. information
    on, 92
*The Cuban Cause Is Just: The Right Shall
    Prevail and in God's Own Time Cuba
    Shall Be Free* (Mathews), 283
*The Cuban Crisis as Reflected in the New
    York Press (1895–1898)* (Wisan), 283
Cuban Junta, 99–100, 104
Cullman, Joseph, 169
Custer, George Armstrong, 117
Custer's Last Stand, 112
customers, advertising to, 124

Daley, Richard J., 27, 39, 47
Davis, Richard Harding, 114
Davis, William, 177
Day's Kidney Pad, 149
*The Death of a President: November 20–
    November 25, 1963* (Manchester),
    282
death sentence, 65
debates: on climate change, 13–14,
    175–76, 184; with Kennedy, John,
    and Nixon, 50; 1960s presidential
    election, 40, 49–50, *50*, 86
Deemer, Mary, 153
defamation, 3
defamed figure, 67–68
deindustrialization, 198
deniers, of climate change, 182–84,
    186; arguments of, 201, *203*; fossil
    fuel companies and, 197; global
    warming and, 197–210; scientific
    community evidence and, 201–3

Department Store Snake, 130
DePaulo, Bella, 1–2
dereliction of duty, 68
derogatory nicknames, 15, 17
destruction, of USS *Maine*, 90, 93, 97, 103–9, *108*, 214, 216
Dewey, George, 109
diagnostic themes, 192
digital literacy, 224
disease mongering, 156
disinformation, 4, 26
divisive, presidential election (2016), 16–17
divorce papers, 232n57
Dole, Bob, 153
domestic affairs, 34
Donaldson, Gary A., 281
Donelson, Rachel, 32, 34
door-to-door salesmen, 259n88
Doubt Is Their Product: How Industry's Assault on Science Threatens Your Health (Michaels), 286
Dr. Johnson Remedy Company, 147
droughts, from climate change, 178
drugs, ethical, 138
Duffy's Pure Malt Whiskey, 153
Dupuy de Lôme, Enrique, 100
Durkheim, Emile, 8

Earth, 181–82, 193–94
echo chamber, 190
economic interests, 91, 203
economic theory, 254n6
Edelman, Murray, 21–22, 280
Edison Electric Institute, 185
editorial opinion-making, 39–40
education, 15–16, 156–57, 224
Egan, Margaret, 8
Eiseley, Jaime de Ojeda, 283
Eisenchiml, Otto, 67–68, 70
Eisenhower, Dwight D., 117
The Election of Andrew Jackson (Remini), 280
Electoral College, 47
e-mails, of scientific community, 206–7

Empire by Default: The Spanish-American War and the Dawn of the American Century (Musicant), 283
energy efficiency, 186
environmental issues, 176, 187, 199
Environmental Protection Agency (EPA), 176, 199
Ephraums, J. J., 285
Ernst, William, 208
ethical drugs, 138, 146
ethics, fake facts and, 33, 224–25
Evening Post, 105
Evening Star, 64
Ewen, Stuart, 125, 283
exaggerated claims, 127–28
executions, soldiers, 35–37, *36*
ExxonMobil, 180, 209–10

Facebook, 128, 217, 223
facts: alternative, 192; conspiracy theories and, 53, 214; epistemic status of, 8; false, 107, 124, 210, 214, 217–18; of Kennedy, John, assassination, 76–77; reality agreement of, 6; about tobacco industry, 15
Facts and Fakes About Cuba (Rea), 89, 282
fake facts, 5, 21, 192; case studies of, 221–22; on Cuba, 90, 94; dissemination of, 216; ethics and, 224–25; falsehoods and, 7, 28, 222; government and, 225; information and, 211; on Kennedy, John, assassination, 82; on Lincoln assassination, 59–60, 62–69; news outlets fighting, 223; phenomenon of, 3
fake news, 5, 106; door-to-door salesmen, 259n88; Jackson, A., and, 31–32; from media, 27, 218–20, 223; in presidential elections, 29–30, 222; public exposure to, 220; truth and, 126
false facts, 107, 124, 210, 214, 217–18

falsehoods, 7, 28, 222

FBI, 81

FDA. *See* Food and Drug Administration

The Federalist Papers, 26

filibusterers, 91, 94

Fillmore, Millard, 27

Fine, Gary Alan, 129, 131, 284

firing squad, of Spain, 247n14

The First Modern Campaign: Kennedy, Nixon, and the Election of 1960 (Donaldson), 281

First Volunteer Cavalry, U.S. *See* Rough Riders

First World Climate Conference, 181

First World War, 117, 119

Food and Drug Administration (FDA), 136, 144

food and drug laws, 145

Ford, Gerald, 49

Ford's Theatre, 55, 59, *59*, 69

Forrester, Jay W., 181

fossil fuel companies, 13, 180, 188–90, 197, 208–9

Foster, Sheila R., 286

Foucault, Michel, 8

Founding Fathers, 21–22

Fox, Sylvan, 83

framing method, 192–93

Francis Parkman Prize, 79

Franklin, Benjamin, 138, 217

"A Frank Statement to Cigarette Smokers" (document), 159

freedom of speech, 218

From the Ground Up: Environmental Racism and the Rise of the Environmental Justice Movement (Cole, L., and Foster), 286

Fuller, Steve, 8

The Fun and Fighting of the Rough Riders (Hall, T.), 114

Fuqua, Stephen O., 119

Gaddis, John Lewis, 30

García, Calixto, 100

Garfield, James A., 105

Gatling gun, 111

German Militarism and Its German Critics (publication), 119

German Revolution, 5

Gettysburg, battles of, 54

global change, 179

Global Climate Coalition, 180

global warming, 195–96; climate change and, 175, 177, 179–80; deniers of, 197–210; economic argument for, 203; exaggeration of, 204–5; Gore's video on, 205; myths about, 199–200; political parties and, 206; pro-business" policies and, 198–99; scientific community and, 202; voters on, 198

Glover, M. W., 144

goals, specific, 14

Goldberg, Alfred, 84–85

Golden Age of Rumors, 128

Gómez, Máximo, 100

Gore, Al, 188–89, 285; climate change comments of, 195–96; criticism of film by, *205*; global warming video by, 205

government, fake facts and, 225

The Government of Germany (publication), 119

grand conspiracy, 67

grassy knoll, 83

The Greatest Hoax: How the Global Warming Conspiracy Threatens Your Future (Inhofe), 186, 285

Greeley, Horace, 58

greenhouse effect, 179, 184–86, 194, 200

Grubb, Michael, 285

The Gumshoe and the Shrink: Guenther Reinhardt, Dr. Arnold Hutschnecker, and the Secret History of the 1960 Kennedy/Nixon Election (Robb), 281

Gunderson, Robert Gray, 280

Hadacol, 154

Hahn, Dan F., 23, 280

halitosis, 156

Hall, Chapman, *137*

Hall, Thomas W., 114

Halpin, Maria, 28
Hamilton, Alexander, 26
Hamlin's Wizard Oil, 152, *152*
Hammond, Charles, 35
Hammond, E. Cyler, 162–63
Hanchett, William, 59, 60, 67–68, 236n3, 281
Hanna, Marcus A., 29
Harold Holzer on Abraham Lincoln (television), 68
Harper's Weekly, 93
Hartnett, Timothy, 169
hat wearing, of Kennedy, John, 244n61
headache capsule, 154
health consequences, 136
Hearst, William Randolph, 105
heartless monster, 37
Heartney, Eleanor, 71
Herbert, Victor, 284
heroes, Spanish-American War creating, 109–10
Herold, David, 55
high school students, 169
Hill, John, 165
Hill & Knowlton, 165–67
Hilts, Philip J., 284
Hockett, Robert, 170
hockey sticks graph, 207–8
Hofstadter, Richard, 19–21
Holt, Joseph, 61, 67
Holzer, Harold, 63, 68, 282
homeopathy, 139, 155
Hoover, J. Edgar, 81
Horn, Daniel, 162–63
Horner, Christopher C., 198, 285
hostile takeover, 30
Houghton, J. T., 285
House of Representatives, U.S., 76
House Select Committee on Assassinations (HSCA), 78
Hubbard, Bryan, 155
Humphrey, Hubert, 45
"Hush'd be the Camps To-Day" (poem), 59

IBM, 133–34
ICE. *See* Information Council on the Environment
illnesses, cures for, 156
imperial powers, of U.S., 115–16
impressions, reinforcing, 23
An Inconvenient Truth (film), 189, *205*
An Inconvenient Truth: The Planetary Emergency of Global Warming and What We Can Do about It (Gore), 285
Indians, 14, 37
individual voices, 18
information: advertising providing, 151–52; age of, 125; in communications, 26; conspiracy theories and manipulation of, 71; corporations and truthful, 123–24; corporations and use of, 12–13; on Cuba, 92; disinformation and, 4, 26; dissemination of, 212; fake facts and, 211; framing method on, 192–93; Internet dissemination of, 26, 221; large groups using, 17; merchandizing of doubt and, 215; messaging of, 219–20; about patent medicines, 138; presidential elections using, 27–28, 280; social media source of, 30; tobacco industry using, 173; weaponization of, 16
Information and American Democracy: Technology in the Evolution of Political Power (Bimber), 280
Information Council on the Environment (ICE), 185
Inhofe, James, 186, 285
Instagram, 217
intelligence gathering agencies, 253n127
Intergovernmental Panel on Climate Change (IPCC), 182
International Relations and Global Climate Change (Sprinz), 285
Internet: false facts on, 210, 217–18; Golden Age of Rumors on,

128; individual voices on, 18;
information dissemination on,
26, 221; misinformation on, 210;
rumors on, 127; social media on,
18; trusted sites on, 16; U.S. use of,
220–21
*Into the Nightmare: My Search for the
Killers of President John F. Kennedy
and Officer J. D. Tippit* (McBride),
282
investigations, of patent medicines,
138–39
IPCC. *See* Intergovernmental Panel on
Climate Change

Jackson, Andrew, 10, 148; adultery
charge on, 32; Battle of New
Orleans and, *38*; charges against,
216; corruption charges against, 33;
divorce papers of, 232n57; domestic
affairs of, 34; executions authorized
by, 35–37, *36*; fake news about,
31–32; fears about, 35; as heartless
monster, 37; Indian expulsion by,
14; nomination of, 31; ointment
complimented by, 153; opposition
research on, 27; rough-and-tumble
frontier hero, 22; as rough-and-
tumble frontier hero, 22; as slave
owner, 35; slave ownership and, 35;
as unfit for office, 33; wife stealing
and, 34
Jackson, Andrew, Jr., 32
Jackson, Rachel, 30
James, William, 125, 156
Jefferson, Thomas, 211
Jenkins, G. J., 285
Jewish bankers, 257n54
JFK (film), 83
Jobs, Steve, 221
Johnson, Andrew, 55, 62, 65
Johnson, Lyndon, 48, 74, 77–79, 117,
120
The Journal, 106
journalism, 109

Journal of the American Medical
Association, 162–63
The Jungle (Sinclair), 144

Kallina, Edmund F., 40, 42, 48
Kallina, Edmund F., Jr., 281
Kammen, Michael, 215, 222
Kavanagh, Dennis, 26, 51
Kelly, Clarence, 81
Kennedy, Jacqueline, 76, 87
Kennedy, Joe, 42
Kennedy, John F., 10, *75*; Addison's
disease of, 41; Camelot period
and, 22; Catholicism of, 14, 42–43;
church and state separation
and, 45; conspiracies role and,
11; hat wearing of, 244n61; as
martyred husband, 87; myth and
misinformation about, 39, 86–87;
Nixon's debate with, *50*; Southern
states challenge to, 44
Kennedy, John F., assassination:
aftermath of, 77; autopsy reports
of, 83–84; Congressional study of,
82–83; conspiracy theories on, 11,
53–54, 74–75; controversy of, 80–85;
cover-up of, 82; facts of, 76–77;
fake facts and misinformation
of, 82; grassy knoll and, 83; high
school boys reaction to, 240n6;
media covering, 73–74; mercy
killing theory of, 84; mythology of,
85–87; police officer and, 243n46;
public opinion on, 87; single bullet
theory, 83; single shooter theory,
79, 87; surveys on, 74; television
covering, 76; U.S. Assassination
Records Review Board and, 73;
Warren Commission on, 78–81, 84;
Wikipedia entry on, 73; Zapruder
film of, 82–83
Kennedy, Robert, 41, 81
*Kennedy v. Nixon: The Presidential
Election of 1960* (Kallina, E. F., Jr),
281

Kentucky Fried Chicken (KFC), 133–34
Kessler, David, 284
KFC. *See* Kentucky Fried Chicken
Kickapoo Indian Sagwa tonic, 151
Killing Lincoln: The Shocking Assassination That Changed America Forever (O'Reilly), 61
Kimmel, Allan J., 283
KKK. *See* Ku Klux Klan
Kline's Painless Cancer Cure, 149
Kluger, Richard, 284
knowledge, preexisting, 70
Koenig, Fred, 283
Koyre, Alexandre, 5–6
Kuhn, Thomas, 8
Ku Klux Klan (KKK), 132, 134
Kunhardt, Peter W., 281
Kunhardt, Peter W., Jr., 281
Kunhardt, Philip B., III, 281
Kunstler, James Howard, 285
Kyoto agreement, 184–85, 187, 192, 201, 276n5
The Kyoto Protocol: A Guide and Assessment (Grubb, Vrolijk and Brack), 285

Laboratory Life (Latour and Woolgar), 8
language, 15, 22–23, 24, 127
Latour, Bruno, 8
leadership, of Roosevelt, T., 110–11
Lee, Robert E., 58
Lefsrud, Lianne M., 192–93
legends, 4
Lexington battle, 247n22
lies, 1–5, 9–11, *10*, 214–15
Lies, Incorporated: The World of Post-Truth Politics (Rabin-Havt), 284
The Life of Andrew Jackson (Remini), 280
Limiting the Magnitude of Future Climate Change (National Research Council), 285
Lincoln, Abraham: Founding Fathers and, 21–22; image transformed of, 57, *57*, 66; opposition research on, 27–28; polling on, 236n7; televised programs on, 68, 76; as unpopular, 57, 65–66

Lincoln and the Power of the Press: The War for Public Opinion (Holzer), 282
Lincoln assassination, 14–15; assassin not tried in, 60; conspiracies role and, 11; conspiracy theories on, 11, 53–55, 62–69; controversy of, 56–69; fake facts on, 59–60, 62–69; at Ford's Theatre, 55, *59*; key players in, 61; media and, 58; misinformation on, 61, 69–70; in newspapers, 63–64; public reaction to, 57–59; Surratt, J., trial in, 65
Lincoln Assassination: Mystery at the Museum Specials (television), 68
The Lincoln Enigma: The Changing Faces of an American Icon (Borritt), 281
Lincoln in American Memory (Peterson), 282
Lincoln Memorial, 61, 69
The Lincoln Murder Conspiracies (Hanchett), 281
Lincoln's Assassination (Steers), 282
literacy, 15
Little Big Horn, battles of, 93
lobbyists, 173
The Log-Cabin Campaign (Gunderson), 280
The Long Emergency: Surviving the End of Oil, Climate Change, and Other Converging Catastrophes of the Twenty-first Century (Kunstler), 285
Looking for Lincoln: The Making of an American Icon (Kunhardt, P. B, Kunhardt, P. W., and Kunhardt, P. W., Jr.), 281–82
López, Narciso, 94–95
luegenpresse (lying press), 5
lung cancer, 159, 168, 170–71
Luntz, Frank, 198
Lydia E. Pinkham's Vegetable Compound, 149, *150*
lying press (luegenpresse), 5

Maceo, Antonio, 100
Madison, James, 26
Maine, USS: crew members of, 96–97; destruction of, 90, 93, 97, 103–9,

108, 214, 216; media on, 105, 109;
    Spanish-American War and, 104–5;
    U.S. response to, 98–99
The Making of Modern Advertising
    (Pope), 284
The Making of the President 1960
    (White), 281
Manchester, William, 76, 282
Manifest Destiny, 91
Mann, Michael, 207–8
Mansfield, Mike, 85
*Manufacturing Tales: Sex and Money in
    Contemporary Legends* (Fine), 284
Marchand, Roland, 127, 283
Marlboro Man, 161, 171, 266n58
Marrs, Jim, 83, 282
Marsh, Leslie, 8
martyred husband, 87
The Martyr of Liberty, 57
mathematics skills, 224
Mathews, Claude, 283
Mazo, Earl, 47–48
McBride, Joseph, 83, 243n46, 282
McCarthy, Joseph ("Joe"), 23
McCormack, John W., 85
McKinley, William, 29, 100
McTaggart, Lynne, 155
mean-spirited lies, 2
measurements, of greenhouse effect,
    194
media: assassinations coverage of, 54;
    as echo chamber, 190; fake news
    from, 27, 218–20, 223; journalism,
    109; Kennedy, John, assassination
    covered by, 73–74; Lincoln
    assassination and, 58; news outlets,
    223; patent medicines problems
    reported by, 146–47; public
    opinion swayed by, 126; scientific
    community opposition using, 197;
    social, 18, 30, 220, 222, 223; Spain's
    image created by, 108; Spanish-
    American War role of, 107; Spanish
    atrocities in, 100–101; on USS
    Maine, 105, 109; Weyler y Nicolau
    reports in, 99; yellow press and, 91,
    245n6. *See also* newspapers

*The Medical Messiahs: A Social History
    of Health Quackery in Twentieth-
    Century America* (Young), 284
medical records, 42
medicines: alternative, 139–42, 155;
    miracle, 142; quack, 136, 146–47,
    153, 157; quakometer and, 155;
    science-based, 141, 146; vaccines,
    146, 156. *See also* patent medicines
medicine shows, 142, 145
Medieval Warm Period, 202
Mendelson, Robert, 203
mercantile legends, 129–30
mercantilism, 125, 254n6
merchandizing of doubt, 215
*Merchants of Doubt: How a Handful
    of Scientists Obscured the Truth on
    Issues from Tobacco Smoke to Global
    Warming* (Oreskes and Conway),
    284
mercy killing theory, 84
messages, 27, 120–21, 169–73, 219–20
metaliteracy, 224
Mexican-American War (1846-1848),
    94, 132
Mexican beer, 132
Meyer, Renate E., 192–93
Michaels, David, 286
military career, of Roosevelt, T.,
    109–10
militiamen, 36
Miller, Darren W., 286
Milstead, Kenneth L., 136
Milton, Joyce, 283
miracle medicines, 142
misinformation, 3; in American public
    life, 213–14; about assassinations,
    67; from candidates, 24–25; about
    climate change, 185–86, 215; in First
    World War, 119; from fossil fuel
    companies, 190; on Internet, 210;
    about Kennedy, John, 39, 86–87;
    on Kennedy, John, assassination,
    82; on Lincoln assassination, 61,
    69–70; from organizations, 17–18;
    about patent medicines, 148–49;
    political parties campaigns of, 28; in

presidential elections (1960), 49–50; scientific community and, 279–80; techniques in, 214–15; tobacco industry using, 160–61; in U.S., 217; U.S. newspapers and, 218–19
misrepresentation, 3, *10*, 10–11
mobile phones, 221
mobilization, action, 192
modern Jezebel, 34
Moore, J. Hampton, 116
moral values, 33
Morano, Marc, 186
Moxie Nerve Food, 149
Mudd, Samuel A., 55, 60
Müller, Franz Hermann, 162
Murrow, Edward R., 167
Musicant, Ivan, 283
mythic expressions, 23
myths, 4

Natex, 153
National Academy of Sciences, 179, 181
National Archives and Records Administration, 78
national campaigns, 40
National Center for Atmospheric Research, 207
national crisis, 20
National Research Council, 285
Navy, U.S., 103
The Necessary Revolution: How Individuals and Organizations Are Working Together to Create a Sustainable World (Senge), 286
negative campaigning, 31
negative images, 17
negative messaging, 27
negativism, 28
New Deal legislation, 15–16
news outlets, 223
newspapers, 27, 145; advertising in, 138; AP and, 246n11; Cuba receiving reporters from, 99; false facts of, 107; Lincoln assassination in, 63–64; misinformation and, 218–

19; Spanish atrocities covered by, 101; in U.S., 218–19; yellow press and, 245n6
news reporters, in Spanish-American War, 251n93
New York Herald, 96–97, 102, 106–7, 114, 236n41
New York Journal, 105
nicknames, derogatory, 15, 17
nicotine, 170, 172
Nietzsche, Friedrich, 6–7, 9
9/11 terrorist attacks, 2–3, 11
1960 LBJ vs. JFK vs. Nixon: The Epic Campaign That Forged Three Presidencies (Pietrusza), 281
*El 98 en el Congreso y en la Prensa de los Estados Unido*s (Eiseley), 283
Nixon, Richard, 10, 23, 42, 118; article publication on, 236n41; Catholicism and, 44; Kennedy, John, debate with, *50*; metal ephemera of, 231n38; sketchy look of, 29; Watergate and, 12
Northrop, Henry Davenport, 116
nostrums (our remedy), 136, 142, 151–52, 156
nuisance suits, 210
Nutrition Cultism: Facts and Fictions (Herbert), 284

Obama, Barack, 29, 190, 206
oceans, warming of, 177
oil-producing countries, 184
ointment, Jackson, A., complimenting, 153
Onof, Christian, 8
opposition research, 27–28
ordinary legends, 4
O'Reilly, Bill, 61
Oreskes, Naomi, 203–4, 284
Oswald, Lee Harvey, 53, 76–77, *77*
Oswald, Marguerite, 84
O'Toole, G. J. A., 282
our remedy (nostrums), 136, 142, 151–52, 156
Overstreet, Harry, 126

pamphlets, 218
papist background, 43
paranoia sells, 71
paranoid mind, 19
Paris climate agreement, 210, 276n5
Parsons, Lynn Hudson, 280
partisan views, of political parties, 25
The Passing of Spain and the Ascendancy of America (Crabtree), 114
patent medicines, 12, 124; advertising on, 136–57; alcohol content of, 142; background of, 141–42; big business of, 142, 156; consumer products beginning as, 139–41, *140*; health consequences of, 136; information about, 138; investigations of, 138–39; media reporting problems with, 146–47; misinformation about, 148–49; outlandish claims about, 148; regulations on, 144; science-based medicines and, 141, 146; testimonials on, 152–54; types of, *140*
Peale, Norman Vincent, 44
Pearl Harbor, 93
penicillin, 146
Pepsi-Cola, 134
perjury, 3
Perriello, Tom, 208
personal life, of candidates, 28–29
personal relevance, 127
Pessen, Edward, 37
Peterson, Merrill D., 282
petroleum industry, 13
P&G, 133–34
Pietrusza, David, 281
Pinkham, Lydia E., *150*, 151
polarization, of politics, 190
Political Communication: Rhetoric, Government, and Citizens (Hahn), 280
Political Language: Words That Succeed and Politics That Fail (Edelman), 280
The Politically Incorrect Guide to Global Warming and Environmentalism (Horner), 285

political parties: ballot box corruption and, 46; campaigning styles of, 212–13; climate change views of, 189; global warming and, 206; misinformation campaigns of, 28; 1960 presidential election and, 51; partisan views of, 25; Tea Party and, 186, 206. *See also* Republican Party
politicians, 15, *24*
politics: commercial case studies and, 13; language of, 15; polarization of, 190; rumors in, 134; science of, 280; systems for, 41, 47
Politics as Symbolic Action: Mass Arousal and Quiescence (Edelman), 280
polling, on Lincoln, 236n7
Pomeroy, Marcus Mills, 66
Pope, Daniel, 142, 284
Pop Rocks, 132
positivism, 6–7
Powell, Colin, 118
Powell, Lewis, 55
PR! A Social History of Spin (Ewen), 283
preexisting knowledge, 70
prejudice, against Catholicism, 48
presidential assassinations, conspiracies in, 11
Presidential Debates: Fifty Years of High-Risk TV (Schroeder), 281
presidential elections: campaigning styles in, 212–13; campaigns in, 28, 31, 40, 98; candidates in, 16–17, 20, 24–25, 27–29; common themes in, 23; communications in, 20–21; fake news in, 29–30, 222; information used in, 27–28, 280; Jackson, A., nomination in, 31; politicians in, *24*; television's role in, 25
presidential elections (1824), 31
presidential elections (1828), 20–21, 30, 32–33, *36*
presidential elections (1960): debates, 40, 49–50, *50*, 86; editorial opinion-making in, 39–40; lies in, 10–11; medical records and, 42; misinformation in, 49–50; political

parties in, 51; on television, 49; voting practices in, 45–46
presidential elections (2016), 16–17
presidential ranking, 236n7
President John F. Kennedy Assassination Records Collection Act, 78
problem solving, 127
pro-business policies, 198–99
prognostic themes, 192
Protestants, 43–45
Pruitt, Scott, 176
public: cigarette smoking sentiments of, 165–66; climate change view of, 188, 216; discourse, 2; fake news exposure to, 220; lies in, 3, 9; Lincoln assassination reaction of, 57–59; reinforcing impressions by, 23; relations, 126, 165; U.S. life in, 213–14; worldview of, 22–23
public opinion, 24–25, 70; on climate change, 188, 216; on Kennedy, John, assassination, 87; media swaying, 126; television swaying, 213, 219
Public Opinion and the Spanish-American War: A Study in War Propaganda (Wilkerson), 283
Pulitzer, Joseph, 105
Pure Food and Drug Act, 144

quack medicines, 136, 146–47, 153, 157
quakometer, 155
de Quesada, Gonzalo, 116
A Question of Intent: A Great American Battle with a Deadly Industry (Kessler), 284

Rabin-Havt, Ari, 185, 284
Radam's Microbe Killer, 146
radio, 145
Rea, George Bronson, 89, 282
Reagan, Ronald, 21, 87, 134, 225
reality agreement, 6
The Real Making of the President: Kennedy, Nixon, and the 1960 Election (Rorabaugh), 281
Redemption Rumors, 129

regulations: fossil fuel companies fighting, 208; on patent medicines, 144; on tobacco industry, 13, 168, 173
religious groups, 134, 213
Remedies and Rackets: The Truth about Patent Medicines Today (Cook), 284
Remington, Frederic, 112
Remini, Robert V., 33, 232n46, 280
Report of the President's Commission on the Assassination of President John. F. Kennedy (government report), 282
Report of the Select Committee on Assassinations, U.S. House of Representatives Ninety-Fifth Congress, 282
Republican National Committee (RNC), 47
Republican Party, 46–48, 186, 206
Richmond Whig, 63
Ridenour, David, 197
R. J. Reynolds Tobacco Company, 170–71
RNC. *See* Republican National Committee
Robards, Lewis, 32–33, 35
Robb, David L., 281
Rockefeller, John D., 209
Roosevelt, Eleanor, 43
Roosevelt, Franklin D., 15, 22
Roosevelt, John, 42
Roosevelt, Theodore, 90, 93; Battle of San Juan Hill role of, 112, *113*; bravery and leadership of, 110–11; Cuban exploits of, 110; governorship sought by, 112–14; military career of, 109–10; Spanish-American War and, *113*; tough cowboy image of, 112, 114–15; vigor and energy of, 115
Rorabaugh, W. J., 281
rough-and-tumble frontier hero, 22
Rough Riders, 90, 110–11, 114
Rough Rider Weekly, 117
Ruby, Jack, 76–77
Rules of Sociological Method (Durkheim), 8

rumors, 4, 12, 214–15; advertising and, 125–26; audience identity in, 128; about corporations, 132; countries involved in, 131–32; distortion in, 128; exaggerated claims in, 127–28; features of, 127–28; Fillmore spreading, 27; about IBM, 133–35; on Internet, 127; plausibility of, 132, 135; in politics, 134; redemption, 129; about Satan, 133

Rumors and Rumor Control: A Manager's Guide to Understanding and Combatting Rumors (Kimmel), 283

Rumors in the Marketplace: The Social Psychology of Commercial Hearsay (Koenig), 283

Sabato, Larry J., 86
salesmen, door-to-door, 259n88
San Francisco Chronicle, 107
San Juan Hill, battles of, 90, 111–12, 113
Satan rumors, 133
Saul's Catarrh Remedy, 149
Schlesinger, Arthur, Jr., 42
Schroeder, Alan, 281
Schwartz, Joel, 204
Schwarzkopf, Norman, Jr., 118
science, of politics, 280
science-based medicines, 141, 146
scientific community: alternative facts and, 192; on climate change, 176–77, 190–97, 202–3; deniers of climate change and, 201–3; e-mails of, 206–7; global warming and, 202; greenhouse gases and, 194; media-savvy opposition to, 197; misinformation and, 279–80; temperature rising and, 200
A Scientific Perspective on the Cigarette Controversy (publication), 167
scientific research, 159–60, 166–68, 173, 181–82
scorched-earth campaign, 98
secondhand smoke, 170–71
Second World War, 117, 119
secularization, 255n12

Seitz, Frederick, 185
self-healing, 141
self-serving lies, 2
Senge, Peter, 286
Seward, William H., 55, 62
Shea, Daniel M., 280
Shenon, Philip, 79–81, 85, 282
Shera, Jesse, 8
Sigsbee, Charles, 105
Sinclair, Upton, 144
Singer, S. Fred, 200, 202
single bullet theory, 83
single shooter theory, 79, 87
situational anxiety, 127
slander, 3, 31
slave owners, 35
Slawson, David, 82
Smith, Al, 44
Smoke Screen: The Truth behind the Tobacco Industry Cover-Up (Hilts), 284
The Smoking Controversy: A Perspective (publication), 170
Snake Oil, Hustlers and Hambones: The American Medicine Show (Anderson), 284
social epistemology, 8
social influence, 128
socially constructed, 6
social media, 220; fake facts on, 223; information source of, 30; on Internet, 18; no barriers on, 222
Social Security, 48
soldiers' executions, 35–37, *36*
Sommers, Sheldon, 170
sound bites, 22, 40
the South, 44
Southern Press, 95
Spain: colonialism of, 90–92; crew members executed by, 96–97; Cuban revolt against, 95–96, 101–2; firing squad of, 247n14; media creating image of, 108; media reporting atrocities of, 100–101; U.S. and war with, 97, 107; U.S. citizens executed by, 94; U.S. tensions with, 103

Spanish-American War (1898), 12, 25, 88, 214; causes of, 91–92; frontier expanding from, 111–12; heroes created by, 109–10; media's role in, 107; messaging controlled for, 120–21; news reporters in, 251n93; revolt beginning of, 98–99; Roosevelt, T., celebrated after, *113*; Spanish firing squad in, 247n14; U.S. and, 89–90; USS *Maine* and, 104–5

The Spanish War: An American Epic 1898 (O'Toole), 282

specific goals, 14

spiders, biting, 131

Sprinz, Detlef F., 285

Squier, Bog, 28

Stalin, Josef, 5

Stanford Encyclopedia of Philosophy (Marsh and Onof), 8

Stanley, Clark, *143*

Stanton, Edwin M., 56–57, 61, 65; conspiracy theory about, 62; as defamed figure, 67–68

statement-without-qualification explanations, 15

Steers, Edward, Jr., 60, 282

Stickney, Joseph L., 116

St. Mary's Infant Asylum, 153

Stone, Oliver, 83

stories, truthfulness of, 5

Strong, George Templeton, 58

Strong, Ted, 117

The Structure of Scientific Revolutions (Kuhn), 8

Stucki, Andreas, 99

Surgeon General, U.S., 163, *164*, 168

Surratt, John, 56, 64–65

Surratt, Mary, 56, 60, 64–65

surveys, on Kennedy, John, assassination, 74

Swaim's Panacea, 149

Swamp Root, 151

Taliaferro, John, 37

talking points, of tobacco industry, *172*

Tea Party, 186, 206

teenagers, 221

telegraph, 26, 58, 62

television, 145; Kennedy, John, assassination covered by, 76; Lincoln program on, 68, 76; 1960 presidential election on, 49; presidential elections role of, 25; public opinion swayed by, 213, 219

temperature, of earth, 182, 200

tent shows, *152*

Ten Years War, 95, 98

terrorist attacks, 9/11, 2–3, 11

testimonials, 152–54, 157

think tanks, 187–88

Tigue, Nancy, 153

Tippit, J. D., 76, 78

TIRC. *See* Tobacco Industry Research Committee

The Toadstool Millionaires: A Social History of Patent Medicines in America before Federal Regulation (Young), 284

tobacco industry, 215; advertisements of, 161–62, 171–72; big business of, 161–62; cancer issue response of, 147, 162–69; facts about, 15; high school students targeted by, 169; information used by, 173; message adherence by, 169–73; misinformation used by, 160–61; public relations, 165; regulations on, 13, 168, 173; scientific research and, 159–60, 166–68, 173, 181–82; talking points of, *172*

Tobacco Industry Research Committee (TIRC), 159, 169

Tonkin Gulf Resolution, 119–20

totalitarian regimes, 5–6

transcontinental telegraph, 62

Trenberth, Kevin, 207

tribal communities, 41

Tropical Fantasy Soda Pop, 132

Trump, Donald, 131, 176, 209, 215, 233n10; derogatory nicknames used by, 15, 17; lies told by, 2; lying press and, 5

trusted sites, on Internet, 16
truth, 267n8; case studies vetting, 16; common perspective shared in, 8; corporate information and, 123–24; fake news and, 126; mistruth and, 222–23; Nietzsche defining, 7; as socially constructed, 6; of stories, 5; of totalitarian regimes, 5–6; untruth, 7; value of, 3; will to, 7, 9
Truth in Advertising Movement, 144
Turner, Thomas Reed, 282
Twitter, 128, 217

UN. *See* United Nations
undesirables, 23
unfit for office, 33
UN Intergovernmental Panel on Climate Change (UNIPCC), 177
Union troops, 55
UNIPCC. *See* UN Intergovernmental Panel on Climate Change
United Nations (UN), 177
United States (U.S.): activists role in, 12; *Black Warrior* vessel of, 95; cigarette smoking in, 168; climate change debate in, 13–14, 175–76, 184; CO_2 emissions in, 13–14; consumer products in, 130–31; Cuba information in, 92; economic interests of, 91; freedom of speech in, 218; imperial powers of, 115–16; Internet use in, 220–21; misinformation in, 217; Navy of, 103; newspapers in, 218–19; oil-producing countries and, 184; public life in, 213–14; ships with contraband and, 93–94; Spain and war with, 97, 107; Spain executing citizens of, 94; Spain's tensions with, 103; Spanish war with, 89–90; USS *Maine* response of, 98–99
unpopular, Lincoln, A., as, 57, 65–66
Unstoppable Global Warming: Every 1,500 Years (Avery), 285
untruth, 7
urban legends, 2–4, 129–30
U.S. *See* United States

vaccines, 146, 156
vendors, 124
Vidal, Gore, 41
Vietnam War, 120
View of General Jackson's Domestic Relations, in Reference to His Fitness for the Presidency (pamphlet), 33
Vindicating Andrew Jackson: The 1828 Election and the Rise of the Two-Party System (Cole, D.), 280
Virginius (American vessels), 95–97
Vital Proteins, 154
vote buying, 46
voter fraud, 46–48
voter registration, 47
voters, on global warming, 198
voting practices, 45–46
Vrolijk, Christiaan, 285

warfare, intelligence gathering agencies and, 253n127
The War Message and the Facts Behind It (publication), 119
Warner, Kenneth E., 171
warning labels, about cigarette smoking, 167
War of 1812, 35
A War of Self-Defense (publications), 119
War Powers Resolution, 120
Warren, Earl, 80, 85
Warren Commission, 76, 78–81, 84–85
Washington, George, 57
Washington Post, 12
Watergate, 12
wealth creation, 209
weaponized, information, 16
Web of Conspiracy: A Guide to Conspiracy Theory Sites on the Internet (Miller), 286
wellness movement, 139, 154, 156
Wells, Gideon, 66
West Virginia, 45–46
Weyler y Nicolau, Valeriano, 98–99
What Doctors Don't Tell You (magazine), 155
White, Theodor H., 40, 48, 281

Whitman, Walt, 59
Who Killed Kennedy (book), 78
Whole Foods, 155
"Who Shot the President?"
  (television), 76
Why Was Lincoln Murdered?
  (Eisenchiml), 68
wife stealing, 34
Wikipedia entry, 73
Wilentz, Sean, 31
Wilkerson, Marcus, 101–2, 283
will to truth, 7, 9
Wilson, Woodrow, 115, 118
Wisan, Joseph, 107, 283
Wisconsin, 45
WMO. *See* World Meteorological
  Organization
Wood, John, 35
Wood, Leonard, 110
Woolgar, Steve, 8

World Meteorological Organization
  (WMO), 182, *183*
World Trade Center, 93
worldview, of public, 22–23
Wynder, Ernest, 163–65

*Yellow Journalism: Puncturing the
  Myths, Defining the Legacies*
  (Campbell), 283
*The Yellow Kids: Foreign Correspondents
  in the Heyday of Yellow Journalism*
  (Milton), 283
yellow press, 91, 245n6
Young, James H., 153, 157, 284
YouTube, 217

Zapruder, Abraham, 82–83
Zarumin, 154
Zicam Cold Remedy, 141

About the Authors

James W. Cortada is a Senior Research Fellow at the Charles Babbage Institute, University of Minnesota. He is a historian of information and its uses in business and American society. He has written more than two dozen books on the role of information. His most recent major publication is *IBM: The Rise and Fall and Reinvention of a Global Icon* (2019), which looks at the company as a large information ecosystem. Some of his other recent publications include: *All the Facts: A History of Information in the United States Since 1870* (2016), *The Essential Manager: How to Thrive in the Global Information Jungle* (2015), and *Information and the Modern Corporation* (2012). He is a member of the editorial boards of *Information & Culture, Library and Information History*, and *IEEE Annals of the History of Computing*.

William Aspray is professor of Information Science at the University of Colorado, Boulder. He is a historian of information, computing, and mathematics. He has written more than two dozen books, including being the co-author of the best-selling history, *Computer: A History of the Information Machine*, third edition (2015). Among his other books is the co-edited *Everyday Information: The Evolution of Information Seeking in America* (2011). He serves on the editorial boards of *Information Research, The Information Society*, and *IEEE Annals of the History of Computing*, and is the former editor of *Information & Culture*.

Cortada and Aspray are busy at work on their next book, *From Urban Legends to Political Fact-Checking: Online Scrutiny in America*.